ADOPTION REIMAGINED

ADOPTION REIMAGINED

An Unconcealed Theology of Huiothesía *(Υἱοθεσία) in Pauline Thought*

RICKY ANDRIES TAN

WIPF & STOCK · Eugene, Oregon

ADOPTION REIMAGINED
An Unconcealed Theology of *Huiothesía* (Υἱοθεσία) in Pauline Thought

Copyright © 2025 Ricky Andries Tan. All rights reserved. Except for brief quotations in critical publications or reviews, no part of this book may be reproduced in any manner without prior written permission from the publisher. Write: Permissions, Wipf and Stock Publishers, 199 W. 8th Ave., Suite 3, Eugene, OR 97401.
Wipf & Stock
An Imprint of Wipf and Stock Publishers
199 W. 8th Ave., Suite 3
Eugene, OR 97401

www.wipfandstock.com

PAPERBACK ISBN: 979-8-3852-5862-8
HARDCOVER ISBN: 979-8-3852-5863-5
EBOOK ISBN: 979-8-3852-5864-2

VERSION NUMBER 110325

The Greek New Testament, Fifth Revised Edition, edited by Barbara Aland, Kurt Aland, Johannes Karavidopoulos, Carlo M. Martini, and Bruce M. Metzger in cooperation with the Institute for New Testament Textual Research, Münster/Westphalia, © 2014 Deutsche Bibelgesellschaft, Stuttgart. Used by permission.

Scripture quotations marked (AMP) taken from the Amplified® Bible (AMP), Copyright © 2015 by The Lockman Foundation. Used by permission. lockman.org

Scripture quotations marked (ESV) are from The ESV® Bible (The Holy Bible, English Standard Version®), © 2001 by Crossway, a publishing ministry of Good News Publishers. Used by permission. All rights reserved.

Scripture quotations marked (KJV) are taken from the KING JAMES VERSION, public domain.

Scripture quoted by permission. Quotations designated (NET) are from the NET Bible® copyright ©1996, 2019 by Biblical Studies Press, L.L.C. http://netbible.com. All rights reserved.

Scripture quotations marked (NASB) taken from the (NASB®) New American Standard Bible®, Copyright © 1960, 1971, 1977, 1995, 2020 by The Lockman Foundation. Used by permission. All rights reserved. lockman.org

Scripture quotations marked "Gutenberg" are from the Gutenberg Bible.

Scripture quotations marked "Coverdale" are from the Coverdale Bible, 1535.

Scripture quotations marked "Darby" are from the Darby Translation, 1890.

Teks Alkitab Terjemahan Baru Edisi Kedua (TB^2) © LAI 2023 Peta Alkitab UBS 1976. Used by permission.

Scripture quotations marked "Bishops'" are from *The Bishops' Bible* (1568), public domain.

Scripture quotations marked "Geneva" are from *The Geneva Bible* (1599), public domain.

Scripture quotations marked "Great" are from *The Great Bible* (1539), public domain.

Scripture quotations marked "Matthew" are from *The Matthew Bible* (1537), public domain.

Scripture quotations marked "Taverner" are from *The Taverner Bible* (1539), public domain.

Scripture quotations marked "Tyndale" are from *The Tyndale New Testament* (1526), public domain.

Scripture quotations marked "Wycliffe" are from *The Wycliffe Bible* (c. 1382–1395), public domain.

Scripture quotations marked "YLT" are from *Young's Literal Translation* (1898), public domain.

Scripture quotations marked "Cambridge" are from *The Cambridge Bible for Schools and Colleges* (Cambridge University Press, c. 1878–1918) and, to the best of our knowledge, are in the public domain.

Scripture quotations marked "Alkitab TB" are from *Alkitab Terjemahan Baru Indonesia (© Lembaga Alkitab Indonesia, 1974)*. Used by permission.

Scripture quotations marked "Alkitab TL" are from *Alkitab Indonesia (© Lembaga Alkitab Indonesia, 1962)*. Used by permission.

Scripture quotations marked "NJB" are from *The New Jerusalem Bible* (© 1985 by Darton, Longman & Todd Ltd.). Reprinted by permission. All rights reserved.

Scripture quotations marked "RNJB" are from T*he Revised New Jerusalem Bible* (© 2018, 2019 by Darton, Longman & Todd Ltd.). Used by permission. All rights reserved.

To
Kenny Tan Tjoan King (†), Margaritje Tjiu Djok Oei (†),
Fe-ing,
Aaron, Matthew, and Jeremy

A challenge to inherited theology

"I WANT YOU TO GO ON PICTURING THE ENLIGHTENMENT OR IGNO-
RANCE OF OUR HUMAN CONDITION SOMEWHAT AS FOLLOWS."
~ PLATO, *REPUBLIC* 7

Contents

Figures and Tables | xi
Preface | xiii
Acknowledgments | xvii
Abbreviations | xix
Brief Conceptual Guide | xxiii

Introduction: The Creator Does Not Adopt Children | 1

The Theological Adoption and the History of Interpretations of *Huiothesia*

CHAPTER 1
What They Say About the Doctrine of Adoption | 29

CHAPTER 2
The History of the Various Interpretations of *Huiothesia* | 73

Biblical Studies of *Huiothesia*: Deconstructing the Doctrine of Adoption

CHAPTER 3
Words Study and Textual Criticism | 93

CHAPTER 4
Galatians: From the Old Being to the New Being | 108

CHAPTER 5
Romans: The Creation of Pneumatic Beings | 134

Constructive Theology: Reconstructing (Unconcealing) Paul's Knowledge of *Huiothesia*

CHAPTER 6
The Person of Jesus Christ and the Holy Spirit | 179

CHAPTER 7
The Pneumatic-Christic Beings | 208

CHAPTER 8
Methodus Salutis Dei | 237

Final Reflections | 243

Bibliography | 265

Figures and Tables

FIGURE 1: The Eternal Creator (Being-Itself) and His Creation | 16
FIGURE 2: Lonergan's Eight Functional Specialty | 24
FIGURE 3: Adamic Humans Are Created with Potentials | 71
FIGURE 4: Relationship of *Nepios*, *Teknon*, and *Huios* | 102
FIGURE 5: *Huiothesía* (the Beginning) and *Huiothesía* (the Consummation) | 172
FIGURE 6: Panentheism, with the God-Human as *Metaxú* | 199
FIGURE 7: God the Son (Infinite Divine) and the Son of God (Finite Human) | 206
FIGURE 8: The Extended Participation of the Sons in the Godhead | 236
FIGURE 9: *Methodus Salutis Dei* (The Historical and Order of Salvation) | 242

TABLE 1: Textual Criticism of Roman 8:23, Apparatus No. 5 23{A} | 104
TABLE 2: Temporary Translation of Galatians 4:1–7 (ATT) | 112
TABLE 3: Temporary Translations of Romans 8:14–23 and 9:4–8 (ATT) | 137
TABLE 4: The Dichotomy in the Concept of Adoption | 256
TABLE 5: The Juxtaposition in the Concept of *Huiothesía* | 256
TABLE 6: A Tabular Comparison Between Adoption and *Huiothesía* | 257

Preface

It is worth considering the possibility that a single word, pivotal to comprehending God's plan for humanity's salvation, might have been subject to interpretation and translation inaccuracies over several centuries since the early days of Christianity in the Latin world. The term "υἱοθεσία" (*huiothesía*), which has been frequently translated as "adoption" in various Bible translations, carries significant theological implications, influencing the doctrines of many and shaping the perceptions of countless believers regarding their relationship with God. However, this inaccuracy may not fully capture the text's original intent, potentially presenting a different interpretation of a truth that could profoundly affect our understanding of divine grace and connection to God. This book respectfully invites readers to explore how recovering the true meaning of "υἱοθεσία," along with its linguistic roots and theological implications, might illuminate the depth of God's creative and redemptive work in humanity.

Because it is difficult to find material that does not read "adoption" into "υἱοθεσία," we must learn the topic from the apostle Paul, who is entirely in control of each occurrence of the word in his epistles. We need to understand his intention—the real issue he wanted to address through his epistles. Irenaeus also discussed "υἱοθεσία," but all translations and discussions that include his writings have been altered and interpreted with "adoption." Consequently, I also refer to secondary sources to debate their interpretation of Irenaeus' *ah* besides quoting him exclusively. We can easily find translated Bibles, books, sermons, and songs that teach theological adoption. Thus, there is no other way; Paul's teachings in his epistles should be considered a primary source for understanding the true meaning of biblical υἱοθεσία, which itself is an *interpretatio christiana* of the υἱοθεσία concept as presented in Diodorus Siculus' account.

The structure of this work follows the eight specialties delineated by Bernard Lonergan in his *Method in Theology*. The initial four specialties highlight the importance of anchoring contemporary theology in its historical roots. The final four specialties engage with current theological and existential questions, facilitating a constructive dialogue between tradition and modernity.

Moreover, essentialist and existentialist theologies assist in comprehending Paul's υἱοθεσία in a novel light, particularly when it pertains to the concepts of essence, state of being, existence, mode of being, human becoming, ontological transformation, the human as *Dasein*, and the Christ as the paradigmatic existence. My introduction to this existentialist theology was through the work of John Macquarrie.[1] This work of mine is influenced by the concepts of Being-Itself and New Creation, as well as de- and re-mythologization, as put forth by Paul Tillich and Adolf Bultmann, while maintaining faith in the historical authenticity of the Messiah's resurrection.

The work addresses the issue of how to be delivered from the human condition (the fundamental aspects of human existence, including sufferings, mortality, imperfection, despair, and the challenges of life) in the present era by drawing upon the teachings of *huiothesía* in the Bible; therefore, the work must adopt an interdisciplinary approach, engaging with a range of perspectives. It seems implausible that a significant proportion of individuals with a background in natural science would adhere to the six-day creationist model. Contemporary science is an integral aspect of our present reality. Our world is not the mythological (etiological) world first described by Mediterraneans, as outlined in the book of Genesis, chapters 1–3.

Therefore, this work integrates other disciplines, such as present-day world-picture (*Weltbild*, contemporary scientific concept of reality), and philosophy with theology.[2] This book is based on deep biblical study but can also be classified as constructive theology.[3] It is both interdisciplinary

---

1. "There is a kinship between existentialism and New Testament thought, so that what we have called the existential approach to theology is likely to lead us to the authentic thought of the New Testament writers." Macquarrie, *Existentialist Theology*, 42.

2. Ian Barbour explains that science and religion can relate as conflict, independence, dialogue, or integration. As for integration, "Science and religion are partners in a common quest for a comprehensive understanding of the world, and the theories and results of science can be brought to bear in fruitful ways on the development of theories in theology, and vice versa." Barbour, *When Science*, 10–12.

3. In his introductory chapter, Veli-Matti Kärkkäinen defines "systematic/constructive theology [as] an integrative discipline that continuously searches for a coherent, balanced understanding of Christian truth and faith in light of Christian tradition (biblical and historical) and in the context of the historical and contemporary thought, cultures, and living faiths. It aims at a coherent, inclusive, dialogical, and hospitable vision. . . . Constructive theology seeks a coherent and balanced understanding." Kärkkäinen quoted Murphy, *Beyond Liberalism and Fundamentalism*, 98–108. "Coherence has not only to do with inner-textual coherence but also with the 'fit' of theological

and transversal.[4] It covers the history of interpretation of υἱοθεσία, biblical theology, systematic theology, and pastoral theology. I document the process of preparing the temporal translations of the Bible passages utilized in chapters 4, 5, and other chapters, but they are not presented here.

The teachings of Irenaeus, Gnosticism, and existentialism all contain notions of human becoming, elevation, or the awakened human.[5] While Gnosticism tends to downplay the humanity of Yeshua, this work places significant emphasis on the human figure of the Christ. I submit that Jesus' human *huio*-ship (consummated sonship, not sonship) plays a key part in serving as the design for how God can save humanity.

This work does not support the idea of a historical Adam and a historical fall. Still, it does support the idea of the historical birth, baptism, ministry, cross, and resurrection of Jesus of Nazareth.[6] It uses anthropological theology from existentialist and essentialist perspectives to address this issue of human facticity (givenness), its predicament, and potentiality. It discusses human nature and how it determines the human relationship to God.

The process of Christian salvation, as described in this work, encompasses both mystical elements—such as human ontological transformation, the concept of *metaxú*, and union with God—and logical aspects, as demonstrated through a structured analysis and rational synthesis of how these themes interrelate according to scriptural teachings on salvation through the doctrine of *huiothesía*.

Furthermore, I affirm that this is my original work. I have not copied or followed anyone else's work or sought assistance from others. Moreover, I wish to state that I have no competing interests or biases against any person, institution, or theological system while working on this publication. This work aims to answer my questions concerning the human condition, and

---

statements with 'reality.'" Kärkkäinen, *Hope*, 1–2.

4. "The term 'transversal' indicates 'a sense of extending over, lying across, and intersecting with one another.'" Kärkkäinen, *Hope*, 3.

5. "The Gnostics had an unique and insightful view of the human being. Existentialist philosophy, Jungian and Transpersonal Psychology, as well as such Eastern religious traditions as Hinduism and Buddhism, all show various degrees of affinity to Gnosticism, particularly when it comes to the Gnostic teachings concerning the human being." Hall, *Wisdom*, 13.

6. *Contra* Strauss. "David Friedrich Strauss (1808–1874) drew out all the consequences from previous historical criticism when he wrote his *Life of Jesus* (1835). . . . But more, he tried to show that the stories of the birth and the resurrection of Jesus are symbols expressing the eternal identity of what is essential in Jesus and God." Tillich, *History of Christian Thought*, 433.

salvation. I hope this will contribute to the ongoing discussion of the doctrine of adoption and υἱοθεσία.

"Pope Gregory I said that only a prophet could understand the prophets. And it is said that only a poet can understand a poet. Who, then, must we be in order to understand Yeshua?"[7] My answer to this analogical and ontological question is

> By God's grace,
>> we must first become Christians, for only the Christians can understand the Christ;
>> we must first become the [mature] sons of God, for only the [mature] sons of God can understand the [mature] Son of God and the triune God.

The doctrine of adoption has the power to obscure the true meaning of Scripture. Yet the gospel of Jesus *the* Christ—who was born a *népios*, matures into the first *huios*, the archetypal image of humanity's consummated ontological transformation—will ultimately be unveiled. The false gospel of adoption must be abandoned.

Ad Dominum meum Jesum.
Ricky Andries Tan

---

7. Leloup, *Gospel of Thomas*, 5.

Acknowledgments

This book originated as my doctoral dissertation, but it has undergone substantial revision in both scope and tone. What began as an academic investigation has developed into a theological work that seeks to reshape a central doctrine long misunderstood in Pauline scholarship. I am deeply grateful to my dissertation advisors—Prof. Joas Adiprasetya, Asigor P. Sitanggang ThD, and Prof. Samuel B. Hakh—and to Casthelia Kartika DTh, my external reader, for supporting my pursuit of a line of inquiry that challenged conventional views and doctrinal assumptions. I also thank Jakarta Theological Seminary for the opportunity to be part of its academic community.

I would like to thank Ms. Béatrice Gerhard from Deutsche Bibelgesellschaft, Stuttgart, for allowing me to quote UBS[5] in this work. While preparing the biblical material, I created provisional translations (ATT). This translation process benefited from the structural analysis approach of Matthew Brook O'Donnell and his collaborators from the OpenText.org project, an open-source tool. However, their original clause annotations are not reproduced in this publication.

I would like to sincerely thank my publication project manager Matt Wimer, who ensured the timely publication of this book through his exceptional effort; Riley Bounds, who has dedicated countless hours to editing and refining this manuscript; Ian Creeger, whose careful typesetting brought this book to its final form; George Callihan, Emily Callihan, and the entire W&S team for their invaluable support and hard work.

To the readers of this book: may these pages invite you not just to reconsider a doctrinal term, but to rediscover the calling and glory of becoming mature pneumatic sons (*huioi*)—new beings—in Christ. May this journey strengthen our faith in the Lord.

Abbreviations

AH	*Against Heresies*
AHT	Andries' *Huiothesía* Translation. An English translation of selected New Testament texts, developed by Ricky A. Tan. This version reflects a distinctive theological framework that reinterprets key Pauline concepts—particularly *huiothesía*—not as "adoption," but as a vision of mature, pneumatic sonship (*huioship*). It emphasizes human ontological transformation into a new state of being, rooted in participatory Christology and the life-giving communion of the Spirit.
AMG	Strong, James, et al. *AMG's Strong's Annotated Dictionaries.* Chattanooga, TN: AMG, 2009.
AMP	Amplified Bible
ANF	*Ante-Nicene Fathers*
ASV	American Standard Version
ATT	Andries' Tentative Translation. This is a provisional English rendering of selected New Testament texts, intended to provide a workable translation for analysis and interpretation, unaffected by previous translations shaped by *adoptio*/adoption framework. To engage the text as closely as possible to the original Greek NT, I have employed a formal equivalent approach, preserving the sentence structure wherever feasible. Occasionally, additional words are placed in square brackets to clarify Greek grammar (e.g., verb moods) or to improve readability. Alternative meanings are presented in parentheses.
AV	Authorized Version
BDAG	Bauer, Walter. *A Greek-English Lexicon of the New Testament and Other Early Christian Literature.* Edited by Frederick

	William Danker. Translated by William F. Arndt and F. Wilbur Gingrich. 3rd ed. Chicago: The University of Chicago Press, 2000.
DRC	Douay-Rheims Bible (Challoner Revision)
ESV	English Standard Version
KJV	King James Version
LAI	*Lembaga Alkitab Indonesia* (Indonesian Bible Society)
LXX	Septuagint
mss	Manuscripts
NASB	New American Standard Bible
NET	New English Translation
NIDNTT	Brown, Collin, et al., eds. *New International Dictionary of the New Testament Theology.* Grand Rapids: Zondervan, 1986.
NIDNTTE	Silva, Moisés, ed. *New International Dictionary of New Testament Theology and Exegesis.* 2nd ed. Grand Rapids: Zondervan, 2014.
NIV	New International Version
NJB	New Jerusalem Bible
NRSV	New Revised Standard Version
PBIK	Sutanto, Hasan. *Perjanjian Baru Interlinear Yunani-Indonesia dan Konkordansi Perjanjian Baru.* Jakarta: Lembaga Alkitab Indonesia, 2010.
RNJB	Revised New Jerusalem Bible
RSV	Revised Standard Version
RV	Revised Version
sn	Study Note (in the NET Bible)
TB^2	*Alkitab Terjemahan Baru Edisi Kedua* (*Indonesian Bible*)
TDNT	Kittel, Gerhard, ed. *Theological Dictionary of the New Testament.* Translated by Geoffrey William Bromiley. Grand Rapids: Eerdmans, 1964.
TDOT	Botterweck, Gerhard Johannes, et al. *Theological Dictionary of the Old Testament.* Grand Rapids: Eerdmans, 1990.
tn	Translator's Note (in the NET Bible)

TR	Textus Receptus
UBS⁴	Aland, Barbara, et al., eds. *The Greek New Testament* (UBS⁴) 4. Rev. ed. Stuttgart: Deutsche Bibelgesellschaft, 1993.
UBS⁵	Aland, Barbara, et al., eds. *The Greek New Testament* (UBS⁵) 5. Rev. ed. Stuttgart: Deutsche Bibelgesellschaft, 2014.
YLT	Young's Literal Translation

Brief Conceptual Guide

This brief guide presents essential terms and concepts to orient readers to the themes explored in the following chapters. It offers a foundational understanding of interpretive variations, especially concerning *huiothesía* theology, preparing readers for a deeper discussion ahead.

SON AND CHILDREN

There are significant differences between the original contexts of the biblical Pauline word "υἱοθεσία" and the mistranslated Latin Vulgate's "*adoptio.*" As a result, specific terms might have different connotations in this context of *huiothesía* compared to the theology of adoption and Reformed theology as a whole.

In the context of biblical Pauline *huiothesía* (υἱοθεσία), the translations "υἱός" and "τέκνα" as "son" and "children" do not correspond to their original meaning. The misinterpretation of *huiothesía* as adoption may have resulted from the mistranslation of these phrases, obscuring the true meaning of *huiothesía*. When I want to emphasize the Pauline meaning of these words, I have to place them next to their corresponding Greek words or use their Greek version. I find that the Pauline "υἱός" can be translated not as "son" but as "mature son," "adult son," "son-heir," "Christic son," "exalted son," "pneumatic son," "perfected son," "eschatological son," or "consummated son." It becomes evident that there is a significant distinction between the phrases "to become a son" and "to become a *mature* son." In addition, the term "τέκνα" has also been mistranslated as "children." In the Pauline biblical context, it can be translated in various ways, including "beloved children," "favored children," or "the elect."

God's children are the *created* human beings and the *uncreated* preexistent Son. In the context of the Pauline Greek *huiothesía*, these God-created children, depending on their positions in God's created family, are referred to as infants or minors (νήπιοι, népioi), beloved children (τέκνα, tekna), and adult sons and daughters (υἱοί, huioi). The teaching of theological adoption misinterprets God's νήπιοι as slaves or sons of Satan. For further study of the terms in the context of υἱοθεσία, please refer to chapter 3.

THE SON OF GOD (THE LORD) AND GOD THE SON (THE WORD)

The phrase "the Christ" or "the Messiah" refers to the human figure (nature) of the person of Jesus Christ, who was born of a woman (he was a human like us) and born under the law (νήπιος, like all other protological Adamic beings), who becomes the consummated Son of Man or the consummated Son of God (ὁ Υἱός τοῦ Θεοῦ, the Christ) after the resurrection. As Luke 20:36 renders, "They . . . are υἱοί of God, being υἱοί of the resurrection."

In the Athanasian Creed, the term "*Deus Filius*" appears as in "*Ita Deus Pater, Deus Filius, Deus Spiritus Sanctus: Et non tres Dii, sed unus est Deus.*"[8] Its formal equivalent translation is "So God the Father, God the Son, God the Holy Spirit. And not three Gods, but one is God." Alternatively, the stanza is translated as "So the Father is God, the Son is God, the Holy Spirit is God. And yet they are not three Gods, but one is God." Thus, the term "God the Son" (Greek: Θεὸς ὁ Υἱός, Latin: *Deus Filius*) refers to the Second Person of the divine Trinity, the eternal, preexistent, divine *Logos*. "The Word" (ὁ Λόγος, *ho Lógos*) is also used to indicate the uncreated divine figure (or nature) who is said to have added to himself the human figure. To mention a few names, Aurelius Augustine[9] and Karl Barth[10] also employed the term "God the Son."

The biblical term "the Son of God (ὁ Υἱός τοῦ Θεοῦ)" and the developed theological term "God the Son (Θεὸς ὁ Υἱός)" refer to a different *figure* (nature) of the *person* of the Son. The former refers to the human Messiah, while the latter refers to the divine Second Person of the eternal Trinity. God makes the sons of God (οἱ υἱοί τοῦ Θεοῦ) similar to the *human* Son of God (ὁ Υἱός τοῦ Θεοῦ) through God's sub-act of υἱοθεσία.

---

8. Logan, *History of the Church*, 10.

9. ". . . than God the Son obedient to God the Father, even to the death of the cross?" Augustine, *On The Trinity*, 336.

10. "God the Father and God the Son are together the origin of the Holy Spirit: Spiritus, qui procedit a Patre Filioque." Barth, *Dogmatics in Outline*, 44.

THE HUMAN SPIRIT

I subscribe to Clarence Larkin's "Threefold Nature of Man,"[11] which schematized the relation between the human body, soul, spirit, and the Holy Spirit. A human spirit and a human soul are distinct, as is the case with the Holy Spirit. The significant role of the "human spirit" is seen in Paul's teaching of υἱοθεσία. The gospel of υἱοθεσία, which has nothing to do with adoption, cannot be understood if one refuses to recognize the human spirit. The interpretation of the theme of υἱοθεσία, which posits that humans are trichotomic beings, is in contrast to the concept of adoption, which does not view a spirit as an essential part of a human being. The former focuses on human *ontological* transformation, while the latter focuses on *legal* transfer. This perspective represents a significant aspect of the work that contributes to its distinctive character in the discussion of υἱοθεσία and adoption.

ADAMIC AND CHRISTIC HUMANS

I subscribe to the notion that there is no historical Adam and Eve but rather a literary Adam and Eve. Accordingly, all conscious beings, regardless of location, including sentient individuals in other galaxies who do not recognize Christ as their Savior, are considered to be temporal, sarkic, protological, Adamic beings—νήπιοι— as are all members of the genus Homo.[12]

Those who are Christic human beings, or υἱοί, are those who believe in and are a part of the mystical body of the person of Jesus Christ, that is, who are transforming into his image. These individuals are immortal, pneumatic, eschatological, able to participate in the communion of spirits, and live in both sarkic and pneumatic modes of existence before the parousia.

MESSAGE

It should be noted that those wishing to read faster may want to forego the discussion of chapter 1 and proceed directly to its heading, "Summary: Articulating My Conceptual Framework." I recommend that the reader first

---

11. Larkin, *Rightly Dividing the Word*, 86.

12. Cf., "The Earth with its human history is a tiny speck in space, a blink of an eye in cosmic time. What does the Earthly history of redemption mean for rational sinners on planets in other galaxies? They have no identification whatsoever with Israel. For that matter, what does redemption in Israel's terms have to do with the Chinese, Indians, and Native Americans before any contact with Israel or Christian culture?" Neville, *Symbols of Jesus*, 143.

familiarize themselves with the introductory chapter before proceeding with the other chapters.

To do the discussion in chapters 4 and 5, I made preliminary translations (ATT) of Gal 4:1–11, Rom 8:14–23, 9:4, and 8. The process of these translations is not included in this publication.

Introduction: The Creator Does Not Adopt Children

"He who knows only his own side of the case knows little of that." ~ John Stuart Mill, *On Liberty*

SETTING THE SCENE

Be prepared to reevaluate every notion we have held about how God has created and saved humans and all other creations within the framework of Christian doctrines. This treatise has intervened to dismantle antiquated notions of human fall and restoration. This biblical and theological study asserts that we, Christians, have misinterpreted our way to salvation. It renders previous doctrines seemingly misguided. Through meticulous investigation, I have reconstructed the concealed truths inherent in the gospel of *"huiothesía"* (υἱοθεσία). These revelations go beyond mere adjustments; they represent a thorough revision of doctrines encompassing both divine creation and redemption.

A Roman gospel has covered the true Christian gospel. It emerged during the early development of Christianity, shaped by errors in translating biblical texts. In his Epistle to the Romans, 8:14, apostle Paul wrote, "υἱοὶ θεοῦ," highlighting the profound implications of Christians' identity in Christ. The *Biblia Sacra Vulgata* wrongly translates it as *"filii Dei,"* which means "sons of God." When we misinterpret the word *"huios"* (υἱός) in Paul's theology as equivalent to *"filius"* in Latin or "son" in English rather than as *"filius maturus"* or "mature son," it leads to a misinterpretation of Paul's gospel of *"huio-thesía"* (υἱο-θεσία). In Rom 8:15, the word "υἱοθεσία" has been inaccurately rendered as "*adoptionis filiorum*" in the *Vulgata*[1] and "adoption" in the 1599 Geneva Bible.[2] Regrettably, these mistranslations, or perhaps more accurately, this misconception, obscure or even replace the biblical substance of Paul's message of salvation with the Roman idea alien to the Greek Bible (or to the gospel of salvation). This erroneous interpretation has served as the foundation for the doctrine of adoption that says that Christians are *adopted sons* of God, which is not valid.

We learn from Alister E. McGrath that efforts were made throughout the Reformation to correct translation problems in Latin Bibles and the corresponding beliefs. However, despite the Protestant Reformers' goal of "bringing theology back into line with Scripture,"[3] the idea of adoption has endured to this day, partly because they (we) support it. Instead, we must keep promoting the Reformers' motto of *ad fontes* ("back to the source," emphasizing a return to the original Bible texts). As Christians, we must point out and correct any contradictions or errors in Bible translations and the theology that goes along with them.

Let us delve into the problem. Which god is our God? The existence of a single creator underlying all of creation is a foundational premise; however, the term "God" is not univocal and carries multiple meanings across different religious traditions. Each religion articulates a conception of God that is distinct from others, reflecting diverse theological interpretations and attributes. This plurality indicates that while there may be one ultimate source of existence, the understanding and description of the divine vary significantly among faiths. Despite our differences, the world has only one Creator.

The concept of the God-Creator, who is traditionally regarded as the sole father or mother of all created beings,[4] has increasingly been marginalized.[5] The mistranslation problem has led to a divergence of opinion

---

1. "*Sed accepistis spiritum adoptionis filiorum, in quo clamamus: Abba (Pater)*" (Rom 8:15). Colunga and Turrado, *Biblia Sacra*, 1100.

2. "But ye have received the Spirit of adoption, whereby we cry, Abba, Father" (Rom 8:15 Geneva).

3. McGrath, *Historical Theology*, 5.

4. Cf., Dille renders, "Among Deutero-Isaiah's many metaphors for God are 'father' and 'mother.' . . . Here [Isa 49:13–21] the image of [Yahweh] as a parent (mother) is explored in interaction with the same vehicle (mother) applied to a different tenor or referent (Zion)." Dille, *Mixing Metaphors*, 1, 129. The tetragrammaton is rendered as "Yahweh" throughout this work for consistency and readability.

5. According to Gunton, "From God's side, the relationship with the world is unbreakable, so long as the world remains. But, given the breach of the relationship from the human side, a new form of mediation is required to deal with the new and dangerous situation. It requires that the one through whom God created the world is now

regarding the fatherhood of God and the categories of sonship (here, it is not *huio*-ship). Those who espouse the doctrine of adoption maintain that the First Person of the Trinity—God the Father—has two categories of sons: natural and adopted. Scott Hahn posits that the First Person of the Trinity (God the Father) becomes the father of the Second Person (God the Son) and that the believers (the sons) are the only ones who God indeed fathers.[6] Non-Christians are not in the family. A considerable number of Christians readily embrace this viewpoint. From a tribalistic (group-oriented) standpoint, they have continued to regard the triune Godhead and the church as a divine family.

According to the doctrine of adoption, unbelievers are regarded as coming from an unknown or Satan's family. This idea suggests the existence of two distinct families, with one being perceived as more favored than the other.[7] To be saved, an *adult* son of an unknown family must be transferred into the Creator's family. This understanding of salvation through divine adoption has led to a growing disconnection from the apostle Paul's gospel teaching on υἱοθεσία.

In the context of the υἱοθεσία presented in Rom 8:15, believers address the Creator as "*Abba*."[8] This term refers to ὁ πατήρ, who is the Creator and Father of all created beings. Therefore, He is the God of both νήπιοι (*népioi*, unbelievers), υἱοί (*huioi*, believers), and the cosmos (the subhuman creations, 8:19–23). In adoption theology, the Father is understood as the father of Christians alone. Such a father is distinct from the Father to whom biblical υἱοθεσία refers, who is the Father of all beings.

In the context of the economic Trinity, the eternal divine sonship of the Second Person of the Trinity towards the First Person of the Trinity is part of the unique internal fellowship of the three Persons of the Godhead, which excludes created humanity. The concepts above are of supreme

---

mediator of reconciliation, which therefore takes center stage in an account of what mediation is." Gunton, *Father, Son, and the Holy Spirit*, 168.

6. Hahn argues, "Divine family life comes naturally only to the Trinity. Thus, for Jesus Christ, it comes naturally, since He is eternally 'one in being with the Father.' His nature is divine, and *only* He is God's Son by nature. So, if we are to become children of God by adoption, we must be remade in the image of Christ." Hahn, *First Comes Love*, ch. 8. Emphasis original.

7. Cf., Scott writes, "All cultures, modern and ancient, draw boundaries between themselves and others, whether it is a matter of defending their turf or building iron curtains. Greeks called everyone who did not speak Greek a barbarian, and Jews divided the world between themselves and the Gentiles. The temptation to draw the line, to dare someone to step across it, seems to be a universal human phenomenon." Scott, *Hear Then the Parable*, 189.

8. Tan, "Call of 'Abba,'" 221–46.

importance when contemplating the everlastingness (sempiternity, eternal in duration towards their end but still temporal in nature because they started in time)[9] of the God-created pneumatic-Christic sons (υἱοὶ) in their temporal external participation in the eternal internal union of the Godhead. The core tenet of the apostle Paul's doctrine of υἱοθεσία is the *huio*-ship (*mature son*-ship) of the created human beings, which mirrors the *huio*-ship of Ὁ Υἱὸς Τοῦ Ἀνθρώπου ("the mature son of human being," that is, the resurrected human Christ).

The opinions of J. Scott Lidgett and Ben C. Blackwell, as indicated below, present a challenge to the study of υἱοθεσία. As cited by Tim J. R. Trumper, Lidgett asserts that the term "adoption as sons" is a concept of Irenaeus.[10] However, this is not accurate. Blackwell makes two errors when he states that the term "adoption (*adoptio*, υἱοθεσία)" is used twenty times in the five books of *Against Heresies*.[11] First, it is erroneous to attribute the concept of adoption to Irenaeus, as the translators of his work are responsible for this interpretation. Second, the terms *adoptio* and υἱοθεσία are not synonymous; therefore, it is incorrect to write "adoption (*adoptio*, υἱοθεσία)." The veracity of their assertions is open to question. Fortunately, portions of Irenaeus' work Ἔλεγχος καὶ ἀνατροπὴ τῆς ψευδωνύμου γνώσεως (*On the Detection and Overthrow of the So-Called Gnosis*)[12] have survived, allowing scholars to compare them with the translations.

Given this known issue, it is prudent to exercise caution when encountering the term "adoption" in Bibles and book translations. When reading

---

9. For "everlastingness," see Padgett, "Eternity," 335–43.

10. See Trumper's 39n. What Irenaeus wrote as "υἱοθεσία" had been read as "adoption of sons," then claimed it as Irenaeus' idea. The claim is an academic bias that conceals the true meaning, when it is not a misreading. Trumper writes, "Beginning with the patristic period, it is probably true to say that the Greek Fathers overlooked adoption less than their Latin counterparts. Lidgett suggests for example that, 'nowhere [sic] can we find more emphatic and constant reference to the "adoption of sons" as the characteristic gift to believers in Christ than in Irenaeus.' Although this claim is more appropriately made of Calvin, nevertheless the adoption motif does figure in Irenaeus' theology as a cognate theme of the Fatherhood of God. Regrettably, however, Irenaeus failed to work through the implications of divine paternity for his theology." Trumper, "Theological History of Adoption: I," 15.

11. Blackwell states, "The term adoption (*adoptio*, υἱοθεσία) arises some twenty times in the five books of AH, with most occurring in Books 3 and 4. The occurrences of adoption in Book 3 are found in Irenaeus' discussion about the nature of Christ and his incarnation (3.16–23), and this was exemplified in our discussion of the exchange formula in 3.19.1 (cf. esp. 3.16.3). While hemost [sic] often associates adoption with Christ in this section, at other times the Spirit is more directly the focus of his discussion." Blackwell, *Christosis*, 59–60.

12. Translation: "Refutation and Overturning of the Falsely Named Knowledge."

what is purported to be Irenaeus' *"Against Heresies,"* it is imperative to exercise caution, as all the lemma υἱοθεσία has been replaced with adoption, and the Greek Bible verses also have been replaced with "translated" Bible verses that convey the concept of adoption. Consequently, when reading a phrase—for instance, an extract from John Behr's writings on Irenaeus concerning adoption—it is necessary to perceive it in the context of υἱοθεσία. The two concepts are distinct from one another.

The following excerpt from Behr can be taken as an illustrative example:

> As Adam was animated by the breath of life, so Christ was vivified by the Spirit, as also will be those who, as *adopted sons* in him, presently have the pledge of the Spirit.[13]

Behr's phrase "as adopted sons in him" suggests a familial affiliation. In contrast, my reading "as οἱ υἱοὶ in him" in the context of the Pauline Greek υἱοθεσία signifies that the adult sons-heirs (οἱ υἱοὶ) are in the Son (ὁ Υἱός, the Christ). The union between *the* Christ (*ha Mashiach* [חישמה]) and Christlike beings (Christic beings) can be understood as a result of the pneumatic compatibility between the two parties.[14] This ontological compatibility arises from the state of being of the Christic beings, which is comparable to the state of being of the Son (ὁ Υἱός, the Christ). This elevated nature brings a novel form of participation in the New Being within the pneumatic realm.[15] No adoption relationship here.

Salvation is God's sub-act of God's act of creation. In the Pauline context of the creation (which includes salvation) of human beings, there are three key concepts: the ontic of a being (essence or nature), its ontological

---

13. Emphasis added. Behr argues, "It is similarly mistaken to equate the pre-lapsarian life of Adam with the life of the Spirit manifested by Christ. That they should be regarded as different modalities of life is demanded by, first, Genesis 2:7, which speaks only of the first man becoming a 'living soul' (ψυχὴν ζῶσαν); second, the apostle Paul, who specifies that it is the last Adam who became a life-creating Spirit (πνεῦμα ζωοποιοῦν), in contrast to the first Adam who was a 'living soul' (1 Cor. 15:45–6); third, the whole movement of Irenaeus's theology of the economy, which moves from 'animation' to 'vivification': as Adam was animated by the breath of life, so Christ was vivified by the Spirit, as also will be those who, as adopted sons in him, presently have the pledge of the Spirit." Behr, *Asceticism*, 95.

14. As is the case with digital television broadcasting, which cannot be received by an analog television, the broadcast and the television must be compatible for the transmission to be successful. In the absence of such compatibility, the existence of both the broadcast and the television is rendered meaningless.

15. Litwa writes, "Participating in divine reality (*pneuma*)." Litwa, *We Are Being Transformed*, 161.

transformation, and existence. In the view of Paul Tillich, existentialism and essentialism are inextricably intertwined.

> On the other hand, a pure existentialism is impossible because to describe existence, one must use language. Now language deals with universals. In using universals, language is by its very nature essentialist, and cannot escape it. . . . Existentialism is possible only as an element in a larger whole, as an element in a vision of the structure of being in its created goodness, and then as a description of man's existence within that framework. The conflicts between his essential goodness and his existential estrangement cannot be seen at all without keeping essentialism and existentialism together. Theology must see both sides, man's essential nature, wonderfully and symbolically expressed in the paradise story, and man's existential condition, under sin, guilt, and death.[16]

The concept of universals in our case of *huiothesía* (υἱοθεσία) is not limited to the category of "humans" but also encompasses the divisions within the human natures, such as "old Adamic protological humans" and "new Christic eschatological humans." The matter at hand is the existence of humans within these two sub-natures, as opposed to atheistic existentialism, which posits that only one human nature exists (the Adamic humans) and that authentic existence can be achieved in that state of being.

Our discussion focuses on the ontological transformation of an individual from one state of being to another and their former and elevated existence. Indeed, specific characteristics are inherent in human nature and remain constant before and after an ontological transformation. The transformation of nature is not equal to the replacement of personhood. Subsequently, each individual retains their particularity (distinctive characteristics) upon attaining the elevated nature. Nevertheless, human beings can undergo an ontological change, given that human life is dynamic, contingent, and shaped by various internal and *external* factors.

A chief external factor that can significantly influence the nature of a person is God's sub-act of υἱοθεσία, which corrects and elevates a person's nature while preserving the peculiarity of his personhood. It develops an old being into a new one by providing a quickened spirit, a sanctified soul, and a spiritual body for its everlasting pneumatic existence. This transformation is called "salvation," a conversion from carnal to spiritual being, which causes a new being to have a new kind of relationship with Being-Itself in the pneumatic reality.

16. Tillich, *History of Christian Thought*, 541.

While we do not have direct access to the original Greek writings of Irenaeus, we have the well-preserved first source, the epistles of the apostle Paul, which explain the apostle's knowledge of the gospel of υἱοθεσία. If we read his epistles in the proper context, we will be amazed at how the gospel of Jesus *the* Christ (Ἰησοῦς ὁ Χριστός) is revealed to us. Paul explained how a mere human can become a Χρίστος (Χρῑστῐᾱνός).

The teaching of human salvation through Paul's gospel of υἱοθεσία may initially appear complex; however, upon thorough examination, it becomes evident that it is, in fact, relatively straightforward and more readily comprehensible than the Roman and Reformed theological adoption, which is alien to Paul himself (or to the gospel itself).

Vernon McGee, who may have consulted a dictionary, wrongly associates the *toga virilis* with adoption and Pauline υἱοθεσία. However, he makes a valid point when he states, "To adopt one's own son . . . *toga virilis* . . . Adoption (the Greek word is *huiothesía*) means to place as a son."[17] Yes, υἱοθεσία is related to "placing as a [mature] son." The argument I wish to advance is that the concepts of the Roman *toga virilis* and *adoptio* are not synonymous with the apostle Paul's biblical term, υἱοθεσία. The first two are rooted in Roman law and culture, whereas Paul's usage reflects a distinct theological meaning. The historical context of these Roman practices has contributed to the development of a Romanized doctrine of adoption, which attempts to explain how a person can be saved. However, equating these Roman concepts with Paul's understanding risks misunderstanding the unique spiritual significance that explains the content of a true gospel he attributes to υἱοθεσία in the biblical sense.

Conversely, Paul places significant emphasis on the symbolic meaning of υἱοθεσία, which has no direct connection to the context of slavery. Furthermore, it is implausible that God would adopt slaves or sons of other families, given that all humans are God's created minor children (νήπιοι) and are always under God's provision. Since their creation, humans have maintained a protological relationship with God. This relationship remains unbroken even when Adamic humans sin. The degree of this relationship is determined by the extent of human protological capacity, which will be enhanced in conjunction with the ontological transformation of human essence. If this is not the case, it is challenging to comprehend how God can save Adamic humans. The concept of adoption necessitates a

---

17. McGee explains, "Adoption has a meaning different from that of our contemporary society. . . . However, the Roman custom in Paul's day was to adopt one's own son. That, you recall, was what was done in the *toga virilis* ceremony. Adoption (the Greek word is *huiothesía*) means to place as a son. A believer is placed in the family of God as a full-grown son, capable of understanding divine truth." McGee, *Galatians*, 69–70.

separation between fallen humans and God. It is unlikely that God, who is love (1 John 4:8), would bestow any of His created children with the status of slave.[18] Only wicked humans can do it. The practice of slavery is a concept that is antithetical to the divine sub-act of *huiothesía*.

In 2002, J. A. Harrill published his exegesis of the Epistle to the Galatians 4:1-7. This passage mentions υἱοθεσία (v. 4:5). He concluded that the celebration of the *toga virilis* (lit., "manly gown") was equal to baptism.[19] God's sub-act of υἱοθεσία to individuals begins with baptism.[20] The Roman *toga virilis* has a meaning associated with the Greek υἱοθεσία, which refers to a new legal status as an adult. If the Latin Bible translators choose to interpret the term "υἱοθεσία" as "*toga virilis*," it will be a more accurate representation than the concept of "*adoptio*." However, this is not the primary meaning of the Pauline metaphorical Christianized "υἱοθεσία," which implies a new essence, a new being, caused by an ontological transformation.

The Roman practice of *toga virilis* and the *adoptio* are two distinct concepts that some proponents of the doctrine of adoption have erroneously conflated. To illustrate this point, consider the following historical events. Emperor Claudius reigned from AD 41 to 54 and held two notable celebrations of the *toga virilis* for Tiberius Claudius Nero Drusus Germanicus Caesar (Nero) and Tiberius Claudius Germanicus (Britannicus).[21] As was previously mentioned, this practice is analogous to Diodorus Siculus' "υἱοθεσία." The context must have been familiar to Paul and the people of the Greek and Latin world, including the Galatians, Romans, and Ephesians, who received epistles that contain the word "υἱοθεσία."[22] The difference between Roman *adoptio* and *toga virilis* is best illustrated by the cases of Nero

---

18. *Contra* Tsang, "In looking at the Roman *paterfamilias*, the similarity between the two perspectives comes from the way Paul used the metaphors of slavery, adoption, and inheritance within Galatians 3 and 4. God as the father acts as the head of the household. On the other hand, while the Roman *paterfamilias* was more legal in its institution, the heavenly Father model of the gospel has a more intimate relationship." Tsang, "'Abba' Revisited," 135.

19. Harrill, "Coming of Age," 252-77.

20. Hušek renders that, "Our adoption as children of God is closely related to baptism." Hušek, "Rebirth into a New Man," 157.

21. Dio recorded, "In AD 51, Nero received the *toga virilis*. . . .In AD 54, Claudius prepared his son, Britannicus, to receive a *toga virilis*, and would announce him as an heir to the throne." Cocceaianus, *Dio's Roman History* 8:15-59, 61-91.

22. St. Paul's Epistle to the Galatians was written in AD 49-50, Romans in AD 58, Ephesians in AD 61-63. Nero becomes Roman emperor in AD 54. See *Ryrie Study Bible: New American Standard Bible*, 1458; another opinion, Paul writes Galatians in AD 48, Romans AD 57, Ephesians AD 62. *ESV Study Bible*, 2147.

and Britannicus, who were Claudius' heirs. In AD 50, Claudius adopted Nero, and in AD 51, he bestowed upon him the *toga virilis*.

In contrast, Britannicus, born to Claudius, was not required to undergo the *adoptio* but only needed the rite of passage of the *toga* of adulthood to become an heir.[23] Claudius did not have to adopt him. To become an heir to the Roman throne, a person needed to undergo both the *adoptio* and the *toga virilis*, unless the individual was a capable natural son of the *paterfamilias*.

In *Bibliotheca Historica* (Βιβλιοθήκη Ἱστορική), Diodorus of Sicily wrote:

> ἑξῆς δὲ μεταλλάξαντος Αἰμιλίου τοῦ κατὰ φύσιν πατρὸς καὶ τούτῳ τε καὶ τῷ Φαβίῳ τοῖς δοθεῖσιν εἰς υἱοθεσίαν ἀπολιπόντος τὴν οὐσίαν, ἐποίησεν ὁ Σκιπίων καλόν τι καὶ μνήμης ἄξιον.[24]

A careful examination of the context—"when Aemilius, *his real father*, died and left his property *to him [Scipio] and to Fabius, the sons* he had given in υἱοθεσίαν"—reveals that "υἱοθεσία" is not "adoption" in this instance. In this case, Scipio and Fabius were the natural sons of Aemilius, who had previously died and left his property to them. The sons who had been granted υἱοθεσία (and thus recognized as having grown up—"matured sons") also can become legal heirs. It is unlikely that the birth father would have proceeded with the adoption of his sons. In this context, the term "υἱοθεσία" is closely related to the concept of the "*toga virilis.*" Nevertheless, the term and context of the *toga virilis* cannot be applied to all of the five instances of υἱοθεσία in the Bible, for example, Rom 9:4. Subsequent analysis will demonstrate that Paul's intention extends beyond literal and legal interpretation.

The apostle Paul employed the term "υἱοθεσία" in a theological context, employing a metaphorical interpretation. He introduced a new layer of Christian meaning, or "*interpretatio christiana*," to the concept of filial maturity, discussing the elevation of human beings from a protological to an eschatological state and its implications, including the freedom from tribal (group-oriented) laws, sins, corruption, and decay. As he did with other words, such as "*agápē*" (ἀγάπη) and "*sōtēría*" (σωτηρία), Paul transformed the original meaning of *huiothesía* (υἱοθεσία) from a celebration of maturity to a spiritual and divine concept, signifying human salvation.

Pauline υἱοθεσία does not describe a new act of God that is separate from the creation, as God has only one primary act. I interpret Pauline υἱοθεσία as a metaphorical description of God's sub-act of elevation. In

---

23. Cocceaianus, *Dio's Roman History* 8:29.
24. Diodorus, *Diodorus of Sicily* 11:385.

the words of Gordon D. Kaufman, it is a sub-act that "moves the creation forward a further step toward the realization of God's purposes,"[25] from the creation of Adamic beings to their transformation (growth, elevation) into Christlike beings. Paul employs the concept of the growth of an infant (νήπιος) into a mature human being (υἱός) to elucidate the ontological change of a person from an old sarkic-Adamic being into the new pneumatic-Christic being. In this context, Adam is symbolically referred to as an infant.[26] This *huiothesía* is an integral aspect of the divine creative process within this temporal realm. It may be interesting to consider Carlo Collodi's metaphor of Pinocchio[27] concerning the idea of an ontological transformation of being. A human being is in a state of becoming or in a continuous process of becoming.[28] What kind of theological transformation does an individual undergo?

---

25. Kaufman explains, "This means for a monotheistic theology that it is the whole course of history, from its initiation in God's creative activity to its consummation when God ultimately achieves his purposes, that should be conceived as God's act in the primary sense . . . he is one who planned 'the end from the beginning' (Isa. 46:10)." On the subject of sub-act he explained, "This does not mean, of course, that every natural or historical event need be or should be regarded as a distinct subact of God; only those events which move the creation forward a further step toward the realization of God's purposes could be properly so designated. . . . It would hardly be appropriate to regard the continuing steady functioning of such process as new 'acts of God'; they are, rather, the product of his earlier (creative) work, still sustained by him no doubt, but now serving as the (relatively completed) foundation on which he can build as yet unrealized superstructures. . . . Only those natural and historical events which directly advance God's ultimate purposes—those which are essentials constituent phases or steps of God's master act—may properly be regarded as (subordinate) acts of God within nature and history. . . . In all these cases the particular is seen in the context of, or a phase of, a more comprehensive whole." Kaufman, *God the Problem*, 137, 144–46.

26. Theophilus sees Adam as an infant literally. Cf. Schaff: "But Adam, being yet an infant in age, was on this account as yet unable to receive knowledge worthily. For now, also, when a child is born it is not at once able to eat bread, but is nourished first with milk, and then, with the increment of years, it advances to solid food. Thus, too, would it have been with Adam; for not as one who grudged him, as some suppose, did God command him not to eat of knowledge. But He wished also to make proof of him, whether he was submissive to His commandment. And at the same time, He wished man, infant as he was . . . to remain for some time longer simple and sincere." Schaff, *Fathers of the Second Century*, 104.

27. Collodi, *Pinocchio*.

28. Ratzinger explains, "This gives the concept of being God's children a dynamic quality: We are not ready-made children of God from the start, but we are meant to become so increasingly by growing more and more deeply in communion with Jesus." Ratzinger, *Jesus of Nazareth*, ch. 5.

I must respectfully disagree with some exegetical approaches that rely on the Roman *toga virilis*, and *adoptio*, or Israeli *bar mitzvah*[29] cultural background to interpret the context of Pauline biblical *huiothesía*. Similarly, a translator or exegete should refrain from using the cultural context of the receiving language to translate the word.[30] Paul has added a theological meaning to Diodorus Siculus' Greek υἱοθεσία, and thus, it is necessary to use its Pauline biblical context to disclose its *theological* meaning.

The term υἱοθεσία is not easily defined due to the prevalence (commonness) of the term "adoption." The seventeen-to-eighteen centuries' long prevalence of erroneous interpretations has resulted in the obscuring of the true meaning of υἱοθεσία by the Roman concept of adoption. Furthermore, biblical scholars have employed it to analyze the Bible's teachings and the Greek patristic tradition. For example, the case of Trumper, Behr, and Blackwell can be cited. There are numerous additional examples. Unfortunately, the extrabiblical Roman tradition of adoption is perceived as a biblical Pauline theology. Nevertheless, examining the biblical context can facilitate reclaiming the apostle Paul's doctrine of *huiothesía*.

Several English Bibles and commentaries define υἱοθεσία as a state of being, "divine-sonship," or having the form of a son.[31] It will be challenging to explain the two occurrences of it in Rom 8 and the one in Rom 9. The issue also concerns the interpretation of other terms, such as "υἱός" (*huios*), "τέκνον" (*teknon*), and "νήπιος" (*népios*), which are essential to an understanding of the context of υἱοθεσία.

Another issue is that numerous scholars who adhere to the doctrine of adoption associate adoption with the Spirit as a single referent. Nevertheless, there are English Bibles that render this verse with a minuscule "spirit," such as the NASB, Douay-Rheims Bible, Darby Bible, God's Word, Webster's Bible, Anderson NT, Mace NT, Worrell NT, Worsley NT, and the Young's Literal Translation. It would appear that the terms "the Holy Spirit" and "πνεῦμα υἱοθεσίας" (which has been mistranslated as the Spirit of adoption) refer to two distinct entities. Moreover, the two occurrences of "spirit," πνεῦμα δουλείας and πνεῦμα υἱοθεσίας in this verse, refer to two distinct states of being of the human spirit. The latter indicates a human spirit capable of participating in the pneumatic union, representing a novel form of communion that transcends the sarkic communion of Adamic humans.

---

29. The term "*bar mitzwah*" itself had not been used in the time of Jesus. *NET Bible*, 1906.

30. *Contra* Mbua, "Conceptualization and Translation," 20.

31. For instance see "Faithful Version," Darby's Translation 1890; Burke, *Message of Sonship*.

I concur with Erin M. Heim's assertion that the term "υἱοθεσία" lacks a singular, univocal meaning.[32] Each instance of "υἱοθεσία" plays a role in the broader concept. However, there are notable discrepancies in our perspectives. I diverge from Heim's interpretation, which asserts that her model is based on the Greco-Roman adoption and Jewish traditions.[33] The latter tradition does not recognize the possibility of adoption. There is a conceptual discontinuity here. Moreover, how can universal salvation be modeled on tribalistic traditions? Pauline υἱοθεσία signifies a universal concept, a transition from infancy to maturity. Furthermore, I disagree with her understanding of "the Spirit of sonship" concerning Rom 8:15. Unlike Heim, I contend that a believer does not receive the Spirit of sonship; rather, they receive a quickened human spirit—also known as an enlivened spirit or a believing spirit—as a launching point of becoming a *mature* son (a υἱός) or a pneumatic being.[34]

Heim perceives υἱοθεσία as a "restoration" of human lost sonship through adoption, much like many adoption advocates do.[35] In my opinion, it is a "constitution" of an ultimate human being (ὁ ἔσχατος [ἄνθρωπος] Ἀδάμ, the last kind of humanity, an eschatological consummated human being, or "human 2.0") from his protological state (ὁ πρῶτος ἄνθρωπος Ἀδάμ, the first kind of humanity, an infant human being, or "human 1.0"); see 1 Cor 15:45 about a living being and a life-giving spirit.

A parallel can be drawn between the construction of a hotel and the creation of humankind. The hotel's design will not be visible until the building is complete. Only the designer, aware of the outcome from the start, can

---

32. Heim argues, "Earlier studies on the Pauline υἱοθεσία metaphors have tended to focus heavily on their background or have tended to synthesize the metaphors into a univocal meaning." Heim, "Light Through a Prism," iv, 318.

33. Heim explains, "Although I argued that the predominant model in play for the υἱοθεσία metaphors in Galatians 4 and in Romans 8 was Greco-Roman adoption, in Romans 9:4 the Jewish sonship tradition as a model for υἱοθεσία is drawn firmly into view." Heim, "Light Through a Prism," 317.

34. Cf. Pate: "The spirit of Christians (the only instance where 'spirit' in Rom. 8 is the human spirit)." Pate, *Romans*, 169. Differing slightly from Pate, I think this is not the only verse where Pauline's πνεῦμα (*pneuma*) refers to a Christian's spirit.

35. Heim renders, "Thus the vertical elements of the υἱοθεσία metaphor regarding how the believers related to God were most prominent in Galatians 4:5. Moreover, Paul grounded his υἱοθεσία metaphor in Galatians 4:5 in the community's shared experience of receiving the Spirit, which intimately connected the Spirit to sonship and solidified their assurance of their spiritual lineage as children of God.... Paul's frame in Romans 8 connects the audience's reception of the Spirit of υἱοθεσία with their experience as co-sufferers with Christ (Rom. 8:17), and with their feeling of eschatological displacement and longing for the completion of their restoration (Rom. 8:23)." Heim, "Light Through a Prism," 316.

see the full plan. However, as the paradigmatic existence, the Messiah, the primogenetic [mature] son of God,[36] enables us to envisage the new nature of humans we will become. God created the Adamic humans in the image of God as a foundation and will build the Christic humankind on it.

Given the disparate perspectives, my analysis will yield conclusions that diverge significantly from those of the proponents of adoption. This work represents a critical examination (deconstruction) of the doctrine of adoption and an attempt to reconstruct (disclose) the knowledge of υἱοθεσία as espoused by the apostle Paul.

CORE CHALLENGE

We turn to Eph 1:5.

> He did this by predestining us to adoption as his legal heirs through Jesus Christ, according to his pleasure and will. (NET)

The 2019 NET Bible Full Note explains, *tn Grk*, "The Greek term υἱοθεσία (*huiothesía*) was originally a legal technical term for adoption as a son with full rights of inheritance. . . . *sn Adoption as his legal heirs* is different from spiritual birth as children."[37] Thus, it says that υἱοθεσία is a legal technical term, and it is different from spiritual birth. That assumption is the fundamental problem. It is not easy to comprehend how a particular Greek word coined by Paul can be interpreted as a reference to Roman culture. If Paul were to refer to Roman culture, he would probably transliterate the term "*adoptio*" into Greek "ἀδοπτῐο" like he did to "Ἀββᾶ" from the Aramaic. The Pauline Greek "υἱοθεσία" is intrinsic to the authentic gospel, whereas "adoption" is an unbiblical Roman cultural construct that bears no resemblance to υἱοθεσία.

The issue I wish to address is the discrepancy between the Pauline Greek υἱοθεσία and the Latin Vulgata's *adoptio*, and *vice versa*. The concept of the Pauline Greek υἱοθεσία is universal in scope, as it denotes the natural progression experienced by all individuals, from infancy to maturity. In contrast, the practice of adoption is not a universal phenomenon; it is culturally contingent and not experienced by every individual or recognized in every society. This distinction underscores the importance of accurately interpreting *huiothesía* within its original Pauline context.

---

36. Jesus is the Christ the Son of God (Ἰησοῦς ἐστὶν ὁ χριστὸς ὁ υἱὸς τοῦ θεοῦ). John 20:31. No comma after "the Christ."

37. *NET Bible*, 2233.

This Roman concept of adoption has already found its way into Western Christian theology through an authorized translation of the Latin Bible. Furthermore, the concept has come to be regarded as "Pauline theology," which further complicates the matter. This depiction of God's method of salvation is inaccurate. Adoption represents the Roman "gospel." It concerns a new legal status. It is of the utmost importance to acknowledge that theological υἱοθεσία represents an ontological transformation into a new being rather than merely a change in legal status.

To make this discussion easier, I break the problem down into the following. First, Tim J. R. Trumper promotes the importance of the doctrine of adoption and "demanded a reorientation of soteriology towards the concept of sonship,"[38] David B. Garner, in 2016, on the contrary, argued for reassessment and deconstruction of the doctrine and dismantling of its inaccurate delivery, false assumptions, and misunderstanding of theological adoption.[39] Like Nigel Johnstone,[40] I ask, "Does υἱοθεσία mean 'adoption' in Gal 4:5?"

Second, the theology of adoption has been constructed upon the terms "*adoptio*" in the Roman Catholic *Biblia Sacra Vulgata* and "adoption" in the Protestant English Bibles. However, the corresponding Pauline original word in the *Novum Testamentum Graece* is "υἱοθεσία." These are two different concepts. Third, the term υἱοθεσία has been interpreted in several ways in the biblical context, including "adoption," "sonship," and "placing of/as a son." It has also been read in the context of the Roman *toga virilis*. However, as God has only one economy, only one of these interpretations may be correct. Fourth, while each instance of υἱοθεσία in the Pauline corpus appears to have its distinct import, a translation of the five occurrences of υἱοθεσία as "adoption" as a judicial act of God would not be accurate. Some may argue that the significance of its occurrence in Rom 8:23 is irrelevant, so they delete it from their *mss* and translation.

According to Jerome, *adoptio* leads to deification.[41] Adoption promises something the gospel does not reveal, thus concealing the true message of God's gospel of υἱοθεσία. The doctrine of adoption applies an alien context to the Bible and does not represent the proper solution to humanity's ultimate concern for salvation. Instead, it obscures the concept of salvation. The doctrine of adoption has influenced the structure of the content of faith and

---

38. Ferguson, "Reformed Doctrine of Sonship," 84; Trumper, "Historical Study," 466.

39. Garner, *Sons in the Son*, xxii, xxv–xxvi.

40. Johnstone, "Does Ὑιοτηεσια."

41. Hušek, "Rebirth into a New Man," 154.

the benefit relationships (logical dependency) of doctrines in the Reformed *ordo salutis*.[42] We will investigate the relationship between υἱοθεσία and the order and history of salvation. The Roman theology of adoption, which functions on a group-oriented level, intends to adopt members of other tribes/believers from different families or none at all as if they were the only members of God's family.

Theories of Theological Adoption

The succeeding statements illustrate the issues mentioned earlier. According to Tim J. R. Trumper, J. L. Girardeau, John Murray, Trevor J. Burke, and John Calvin,

> the exposition of adoption must reflect the actual language of the New Testament (NT), especially the uniqueness of Paul's term (*huiothesía*), from which the adoption model derives its name (Rom. 8:15–16, 22–23; 9:4; Gal. 4:4–5; Eph. 1:4–5).[a] In keeping with this, I have refused to draw on extra-Pauline NT texts, including John 1:12.[43]

> Regeneration is a creative act, adoption is not. By regeneration we are created children of God in Christ Jesus; by adoption we are, as the already *created* children of God, *authorized* to take our place in his family.[44]

> Firstly, adoption is never separable from justification and regeneration. The person who is justified is always the recipient of sonship. And those who are given the right to become sons of God are those who, as John 1:13 indicates, were born . . . but of God; secondly, adoption is, like justification, a judicial act. It is a bestowal of a status, or standing, not the generating within us of a new nature or character. It concerns a relationship and not the attitude or disposition which enables us to recognize and cultivate that relationship.[45]

> Salvation, as expressed in Paul's metaphor of adoption, is the taking of an outsider—one who does not belong—and bringing

---

42. For instance, see Grudem, *Bible Doctrine*, 281–82.

43. Trumper, "Fresh Exposition of Adoption," 61. Trumper's note *a*: "I recognize the danger of building a theology on a specific biblical term. As Vern S. Poythress warns, a biblical term may become technical when used theologically. We must ensure, then, that its technical use retains its core biblical meaning."

44. Girardeau, *Discussions*, 475. Emphasis original.

45. Murray, *Redemption*, 132–33.

him into a new family, "the household of faith" (τοὺς οἰκείους τῆς πίστεως, Gal. 6:10).⁴⁶

Calvin affirms that "Father" is the term "which applies only to the members of Christ." Again, his comments on Isa 63:16 confirm the view that sonship, properly speaking, is the "peculiar privilege of the Church." A similar delimitation is made concerning Malachi's question, "Have we not all one Father?" (2:10), where for Calvin the "all" is exclusively a reference to the Jews.⁴⁷

Addressing the Issue

I perceive the Godhead as the Creator and Father of all intelligent beings and all subhuman creations. The Valdes Catechism of 1549 teaches: "In the first place, let them recognize God as Father, generally, by human *generation*, and particularly, by Christian *regeneration* (Gen. 2; Rom 8)."⁴⁸ God is always the Father of all created beings, including those of Christ-faith and those of other faiths or no faith.

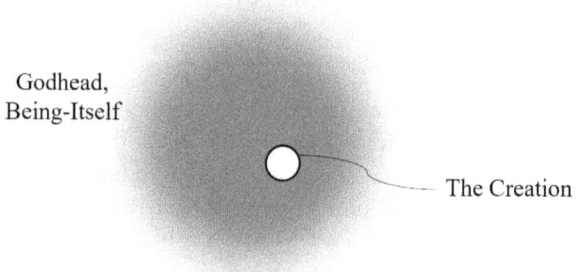

FIGURE 1: The Eternal Creator (Being-Itself) and His Creation

Remember the First Helvetic Confession, chapter 10, "The Eternal Counsel of God Concerning the Renewal of Man," which says,

> Thus, through his fault, man was given over to damnation and incurred just indignation; nevertheless, *God the Father never ceased to care for him*. This is manifest from the first promises,

---

46. Burke, "Adopted as Sons (ΥΙΟΘΕΣΙΑ)," 271.
47. Westhead, "Adoption," 104.
48. Dennison, *Reformed Confessions* 1:529. Emphasis added.

and the whole law (which stirs up but does not extinguish sin), and from Christ who was ordained and appointed for that purpose (Eph. 1; Rom. 7).[49]

God has always cared for His created children and has never abandoned them, even when they fall. God never excommunicated Adam or allowed him to become a son of another family. God expelled Adam and Eve from Eden (Gen 3:21–24), not from the God-created family and household (the creation). Both fallen and unfallen human beings are members of the κτίσις (creation, the material universe), and all the κτίσις are always in God (panentheism). In the beginning, God started the κτίσις, but God has not completed the establishment of it. God is improving it, including improving God's created children until their consummation at the parousia. Under these settings, it is difficult to maintain the doctrine of adoption, which requires the condition that humans are separated from God because of Adam's fall and their sins.

Salvation, like creation, is an act of the Godhead on the principle of *opera Trinitatis ad extra sunt indivisa*—the aspect of classical theism that asserts that the acts of the triune God are indivisible outside of Godself.[50] In John Frames' words, "All of God's activities in the world, therefore, are Trinitarian—the result of the complex interplay between the three persons."[51] Before His death and resurrection (before fully becoming the human Messiah, the Christ), God the Son incarnate, using human language, calls "*Abba*" to God the Father in their Trinitarian relationship. Humans are outside of this unique relationship. In the context of υἱοθεσία, in terms of extended relationship, Christian believers (the beings outside Being-Itself)—as the object of salvation—also call "*Abba*" to God the Father because these created beings observe and imitate the actions of God the Son incarnate.

I observe that science can support theology through dialogue and integration. The arguments in this work start from a religious tradition and then argue that a particular belief needs to be reformulated in the light of its true theological significance and contemporary knowledge. Ian G. Barbour calls this "a theology of nature."[52] Thus, for this writing, I use philosophical,

---

49. Bullinger et al., *Reformed Confessions* 1:342. Emphasis added.
50. Adiprasetya, *Berteologi*, 224.
51. Frame, *Systematic Theology*, 507.
52. Barbour argues, "Science and religion are partners in a common quest for a comprehensive understanding of the world, and the theories and results of science can be brought to bear in fruitful ways on the development of theories in theology, and vice versa." Barbour, *When Science*, 10–12.

anthropological, scientific, and theological categories in my quest for a comprehensive worldview (*Weltanschauung*) as a believer in Christ.

After exploring the theoretical frameworks of other writers, I developed the key concepts and perspectives that will guide the work and help frame the problem.[53] The main point of distinction—which creates novelties—is that this work goes beyond a literal interpretation of the metaphor of υἱοθεσία (read: *adoptio*). I view υἱοθεσία, νήπιος, τέκνον, and υἱός as Pauline symbolic language concerning ontological transformation. Gerald O'Collins points out that figurative language leads us to ultimate realities more than abstract concepts.[54] Thus, υἱοθεσία, which semantically explains a change (growth) from a νήπιος to a υἱός, figuratively leads us to the meaning of an ontological transformation of an old being. This ontological transformation (elevation, exaltation) enables a person to enter the spiritual realm.

This work does not convey the concept of tribal religions, in which some adherents perceived themselves as children of their gods and others as slaves or children of other gods. Such religions adhere to the Old Testament descriptions of tribal laws enforced by tribal gods. Compare this with Josh 24:15: "Choose this day whom you will serve, whether the gods your fathers served in the region beyond the River, or the gods of the Amorites." These are the faiths of these νήπιοι (infants, corporeal Adamic humans). Those who adhere to tribal religions are firmly anchored in their mythological origins, yet scientific minds will gradually diverge from them.[55]

I subscribe to the theistic theory of evolution and polygenesis. Thus, I perceive that there is no historical Adam, only a literary Adam. The accounts of a literary Adam in Gen 1 and 2 are etiologies. Many civilizations have tribalistic etiologies.[56] These narratives elucidate the genesis of their

---

53. Roberts, *Dissertation Journey*, 163–77 (emphasis original); the doctrine under my examination is not the theory that was employed to do the research, but it is the problem. This research agrees that "some qualitative studies *do not employ any explicit theory*"; see also Creswell and Creswell, *Research Design*, 62, 64.

54. O'Collins renders, "We are guided toward ultimate realities by symbolic language, even more than by abstract concepts. Faced with analogies, metaphors, and symbols, theologians must listen to the philosophical experts on language and religious language." O'Collins, *Rethinking Fundamental Theology*, 335.

55. Fowler argues, "Faith stage transitions are not automatic or inevitable. They may occur more slowly in one person or group than another, and some persons find equilibrium at earlier stages than do others." Fowler, *Stages of Faith*, 133–50, 151–73, 276.

56. There is a mythological etiology (Greek αἰτιολογία, "giving a reason for") of the creation of the *Manusia Jawa* ("Javanese People") in Indonesia. This is recorded in *Tantu Penggelaran*. The first, third, and sixth paragraphs of it are translated and quoted below: "Hopefully, nothing gets in the way. . . . Long Bathara meditating. He sent Sang Hyang Brahma and Wisnu to make humans. Hyang Brahma and Wisnu did not refuse,

respective universes and how their creators brought forth humankind and the myriad of other entities that populate these worlds.

I perceived that the story of the literary Adam represents the condition of all conscious beings. The protological "humankind" is denoted by the collective noun "*adam*" in Hebrew.[57] Every conscious being's existential circumstance is portrayed in *adam*'s fall. Søren Kierkegaard asserts, "Every individual is itself and the race, and that the later individual is not significantly differentiated from the first man."[58] Humankind *(adam)* sinned; everyone sins.

It can be posited that a complete human being is comprised of three distinct constitutive elements: the body, the soul, and the spirit. It is believed that the will of the flesh and the spirit are in constant conflict, attempting to dominate the soul.[59] However, a latent (dormant) spirit cannot win the conflict; vivification is necessary.[60]

Aims and Objectives

In light of the considerations mentioned above, through this work, I endeavor to contribute a novel perspective to the discourse on Pauline biblical υἱοθεσία while also facilitating the comprehension of the Christian proclamation of salvation (kerygma) among individuals with a scientific

---

and they made humans, soil clumped in fists to make humans who were very perfectly beautiful as the image of a god. The male human was made by Sang Hyang Brahma, the female human was made by Sang Hyang Wisnu. Everything is wonderful. . . . Then my son, Sang Hyang Wiswakarma, comes down to the land of Java, makes a house to be imitated by humans, then he will be called 'Undagi.'" Nurhajarini et al., *Kajian Mitos*, 72–73.

57. Mills, "Adam," 3.

58. Kierkegaard, *der Begriff der Angst*, 105, as quoted in Niebuhr, *Nature and Destiny of Man* 1:263.

59. Cf. Fokin: "Origen sometimes regards the soul as "something middle" (*quasi medium quoddam*) between flesh and spirit." Fokin, "Relationship," 603–4.

60. Dodd argues, "The only way for man to rise from the lower life to the higher is by being born ἐκ πνεύματος [from *pneuma*], which is also to be born ἐκ τοῦ Θεοῦ [from God]. This rebirth is made possible through the descent of the 'Son of Man' from τὰ ἄνω [the things above (heavenly realm)] to τὰ κάτω [the things below, on earth (earthly realm)]. This descent is otherwise expressed in the terms, ὁ λόγος σὰρξ ἐγένετο [the logos became flesh]. The Logos, being Θεός [God], has the nature of πνεῦμα [spirit], and consequently is said to be both ἀλήθεια [truth or disclosure] and ζωή [life]. Being πνεῦμα [spirit] (not, of course, being 'the Holy Spirit'), He became σάρξ [flesh], partook fully in the experience of this lower world, and gave himself to death (the characteristic mark of σάρξ [flesh]), in love for mankind." Dodd, *Interpretation of the Fourth Gospel*, 226.

disposition. As Robert S. Candlish observed, "I do not mean to teach a new doctrine. I seek to know the mind of Christ."[61] Likewise, the doctrine in question is already present in the Bible. It is necessary to elucidate the concept of biblical υἱοθεσία and to construct a content of faith (*notitia*) based on biblical interpretations that are free from the Roman idea of adoption and, in addition, corresponding to the contemporary world-picture (*Weltbild*), or modern scientific thoughts. This approach may be "time-based contextualization," which employs the contemporary context and knowledge in interpreting biblical accounts.

This work aims to abandon the Roman gospel of *adoptio* and reconstruct the Pauline Greek υἱοθεσία that it has covered to unconceal the gospel of salvation that the apostle Paul was made aware of and desired to spread to others. Additionally, the work aims to identify the role of υἱοθεσία within other doctrines and to raise awareness among Bible translators, interpreters, and exegetes about the significance of Pauline υἱοθεσία. This work encourages the intellectual conversion[62] of those who advocate adoption and those who have left the faith. In this work, the term "υἱοθεσία" is employed in a manner that extends beyond the meaning recorded by Diodorus Siculus. I will momentarily define it as "developing a mature pneumatic human being."

Key Questions Explored

This work will explore four key questions designed to address the objections raised against the current framework. The first two questions focus on evaluating the doctrine of adoption through a theory-first approach. The last two questions are designed to stimulate the development of a new doctrinal framework, offering a fresh perspective to replace the existing paradigm of theological adoption.[63]

The initial question addressed in chapter 1 is as follows: What insights does the adoption narrative offer that prompts some individuals to question

---

61. Candlish, "Fatherhood of God," 7.

62. Barden explains, "Intellectual conversion is a radical clarification and, consequently, the elimination of an exceedingly stubborn and misleading myth concerning reality, objectivity and human knowing. . . . As radical clarification, it is a discovery. As the elimination of a myth, that is, of a mistaken account, it is the eradication of an error." Barden, "On Intellectual Conversion," 125.

63. Cf. White: "In 'theory testing' ('theory-first') studies, hypotheses are derived from a theory and are then subjected to empirical testing. In contrast, the aim of 'theory generation' (or 'theory-after') research is to produce theories as the result of the investigation." White, *Developing Research Questions*, 25.

its veracity? The second question, discussed in chapter 2, is as follows: When and how did the term "υἱοθεσία" become "adoption?" The third question, which is discussed in chapters 3, 4, and 5, is as follows: What is the most accurate translation of υἱοθεσία? The fourth question, which is discussed in chapters 6, 7, and 8, is as follows: What does the term "υἱοθεσία" teach, both literally and metaphorically (theologically)? In the conclusions, this work discusses Lonergan's final specialty: communication, which concerns practical theology.

The Limits and Reach

It is beyond my control to address the following constraint. Concerning Pauline υἱοθεσία, no specific books or articles have been identified and fully collected that discuss υἱοθεσία in its own right. However, biblical υἱοθεσία is commonly interpreted as adoption. Consequently, before I can reconstruct the theological (metaphorical) meaning of υἱοθεσία, I must rely on biblical exegesis, commentaries, some translations of the vernacular Bible *Versions*, and Greek dictionaries to reveal the literal sense. On the other hand, I have not come across any particular texts that specifically refute the adoption idea. In the preface to his work, David B. Garner raises concerns about theological adoption. Nevertheless, said work discusses theological adoption.

This situation compels me to assess the claims of sonship, adoption, and *toga virilis* in light of the Greek New Testament. I impose limitations. The primary biblical texts under examination at this stage are the Pauline chapters that contain the term "υἱοθεσία." In a textual criticism work in chapter 3, I addressed the omission of the word "υἱοθεσίαν" in Rom 8:23. This omission can inform us about the region of churches, the specific era in which the variation emerged, and the dissemination of the manuscripts that do not support the reading of υἱοθεσίαν in that verse. Some may argue that the term "υἱοθεσία" cannot appear twice in the same passage. However, another limitation is the absence of any higher criticism analysis in this work. While the concept of election is discussed in Romans chapter 9, it is addressed here only in relation to υἱοθεσία. Additionally, this work does not explore the *huio*-ship of the angels.

Theological Weight of the Title

Instead of talking about adoption, the apostle Paul wants to preach about "human elevation." He posits that humanity has the potential to transcend its current protological state of existence, which he refers to as "fleshly life" and "decay," through a process of ontological transformation into everlasting pneumatic eschatological being. *Huiothesía* (Υἱοθεσία) has been interpreted as adoption; therefore, before I can reconstruct or unearth the apostle's knowledge of *huiothesía* (υἱοθεσία), I must first deconstruct the gospel of adoption to demonstrate its fallacy.

Given the pervasive conviction among many that the doctrine of adoption is unalterable and definitive, it is probable that this endeavor will be met with skepticism, as evidenced by my observations during my research. Indeed, Christian dogmas about the triune God and the preexistent Son's incarnation are immutable. However, other aspects of faith are open to discussion, and this work will attempt to address such elements.

The content of our faith is not fixed or definitive. John Macquarrie argues that no final theology can be regarded as definitive upon which we can ultimately repose. Given that every theology is historically and culturally conditioned, the most that can be hoped for is to express the content of our faith in the "clearest and most coherent language available" at the time.[64] In the view of Donald G. Bloesch, theology has two distinct aspects: apologetic and dogmatic. The former is concerned with refuting erroneous beliefs through polemics and the defense of the faith, while the latter is focused on elucidating the correct interpretation of religious doctrine.[65] This work examines both the apologetic and dogmatic aspects of Paul's theology of υἱοθεσία.

The well-known translation problem is not a novel phenomenon. The following are the novelties of this work: it illustrates the philosophical and contextual challenges of adoption and unconceals the true meaning of Pauline biblical υἱοθεσία. It approaches the problem from a variety of perspectives. In contrast to the dualistic view of adoption advocates, I adopt a panentheistic viewpoint, which posits that all is in Being-Itself. Accordingly, "father" and "family" are imbued with symbolic connotations rather than constrained by their legal, literal meanings. This work demonstrates how existentialist and essentialist theologies facilitate the revelation of the gospel of υἱοθεσία.

Following the contemporary *Weltbild* (in particular, in paleoanthropology and cosmology), I demonstrate how the concept of a historical Adam/fall can be eliminated from this work, while this work places particular emphasis on the primacy of each person of the Godhead and the incarnation of the preexistent Son. Furthermore, it differentiates Paul's

---

64. Macquarrie, *Principles*, 20.
65. Bloesch, *Theology of Word & Spirit*, 127.

theological υἱοθεσία from the Roman *toga virilis*, adoptive sonship, and Diodorus Siculus' υἱοθεσία, which is limited to a literal and legal sense. This work redirects the focus of soteriology from adoption to the concept of υἱοθεσία.

One of this revelation's (unconcealment, *alêtheia*, truth) many distinctive features is the trichotomic view of humans, distinguishing the idea of Pauline theological υἱοθεσία from his translator's Roman *adoptio*. The adoption and υἱοθεσία debates take on new dimensions when the human spirit is included as an indispensable and irrefutable variable in the discussion of God's sub-act of salvation. This *alêtheia* shows that υἱοθεσία and *adoptio* are two diverse topics. It also prompts some further research in some areas, including Bible translation, particularly in the sections that deal with the Pauline context of υἱοθεσία, υἱός, νήπιος, and τέκνον. The study of textual criticism of vernacular Versions is an intriguing field of inquiry, as it offers the potential to either corroborate or challenge existing interpretations of the translation of υἱοθεσία. It calls for extensive efforts in constructive theology, such as reworking the *historia salutis* and *ordo*. On the theme of υἱοθεσία, we can also reread Irenaeus' translated writings without the idea of adoption. Before being shared with a wider audience, this work has to be further investigated from a practical theological perspective.

This work shows that the idea of salvation as an act of returning to Adam's prelapsarian perfection (restoration) is not supported by Paul's teachings on υἱοθεσία. It conveys to believers that while humans are initially created in a state of protological (foundational) perfection, they are destined to achieve ultimate eschatological perfection, a state attainable solely through faith in Christ. Humans cannot fall from ultimate perfection but from protological perfection, as evidenced by Adam's fall, indicating the created humans had not yet attained ultimate perfection (*huio*-ship). Humans are seen as "human becoming," with the prelapsarian state of foundational perfection as a starting point for future development rather than the final state.

Ultimately, this work represents two distinct intellectual conversions: first, a transition from adoption to υἱοθεσία; and second, a shift from viewing adoption merely as a benefit within the *ordo salutis* to understanding υἱοθεσία as the *Methodus Salutis Dei*—a framework that emphasizes the significance of both the *ordo salutis* and the *historia salutis* (history of salvation, *Heilsgeschichte*) as an integrated whole.

FROM TEXT TO THEOLOGY: A WAY THROUGH

This interpretive and interdisciplinary work of literary research may be described as basic or pure research[66] involving the testing and development of theories and hypotheses. This basic research contains highly abstract and specialized concepts.[67] It applies Bernard Lonergan's *Method in Theology* to map the research process.[68] It utilizes critical biblical exegesis as a dialectical specialty, incorporating apologetic and dogmatic elements.

ORGANIZATION OF THE BOOK

Let us refer to Lonergan's Eight Functional Specialties in Table 1. Following the identification of an issue with the translation of *huiothesía* (υἱοθεσία), I begin with special research.[69] It encompasses collating data pertinent to the doctrine of adoption and *huiothesía*, including books, articles, and Bibles.

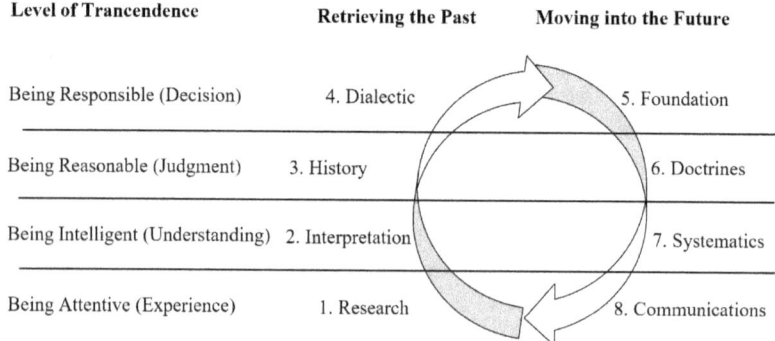

FIGURE 2: Lonergan's Eight Functional Specialty

The initial chapter of this work then turns to the second specialty, namely interpretations. It aims to gain insight into the doctrine of adoption from its proponents, identify their theoretical frameworks, identify any gaps in their arguments, and construct the conceptual framework of my work. The initial chapter addresses the initial question: What insights does the doctrine of adoption offer that prompt some individuals to question its veracity?

---

66. Leedy and Ormrod, *Practical Research*, 45.
67. Kumar, *Research Methodology*, 30.
68. Lonergan, *Method in Theology*.
69. Cf., Lonergan, *Method in Theology*, 127.

The second chapter deals with the third specialty, namely history. This section presents a brief history of the interpretations of the term *huiothesía*. Adoption is not the sole interpretation. This section addresses the second question: When and how did the term "υἱοθεσία" evolve into the concept of "adoption?"

From that point, I proceed with the analysis by examining Paul's intention in writing this word, "υἱοθεσία." It falls within Lonergan's specialty four, dialectic, and five, foundation. Given the extensive material in this section, I divide it into three chapters: 3, 4, and 5. In these chapters, I will present dialogues between myself and other interpreters during the exegetical process. This section is designated as the dialectic or debate. In the foundation, I present my position. Chapter 3 discusses some words and the omission of "υἱοθεσίαν" in Rom 8:23; chapter 4 examines υἱοθεσία from the Letter to the Galatians; and chapter 5 discusses υἱοθεσία in the Letter to the Romans. These chapters conclude the process of determining the appropriate translation of υἱοθεσία.

The third section holds chapters 6, 7, and 8. Lonergan states that it is no longer sufficient to merely recount what others have proposed, believed, or done. It must elucidate which doctrines are true; how they can be reconciled with each other and with the conclusions of science, philosophy, and history; and how they can be effectively communicated to members of every class in every culture.[70] The chapters in this section are devoted to the theory-after or doctrine generation, which is Lonergan's specialty number six. This synthesis of findings results in a proposed doctrine, a remythologized doctrine of υἱοθεσία.[71] Chapter 6 discusses υἱοθεσία of ὁ Υἱός (*ho Huios*, the consummated Son, the Christ). Chapter 7 elucidates the concept of υἱοθεσία concerning the Christic beings or οἱ υἱοί (*oi huioi*). Chapter 8 then delves into the systematic aspect of the doctrine. These chapters address the fourth problem and its associated question: What does υἱοθεσία teach, both literally and theologically (symbolically)?

The concluding chapter offers a synthesis of the preceding discussions, elucidating the contemporary relevance of Paul's gospel of υἱοθεσία. Additionally, it presents a comparative analysis of the concept of υἱοθεσία with other biblical passages, including its implications for transhumanism.

---

70. Cf., Lonergan, *Method in Theology*, 267.
71. Tillich, *Systematic Theology* 2:112.

THE THEOLOGICAL ADOPTION AND THE HISTORY OF INTERPRETATIONS OF *HUIOTHESIA*

CHAPTER 1

What They Say About the Doctrine of Adoption

"The most erroneous stories are those we think we know best—and therefore never scrutinize or question." ~ Stephen Jay Gould

OVERVIEW

In the United States, the formulation of this doctrine of adoption was initiated by J. L. Girardeau in 1905.[1] His son-in-law, Robert A. Webb, subsequently expanded upon this doctrine in his work *The Reformed doctrine of adoption*. This book was published in 1947.[2] In conjunction with these developments, the Roman Catholic Church in the USA formulated the teaching on adoption that can be found in the 1907 Catholic Encyclopedia.[3] Roman Catholic academics such as Michael Peppard[4] and a former Protestant minister, Scott Hahn,[5] are among those writing about adoption.

---

1. Girardeau, *Discussions*, 428–521.
2. Webb, *Reformed Doctrine of Adoption*.
3. Sollier, "Supernatural Adoption," 148.
4. Peppard, "Eagle and Dove"; Peppard, *Son of God*; Peppard, "Adopted and Begotten," 92–110.
5. Hahn, *First Comes Love*.

The doctrine of adoption may be understood as a misinterpretation of the Pauline biblical account of *huiothesía* (υἱοθεσία), exhibiting a multitude of intricate irregularities that render it challenging to comprehend. In the idea of adoption, the act of creation by God is followed by the fall of Adam and Eve, which results in their enslavement or incorporation into another family. For their descendants to be safe, God must adopt them and bring them back into His family. This process results in a change in their status from fallen God-created children to God-adopted children. Unfortunately, the concept of a νήπιος (*népios*) becoming a υἱός (*huios*) is not addressed. In contrast, the fate of Pinocchio is more favorable in this regard. He undergoes an ontological transformation of his puppet nature, becoming more aligned with his father's human nature. Furthermore, the notion of deification in adoption[6] introduces an additional layer of complexity regarding the possibility of deifying old sarkic-Adamic temporal beings.

It is not appropriate to take the term "sons of wrath" literally because it has a symbolic significance. It means "people who are facing divine judgment or God's wrath as a result of their deeds." This situation can only take place when these sons are God's children. The phrase "sons of wrath" refers not to sons of another family but to "disobedient children" in the family of God. This book's metaphorical view avoids such a literal, oversimplified reading that can lead to misunderstanding.

If God is omnipotent and can create all things, it would seem illogical for Him to adopt children. It is central to recall that "from him and through him and to him are all things,"[7] and that "he is before all things, and in him all things hold together."[8] Those who espouse the doctrine of adoption view the church as the entity that adopts; for proponents such as M. J. Gorman, the church can be considered an alternative family. Additionally, he refers to it as a "fictive family."[9] Suppose the church is a family (that replaces Israel).

---

6. See Hušek, "Rebirth into a New Man."

7. Rom 11:36 ESV.

8. Col 1:16–17 ESV.

9. Gorman writes, "We see it also in the way Paul understands believers as descendants, or children, of Abraham by faith, and thus also as children of God (Gal. 3:23–29). Paul capitalizes on the Roman practice of adoption to express the reality that this status of becoming God's children is due to a special act of divine fatherly grace, the result of which is full access to the father's inheritance—that is, sharing with the elder Son, Jesus, in the future glory of the Father (Rom. 8:12–17). Because all members are adopted into this family, all are equal: male and female, Jew and Gentile, black and white, European and Latino/a, etc. The church is an alternative family, what sociologists call a 'fictive family,' one constituted not by sharing in the blood of biological parents but in the blood of Jesus." Gorman, *Reading Paul*, ch. 10.

In that case, we return to the problem of a tribal (group-oriented) religion,[10] as in the Tanakh (OT), which the universal God-Creator wants to abolish. Such a concept suggests that the church is one of many tribal religions. Such a family offers salvation only to its members; in contrast, Jesus Christ is *Salvator Mundi*, "Savior of the World"; thus, the entire world is His family.

Thus, for the concept of adoption to be effective, it is necessary to assume that the devil is a father alongside God,[11] as is the case in dual cosmology. It degrades the divine ὁ πατήρ, because when it acknowledges the existence of an additional principal as the head of the alien family (the unknown family, the devil's family) in addition to a monotheistic Creator, it devalues the Infinite God (Being-Itself) to the status of a mere god (a being). Such a concept is at odds with the traditional Christian belief that "God is one"[12] and that "there is no other besides him."[13] The unknown family is presented as an adversary, yet paradoxically, it is willing to relinquish children for adoption. In the context of the doctrine of adoption, it can be argued that God saves the children of the enemy rather than those of God.[14] This approach employs many categories for God's children and God's roles, a phenomenon that is most evident in the work of Robert A. Webb.

The doctrine of adoption suggests a legal relationship, a familial transfer, and an adamic-temporal sibling relationship with the *pre*-resurrected Jesus (not with the resurrected Christ who is the [consummated] Son of God [ὁ Υἱός τοῦ Θεοῦ]). It is not a *pneumatic* union as in the mystical body of Christ. This logical situation arises from the absence of any discussion of ontological transformation, but new legal status only, so that the adopted sons continue to exist in the protological state (*népio* state, or "the state of estrangement"). This state renders them incapable of participating in a pneumatic fellowship. This viewpoint is not fully appreciated by those who espouse the doctrine of adoption or are unaware of it. They often assert that

10. See Amerson, "Church as Tribe," 91–104.

11. MacArthur states, "Since unregenerate people are by nature children of the devil, the only way they can become God's children is by spiritual adoption." MacArthur, *Galatians*, ch. 7.

12. Gal 4:20 ESV.

13. Mark 12:32 ESV.

14. Cf. Ratzinger, "Jesus' going out, on the other hand, presupposes that creation is not a fall, but a positive act of God's will. It is thus a movement of love, which in the process of descending demonstrates its true nature—motivated by love for the creature, love for the lost sheep—and so in descending it reveals what God is really like. On returning, Jesus does not strip away his humanity again as if it were a source of impurity. The goal of his descent was the adoption and assumption of all mankind, and his homecoming with all men is the homecoming of 'all flesh.'" Benedict, *Jesus of Nazareth: Part Two*, ch. 3.

the adopted son must be legally an adult son, implying that the maturity required for membership in God's family is attained outside God's family. Such an idea is not the case in the gospel. God brings God's created infants to maturity while they are in God's created family—this *ktisis*.

Many proponents of adoption draw support from a misreading of John 1:12, which states, "to become children of God." They interpret this to mean that unbelievers are not God's children and that they become children of God when they have been adopted. In contrast, the phrase "τέκνα θεοῦ γενέσθαι" is about the rebirth (elevation) of God's finite sarkic infants (νήπιοι, *népioi*) to become the beloved spiritual children (τέκνα, *tekna*), which are born of the Spirit.[15]

SCHOLARLY PERSPECTIVES AND INTERPRETATIONS

This section examines the assumptions that theologians and scholars rely on when developing their theories, the context in which they operate, their interpretations of biblical verses and passages, and how they relate the topics in support of or against the main issues and the construction of their *theoretical* framework. Furthermore, this work examines the vocabularies employed, their respective fields of meaning, and their distinctions. These distinctions can be subtle and require accuracy to distinguish them.

From the various interpretations of υἱοθεσία, it is uncertain whether "adoption" is the appropriate term. Initial readings suggest that the current authors of adoption engage in *eisegesis*, relying on the Latin and English translations of certain traditions, like the Reformed and Roman Catholic. In my view, a proper exegesis must be based on the original languages of the Bible, especially when there is a known issue of translations. Besides υἱοθεσία itself, it is essential to consider both the literal and symbolic meanings of the words associated with it.

I want to highlight here that those versed in the meaning of the terms "*népios*," "*tekna*," and "*huios*" in Paul's concept of *huiothesía* can discern that the proponents of adoption are discussing the topic of *adoptio* outside the scope of Paul's biblical *huiothesía*. Given that the Roman *adoptio* differs from the Roman *toga virilis*, the case might be different if the *Vulgata*

---

15. See John 3:3–8; cf. Russell: "Accordingly, believers are called 'children of God.' Unlike Paul, John never calls them 'sons of God.' The phrase υἱὸς τοῦ θεοῦ is reserved for the unique Son; believers are τέκνα τοῦ θεοῦ—perhaps John's equivalent to the distinction between Son and sons which Paul expresses by his image of adoption." Russell, *Doctrine of Deification*, 88.

employs the idea of *toga virilis* in place of *adoptio*, which would facilitate the comparison of biblical *huiothesía* to the Roman *toga virilis*.

Since adoption and *huiothesía* are unrelated, aligning their ideas and terminologies is challenging. Initially, some readers may face difficulties in maintaining their engagement with the text due to their lack of familiarity with the concept of biblical *huio-thesía*, which may be compounded by their prior knowledge of the terms and concepts associated with adoption, potentially leading to a *primacy bias*.

John L. Girardeau

According to John L. Girardeau, the doctrine of adoption has been overlooked by some, and its interpretation varies among leading theologians.[16] He begins his argument by referring to the debate among Robert Candlish,[17] Wright, and Thomas Crawford[18] on the Fatherhood of God. Thornwell's statement that "by nature, man is not a son of God, but simply a subject and servant" is quoted.[19] As Thornwell states, Adam can become an adopted son through his deeds, which Crawford has responded to. However, I support Girardeau's stance that before the topic of adoption is considered, we must address "man's natural relation to God." "Is he, in any sense, a *son* of God by nature?"[20] The issue in the preceding discussion is whether we interpret "son" according to Pauline *huios* (υἱός) or according to its English definition. The two are not the same. Remember the emphasis on the difference in meaning between the two, explained in the Brief Conceptual Guide. In Pauline theology, Adam and his descendants ("we") are *infants* (νήπιοι, *népioi*, protological beings) of God by creation. This way, we are created sons (in English definition) of God, but it is not at all appropriate to classify that all created sons are theologically adults (υἱοί, *huioi*, eschatological beings) of God.

It would appear that Girardeau's concept is deficient in the context of Adam as a created, protological, and natural human (νήπιος). Girardeau asserts that until recently, the prevailing opinion among commentators and theologians was that man was, in some sense, a son of God by nature. However, he notes that there were a few exceptions to this consensus.[21] Girardeau

16. Girardeau, *Discussions*, 428–29.
17. Candlish, *Fatherhood of God*.
18. Crawford, *Fatherhood of God*.
19. Girardeau, *Discussions*, 429.
20. Girardeau, *Discussions*, 429. Emphasis added.
21. Girardeau, *Discussions*, 430.

asserts that the creative act must make man a son of God.[22] These arguments suggest that Girardeau (and all the proponents of adoption) may not fully comprehend the Pauline Greek theology of God's infant (νήπιος) becoming God's mature son which symbolically teaches about God's protological son becoming God's eschatological son (υἱός).

Girardeau distinguishes between the natural and spiritual relationship of a son to God. He asserts that the natural relationship cannot be destroyed since "the sinner is a son of God."[23] However, Girardeau states that "man by his fall ceased to be a son of God" and became "a child of *wrath*."[24] Thus, for Girardeau, the natural relationship remains, but it has been destroyed spiritually and legally and requires restoration.[25] Does Adamic humanity have a natural relationship with the divine? The answer is "yes." Does Adamic humanity have a pneumatic relationship with the divine? The answer is, "As yet, human beings do not everlastingly participate in the eternal pneumatic union."

Adoption demands a separation between God and His created sons, and then it adds the requirement of a restoration to be saved. In Paul's concept of *huiothesía* (υἱοθεσία), humans (νήπιοι and υἱοί altogether) are always members of the created family of God, that is, the shared inhabitable world with God as the Father and Creator. In the beginning, human beings (νήπιοι) have a natural relationship with God, and later, God develops it into a pneumatic union following their *huiothesía* (υἱοθεσία). Salvation is not the restoration of lost imaginary sonship but the growth into a new state of being. An ax can do what it is intended to do, much like an old being is capable of doing old tasks, and a new being can do new tasks that the old being cannot do. A sarkic person can do sarkic things; a pneumatic person can do pneumatic things.

The concept of adoption becomes complicated when Girardeau discusses moral government and moral discipline, son and servant, and God as Judge and Father. These categories are "predicative nouns" designed to respond to roles and positions. These categories have nothing to do with "being," which refers to the whatness (essence) of a human being. Regardless of a person's predicates as an adopted son of God, he remains the same being. Girardeau creates unnecessary complexity by attempting to place adoption in the context of salvation by restoring human prelapsarian status.

---

22. Girardeau, *Discussions*, 431.
23. Girardeau, *Discussions*, 431.
24. Girardeau, *Discussions*, 432. Emphasis original.
25. Girardeau, *Discussions*, 433.

It is reminiscent of Richard Swinburne's "Simplicity as Evidence of Truth."[26] Due to the complexities of addressing the need for adoption, Girardeau attempted to simplify his argument by stating that "he [Adam] was simply a servant."[27] If that is the case, then the argument becomes even more difficult in the context of adoption. If Adam was a servant (not an infant), then there *is* a need for adoption, but then there is no lost prelapsarian sonship, and no restoration is necessary. The idea of adoption and restoration are mutually exclusive; they cannot be integrated.

Girardeau distinguishes adoption from regeneration and justification.[28] He explains that "regeneration is not conditioned upon faith; adoption is."[29] He incorporates the Johannine concept of "to become the sons of God," which he interpreted as "to become [*adopted*] sons of God."[30] It is an eisegesis problem. For him, "regeneration is a creative act, adoption not," but these God-created children in Christ Jesus "require adoption to be *authorized* to partake in God's family."[31] Girardeau separates regeneration from adoption, where he sees the latter from formal or legal aspects. The relation of justification, regeneration, and adoption can be seen when he says, "The regenerate children of God do believe in Christ in order to be justified.... They believe in Christ in order to be adopted."[32] He clarifies that believers cannot fully actualize the union with Christ without justification and adoption. Still, the vital relationship with Christ functioned in regeneration as a guarantee of eternal life.[33]

I contend that Paul's teaching of υἱοθεσία (which is not adoption) fundamentally addresses the ontological transformation of humans. This focus is primarily concerned with the nature and existence of human beings to address the issues of sin, decay (corruption), and temporality rather than attempting to resolve these problems through legal status. Human salvation is not solved by fulfilling a legal requirement but by becoming a new being who cannot sin, does not decay, and thus can live everlastingly.

---

26. Swinburne states, "The simplest hypothesis proposed as an explanation of phenomena is more likely to be the true one than is any other available hypothesis, that its predictions are more likely to be true than are those of any other available hypothesis, and that it is an ultimate a priori epistemic principle that simplicity is evidence of truth." Swinburne, *Simplicity*, 1.

27. Girardeau, *Discussions*, 444.
28. Girardeau, *Discussions*, 473.
29. Girardeau, *Discussions*, 473.
30. Girardeau, *Discussions*, 474.
31. Girardeau, *Discussions*, 475. Emphasis original.
32. Girardeau, *Discussions*, 477.
33. Girardeau, *Discussions*, 478.

Although the doctrine of adoption does not explain how unbelievers become believers, it is assigned to "regeneration" to answer this question. In contrast, the doctrine itself develops its teaching on the word "υἱοθεσία." Girardeau offers definitions:

> Regeneration is a *real translation*; adoption a *formal translation*. By the former we really become God's children, are really taken out of the family of Satan; by the latter we are formally, that is, legally and authoritatively, translated from the devil's family into God's.[34]

Adoption has legal characteristics. The rest of Girardeau's argument discusses the necessity of adoption *and* regeneration. One possible hypothesis is that the regeneration [of the human spirit] is one of the benefits of the *ordo salutis*, which, when considered alongside the other benefits, can help to elucidate the concept of *huiothesía*. We will get back to this in chapter 8.

Robert Alexander Webb

This fourth volume of R. Webb's lectures, published by J. L. A. Richardson, focuses on adoption and expands upon Girardeau's work.[35] While Webb claims that this doctrine is based on the Bible,[36] his argument relies more on *eisegesis* than biblical exegesis. Moreover, no evidence suggests that he consulted the Greek NT Bible. Webb also rejects the idea of God's natural and universal fatherhood. It is possible that he started with a concept related to slavery and mistakenly applied it to God's system, which is an error in methodology.

Webb sees a profound and fundamental difference between moral government and moral discipline. He argues that a theology that ignores or combines the two is fundamentally flawed in its understanding of the nature of God and human relations. Webb distinguishes between a servant under moral government and a son under moral discipline.[37] This fundamental argument is the concept that leads to his views on what he believes to be biblical adoption. We see the lack of ontological discussions in his work.

---

34. Girardeau, *Discussions*, 475. Emphasis original.

35. Richardson writes, "The subject of Adoption was one that intrigued Dr. Girardeau and was developed by Dr. Webb to the highest point of excellence." Webb, *Reformed Doctrine of Adoption*, 8.

36. Webb, *Reformed Doctrine of Adoption*, 18.

37. Webb, *Reformed Doctrine of Adoption*, 24.

Webb claims that the doctrine of paternalism has a damaging effect on the doctrine of sin. This doctrine sees offenses against God as filial disobedience and must be treated as such if God is only a Father and a human is only His son.[38] Thus, for Webb, created human beings are not yet sons of God. Webb argues that the doctrine of divine paternalism does not require the doctrine of atonement.[39] This argument is the basis for discussing sons by atonement in his ninth and tenth lectures. He reasons against what he calls "sentimental theology." In lecture eight, he skillfully discusses and rejects the idea of sonship through love. In lecture two, entitled "The Son and the Servant," Webb argues that the son and servant differ in origin,[40] natures, the form of government and careers, obedience, reward, and freedom.[41] The initial two points—origin and nature—might be pertinent to our attention on how sons and servants can differ in their origin and nature if one Creator creates them.

Webb says God-created children are not automatically considered God's sons. This argument emphasizes the need for adoption. The context of slavery is essential within Webb's argument, as it played a crucial role in developing this doctrine. I see that it is challenging to perceive God as the Creator in the setting of adoption and slavery.

Webb employs terms associated with social hierarchy and relationship status. In lectures three and four, "The Sonship of the First Adam" and "Objections to Adam's Sonship," he questions whether Adam, being created and unfallen, is a son subject to *moral discipline*, a servant subject to *moral government*, or both.[42] However, it remains unclear how Adam can

---

38. Webb, *Reformed Doctrine of Adoption*, 24. Correction: His son.

39. Webb, *Reformed Doctrine of Adoption*, 25.

40. Webb argues, "The son and the servant differ from each other as to their origins. Sonship comes in one but two ways: by creation or generation, and by adoption. One person, however, may become the servant or subject of another in a great variety of ways—by creation, by birth, by theft, by war, by purchase, and the like, but nowhere is it necessarily implied that one person becomes the subject and servant of another in consequence of birth, simply because he happens to be born in his house and of his loins. Such a birth, would, per se, constitute sonship; but if it should bring servitude, such a consequence would be accidental and abnormal." Webb, *Reformed Doctrine of Adoption*, 31.

41. Webb, *Reformed Doctrine of Adoption*, 32–39.

42. Webb further argues, "That Adam was created as a subject of God's government, in possession of holy and righteous citizenship in his kingdom, is not even put into debate.... Whatever God as Creator makes, he must rule.... Adam, unfallen, was created the servant of God, a subject of His government, under His moral law, and liable to punishment in case of disobedience.... The real debate respects the filial relation. Was Adam in Eden, a son, as well as a servant?" Webb, *Reformed Doctrine of Adoption*, 41–42.

simultaneously be a son and a servant. While a son may serve his father, he does not necessarily have to be a servant. Why should Webb introduce the status of a *servant* here as different from a son when referring to the same individuals in a relationship? Conversely, it can be argued that the nature of the individual in question determines the nature of the relationship that they can have with God.

Lectures three and four, as well as lecture two, lack coherence. Lecture two refers to two people with distinct statuses and origins, with the ability for one to be adopted into the family. In contrast, lectures three and four describe a family with one child possessing two statuses. These concepts are ambiguous. It seems likely that Webb prepared several alternative options intending to establish a foundation for the doctrine of adoption.

Webb creates unnecessary difficulties, which may lead to further complications. The question remains whether or not it is appropriate to worship a father who condones the slavery of his sons for disobedience and whose children must wait thousands of years to be adopted by him. According to Webb, "Adam, *unfallen*, was created the *servant* of God, a subject of His government, under His moral law, and liable to *punishment* in case of disobedience." He asks, "Was Adam in Eden a son as well as a servant?"[43] Is there any loving father on earth who would give birth to a son as a servant? This concept is central to Webb's Reformed doctrine of adoption. What is the significance of a *status* as a created son and servant before a fall? Webb emphasizes Adam's status rather than his ontological being.

Robert S. Candlish has correctly argued that Adam was not a created son of God in his holy state.[44] Webb's argument is left incomplete in this first part.[45] It is important to note that Webb did not publish these lecture notes; instead, Richardson published them as a book. I sense that some of the arguments presented in the notes may remain unfinished or that one is an alternative to the other.

In the second part, Webb stated:

> The Scriptures, in both Testaments, over and over again, designate God as "Father," and speak of a people as the "children" and

---

43. Webb, *Reformed Doctrine of Adoption*, 42. Emphasis added.
44. Webb, *Reformed Doctrine of Adoption*, 42.
45. For Webb, "if, then, there is nothing inherently incompatible in the notion of sonship and servitude as cohering upon the same person at one and the same time;—if . . . then, in the light of all this, we are entitled to infer, in the absence of proof to the contrary, that the original government of God in Eden was patriarchal—a government in which He was at once both a Father and a Sovereign, and in which Adam was at the same time a son and a subject . . . such a reasoning, at best, is but problematical and presumptive. By itself it is not conclusive." Webb, *Reformed Doctrine of Adoption*, 46.

"sons" of God. . . . A distinction should be made between the special sonship of believers and the general sonship of men.[46]

This statement is a crucial theoretical framework of Webb's. It demonstrates his understanding of "sonship," an English term distinct from the Greek "*huio*-ship." If Webb knows the meaning of "*huios*" in "*huio-thesía*," he will not differentiate between the two forms of sonship he has previously discussed. In contrast to his, I formulate a conceptual framework that refers to the Greek words νήπιοι, τέκνα, and υἱοί, and distinguish them from one another based on their usages in the paragraphs of the Greek NT where the word υἱοθεσία appears.

Webb does not accept that the Bible presents God as the father of all people in any way.[47] He makes six points, the first of which refers to Luke 3:38, which characterizes Adam as the son of God in a metaphorical sense. From his phrase "that the human sonship of Christ was created by the Holy Spirit out of the substance of the Virgin,"[48] again we know that Webb ascribes an English meaning to the terms "son" and "sonship." The biblical term "υἱός" has a range of meanings, but "υἱός" in "υἱοθεσία" should be interpreted in the context in which it is used. The term "υἱός" used in Jesus' genealogy (Luke 3:23b) is equivalent to the Hebrew term "*ben*," which denotes the relationship between a father and his child, "son," but it is distinct from the term "υἱός" (an *adult* son) which is used in the context of Pauline

---

46. Webb, *Reformed Doctrine of Adoption*, 47.

47. Webb, *Reformed Doctrine of Adoption*, 47.

48. Webb renders, "This is a genealogical record. . . . If creation were an impossible mode of constituting the filial relation, then Adam could not be the son of God in any other than a metaphorical sense. But sonship may be constituted by creation, for the sonship of believers is so originated. Regeneration is characterized by a 'new creation.' The sonship of believers does not originate by a naturalistic generation, but by the supernatural and sovereign will of God. . . . The table on its surface shows Adam to have been the son of God as Seth was the son of Adam. .˙. . For sonship may be constituted by creation as well as by generation, the proof is the fact that the human sonship of Christ was created by the Holy Spirit out of the substance of the Virgin. Neither the Divine Sonship of Christ nor His human sonship were generated in a naturalistic way. His Divine, or monogenistic, sonship was eternally and inscrutably generated, and his human sonship was created by the supranatural agency of the Holy Ghost, if we may believe the doctrine of the miraculous conception. Adam was not the begotten, but the created, son of God. Christ, as to His human nature, was not the begotten, but the created, son of God. Luke's table teaches the fact of Adamic and Christic sonships, but not their modes. . . . Luke thus carries the genealogy of the Second Adam back to the first, and thence on to God. Here is at last a stopping place. The crown and glory of human ancestry—*Adam the Son of God.*" Webb, *Reformed Doctrine of Adoption*, 47–51. Emphasis original. Here we learned about Divine and human sonship of Christ, Adamic and Christic sonships.

υἱοθεσία. The latter metaphorically conveys the idea of a regenerated being, a mature or eschatological human.

At the second point, Webb cites Acts 17:28, 29, which states, "For we are indeed his offspring." In this speech at Mars Hill, "the idea of the divine paternity... man is the son of God."[49] Webb adds, "Forasmuch then as we are the offspring (Τevoς, race, progeny, family, lineage) of God..." Contrary to Candlish's opinion, Webb concludes, "We are obliged to think that Paul meant to transfer the language of the heathen poet to the pages of inspiration and cause it for all time to come to do duty in the interest of the dogmatic thought of God's church."[50] Still, I think it was not about Christians, but Paul makes the argument once he recognizes that all humans are God's created children.

In his third point, according to Gen 1:27, Webb contends that, "made in the likeness of God, treated by God as if he were a son, all natural expectations would be disappointed if he be not a son."[51] His phrase "as *if* he *were* a son" means that Adam was not a son. However, his argument depends on the assumption that "son" in this context refers to the English significant or the Greek term "υἱός." Again, Webb meant "son" in English. The Greek term "υἱός" may not be the case since even Jesus, in His incarnation, was born of a woman (a mere human) and under the Law (a child in need of a guardian and manager), indicating that He was incarnated as a νήπιος. Jesus assumed the nature of humanity that He wanted to save—the nature of these νήπιοι (protological Adamic beings). Adam was not a υἱός (an adult son-heir) but a νήπιος (an infant).

At the fourth point, Webb distinguishes between general and redemptive sonship of man, emphasizing the distinction between a *created* and *born* sonship. Webb cites Mal 1:6; 2:10; Isa 63:16; 64:8; Deut 32:6; and Jer 3:4. While admitting that "Father"[52] can have a true and proper meaning, the term is ultimately symbolic and cannot be taken literally. The nation of Israel is considered a *covenantal son* due to the provisions of the Torah, as stated in Exod 19–24. This covenant has been bestowed upon them, and

49. Webb, *Reformed Doctrine of Adoption*, 55.
50. Webb, *Reformed Doctrine of Adoption*, 51–57.
51. Webb, *Reformed Doctrine of Adoption*, 58.
52. Webb argues, "The Scriptures do teach the sonship of a nation. But does Israel become the people of God by a 'begetting?'... Israel was not the begotten, but Israel was the created son of God?... All could say, 'O Lord, thou art our Father.' Yet some of the nations were not converted. If the nation could call him 'Father,' the individual people in the nation could call him by that endearing title.... They call God 'Father' in the true and proper meaning of that term." Webb, *Reformed Doctrine of Adoption*, 61–63. Here, we learn the following terms: general sonship as distinguished from redemptive sonship, and created sonship as distinguished from born sonship. Do they exist?

as a result, Israel can form a relationship with the Father through the dispensation of the Law. God initiates this relationship: "Out of Egypt I called my son" (Hos 11:1). It describes a kind of relationship and that God cares for God's chosen people. We should see Israel in the context of υἱοθεσία in Rom 9. However, how should we interpret Webb's earlier reference to "*born sonship*?" In Paul's υἱοθεσία, there is no such thing as born sonship; instead, it is born *népio-ship, infantship*, or *minorship*. Webb aims to differentiate between the sonship of a believer and an unbeliever. However, he overlooks that Adam was a created minor (νήπιος) who would inevitably fall at any point in his existence. If "sonship" is a translation of "*huio*-ship," then in the context of υἱοθεσία, born sonship is nonexistent as no human being is born as an adult son-heir (υἱός).

It can be argued that, in addition to God's unique Son (*monogenes*, μονογενής), God's one-of-a-kind Son, there is only one other type of child of God, namely the created (*népioi*) ones. Webb refers to the Second Person of the triune God as the begotten Son. This designation can be more accurately rendered as the preexistent Son. This divine *Huios* assumes human nature through the incarnation. Webb's categorization and definitions present some challenges. Additionally, he fails to acknowledge that Gal 4 states that the same minor must transition from his *immature* childhood (*népio*-hood) to his *mature* sonhood (*huio* hood) before he is eligible to receive the rights to inherit from his father.

At his fifth point, Webb begins with a statement:

> The next proof-text puts into sharp contrast "the fathers of our flesh" and "the Father of our spirits": we have had fathers of our flesh which corrected us, and we gave them reference: shall we not much more be subject to the Father of spirits and live? (Heb. 12:9).[53]

He proposes that an individual may be classified in numerous ways and asserts that these categorizations are distinct entities. For instance, one Creator may be understood as two kinds of fathers with different functions, or Adam as a servant and a son (with English significance). In my view, this mode of reasoning is misguided. Webb then proceeds to examine the genesis of the soul from the perspectives of creationism and traducianism. I contend that this discussion of the human soul is paramount in determining whether protological humans will become incomplete or totally annihilated. However, this topic will not be addressed in any further detail here.

---

53. Webb, *Reformed Doctrine of Adoption*, 63.

The sixth point, which shifts the subject to the parable of the prodigal son, asserts that "it is a picture of the fall and rise of a son of God."[54] However, I contend that the story does not pertain to the fall of Adam. Rather, this parable relates to a υἱός (a person who has been saved) who lives κατὰ σάρκα (kata sarka) after receiving his share of the inheritance, yet is still welcomed into the house.

After lecture three, Webb posits that Adam and his descendants maintain two primary relationships with God: servile and filial. "Both relations were contingent and dependent; both were probationary and mutable. Therefore, if he fails, he fails in both relations, the same if he is faithful."[55] However, the statement is ambiguous; as Webb previously stated, a person cannot be both a servant and a son. It is unclear how failure in one relationship impacts the other.

Webb may be testing various arguments. It is surprising when he begins lecture four, entitled "Objection to Adamic Sonship," by arguing that the servile and the filial relations are inherently incompatible and mutually exclusive. Webb concludes:

> But adoption is one of the very choicest favors which accrued under the gospel; and the conclusion would seem to be irresistible that adoption must have a place under the covenant of works in order for it to be ranked as one of the blessings *lost by the fall* and *regained by Christ*.[56]

Consider his idea that sonship can be lost and reclaimed. Here's where we differ. Adamic humans are in their *népio*-ship (infancy, not sonship), which is why they sin (fall). They are saved when they gain the *huio*-ship (not sonship) like the *huio*-ship of the human Messiah. This concept of sonship is very confusing because it is part of misreading the NT word υἱός. What is "sonship?" If a creative sonship can be lost, there is no hope of being saved through an adoptive sonship.

In lecture five, "Fallen Sons," Webb distinguishes between different forms of government, i.e., a ruler and a father. A ruler is the head of a magisterial or rectorial government. At the same time, a father leads a paternal and domestic government. The patriarchal form combines both; its subjects are citizens and sons simultaneously. Webb also differentiates between a kingdom, a house, a citizen, and a son. Humans failed his trial with the forbidden fruit, falling under both forms within the patriarchal system.

---

54. Webb, *Reformed Doctrine of Adoption*, 67–69.
55. Webb, *Reformed Doctrine of Adoption*, 69.
56. Webb, *Reformed Doctrine of Adoption*, 77–78. Emphasis added.

He is an expatriated citizen, a fallen and disinherited son.[57] However, if we consider only God, Adam, and the entirety of creation, how can we distinguish between a kingdom and a house if all the members of the *domains* are identical? It is possible if the two domains exist in a super domain. Still, if all elements are in a super domain and there are no other domains, then this concept of Webb is not possible. Webb's model applies only in a dualistic world with a lesser God but is not valid in a panentheistic world where only one Creator exists.

Consider a mathematical Venn diagram[58] as an analogy for God and His creation. Assume the sample space SK represents God's kingdom, and the set A represents all creation. Within A, there are subsets. There is a subset with element a for Adam, a subset b for angels, a subset c for subhuman creations, and so on. If we have another sample space SH for God's house, with identical spaces, sets, and elements as SK, then both sample spaces SK and SH exist without distinction. Hence, we have only one sample space S, which is equivalent to both SK and SH. Both sample spaces are identical regarding their space, sets, and elements. Therefore, it can be inferred that the *house* should be the *kingdom* and vice versa. However, determining this relationship is more complex when considering a sample space, SP, where P represents the patriarchal form, a combination of two sets, R for ruler and F for father, where all elements in R and F are the same.

Webb argues about the way to differentiate between a *kingdom* ruled by God and a *household* led by a father. He seeks to distinguish an angry God from a loving father as two distinct essences of God. This way, Webb creates two different beings. According to Webb, there are two other essences; thus, one God has two forms of governance. However, if one being has two different essences, how can we define that being in terms of its whatness? If the essence of a ruler is different from that of a father, then both cannot refer to the same *Being*, namely God. If the essences are identical, there is no difference between the ruler and the father. The objective of establishing these distinctions is to facilitate the possibility of separation from God and the necessity of adoption to reestablish the relationship and to provide a framework for a person's transition from one domain (family) to another.

How does Webb distinguish between the offices of a person before and after Adam sinned? Is Webb's concept parallel to the modern system, where an individual is a member of a family and a citizen of a state or nation? Are they comparable? After the fall, for him, humanity is identified

---

57. Webb, *Reformed Doctrine of Adoption*, 79–80.

58. For the theory of Venn diagram, check, for instance, Kreyzig, *Advanced*, 1055–57.

as an *outlawed subject* and *repudiated son*, as well as a *vicious servant* and *depraved son*. How should these four offices of a person be interpreted? To support his argument, Webb cites John 8:37–48. For us to argue with Webb, our homework is to analyze the spectrum of meaning of the term "father" and the expression "your father, the devil."

In lecture six, titled "The Sonship of the Second Adam," Webb expounds on Christ's monogenetic Sonship, emphasizing the unparalleled nature of the only begotten Son of God and Christ's status as the Firstborn. Webb asserts that

> if there be, therefore, any angelic sons of God, or if there be any human sons of God, they must be sons in some other mode than by generation—as by creation, or by providence, or by redemption—for Jesus is pointedly and repeatedly said to be "the only begotten Son of God." If any angel, if any man, if any creature were made a partaker of this sonship, Jesus would from that time forth cease to be God's only Son, and would have brethren in the same relation with himself.[59]

Christ is the preexistent mature Son (Υἱός), while a believer is an imitated mature son (υἱός). A believer attains similar human *huio*-ship by taking on the assumed created nature of the one and only preexistent Son. At the end of time, a believer will remain a created human soul with a quickened (enlivened, vivified) spirit and new body, experiencing spiritual communion with the Son of God. The believer shares only a prolonged fellowship through the Spirit of Christ without entering into the fellowship of the Godhead. The believer obtains his sonship or "*huio*-ship" by quickening his spirit, but this *huio*-ship and its fellowship are only "replicas." The *huio*-ship of created beings differs from that of the preexistent Son. A further discussion of this topic will be presented under the heading of "Dual Sonships of the Person of Jesus Christ."

In lecture six, parts two and three, Webb delves into the significance of Christ's role as a mediator, His Sonship as the Second Person of the divine Trinity, and His humanity. This topic holds great importance in the teaching of υἱοθεσία. Webb's writing warrants consideration. He writes,

> The incarnation does not alter or modify the constitution of the Trinity. The Trinity is not theanthropic; nor is the Father theanthropic. The divine nature interpenetrates the human nature in

---

59. Webb, *Reformed Doctrine of Adoption*, 96.

Christ, but the human nature does not flow through the divine nature.[60]

I concur with Webb's statement regarding the Theanthropos, except that I perceive the designations "the Son of God" and "the Son of Man"[61] pertain to the human nature of Christ, the Messiah. Rather than referring to "the Son of God," we should discuss the divinity of the Second Person of the eternal Trinity (God the Son) as the preexistent Son of God.

> When the Son of God became the Son of Man, the union of the Logos with a human nature did not disturb, annihilate, or modify the original trinitarian relation of the Second Person to the First Person of the Trinity. His monogenetic sonship abides pure, unmixed, uncorrupted and unqualified. But as a Theanthropos, He is also the Son of God. Are the two relations identical—the sonship of the Logos, which is trinitarian, and the sonship of the Theanthropos, which is mediatorial?[62]

Contrary to the assertion that "the Son of God became the Son of Human," my analysis suggests that the preexistent Son of God "becomes" a νήπιος (an infant, used to be read as a servant) of human nature, which later becomes the υἱός (used to be read as a son) of human nature. I share Webb's perspective that Trinitarian sonship (*huio*-ship) was established for eternity, while messianic sonship (*huio*-ship) "was constituted in time that the world of sinners might have a Redeemer."[63] I recognize that the issue of sonship in the Theanthropos is crucial in the conversation surrounding υἱοθεσία, as salvation is reliant on the human sonship (*huio*-ship) aligning with that of the Theanthropos. As such, our attention ought to be focused on the messianic role of the Second Person of the Holy Trinity, specifically on the historical events leading up to His human figure's transformation into God's first human υἱός (son).

In lecture seven, "Sons by Incarnation," Webb examines the coexistence of humanity and divinity in the person of Jesus Christ. In his section six, Webb states,

> Now the problem is to introduce the individual sinner into the new Theanthropic family. His present membership, because of a false development, is in the family of Satan; he stands in need of a transition from the false household into the true and ideal

---

60. Webb, *Reformed Doctrine of Adoption*, 100–1.
61. "Son of Man" as a messianic title derived from Dan 7:13.
62. Webb, *Reformed Doctrine of Adoption*, 101.
63. Webb, *Reformed Doctrine of Adoption*, 103.

family. The incarnation is the foundation of this translation; but it is the mission of the Holy Spirit to actually affect the great and fundamental change.... The Spirit does not beget a person anew by implanting Christ into him. By the Spirit he is implanted into Christ. The Son of Man glorified is the principle of regeneration. He is the one new Man—the regenerate personality.[64]

From that quote, we can see how a person is transferred from one family to another and how Webb connects this to the incarnation. We should examine how a believer can achieve sonship by regaining what was lost, quickening the spirit, or indwelling the Spirit of Christ. It is important to note that believers do not attain the exact personhood of Jesus Christ, only a shadow, nor do they possess His divine nature. They—as created beings—become like Him in His perfect, consummated humanity.

In Lectures Eight to Tenth, "Sons by Love versus by Atonement," Webb begins by stating that God is love and concludes with this idea.

I think this theory . . . is fundamentally and radically wrong . . . and utterly unbiblical. . . . The Divine wrath is the Divine holiness in one phase or mode of it; and the Divine love is the same Divine holiness in another phase or mode of it. . . . Accordingly, the two feelings of love of holiness and hatred of evil *coexist* in the character of God, the most perfect of beings, and in that of angels and redeemed men. . . . "Wrath" . . . occurs as often in our Scripture as do "love."[65]

A deity of wrath is perpetually in search of victims. He is not disinclined to exact retribution. It is unlikely that a God of wrath would send His Son to save the world. If God is wrathful, it is difficult to comprehend why He would desire to save sinners. God elects to bestow His benevolence. It is not inherent to God to be wrathful. God is not characterized by wrath, but rather by love.[66] The apostle John also attested to this truth, stating, "God is love" (ὁ θεὸς ἀγάπη ἐστίν, 1 John 4:8). God is a benevolent father figure who cares for His creations, including humanity and the natural world. Nevertheless, without the incarnate Son, sinners will only experience God's love in a limited capacity during their physical temporal existence. In Jesus, believers encounter an eternal and loving God. The atonement for sin on the cross is evidence of the love of Christ. The preservation of humanity by

---

64. Webb, *Reformed Doctrine of Adoption*, 116–17.

65. Webb, *Reformed Doctrine of Adoption*, 127, 132, 135. Emphasis added.

66. Cf. Becker, *Pedoman Dogmatika*, 60–61. Becker addresses the Lutheran view on the essence of God.

God is a consequence of His profound love,⁶⁷ as evidenced by His bestowal of common grace. Even His wrath is motivated by a desire to protect and preserve.

In lecture nine, Webb asks, "Man being a depraved, disinherited, and outcast child of God, how can he be reinstated in his lost sonship, and be reinstated with filial rights and privileges in the house of God?"⁶⁸ The method of atonement is briefly discussed before being expanded upon in lecture ten. Adam is characterized as a νήπιος, thereby negating the conceptual possibility of forfeited *huio*-ship; consequently, no necessity exists for the reinstatement of *huio*-ship.

Webb does not appear to reference his Greek New Testament. He appears to only refer to the English Bible, possibly the KJV. Consequently, his argument, which references the biblical phrase "that ye may be children of your Father which is in heaven" (Matt 5:45),⁶⁹ fails to recognize that Matthew is not discussing becoming children but rather becoming "υἱοί" (*mature* sons). Due to this oversight, his argument may lead to different conclusions. However, he presents compelling arguments. He explains his reasoning about sons benefiting from atonement through love.

In lecture eleven, entitled "Sons by Regeneration," the following statement is noteworthy due to the potential for interpretation variations. The statement in question is as follows:

> The mediatorial work of Christ directly and immediately makes God the Father of believers, but indirectly and mediately, through the Spirit, renders believers the sons of God. Jesus died to reconcile God to men; the Spirit was granted to reconcile men to God. The atonement made God a Father; the Spirit made man a son. Christ's work is subjective to God, but objective to men; the Spirit's work is objective to God, but subjective to men.⁷⁰

These ideas invite further exploration. Here, Webb discusses the theme of being born again in John 3, demonstrating that his views on adoption derive from Pauline and Johannine teaching.

Webb also talks about regeneration.

> There are some thoughts behind the word of regeneration. If regeneration is strictly "creative," then something is originated in it by supernatural power; if it is construed as "resurrective,"

---

67. Bray, *God Is Love*, 473.
68. Webb, *Reformed Doctrine of Adoption*, 148.
69. Webb, *Reformed Doctrine of Adoption*, 168.
70. Webb, *Reformed Doctrine of Adoption*, 178–79.

then something which was death is in regeneration made alive again; if it is defined as "vocative," in its essential nature, then something is called into existence when the soul is regenerated; but if it is interpreted as a literal "generation," then something is born when the sinner is converted by the Spirit into a son of God.[71]

The rest of the discussion maintains the focus on varying perspectives. Let us consider that regeneration, from the context of υἱοθεσία, should be the vivification of the human spirit. Following this spirit activation, a person can be resurrected from death.

It appears that Webb comes from a fundamentalist circle that frequently depicts God as a God of judgment and punishment rather than as a merciful and compassionate God.[72] God's love is the motivation behind both the creation and the redemption of His creation. The God of wrath does not save the object of his anger but punishes them. However, he does save Adamic human beings. It can be interpreted as an act of love. The doctrine of adoption lacks coherence in its own right. James E. Cousar concludes his analysis of Webb's book as follows:

> Yet he speaks of this same "natural and created sonship" as having been "annulled by the fall." . . . But how can a relationship that was "terminable" and which was "forfeited," "annulled," and "cancelled," still be said to exist?[73]

If God had annulled humans' sonship, He would have no relationship with them. Theological adoption is a human idea; the Bible does not discuss it. Rather, υἱοθεσία, which is often inaccurately translated as "adoption," pertains to the process of "human becoming" from infancy to adult human form, as seen in the case of the Messiah.

John Murray

John Murray writes about a chapter on adoption in the second section of his *Redemption: Accomplished and Applied*, published in 1955.[74] For Mur-

---

71. Webb, *Reformed Doctrine of Adoption*, 184.

72. To read about the topic of "fundamentalist," see Hill at al., *Faith, Religion & Theology*, 326.

73. Cousar, "Reformed Doctrine of Adoption," 236.

74. Murray, *Redemption*, 132–40.

ray, adoption is not an aspect of justification or regeneration. He defines regeneration as the renewal of our *hearts* in the image of God.[75]

Murray sees adoption from Pauline and Johannine's perspectives. He begins:

> Firstly, adoption is never separable from justification and regeneration. The person who is justified is always the recipient of sonship. And those who are given the right to become sons of God are those who, as John 1:13 indicates, were born . . . but of God; secondly, adoption is, like justification, a judicial act. It is a bestowal of a status, or standing, not the generating within us of a new nature or character. It concerns a relationship and not the attitude or disposition which enables us to recognize and cultivate that relationship.[76]

If υἱοθεσία involves the bestowal of *spirit* from above, or γεννηθῇ ἄνωθεν (be born from above, John 3:3), then the bestowal of spirit occurs *within* the individual's soul as a transformative act of God. It is not a legal or judicial status imposed externally but a personal transformation experienced through receiving the regenerated spirit from their Creator. The Spirit of Christ can now reside within the person's regenerated spirit. Regeneration brings about a transformation of being. However, problems arise when adoption is distinguished from regeneration.

Murray continues, third,

> those adopted into God's family are also given the Spirit of adoption. . . . The Spirit of adoption is the consequence but this does not itself constitute adoption.[77]

Here, Murray distinguishes between the adoption and the bestowal of the Holy Spirit. Our concepts diverge. I view that it is the bestowal of the quickened human spirit—not the bestowal of the Spirit of adoption—that makes a person a pneumatic son (υἱός). Once a person becomes a υἱός (pneumatic human), they can then receive the Holy Spirit to initiate the spiritual union.

Murray elucidates his fourth point:

> There is a close relationship between adoption and regeneration. So close . . . that we are sons of God both by participation of nature and by deed of adoption. . . . There are two ways whereby we may become members of a human family—we may be born

75. Murray, *Redemption*, 132. Emphasis added.
76. Murray, *Redemption*, 132–33.
77. Murray, *Redemption*, 133.

into it or we may be adopted into it. The former is by natural generation, the latter is by legal act.[78]

The fourth point above presents a significant issue with Murray's concept of adoption, which relies on a human adoption analogy. God does not adopt in the way that a human family does. It is because there is no family other than God's, or there is no God who adopts children. The entire foundation of this notion is affected when we alter this concept. The only means by which one can become a member of the Creator's family is through a state of infancy, much like Adam when he was first created as a νήπιος. Regarding regeneration, is it possible that this concept explains an aspect of adoption (read: υἱοθεσία)? Murray argues that

> regeneration is the prerequisite of adoption. It is the same Holy Spirit who regenerates who is also sent into the hearts of the adopted, crying Abba Father. But adoption itself is not simply regeneration, nor is the Spirit of adoption—the one is prerequisite, the other is consequent. Adoption, as the term clearly implies, is an act of transfer from an alien family into the family of God himself. This is surely the apex of grace and privileges.[79]

From this quoted definition, there appears to be an assumption of another family besides God's, which I disagree with. This assumption defines the nature of God's fatherhood. In my view, God's sub-act of υἱοθεσία initially regenerates (resurrects the human spirit), paving the way for sonship (*huio*-ship).

Murray dismisses the notion, sometimes found in contemporary theology, that people can come to partake in Christ's Sonship and thus participate in the divine life of the Trinity through adoption. We ought to concur with his view that "the preexistent Son" is the only begotten, and no one shares in His Sonship, just as God the Father is not the Father of any other in the sense that He is a Father of the only begotten and eternal Son."[80] We should regard Christ in His *humanity* as the first consummated Son (υἱός), and He has many *earthly* brothers. He brings these brothers to the Father through His birth of a woman, as part of a human family.

We must identify who the Father is. Murray cites the expression "we cry '*Abba*, Father!'" and clarifies that this signifies a particular relationship rather than a universal Fatherhood of God.[81] Murray distinguishes between

---

78. Murray, *Redemption*, 133.
79. Murray, *Redemption*, 133–34.
80. Murray, *Redemption*, 134.
81. Murray, *Redemption*, 134.

God's fatherhood by *creation* and fatherhood by *adoption*.[82] If all humanity is descended from the created Adam, how can we determine the two ontologically? What is the adoptee if not the God-created child? Murray goes on to argue about distinguishing God's Fatherhood in the remainder of his chapter 6. Nevertheless, before the creation and (what the proponent calls) adoption, God is always a universal Father; before and after, one can call "*Abba*, Father!"

Consider the possibility that God's sub-act of constituting eschatological human (υἱοθεσία, often misunderstood as adoption) may include regeneration as one of its benefits. Murray's framework distinguishes adoption from regeneration, emphasizing that regeneration must occur before adoption. However, Murray does not discuss the differing statuses of νήπιοι, τέκνα, and υἱοί, treating them as though they have the same meaning. Additionally, he employs a contemporary definition of adoption as transferring a child from one family to another. He accepts the universal fatherhood of God to the human race in terms of creation and provision, while differentiating between God's Fatherhood to Christ the Son and believers. No exegesis of the Greek text is presented.

Herman Ridderbos

Herman Ridderbos examines the concept of adoption in his 1975 work *Paul: An Outline of His Theology*, specifically in section 35 entitled "The Adoption of Sons. The Inheritance." In the first paragraph, he states, "The new relationship between God and men . . . finally finds expression in the important concept adoption of sons (υἱοθεσία)."[83] However, we hold a distinct view.

Since the beginning, the relationship between God and humans, regardless of their state of sin, has been metaphorically depicted as that of a Creator Father and His created *minor* children (protological transient sarkic beings). These minors (infants), as the term clearly implied, are not yet mature, as they remain in an initial stage of humanity and require further development to become mature sons (eschatological everlasting pneumatic beings) who are also everlasting heirs. The process[84] of developing them into sons-heirs (υἱοί) is known as "υἱοθεσία," or the constitution of a mature son, and it involves an ontological transformation of being.

82. Murray, *Redemption*, 134.

83. Ridderbos, *Paul*, 197.

84. Ridderbos explains, "The adoption of sons embraces more; it spans the present as well as the great future." Ridderbos, *Paul*, 200.

Please take a look at this sentence below:

> The adoption of sons is here described, therefore, as the object of the great eschatological redemptive event and as the direct result of redemption, just as that is said elsewhere of justification (Rom. 3:25, 26; 4:25) and of reconciliation (2 Cor. 5:18, 19). And as elsewhere God's grace and love are designated as the principle of justification and of reconciliation, so the apostle says in Ephesians 1:5 that God in his love destined us beforehand to the adoption of sons.[85]

Let's look at the first phrase, "*the object of* the great *eschatological* redemptive event." At the end of his chapter, we find Ridderbos writes, "When we consider in greater detail the passages where Paul expressly speaks of the sonship of believers and of their adoption as sons, it becomes clear at once that he is again thinking in redemptive-historical, eschatological categories."[86] Unlike Webb and Murray, who see adoption as a benefit of *ordo salutis*, I see that it seems that Paul's concept of υἱοθεσία provides a unifying framework for understanding both the *historia salutis*, as elucidated in Gal 4, and the *ordo salutis*, as portrayed in Rom 8.

When discussing the idea of salvation, it is true when he writes,

> Scholars have accordingly been able to say of these various central concepts with a certain degree of justices that they are only different figures for the same thing and are related to each other as concentric circles. However, this does not alter the fact, evident already from the preceding, that each one of these descriptions has its own specific significance and that only by means of the determination of that significance can the rich content of the gospel be illuminated. This applies as well to the concept adoption of sons.[87]

I see that υἱοθεσία (not adoption) represents the fundamental tenet of the gospel, with its origins tracing back to the initial promise regarding "her seed,"[88] a human child who will serve as the Redeemer of humanity. The apostle Paul explains human salvation through υἱοθεσία in the middle of his prominent Letters to the Romans and Galatians.

According to Ridderbos,

---

85. Ridderbos, *Paul*, 197.

86. Ridderbos, *Paul*, 198.

87. Ridderbos, *Paul*, 197. Ridderbos refers to Villiers, *Die betekenis van huiothesia in die briewe van Paulus*, 3. This source has been quoted several times in this section 35.

88. Gen 3:15.

The term stems from the Hellenistic world of law; its content, however, must not be inferred from the various Roman or Greek legal systems, nor from the adoption ritual of the Hellenistic mystery cults, but must rather be considered against the Old Testament, redemptive-historical background of the adoption of Israel as son of God.[89]

The concept of *huios* can be defined by reference to Gal 4:1–2. The adoption of the Israelites is not to establish a relationship of *huio*-ship; rather, it is to establish a relationship of *tekno*-ship. It is crucial to acknowledge that the process of becoming a υἱός (an adult son-heir, an eschatological being) is inherently individualistic and not applicable to a collective entity such as a family, nation, or the church. It thus follows that the church is unable to assume the role of the children of Israel as the favored children of the flesh (τὰ τέκνα τῆς σαρκὸς, Rom 9:8). As delineated in Eph 1, the function of this nation is to facilitate the presentation of the [mature] Son of a Woman (the eschatological being), who was born under the law (νήπιος) and subsequently became the inaugural mature Son of God, bearing the responsibility of bringing numerous son-heirs to the Father. In this temporal reality, these Christic sons congregate as the church.

Trevor J. Burke

Trevor J. Burke is an author who specializes in adoption and sonship. We have done several annotations on his writings. In his "Exegesis 14," Burke asserts that the conflict discussed in Rom 7 and the life of a Christian who lives by the Spirit in Rom 8 are components of regular Christian life. He explains what it means to live by the Spirit in Rom 8 and how this pertains to those who have become adopted as sons of God.[90] Burke continues:

> Hence, it would not be unreasonable to suppose that the adoption motif itself is eschatological in character, since it is connected with the gift of the Spirit and obviously refers to those who are "in Christ," and are justified. We shall look at this more closely in our exegesis which we will approach serially because of the apostle's close reasoning.[91]

The assertion that the "adoption motif is eschatological" gives rise to two key concerns. First, the use of υἱοθεσία (Rom 8) to refer to adoption is a

89. Ridderbos, *Paul*, 197–98.
90. Burke, "Exegesis 14," 25.
91. Burke, "Exegesis 14," 25.

mistranslation; thus, there is no correlation between the two; it is incorrect to equate υἱοθεσία with adoption. Second, the term υἱοθεσία is not exclusively eschatological in nature; it does not solely pertain to the period between the two advents of Jesus Christ. The sub-act or process of υἱοθεσία, as initiated by God, commences with the creation of the first human beings as infants (νήπιοι). Consequently, the concept of υἱοθεσία encompasses the history of creation, revelation, and salvation of protological humans to eschatological humans, extending from the event in Eden to parousia. However, given the inherent subjectivity of preconceptions and understandings, there may be a range of interpretations.

Burke asserts that Diodorus, who offers a paraphrase of Polybius, employs the term "adoption." This claim, however, is a form of eisegesis that obscures the underlying facts. He writes:

> When Aemilius, his real father, died and left his property to him and to Fabius, the sons he had given in *adoption* (*huiothesían*), Scipio performed a noble act, which deserves to put on record" (Diod. Sic. 31.27.5; my emphasis). Diodorus also employs the expression in the Greek myth of Zeus, who persuaded his wife Hera to adopt Heracles (Diod. Sic. 39.2).[92]

As previously stated in this book's introduction, Diodorus, who wrote in Greek, did not address the topic of adoption. A biological father has no valid reason to adopt his sons who are currently residing with him. In Aemilius' context, υἱοθεσία can be likened to the Roman *toga virilis*. Paul borrowed υἱοθεσία and gave it a Christian meaning.

The theoretical framework proposed by Burke is clearly discernible. He posits that Paul proceeds to present an ecclesiological emphasis in which υἱοθεσία functions inclusively—adoption into God's family (Eph 2:20; Gal 6:10)—that unites Jews and gentiles into one household. The objective is for God's children to conduct themselves in a manner that brings glory to their adoptive Father and His family name.[93] Those who espouse this concept reject the notion of universal human brotherhood, which posits that every human is inherently part of a family—God's created family. Furthermore, Christians are not grouped with those who lack a Christ-faith, including non-believing Jews. Christians form a distinct new category within God's family structure, known as the υἱοί, which differs from the νήπιοι.

Those who adhere to the tenets of Gen 1 must acknowledge that Jews and gentiles, as descendants of Adam, are already members of God's created family, regardless of whether they are subject to the law or the laws

---

92. Burke, *Adopted into God's Family*, 22.
93. Burke, *Adopted into God's Family*, 99.

(τὰ στοιχεῖα τοῦ κόσμου). In his concept of *"adoption into God's family,"* Burke suggests that God initially failed with His initial family, subsequently creating a new family to replace it and adopting children from the first family into this new family. From this perspective, one might perceive God as overseeing two distinct families or allowing another paternal figure to assume leadership of the original family. This concept may prove challenging to comprehend. The doctrine of adoption posits that a father may renounce his familial responsibilities or abandon his children. However, it would be unwise for humans to follow this example and abandon their original family in the face of failure or attempt to manage two families simultaneously. From the creation of Adam until the present day, the Christian concept of God the Father as the Creator and Sustainer of a single family has remained a cornerstone of religious belief. He pledged to this family regarding "her seed."

In his book *The Message of Sonship*, Burke explores various aspects of sonship, including the process through which a believer obtains it through adoption. Burke utilizes the following background for his concept.

> The adoption procedure involved, in the first instance, the severing of the old *potestas* followed by the establishing of the paternal authority of the new father. This was carried out by the *paterfamilias* selling off his offspring into civil bondage (*in mancipio*), thereby making him a slave. On the release of his son the latter was still the property of the father and could by right be sold into bondage by him again and again. In order to avoid the son becoming a kind of familial football a law was laid down in the Twelve Table (established by the second Decemvirate c. 450 BC) which stated that when a son was sold three times by his father the latter ceased to have any authority over him.[94]

In his writings, the apostle Paul established the Christian context of υἱοθεσία, as evidenced in Gal 4 and Rom 8. However, Burke disregarded this biblical context in favor of an extrabiblical one. The biblical concept of υἱοθεσία has been supplanted by a Roman construct of family and adoption. In conclusion, Burke asserts that

> it was from this law that the *adoptio* was derived. We can immediately see the relevance this background has for Paul—himself a Roman citizen who only uses his adoption term in letters written to churches under Roman rule—who is of the view that it

---

94. Burke, *Message of Sonship*, 142–43.

is God the Father who begins the procedure of bringing us into his household.[95]

In his theoretical framework, Burke presents a compelling argument in favor of this position. It is, however, important to note that Paul never uses the word "adoption" in his Greek text of the New Testament, but instead employs the term "υἱοθεσία." The erroneous choice of "*adoptio*" by Latin translators to translate "υἱοθεσία" is a significant error in the field of biblical studies. The context identified by Burke does not apply to υἱοθεσία but rather to Roman *adoptio*, which is unrelated to Paul's intention with υἱοθεσία. Moreover, in this context, it is crucial to examine the implications of the alien family (the unknown family), which effectively owns us as sinners, having the capacity to sell us on three occasions, even when this unknown father did not create us. It is inadvisable to use a translation with unfamiliar cultural or contextual elements as a foundation for biblical exegesis.

The concept of a Roman *paterfamilias* is not analogous to the biblical concept of God the Father. The concept of slavery does not form the context of Pauline υἱοθεσία, which pertains to the adoption of an individual into a free family unit or the purchase of their freedom. In contrast, the context is that of the minority (protological Adamic humans) and the majority (eschatological Christic humans), where minor children gain independence from their birth father upon reaching adulthood. An erroneous interpretation of the context may lead to the formulation of an erroneous doctrine.

Tim J. R. Trumper

Below are reviews of one of Trumper's writings, entitled "From Slaves to Sons!," which describes the writer's desires for the doctrine.

> The doctrine of adoption is in the process of a long overdue comeback; one that promises a more exact understanding of what the Bible (specifically Paul) teaches: Eph. 1:5; Rom. 9:4; Gal. 4:4–5; Rom. 8:15, 23. As a Reformed/reforming Christian I welcome this, for no other wing of the church has done as much with the doctrine in either the pre- or post-Reformation eras.... Over recent centuries, the Calvinistic tradition has lost sight of adoption, chiefly because of our understandable... preoccupation with our defense of justification. We have rightly

---

95. Burke, *Message of Sonship*, 143.

stressed what we are saved from, but at the expense of what we are saved to.[96]

Thus, Trumper thinks that adoption is "a more exact understanding of what the Bible (specifically Paul) teaches." Is that true? What are the consequences if we misunderstand it? Trumper distinguishes Paul's conception from John's.

> Whereas John's model speaks of the birth of the children of God (*tekna tou theou*) into the kingdom—emphasizing their subsequent growth into the image of the Son (*huios*)—Paul's refers to the adoption of God's (mature) sons into his family, and indicates the new status they have in Christ, and all that goes with it: acceptance, assurance, liberty, prayer, obedience and hope (the inheritance).[97]

In fact, Paul emphasizes believers' subsequent growth into the image of the Son (υἱός). It is the main context of Rom 8, which explains the constitution of τὰ τέκνα τοῦ Θεοῦ in two steps (vv. 15 and 23) to be conformed to the image of His Son (v. 29). Trumper's idea of adoption is not found in Paul's view. Paul does not mention any sense of adoption at all.

Trumper continues:

> In predestination (the *material* cause of adoption), the Father named for himself a seismic family (Eph. 3:15). By, or literally through (*dia*), Christ (v. 5; cf. v. 7), he determined the transferal of the elect from the devil's household into his own. In time, the sons of disobedience would through faith (the *instrumental* cause) become the sons of God and experience his warm paternal embrace (*eis auton* v. 5). Enough to say that the gospel begins with grace, but culminates hereafter in glory (the final cause): ours, but ultimately our Father's (v. 6).[98]

In his conceptualization, which is shared by other Reformed scholars, there is the devil's household, comprising the sons of disobedience, and the Father's family, comprising the sons of God. The doctrine of adoption is inextricably linked to the concept of two families, which also encompasses the idea of human separation from God. In contrast to Trumper, who advocates for the doctrine of adoption, I am skeptical of its biblical foundation.

---

96. Trumper, "From Slaves to Sons!," 17.
97. Trumper, "From Slaves to Sons!," 17.
98. Trumper, "From Slaves to Sons!," 17. Emphasis original.

Nigel Westhead

Nigel Westhead's "Adoption in the Thought of John Calvin" explores Calvin's views on the Fatherhood of God and adoption. The paper includes "Adoption and the Trinity," "Adoption and the Covenant," and "Adoption and Justification." Like Trumper, Westhead bemoaned that adoption has been more commonly misunderstood than properly elucidated.[99]

Under Adoption and Trinity, Westhead explains the types of sonship. He quotes that according to Calvin, Adam was in the state of "creative sonship," but

> because of the fall we are not now sons, for "our sin [is] just cause for his disowning us and not regarding or recognizing us as his sons." But the Father-son relationship is reestablished by the message of the cross, which we ought to embrace "if we desire to return to God our Author and Maker from whom we have been estranged, in order that he may again begin to be our Father" *(Inst.* 2:6:1).[100]

It is difficult to comprehend how human sin can result in God disowning His created children. The notion that God disowned the people after the fall is a fallacious interpretation. Furthermore, it is unclear why God would desire to save those who have been disowned. One might inquire whether this is due to divine love. If this is the case, it would appear that God's love for Adam should have resulted in his forgiveness, thereby eliminating the necessity for a Savior to come. Calvin posits that the relationship with the Father can be restored through the cross.

Still, I argue that forgiveness on the cross alone is insufficient to address the consequences of the Adamic human facticity; it suggests that there is an underlying cause that requires attention. It is therefore proposed that the capacity for *sin* and *temporal existence* inherent to the Adamic human must be eradicated. It is not feasible for the adoption into a new family to eliminate them. The solution to the problem of Adamic facticity must originate and be resolved from the position of the Adamic human, as represented by God the Son through His incarnation. In the authentic doctrine of υἱοθεσία, the path to salvation is laid by Jesus of Nazareth through His baptism and resurrection (Rom 8:15 and 23) that makes Him a υἱός. His crucifixion resulted in His subsequent resurrection into a new being.

It seems Calvin misunderstood the situation. There is only one form of *huio*-ship for human beings. The other one is for the divine *Huios*.

---

99. Westhead, "Adoption," 102.
100. Westhead, "Adoption," 102.

It is, we might say, in this "redemptive" sonship that for Calvin adoption properly consists. A "sure" adoption is only to be received by coming to Christ the Head. This redemptive sonship is so far superior and qualitatively different as to permit Calvin to aver that creative sonship is not sonship at all, for "to neither angels nor men was God ever Father," but he becomes so only "by free adoption" *(Inst.* 2:14:5). "The adoption of all the godly is gratuitous and does not depend on any regard to works."[101]

When God creates humans, He becomes a Father. However, it is vital to note that a father capable of procreating without assistance does not require the adoption of his offspring. Calvin's creation of these two categories of sonship (redemptive sonship and creative sonship) stems from a misunderstanding of Adam's infancy, his *népio*-ship.

Our relationship with God is not "reestablished" to an earlier state before the fall but rather "constituted" into a new state. It is not by restoring humans to their prelapsarian state that they are saved, but rather by constituting them as new beings. God elevates those whom He created to become mature sons (υἱοί). Due to the absence of an understanding of the concept of *népio*-ship and *huio*-ship, Calvin proposed the elevation of Adamic human sonship to what he termed "redemptive sonship." There has been a misinterpretation of Paul's concept of *huiothesía* (υἱοθεσία), caused by the incorrect assumption that the Latin concept of *adoptio* is the correct interpretation. The Latin translation of *huiothesía* has contributed to this misunderstanding of the Messiah's gospel by obscuring the true meaning of the original idea of salvation.

When discussing Calvin's perspective on the Fatherhood of God, it becomes complex. In Calvin's view, the term "Father" is exclusively applicable to members of Christ, while the reference to "all" in Mal 2:10, "Have we not all one Father?," is understood to pertain solely to Jews.[102] This concept is a consequence of his conviction that only through the act of being adopted into God's divine family can humans achieve salvation. Additionally, he attempts to establish a correlation between this concept—Christians as adopted sons of God—and his interpretation of the adoption of the nation Israel by referencing Rom 9. He incorporates his idea of adoption (similar to the approach taken by the *Vulgata* interpreter) into the biblical text, which is an illustration of eisegesis. Rather than reading the Bible, he reads his own thoughts into it.

---

101. Westhead, "Adoption," 103–4.
102. Westhead, "Adoption," 104.

John Calvin was a jurist who addressed civic matters through the medium of legal discourse. During his era, Latin was the prevalent language among educated Europeans, and he demonstrated a high level of proficiency in it. His proficiency in Latin and familiarity with the *Vulgata* may have shaped his interpretation of the Bible. It is possible that he was well versed in the concept of the Roman *adoptio* but less familiar with the idea of υἱοθεσία when he subsequently engaged with the Greek text. Calvin's systematic approach to theology and ecclesiastical reforms was significantly influenced by this background. Latin was used in the composition of his *Institutes of the Christian Religion* (*Institutio Christianae Religionis*). He was fluent in Greek, which he used to read the NT Bible, but his main language for academic and theological discussions was Latin. Because of his training in Latin and law, he consequently concluded that *adoptio* is a legitimate way to solve the salvation issue. Upon encountering the challenging term "υἱοθεσία," and the *Vulgata's* translation, his cognitive processes led him to perceive it as an iteration of the Latin word "*adoptio*" without questioning it.

The referenced Calvin passage presents certain issues that require further examination. If the assertion is made that God is the father of Christians only, then it follows that those who do not adhere to Christianity are also excluded, including the Jews. Then we have a problem with "υἱοθεσία" in Rom 9. Calvin's perspective suggests that non-Jews and non-Christians have a distinct paternal figure, but upon conversion to Christianity, they all share the same paternal figure, regardless of ethnicity. In alignment with Calvin's tribalistic (group-oriented) conceptualization, individuals who do not adhere to the Jewish or Christian faith are devoid of a paternal figure or possess a different one.

If we accept that the God of Gen 1 is limited to being the father of the Jews and Christians, then we must conclude that all other humans are excluded from having any relationship with this Creator Father. Consequently, it follows that God cannot save them. The argument is presented that the Creator and His revelations are intended for all of humanity. This is based on the premise that the God of Gen 1, who creates all humankind, makes a promise in Gen 3 that applies to all of God's created children. The reading of Genesis must be approached from a universal perspective, rather than from a tribalistic (group-oriented) perspective. God is the Creator of all beings and thus the Father of all beings.

Still, although all humans are created in the image of God, only those who are in Christ (υἱοί, mature sons; see Gal 3:26) who conform to the image of Christ (Rom 8:29 and 1 Cor 15:49) can address the Creator of all things as "*Abba*," which is a unique term reserved for υἱοί. This is not about attaining the status of God's "sons," but rather about becoming "mature sons" (eschatological sons) who address God the Father with a special term, "*Abba*." Calvin presents an alternative viewpoint, as follows:

> Moreover, it is quite unfitting that those not engrafted into the body of the only begotten Son are considered to have the place and rank of children *(Inst.* 2:6:1). . . . With what confidence would anyone address God as "Father?" . . . no one, unless we had been adopted as children of grace in Christ *(Inst.* 3:20:36).[103]

The inability of humans to refer to the Creator as "*Abba*" does not imply that the Creator is not the parent of all beings. The fundamental nature of Being-Itself is not contingent upon how humans describe or refer to it. The term "Father" is not a status attributed to God; rather, it is a manifestation of His existence, reflecting His active choice to embody a paternal role.

The relationship between humans and the Creator God is not analogous to the relationship between humans and their earthly parents. Unlike the latter, there is no biological familial relationship between humans and the Creator God. The concept of human beings as natural offspring of God is a symbolic one; as a result, there cannot be a legally binding adoption in the conventional sense. The concept of God as the Creator can be likened to that of a father figure towards His creations. The assertion by Christian believers that they are the only true children (through adoption) who can address God as their father gives rise to many issues. This concept is analogous to one found in tribal religions, in which each tribe has its deity (portrayed as a father figure) and one must confess to that deity to be accepted into the tribe. This is reminiscent of the pledge made by Ruth to Naomi (Ruth 1:16–17) and Joshua (Josh 24:15).

Since the first phase of creation, God the Creator has been a Father to all His created minors (νήπιοι), even if they do not believe in Him or Christ. Ignoring the truth is to claim that He is only the Father to the elect. It is important to avoid twisting the gospel's message in a direction contrary to the gospel itself. It is against God's will for salvation. The promise of salvation is extended to all conscious beings, figuratively represented by Adam and Eve, as recorded in Gen 3:15. Those who are truly children of the *Creator* are those who were *created* and raised to maturity, not those who are *adopted* in the proper sense of the term.

The doctrine of adoption's exclusive father can be considered a lesser god and, thus, only a being. The overarching objective of Christianity, as a universal faith, is to supplant the group-oriented religions of the Old Testament, rather than introduce a new tribalistic one. Calvin's doctrine of

---

103. Westhead, "Adoption," 104.

adoption is at odds with the fundamental tenets of Christianity. The designation of God as the father of adopted children establishes limitations on His nature, effectively reducing Him to the status of a mere deity.

Westhead then explained the mechanics of Calvin's adoption.

> Adoption is the category Calvin used to describe the status one enters into upon release from the law. But this is achieved by Christ himself becoming a curse for us, being made subject to the law, "that we should not be borne down by an unending bondage, which would agonize our consciences with the fear of death." . . . Our access to the Father in prayer is a way "opened to us by the blood of Christ, [that] we may rejoice fully and openly that we are the children of God." It is precisely because adoption is the fruit of the cross that we must "embrace it [*i.e.* the cross] humbly" if our sonship is to be restored (*Inst.* 2:6:1).[104]

In his gospel of adoption, Calvin avoided discussing sonship as a new being but rather as a *restored* relational status. I argue that the new relationship undergoes an "augmentation" in the individual's nature, representing a revival of the previous version of creation and its capability to participate in an elevated kind of relationship with the Creator. It means, in Calvin's view, that the restoration is external to the individual, who lacks efficacy because "the son in a certain sense" and "the son in a fuller sense" will inevitably relapse, constantly disrupting the relationship and thus necessitate the second, third, and n^{th} cross both here and in the *aeon* to come. The recurring need for the cross cannot be remedied solely by defining the efficacy of the cross without a change of nature within man's constitutive elements. Only new beings can prevent future falls. In the realm of redemptive sonship that adoption entails,[105] salvation is described as transferring a person from one legal stand to another.

As a conceptual framework for analysis, consider the following comparison. It is a fallacy to assume that purchasing a Mercedes-Benz C-Class 1496 cc will result in the vehicle becoming a Mercedes-Benz Maybach *Sonderklasse* 5980 cc. An ontological transformation is not contingent on the transfer of payment, legal documentation, ownership, or even the alteration of the vehicle's exterior to resemble that of a Maybach S-Class. Despite such changes, the vehicle will not automatically assume the characteristics of a Maybach S-Class. A 1.5-liter engine is incapable of producing the same amount of power as a 6-liter engine.

---

104. Westhead, "Adoption," 104–5.
105. Westhead, "Adoption," 103.

Similarly, an adopted son is, in essence, the same individual (the same protological human) following the adoption. It can be observed that the ontological transformation of Adamic beings into Christic beings is a central tenet of Christian theology concerning salvation. Only those who embody the qualities of Christ (Christic beings) can engage in actions that align with the teachings of Christ. This is a matter of fundamental importance to the concept of human salvation.

This leads to the question of how Adam, who was a created son, could have fallen. If the term "sons" can be used to describe a state of fallibility, then it follows that humanity has no hope of salvation. Fortunately, Calvin's use of the term "son" does not correspond to Paul's use of the term "υἱός." It is only those who are in a state of minority (νήπιοι) who are susceptible to falling. Accordingly, the primary objective is to achieve the state of a υἱός, or eschatological son, which represents the fully elevated human being immediately before entering an everlasting existence. The fall is a natural phenomenon that occurs in all minors (νήπιοι), from Adam and Eve to subsequent generations. To achieve salvation, this creation must progress from its original form to its ultimate state of consummation. It seems reasonable to posit that few would desire to return to a state of ignorance, akin to that of Adam before the fall, where he was unaware of his nakedness and the distinction between good and evil. In such a situation, it would be impossible to engage in productive activities.

What "nature" are we talking about?

> What is equally essential to the procurement of our adoption for Calvin is not only that Christ takes our place to release us from the law of God, but that he takes our nature through incarnation, so that "what he has of his own by nature may become ours by benefit of adoption" (*Inst.* 3:20:36).[106]

The assumption of the human condition by Christ was not intended only to release humanity from the Torah through the forgiveness of sins on the cross. It intends more. Forgiveness represents merely one aspect of this complex phenomenon of ultimate salvation. Conversely, it can be proposed that God elevated human nature from its original sarkic state to a new pneumatic state, thereby rendering the sarkic state obsolete and establishing the pneumatic state as the dominant force. This would render the law disposable. The original sarkic state was defined by sarkic desire; however, this is no longer the case in the new pneumatic state that will be defined by pneumatic desire. I propose that the aforementioned quotation be modified

---

106. Westhead, "Adoption," 105.

as follows: "but that He takes our nature through the incarnation, so that 'what He has achieved in His assumed human nature may become ours by ontological transformation through υἱοθεσία.'" The assumption of the human condition by Christ is of greater importance in that He elevates human nature into the state of *huio*-ship, which frees humanity from temporality (decay, annihilation) through His resurrection. This can be defined as the ultimate salvation. Thus, there is no interchange of nature, as only human nature can be possessed by humans. Acquisition of a different nature would render humans something other than human. The essence of humanity cannot be altered; however, it can be elevated.

The following statement serves to illustrate Calvin's rejection of the concept of universal brotherhood and the notion of universal fatherhood.

> It is *quite unfitting* that those not engrafted into the body of the only begotten Son are considered to have *the place and rank of children* (Inst. 2:6:1).[107]

Once more, Calvin has such an idea because he lacks the concept of Paul's νήπιος, τέκνον, and υἱός. Furthermore, he is unaware that individuals with a sarkic nature who do not undergo the ontological transformation through υἱοθεσία are corporeal beings, constrained to participate in a physical fellowship within the confines of this temporal physical reality only. They are thus unable to engage in a spiritual union within the eternal spiritual reality. However, despite their corporeal existence, they remain part of the human family under their status as created children of God. Individuals with a sarkic nature are unable to be incorporated spiritually into the spiritual body of Christ.

Still, Calvin rendered,

> Flesh alone does not make the bond of brotherhood.... When we say that Christ was made man that he might make us children of God, this expression does not extend to all men. For faith intervenes, to engraft us spiritually into the body of Christ (Inst. 2:13:2).[108]

What is the process by which Christians may be grafted into the body of Christ? Humans require a spiritual union with the Godhead through the Messiah and the Holy Spirit for the attainment of salvation. Consequently, external and moral relationships are deemed insufficient for attaining this state.[109] The question arises as to how those of a sarkic nature, who are

---

107. Westhead, "Adoption," 106. Emphasis added.
108. Westhead, "Adoption," 106. Emphasis added.
109. Cf. George, *Theosis*, 21.

confined to a transient, corporeal, fleshly existence, can be grafted spiritually. The nature of the relationship between humans and God is a function of human nature. In other words, it is human nature that determines the form of relationship between humans and God. Adoption does not affect a transformation of the sarkic-Adamic humans; thus, adopted children are only capable of maintaining external, legal, and moral relationships without attaining a personal spiritual union with God. Without an ontological change, adopted children are merely human beings of τὰ κάτω (things below—earthly, transient, sarkical, protological); they are not ultimately saved because they cannot enter the pneumatic union and reside in the heavenly realm (τὰ ἄνω).

Proper translations, interpreting the context accurately, can resolve the issue of who the "children" and the "father" are. Christ's purpose is not to make people become children of God but to transform the *beloved* children (τέκνα) who are in their immature state (νήπιοι, old sarkic beings) into mature son-heirs (υἱοί, new pneumatic beings) of God. And also, there is no such thing as "the Spirit of adoption" as the phrase is made up of wrong translations of the "πνεῦμα υἱοθεσίας."

> The major function of the Holy Spirit in relation to adoption is to create within the believer a filial confidence—an assurance or persuasion of being a son or daughter of God. Our assurance of God's paternal care for us "is made certain by the Spirit of adoption." . . . The Holy Spirit is called the Spirit of adoption precisely "because he is the witness to us of the free benevolence of God" (*Inst.* 3:1:3).[110]

Although I read "a spirit of the constitution of mature son/daughter" instead of "the Spirit of adoption," I fully agree that the Holy Spirit is responsible for convincing a believer of her status as a daughter-heir of God. As the unitive Being,[111] the Spirit enables believers to fellowship with the Son.

Westhead begins the next section, Adoption and the Covenant:

> A second major aspect of Calvin's thought, in addition to the Trinitarian dimension, is what we might call the "covenantal" or perhaps the "redemptive-historical." . . . In a word, we have to take cognizance of the fact that Calvin's understanding of

---

110. Westhead, "Adoption," 106.

111. Macquarrie explains "the Holy Spirit as unitive Being. This already indicates how the work of the Spirit is to be conceived. It is the work of maintaining unity and, where need be, renewing it, throughout the whole extent of Being and beings. Thus the work of the Spirit is simply another aspect of the reconciling work of God, and so another aspect of the work of Christ." Macquarrie, *Principles*, 332.

adoption is arrived at by employing what has been called the biblico-theological method. What results does this method yield as used by Calvin for the doctrine of adoption? To answer this question it is important to remind ourselves of the broader covenantal framework in which Calvin's understanding of adoption in particular is set. For Calvin, any transition or development in the notion of sonship across time must be set against the relationship between the old and new covenants.[112]

Recall the plea of David Garner that "urges renewed reflection on the biblical concept of adoption."[113] The concept is an unbiblical eisegetical attempt to read the NT Bible. It is "biblical" only when it refers to *Vulgata*, Calvin's translation, the Geneva Bible, the KJV, the ESV, and other translations that render υἱοθεσία as "adoption as sons." Later, I will show that υἱοθεσία (on which the teaching of adoption is based) is an activity of the triune God from the first days of creation to the eschaton. The Creator God made a promise to all humans, as recorded in Gen 3:15. This promise was fulfilled in its entirety through the event of Christ, who is referred to as the Son.

About the Old Testament and New Testament, Westhead wrote,

> In principle these covenants are essentially one. . . . Calvin's arguments for the inherent oneness of these two administrations are summarized in his usual vivid manner: "Let us, therefore, boldly establish a principle unassailable by any stratagem of the Devil: the Old Testament . . . that the Lord had made with the Israelites had not been limited to earthly things, but contained a promise of spiritual and eternal life . . . away with this insane and dangerous opinion that the Lord promised the Jews . . . nothing but a full belly, delights of the flesh, flourishing wealth, outward power, fruitfulness of offspring and whatever the natural man prizes! (*Inst.* 2:10:23)."[114]

And that

> the Old Testament refers to one nation, the New to all. The final difference between the two covenants bears more directly on the subject of adoption. . . . The Old Testament struck consciences with fear and trembling, but by the benefit of the New they are released into joy. The Old held consciences bound by the yoke

---

112. Westhead, "Adoption," 107–8.
113. Garner, *Sons in the Son*, xxv–xxvi.
114. Westhead, "Adoption," 108.

of bondage; the New by its spirit of liberality emancipates them into freedom (*Inst.* 2:11:9).[115]

Here, we see that Calvin saw adoption as the *historia salutis*, from the Old Testament to the New Testament. He also stated that the NT is for all nations. In Rom 11:11–24, Paul discusses the addition of all nations, the gentiles (a wild olive branch), to the olive root. We need to resolve what the olive tree symbolically represents: the nation of Israel, the old covenant, the promise, or the Messiah of Israel. How does this olive metaphor relate to υἱοθεσία, or are they addressing separate ideas? We leave this topic for another discussion.

Westhead continues,

> Here again Calvin institutes a threefold contrast between the adoption of Old and New Testament believers. First, the Jews were "under the custody of the law . . . [which] . . . did not restrain them from faith; but, that they might not wander from the fold of faith, it kept possession of themselves." Again this does not mean that the ancient believers were not "sons," for when Paul speaks of believers who lived "before faith came" (Gal. 3:23), he does so, says Calvin, "not in an absolute, but in a comparative sense." Again, "while they had the mirror, we have the substance," but, "whatever might be the amount of darkness under the law, the fathers were not ignorant of the road in which they ought to walk." Secondly, believers under the law were "children" under a "schoolmaster," being trained for more mature years: The law was the grammar of theology, which, after carrying its scholars a short way, handed them over to faith to be completed. Thus, Paul compares the Jews to children, and us to advanced youth. Just as a child is not so indefinitely but comes to adulthood, so he is not expected to be under the schoolmaster all his life. Here again, we believers of the new dispensation, "under the reign of Christ, [need] no longer any childhood . . . consequently, the law has resigned its office." Thirdly, Paul explains and illustrates the difference that exists between us and the ancient people . . . by introducing a third comparison, drawn from the relation which a person under age bears to his tutor. For Calvin, Old Testament believers resemble "slaves." They are in fact "sons," since the period of guardianship lasts only until the time appointed by the Father, after which they will be free. "In this respect," says Calvin, "the fathers under the Old Testament, being the sons of God, were free; but

---

115. Westhead, "Adoption," 109.

> they were not in possession of freedom . . . [until] the coming of Christ." Pursuing this line of thought on Galatians 4:24, Calvin terms the covenant symbolized by Hagar as "legal" and that by Sarah as "evangelical," the former "makes slaves," the latter "makes freemen."[116]

For Calvin, there are *two* kinds of adoption such as the adoption of the Old and New Testaments. I guess this problem arises because "adoption" has a univocal meaning. In contrast, I see there is only *one* continuous process of developing υἱός (υἱοθεσία), which starts in the Old Testament and is completed in the New Testament. In some parts, it seems that Calvin has correctly grasped some of Paul's idea of υἱοθεσία, but it looks incoherent with his other arguments about adoption.

Westhead closed this heading with this.

> In a word, the climax of this grace of adoption is renewal in God's image. This image, as we have seen, is the ground of our being children of God by creation. This was only sonship "in a certain sense," but now the final phase of adoption brings us into sonship in its fullest and richest sense, being conformed not to Adam but to the last Adam, Jesus Christ.[117]

There is no such thing as a "*huio*-ship in a certain sense." I see the culmination of the constitution of an eschatological son as the conformity to the image of Christ the Son. The first image, as we have seen, was the ground of our being created children of God (νήπιοι). It is not sonship but Adamic minorship (*nēpio*-ship), but now the final phase of the constitution of an eschatological son (υἱοθεσία) brings us into mature or pneumatic sonship (*huio*-ship) in its fullest new being of a recreated and elevated human.

In the subsection "Adoption and Justification," Westhead writes, "We must now look briefly at a third aspect of Calvin's thinking in the area of adoption, namely, the relationship between adoption and justification. This issue arises since in the history of dogmatics, adoption has not always been viewed as distinct from justification, but rather as a subordinate aspect of justification."[118] Some scholars posit that adoption is an integral component of the *ordo salutis*. However, it is erroneous to assume that adoption is equivalent to the Pauline υἱοθεσία, and *vice versa*. Paul addresses the topic of υἱοθεσία in Rom 8, associating it with the *ordo salutis*. However, in his discourse in Gal 4, he refers to the *historia salutis*. It is erroneous to

---

116. Westhead, "Adoption," 109–10.
117. Westhead, "Adoption," 112.
118. Westhead, "Adoption," 112.

assert that believers are adopted children in God's family; rather, they are created humans transforming into new beings, symbolically designated as "son-heirs."

Discrepancies in Theological Adoption

Trevor J. Burke observed that there were inconsistencies among the advocates of adoption. He enumerated the Reformed theological discrepancies of Francis Turretin, John Leith, R. A. Dabney, L. Berkhof, A. Kuyper, J. Murray, A. Hoekema, and so forth.[119] Burke's approach to adoption was grounded in the Pauline concept of υἱοθεσία. Additionally, Burke composes another volume that elucidates the concept of sonship, employing the Old and New Testaments and incorporating the apostle John's concept of ἄνωθεν (John 3:3) to substantiate his argument.[120] Some academics, such as Burke himself, associate υἱοθεσία with the idea of adoptive sonship.[121] I must respectfully disagree with that assertion. The concept of sonship represents a state acquired by individuals previously not considered sons of God's family. It differs considerably from the idea of *huio*-ship, which means a state of maturity and is bestowed upon individuals previously minors within God's family.

Trumper maintains that any concepts that extend beyond Paul's teachings must be excluded from the discourse on adoption.[122] From the Greek NT, we can see clearly that in John's perspective, the state of *huio*-ship does not apply to believers but to the Messiah alone; instead, *tekna*-ship is the pertinent consideration. Given the considerable diversity of the ideas of Paul's *huio*-ship and John's *tekna*-ship, I advocate that it is necessary to distinguish between them. Still, they are frequently referred to as "sonship" in English translations of the Bible. Accordingly, when discussing υἱοθεσία, it is preferable to employ the term "*huio*-ship" rather than "sonship." However, there are similarities between John's ἄνωθεν and Paul's υἱοθεσία.

---

119. Burke, *Adopted into God's Family*, 23–29.
120. Burke, *Message of Sonship*.
121. Burke, "Characteristics," 62–74.
122. Trumper, "Fresh Exposition of Adoption," 61–62.

SUMMARY: ARTICULATING MY CONCEPTUAL FRAMEWORK

Our review aims to identify and examine the definitions and the theoretical framework. In the context of theological teachings on adoption, the concept of God creating Adam as His *son* is a fundamental tenet. However, following Adam's fall, he lost his *status* as God's son and became a member of an unidentified family, potentially Satan's. In the theology of adoption, all subsequent human beings are considered descendants of historical Adam and thus bear the burden of his transgressions. In this context, the term "salvation" is used to describe the act of God adopting these lost children and reinstating them to their original pre-fall status as God's sons. Consequently, the concept of salvation is inextricably linked to the original situation in the garden of Eden. It is about restoring the status of lost sonship and transferring individuals from an unknown family to the family of God. It is crucial to acknowledge that the term "son" possesses a unique connotation that differs from Paul's usage of νήπιος and υἱός. Consequently, the precise meaning of the term "son" remains ambiguous. In this adoption's theoretical framework, human beings require the process of adoption to become (to be restored to) the status of sons of God. It is back to point zero, no growth.

It would be a significant challenge to alter the interpretation of υἱοθεσία to mean "adoption" without compromising the content, integrity, and coherence of the Christian gospel. To assert that this biased interpretation is the primary meaning of the gospel is to cause significant harm. Those who espouse this interpretation must resort to eisegesis and intricate arguments to defend their engineered idea. Regardless of the degree of care taken in its construction, the resulting complexity is an inherent flaw. Therefore, it is also challenging to reestablish the authentic meaning of Pauline υἱοθεσία.

This adoption framework presents several problematic aspects. The question thus arises as to how Adam, if he was indeed a "son" of God, could have fallen. If Adam was capable of falling from this state when he was God's son, which would make him a member of an unknown or Satan's family, why do we revert to the prelapsarian state for salvation? It is not assured that these restored children will not fall again as Adam did. The act of restoring or reinstating a being to the Eden condition that existed before the occurrence of a fall results in the recurrence of falls. If Adam and his descendants lost their status as God's children and became part of Satan's family, it is unclear how God, who has no relation to this unknown family, could adopt these children. One might inquire as to why God permitted His created children to become members of another family in the first place.

The following is my conceptual framework. Sin and decay represent intrinsic negative potentials that are fundamental to the Adamic primordial nature. However, this nature also possesses the capacity for development, albeit constrained by its inherent limitations, which can be characterized as Adamic facticity. This perspective underscores the duality of human existence, where the growth potential exists alongside the acknowledgment of existential boundaries.

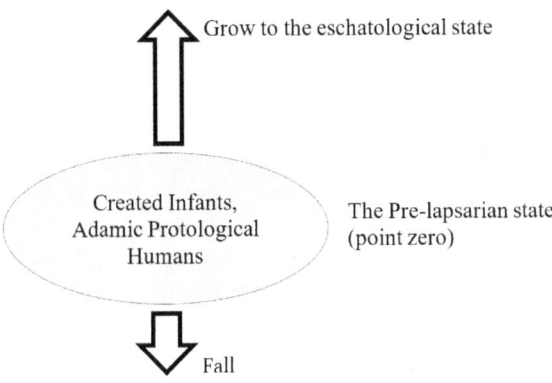

FIGURE 3: Adamic Humans Are Created with Potentials

There exists a transitional state in the ontological transformation of human beings. It is recognized that even after an individual has embraced a new nature, they may still engage in behaviors characteristic of their former nature. For instance, one might assert that they no longer require repentance, a stance that can be interpreted as sinful. This observation highlights the complexities and contradictions inherent in the process of transformation within human existence.

This conceptual framework posits that the dilemma concerning protological humanity extends beyond the mere existence of sin; it fundamentally revolves around the concept of temporality. The existence of flawless beings who are nonetheless temporal presents a paradox, as God's capacity to share divine love with humanity in an eternal context is inherently limited by their temporal nature. It is incongruous for an Eternal Being to engage with beings defined by temporality. Consequently, from the beginning, God intends to create the object of His love singularly and everlastingly, without the desire for replacement or repetition in that creation. This perspective emphasizes the intrinsic relationship between divine love and the nature of existence itself, highlighting the significance of permanence in the context of God's creative will. Salvation encompasses not only liberation from sin but also liberation from temporality. God's act of *creation* includes *salvation* through sub-act of υἱοθεσία—it is an elevation of beings.

To be free from sin and temporality, humans must achieve a new state of being that is entirely distinct from their previous state. Adamic protological humans (νήπιοι), symbolically represented by literary Adam, have the potential to either fall or grow. In the event of a fall on the part of Adamic humans, their natural relationship with God remains intact, as it is only those who have a prior relationship with God who can be saved. Regardless of whether they engage in sinful behavior, Adamic humans remain part of God's created family in the created existence.

Concerning 1 Cor 15:44–51, the objective of human creation is to attain the state of pneumatic eschatological humans, or biblically depicted as "mature sons" (υἱοί) or "heavenly humans." Upon attaining this state, humans become fully actualized spiritual beings and partake in a pneumatic union with the Godhead. This eliminates the possibility of sin or falling again, and breaks the process of decay (annihilation) but growth. At this juncture, the *potential* for communion with the Godhead has been *actualized* and transformed into an actual ability. The protological state of being of the human being serves as the foundation for the establishment of the eschatological state of being. The ontological transformation is symbolically articulated through a pattern of progression, wherein the Adamic humans (νήπιοι, infants) undergo eschatological maturation from a state of infanthood to adult son-heirs (υἱοί).

My conceptual framework is consistent with Irenaeus of Lyons' teaching of human growth.[123] The Creator bestows growth upon the created sarkic-Adamic protological beings (νήπιοι). Accordingly, I contend that the process of growth from a protological Adamic being to an eschatological Christic being is best understood as a process of God's sub-act of υἱοθεσία.

---

123. Presley writes, "His economic report describes God as the Creator of the world (Gen 1:1), the Creator of humankind (Gen 2:7), and humankind as infused with the "faculty of increase" (*donauit incrementum*), echoing Gen 1:28 characterizing the progressive sanctification of God's creature. (*Haer.* 2.28.1). . . . The lesser creature (Adam) is blessed by the greater Creator (God), which entails growth and increase (Gen 1:28) toward God." Presley, *Intertextual Reception* 8:79.

CHAPTER 2

THE HISTORY OF THE VARIOUS INTERPRETATIONS OF *HUIOTHESIA*

"THE MEANING OF A WORD IS ITS USE IN THE LANGUAGE." ~ LUDWIG WITTGENSTEIN

OVERVIEW

Tim J. R. Trumper's work focuses on the historical development of the doctrine of adoption, rather than on the evolution of its interpretations and translations.[1] Regrettably, the author fails to pose a fundamental question: At what point and in what context did υἱοθεσία evolve into adoption?[2] It should be noted that "adoption" is not the only translation of "υἱοθεσία." In historical contexts, there have been several different interpretations and translations of the term "υἱοθεσία," including "*adoptio*," "*toga virilis*," "sonship," and "the placing as/of a son."

The Weymouth New Testament Bible offers a distinctive translation of the term "υἱοθεσία." It reads in Gal 4:5 "so that we might receive *recognition* as sons."[3] This expression is found in Rom 8:23, too. But Weymouth's Rom 8:15 and Eph 1:5 read "adopted as sons," and Rom 9:4 reads

---

1. Trumper, "Theological History of Adoption: I"; Trumper, "Theological History of Adoption: II," 177–202.

2. See Tan, "Call of 'Abba,'" 241.

3. Weymouth, *New Testament in Modern Speech*, 454. Emphasis added.

"God's sons."[4] It shows that Paul's "υἱοθεσία" does not have a univocal meaning like "adoption" for all its appearances. This chapter will discuss some developments in the history of the translations and interpretations of Pauline υἱοθεσία, as well as issues related to a certain translation variation—adoption.

BEFORE THE PROTESTANT ERA

Irenaeus, an Interpreter of Paul, Did Not Write Theological Adoption

The Roman *adoptio* has been erroneously incorporated into the υἱοθεσία teaching of Paul. The reason it was not translated to *toga virilis*, despite its similar significance to υἱοθεσία, is likely because *toga virilis* cannot be applied to Rom 9:4 and 8:23. Nevertheless, the concept of *adoptio* has also led to the misinterpretation of Paul's υἱοθεσία and Irenaeus' explanation of it. The following is a paragraph from Irenaeus' *Against Heresies*, taken from book 3.

> For it was for this end that the Word of God was made man, and He who was the Son of God became the Son of man, that man, having been taken into the Word, and receiving the adoption, might become the son of God. For by no other means could we have attained to incorruptibility and immortality, unless we had been united to incorruptibility and immortality. But how could we be joined to incorruptibility and immortality, unless, first, incorruptibility and immortality had become that which we also are, so that the corruptible might be swallowed up by incorruptibility, and the mortal by immortality, that we might receive the adoption of sons?[5]

The translators' idea of becoming the adopted son of God as a means to attain incorruptibility and immortality is different from Irenaeus' concept of God's economy. It is God's sub-act of υἱοθεσία, not a new status by adoption, that makes Adamic humans incorruptible and immortal.

Despite that, some interpreters claim that the reading of "*adoptio*" can be traced back to Irenaeus (AD 120–202) because his work Ἔλεγχος καὶ ἀνατροπὴ τῆς ψευδωνύμου γνώσεως (*On the Detection and Overthrow*

---

4. Weymouth, *New Testament in Modern Speech*, 368, 370, 463.

5. ANF 1:448–49.

of the So-Called Gnosis), translated into Latin as *Adversus Haereses*, speaks of adoption. Is this true?[6] David B. Garner points out that, with the notable exception of Irenaeus, a study of the church fathers reveals little mention of υἱοθεσία. "*Adoption as sons*" (as Garner altered the term from "υἱοθεσία," as he referenced J. Scott Lidgett) represents the dominant motif in Irenaeus' theological construction of the comprehensive range of redemptive privileges. Though Irenaeus gave *adoption* the formative significance it had in the early church, Origen (c. 185–254) and Athanasius (c. 297–373) also contributed to the Alexandrian tradition with similar notions of God's Fatherhood and Jesus' redemptive *Sonship*.[7]

Because of such a claim, these writers use the two words "υἱοθεσία" and "adoption" interchangeably. The assertions regarding Irenaeus and adoption are erroneous. Irenaeus wrote in Greek about υἱοθεσία, not about *adoptio*. The translators presumed that the two terms were equivalent. The term "theological adoption" is an inadequate interpretation of "υἱοθεσία."

To illustrate, consider the replacement of the term "adoption" from *ah* with the concept of "υἱοθεσία" (the making of a υἱός).

> He at one time conferring with His creature, and at another propounding His law; at one time, again, reproving, at another exhorting, and then setting free His servant, and adopting him as a son (*in filium*); and, at the proper time, bestowing an incorruptible inheritance, for the purpose of bringing man to perfection? For He formed him for growth and increase, as the Scripture says: "Increase and multiply."[8]

In this example, we can try to replace the phrase "adopting him as a son (*in filium*)" with "making him into a υἱός (*in maturum filium*, into a mature son, or as an adult son)." We can sense the difference, and if we look at the overall theme of *ah* 4.38 titled "Why man was not made perfect from the beginning," it becomes evident that Irenaeus is articulating the

---

6. Cf., at its preface of book 1, *ANF* 1:315n1 writes, "The Greek original of the work of Irenæus is from time to time recovered through the numerous quotations made from it by subsequent writers, especially by the author's pupil Hippolytus, and by Epiphanius. The latter preserves (*Haer.* 31. secs. 9–32) the preface of Irenæus, and most of the first book. An important difference of reading occurs between the Latin and Greek in the very first word. The translator manifestly read ἐπεί, *quatenus*, while in Epiphanius we find ἐπί, *against*. The former is probably correct, and has been followed in our version. We have also supplied a clause, in order to avoid the extreme length of the sentence in the original, which runs on without any apodosis to the words ἀναγκαῖον ἡγησάμην, 'I have judged it necessary.'" *ANF* 1:315.

7. Garner, *Sons in the Son*, 21.

8. *ANF* 1:474. Gen 1:28.

concept of *growth* and *increase*, the process of human becoming (or the idea of God bringing man to the planned goal), which are inextricably linked to the notions of incorruptibility and immortality. From this chapter of the *ah*, we learn from Irenaeus that God created humans as infants (νήπιοι, protological Adamic human) and that God the Son came to us also as an infant (νήπιος), thus enabling us to behold Him.[9] This correctly interprets Paul's teaching.

Luckily, this section of *ah* 4.38 serves to safeguard the original interpretation of υἱοθεσία put forth by Irenaeus from the influence of inadvertent mistranslations. Irenaeus provides further clarification.

> God had power at the beginning to grant perfection to man; but as the latter was only recently created, he could not possibly have received it, or even if he had received it, could he have contained it, or containing it, could he have retained it. It was for this reason that the Son of God, although He was perfect, passed through the state of infancy in common with the rest of mankind, partaking of it thus not for His own benefit, but for that of the infantile stage of man's existence, in order that man might be able to receive Him.[10]

Note the phrase "the infantile stage of man's existence," which is important to understand the concept of Pauline υἱοθεσία. This arrangement of creation is part of God's wisdom. In the following translated passage from Irenaeus, attention is drawn to phrases such as "receive growth and a long period of existence" and "ascending towards the perfect." Thus, humans are not going back to the protological perfection in Eden.

> His wisdom [is shown] in His having made created things parts of one harmonious and consistent whole; and those things which, through His supereminent kindness, receive growth and a long period of existence, do reflect the glory of the uncreated One, of that God who bestows what is good ungrudgingly . . . the Son carrying these into execution and performing the work of creating, and the Spirit nourishing and increasing [what is made], but man making progress day by day, and ascending towards the perfect, that is, approximating to the uncreated One.[11]

---

9. *ANF* 1:521.
10. *ANF* 1:521.
11. *ANF* 1:521–22.

These expressions of Irenaeus encapsulate the notion of human development and the journey towards spiritual perfection, reflecting Irenaeus' theological framework.

In his fourth section, Irenaeus discusses divinization, immortality, and incorruptibility, and asserts that it is God, and not created beings, who "shall overcome the substance of created nature."

> For we cast blame upon Him, because we have not been made gods from the beginning, but at first merely men, then at length gods; although God has adopted this course out of His pure benevolence, that no one may impute to Him invidiousness or grudgingness . . . while at the same time by His prescience He knew the infirmity of human beings, and the consequences which would flow from it; but through [His] love and [His] power, He shall overcome the substance of created nature.* For it was necessary, at first, that nature should be exhibited; then, after that, that what was mortal should be conquered and swallowed up by immortality, and the corruptible by incorruptibility, and that man should be made after the image and likeness of God, having received the knowledge of good and evil.[12]

God facilitates the growth and maturation (elevation) of His chosen children. It is not within His purview to adopt individuals who have already reached adulthood in another family, as is the practice in Roman culture. The concept of adoption is incompatible with the notion that God nurtures His children until they reach the age of maturity.

On the subject of Pauline υἱοθεσία, it would be beneficial to concentrate on the maturation and growth process that symbolizes the conquering of the Adamic characteristics of created protological human nature. A newly established legal standing does not alter a person's essence and existence, also it might not alter a person's level of maturity—as demonstrated by the example of an infant king. It is crucial to bear in mind that existence and essence (substance, *ousia*) are what matter most when it comes to salvation, not legality. Salvation is about transforming a person from the inside out, ontically.

The apostle Paul employs symbolism through a metaphor of family life, which he refers to as *huiothesia* (υἱοθεσία), to connect the abstract theological concept of salvation to well-known ideas that *everyone* experiences in their natural life. As a metaphor, it can both reveal truths to those who are

---

12. ANF 1:522. *"That is, that man's human nature should not prevent him from becoming a partaker of the divine." We will subsequently address the manner in which this can be accomplished.

receptive to understanding them and conceal meaning from others who are not. The listener's level of openness, preexisting bias,[13] and desire to explore the deeper meaning are frequently determining factors in how well they understand this metaphor. It has several levels of significance that those who take things at face value or do not try to grasp the underlying message might miss. The problem is more severe when we misread and mistranslate the biblical word υἱοθεσία into a cultural concept that differs from its original and then take it at face value of the newly translated concept. Such a problem creates a false gospel of salvation. The apostle Paul's υἱοθεσία is not the Latin *adoptio*.

The original Greek of *Against Heresies*, as preserved by Theodoret, differs considerably from the Latin translation.[14] Fortunately, the availability of numerous quotations from the original Greek of book 1 allows for its reconstruction.[15] However, it may not be feasible to reconstruct the remaining books in which the term "υἱοθεσία" is mentioned. Alternatively, it would be prudent to consider "υἱοθεσία" when encountering the word "adoption" in the translations. For this study, we must first eliminate this preexisting bias, which assumes that υἱοθεσία is adoption and *vice versa*. It is crucial to reiterate that υἱοθεσία and adoption are two completely different themes. "Adoption is not υἱοθεσία, v.v."

The concept of the adoption of the elect is found in Gnosticism. Elaine H. Pagels wrote, "According to their own choice, they become children of God or of the devil—whichever they choose—not 'by nature' but, as Heracleon says, 'by adoption.'" In Pagels' analysis, "Heracleon's theory of adoption" may have been inspired by Rom 8:12–15.[16] As Irenaeus puts it, humanity has never been able to "escape the hands of God," as it were, in the sense that the Son and the Spirit have always been present in our lives. In

---

13. For instance, a legal professional will analyze the matter from the perspective of the law, whereas a construction project manager will consider it from the standpoint of construction methodology.

14. See 9n of *ANF* 1:448. "The original Greek is preserved here by Theodoret, differing in some respects from the old Latin version: καὶ ἀποστεροῦντας τὸν ἄνθρωπον τῆς εἰς Θεὸν ἀνόδου καὶ ἀχαριστοῦντας τῷ ὑπὲρ αὐτῶν σαρκωθέντι λόγῳ τοῦ Θεοῦ. Εἰς τοῦτο γὰρ ὁ λόγος ἄνθρωπος . . . ἵνα ὁ ἄνθρωπος τὸν λόγον χωρήσας, καὶ τὴν υἱοθεσίαν λαβὼν, υἱὸς γένηται Θεοῦ. The old Latin runs thus: '*Fraudantes hominem ab ea ascensione quæ est ad Dominum, et ingrate exsistentes Verbo Dei, qui incarnatus est propter ipsos. Propter hoc enim Verbum Dei homo, et qui Filius Dei est, Filius Hominis factus est . . . commixtus Verbo Dei, et adoptionem percipiens fiat filius Dei.*' [A specimen of the liberties taken by the Latin translators with the original of Irenæus. Others are much less innocent.]" *ANF* 1:448.

15. Reimherr and Cranz, "Irenaeus Lugdunensis," 7:16.

16. Pagels, *Gnostic Paul*, 35.

contrast, the doctrine of adoption posits the necessity of a second family for the concept to be valid. This would entail that humans must be the sons of another family, thus escaping the hands of God.

> For never at any time did Adam escape the hands* of God, to whom the Father speaking, said, "Let Us make man in Our image, after Our likeness." And for this reason in the last times (fine), not by the will of the flesh, nor by the will of man, but by the good pleasure of the Father, His hands formed a living man, in order that Adam might be created [again] after the image and likeness of God.[17]

If we consider the possibility that adoption is part of Gnosticism, it seems improbable that Irenaeus subscribed to or taught the doctrine of adoption in his *On the Detection and Overthrow of the So-Called Gnosis*. The exaltation of human nature is the defining factor of salvation. The granting of a new status as an adopted child of God is a foreign concept to the gospel.

We have learned from *ANF*'s footnote number 9 of page 448 that the case of υἱοθεσία is an example of the liberties taken by the Latin translators with Irenaeus' *ah* text. Take the phrase "καὶ τὴν υἱοθεσίαν λαβών, υἱὸς γένηται Θεοῦ." It means "and having received the υἱοθεσία, should become a υἱὸς of God." The Latin "*et adoptionem percipiens fiat filius Dei*" means "and by receiving the adoption, he becomes the son of God." If one can distinguish between the concepts of becoming a υἱός (a mature son-heir) in the context of υἱοθεσία and becoming an adopted son in the context of adoption, the situation becomes clear. There are substantial differences between the two. A more nuanced understanding of these differences can be achieved by examining the context of the Latin adoption and comparing it with the Greek context of Pauline υἱοθεσία. A more detailed examination of this topic will be presented in chapters 3 and 4.

It is implausible that Irenaeus espoused two mutually exclusive ideas that relate to υἱοθεσία. However, it is conceivable that the alternative notion, *adoptio*, originated not with him but with his Latin interpreters because he wrote his books in Greek. It may be possible to retranslate Irenaeus' sentences (the term "adoption" has more than twenty appearances in *ah*) using the available Greek fragments. However, at this point, it is necessary to first complete the main task. The objective is to recover Paul's gospel of "υἱοθεσία" as elucidated in the Pauline Epistles by taking off the veil of adoption.

If this is not done, the clause "καὶ τὴν υἱοθεσίαν λαβών, υἱὸς γένηται Θεοῦ" will be retranslated as "and having received the adoption,

---

17. ANF 1:527. *Viz., the Son and the Spirit.

should become a son of God," because everyone thinks that υἱοθεσία is adoption, which will render the effort futile. Consequently, it is necessary to utilize the primary source of υἱοθεσία, viz., the apostle Paul's epistles, in order to ascertain the true meaning of υἱοθεσία. Nevertheless, at this juncture, it is sufficient to recognize Irenaeus' central concept of "human becoming" or "human growth."[18]

Adoptio Before the Era of *Vulgata*

According to Jean Gribomont, countless *Vulgata* manuscripts bear evidence of previous translations, as do numerous manuscripts containing books of the Bible from the *Vetus Latina*.[19] On Jerome's work, H. A. G. Houghton advises, "The *Commentary on Galatians* is, therefore, a potential witness for the Old Latin tradition of this Epistle."[20] So we must see if the "*adoptio*" comes from *Itala* Bibles (*Vetus Latina, Old Latin*). However, if the *Itala* is a collection of texts, the *adoptio* may not be the only translation. Those who have access to the various *Itala*, like the *It*[a] version of the fourth century[21] (the oldest *Itala* manuscript preserved today), can examine the translations of "υἱοθεσία." The formation of a translation tradition has the potential to create a new theological tradition or a divergence from the true biblical teaching.

The Rise of *Adoptio* and Christians' Understanding of God's Economy

The fourth century marked a pivotal moment in history, as the concept of the Roman "*adoptio*" first appeared in the Bible and Christianity was officially recognized as a legal religion throughout the Roman Empire. As Western Christianity expanded throughout the Roman Empire, the *Vulgata*, which included the reading of "*adoptio*," benefited. This is the standard Bible Version that is used in the liturgy of the Roman rite. Subsequently, Augustine incorporated the concept of adoption into his writings.[22]

---

18. Blackwell writes, "Central to Irenaeus' anthropology is also the concept of progression from infancy to maturity, which culminates in, among other things, incorruption." Blackwell, *Christosis*, 64.

19. Gribomont, "Translations of Jerome and Rufinus," 4:198.

20. Houghton, "Biblical Text," 1–2.

21. For the list of *Itala* manuscripts, see Aland et al., *Greek New Testament* (UBS[5]), 888.

22. Augustine argues, "But the Trinity cannot in the same way be called the Father,

The teaching of adoption and υἱοθεσία construct different Christian worldviews (*Weltanschauung*) of the human condition and how humanity can be freed from its facticity. Unlike υἱοθεσία, adoption does not have the idea of infants becoming adult humans, which metaphorically describes an ontological change. In theological adoption, before being adopted into God's household, the adopted son grew up in another family—in another economy. It is a dualism, where there are divine and demonic powers.

There is more than one soteriological concept.[23] But God cannot operate in two or more economies at once.[24] There must be one economy of God, but many human interpretations. I argue that a framework called υἱοθεσία was revealed to clarify God's intention to unite Godself with God's created children through His Son. This particular framework does not describe two or more concepts but one. Perhaps we need to look beyond our Western traditions to find the meaning of υἱοθεσία. Remember the Reformation's motto, "*ad fontes.*" How close do we want to get to the fountain (source)? We must return to the Greek NT Bible, where God's economy of υἱοθεσία first appears.

Human's Effort to Alter God's Word

Referring to the UBS[5] apparatus of Rom 8:23[25] and the textual criticism's evaluation, we learn that Ambrosiaster (Pseudo-Ambrosius), in the fourth century, made a deliberate change in the copying and transmission of the Bible by omitting the word "υἱοθεσίαν." Three of the lettered uncials follow his variant. They are D from the sixth century, F and G from the ninth century, and five versions of *Itala* from the fifth to eleventh centuries of the Western text type.[26] The scribes of this small number of manuscripts—less

---

except perhaps metaphorically, in respect to the creature, on account of the adoption of sons." Augustine, *On the Trinity*, 157.

23. See Holcomb, *Christian Theologies of Salvation*.

24. Cf. Behr, "Of Irenaeus's theology, the ground-plan or plot (ὑπόθεσις) of Scripture and of the truth itself: that there is one God who has acted continuously in one economy, unfolded in Scripture, to bring his creation to share in his own life.... In *AH* 1.10.3 Irenaeus specifies that it is only within the overall economy of the true hypothesis of Scripture that theologians are to pursue their theological reflections.... Neither in protology nor in eschatology does Irenaeus ever characterize or assimilate man or human life to the angelic: it is man, and *the becoming fully human* in communion with God in Christ, that is the center of the divine economy and of Irenaeus's theology" Behr, *Asceticism*, 19, 34, 43. Emphasis added.

25. Aland et al., *Greek New Testament* (UBS[5]), 522.

26. Greenlee informs, "No reading with solely Western support could be accepted as original without serious question." Greenlee, *Introduction*.

than 16 percent of the total number of witnesses and distributed only in the Western text type—*may* have thought "υἱοθεσία," which they read as "*adoptio*," should occur only once, that is, in v. 8:15. The 2019 Revised New Jerusalem Bible (RNJB) of the Roman Catholic Church continues the effort to omit the word "υἱοθεσία" in v. 23. Romans 8 explains the salvation of each individual, so these scribes might wonder why God would adopt the same person twice. I argue that these two occurrences of υἱοθεσία have different significances that lay the ground for Paul's already/not yet (human salvation has already started but not finished yet) theology.

Remarkably, a misleading preexisting bias leads to a conceptual problem. The case suggests that some Western scribes and scholars have tried to read the concept of Roman *adoptio* into this particular passage. Certain academics continue to advocate for this goal even now as if Roman *adoptio* were the gospel that explains the Christian way to salvation. Jerome's *Vulgata* reads "*ut adoptionem filiorum reciperemus*" (lit., the adoption of children to receive)[27] as a translation of a phrase in Gal 4:5, "ἵνα τὴν υἱοθεσίαν ἀπολάβωμεν" (so that the *place* of a υἱός—the position of an adult son-heir—we might receive).

Huiothesía in Other Vernacular Bible Versions

There are different voices from the vernacular Bibles on υἱοθεσία. An Aramaic *Version* translated into plain English renders this in Gal 4:5, "and that we would receive the *position* of children."[28] I think it can be corrected to "and that we would receive the *position* of a υἱός," which describes the literal meaning of the verse. John Wesley Etheridge comments on his Peshitta translation of Rom 8:15, "the adoption as sons." He writes, "*Rucho da-simath benayo*: The Spirit of the constituting of sons."[29] It can be rewritten as "the spirit of the constituting of *a* υἱός (a new being)." The Coptic NT renders, "For ye received not a *spirit* of servitude unto a fear again; but ye received a *spirit* of sonship."[30] Note the small "*s*" of "spirit," and there is no word for "adoption."

Later, we can read the other verses in these Bibles to see what they have to say about υἱοθεσία. It is crucial to find out how υἱοθεσία is rendered in the other vernacular Bibles, such as the Armenian, Georgian, and Ethiopic.

---

27. Gal 4:5, "*Ut eos, qui sub lege erant, redimeret, ut adoptionem filiorum reciperemus.*" Colunga and Turrado, *Biblia Sacra Vulgata*.

28. *Original Aramaic New Testament*. Emphasis added.

29. Etheridge, "Peschito Syriac."

30. Horner, *Coptic Version* 4:83. Emphasis original.

"Adoption" Is Not a "Mere Legal Adoption"

Desiderius Erasmus (c. 1466–1536) wrote about "adoption," but never meant it as adoption. This sentence is quite strange. So, we must be cautious when we read his paraphrases of Rom 8:11–17, where he writes, "Instead, you have received the Spirit of God, through whom you have been adopted into the number, not of servants, but of the sons of God."[31] He is not talking about an outsider being adopted as a son into that family, but "into the number" (into a different classification), which perhaps is a change of one's position within the family, receiving the position as υἱός. Nevertheless, in his paraphrase of Gal 4:1–6, the phrase "whoever adopts someone else" explains the context of adoption as in the *Vulgata*. "Consequently, whenever God imparts the Spirit of his Son to someone, that one is no longer a slave but a son. . . . For whoever adopts someone else and gives him the name of son receives him into the right of the inheritance."[32] We must realize that he was paraphrasing the verses of the *Vulgata* on adoption; it was not his commentary.

In another book, Erasmus clarifies the context. In annotations to Rom 8:15, he distinguishes "adoption" from a "mere legal adoption." He does not mean something like adoption *from* another family. I copied his explanation verbatim, including its editorial notes in brackets, as follows:

> If we take [the Vulgate's phrase] to mean the adoption of those who were previously sons of Satan, *the Scripture does not intend this*. If we understand that we are being adopted sons of God, *the Latin expression is inappropriate*—one would have to say rather the spirit of "adoption into [the place of] the sons of God." But just as Paulus can adopt the son of Scipio into the position of his own grandson, so he can adopt Scipio's grandson into the position of his own son. To avoid this difficulty, some have translated spiritum adoptionis [the spirit of adoption], because the chief kind of adoption is adoption into the position of son. Thus the shorter expression is understood to stand for the primary type. But the very tone of the Apostle's discourse indicates that here it is a question of those adopted into the privileges of sons. A further point: the genitive "of God" has been added though it is not found in the Greek codices. For he is not distinguishing here the sons of God from the sons of men, but rather *the sons of grace from the servants of the Law*.[33]

---

31. Erasmus, *Paraphrases on Romans and Galatians* 42:47.
32. Erasmus, *Paraphrases on Romans and Galatians* 42:116.
33. Erasmus, *Annotations on Romans* 56:210. Emphasis added.

Erasmus noticed the addition of the genitive "of God" because he knew humans were already in God's family, for no one was previously the son of Satan. He did not change the word "adoption," but he read it according to the context of υἱοθεσία. I am afraid I must disagree with how Erasmus approaches this problem, but I realize that he cannot change a dot in the *Vulgata*. In modern times, some scholars can even publish their translations of the Bible,[34] but during his time, it may not have been possible; recall the execution of William Tyndale (c. 1494–1536). I draw attention to the small "*s*" when Erasmus quotes "*spiritum adoptionis*." The human spirit is a critical variable involved in the context of υἱοθεσία (Rom 8:15).

FOLLOWING THE PROTESTANT ERA

Printing Machines and Adoption

Before the invention of the printing press, the distribution of manuscript Bibles was very limited. Scribes could only duplicate manuscript Bibles, which took a long time to complete. When Johann Gutenberg printed the first Bible in 1450, it was sold for about three years of a clerk's salary. By 1500, more than one thousand European printers printed Bibles, religious books, and indulgences. This invention transformed European societies from illiterate to literate.[35] In our case, the printing of *Vulgata*[36] can be read as the spreading of the "*adoptio*."

Tyndale's English New Testament Bible was first printed by Schoeffer in Worms, Germany, in as many as six thousand copies and was sold in England by April 1526. Subsequent editions were published in 1530 and 1534, and a revision in 1535.[37] Tyndale and the English Bibles after it translated υἱοθεσία as "*adoption*."[38] Unlike the Greek Bibles, these English Bibles—in-

---

34. For instance, Wright, *Kingdom New Testament*.

35. Ede and Cormack, *History of Science in Society*, 95.

36. The first printed text of Vulgate, the famous 42-line-per-page Bible printed by Johannes Gutenberg in Mainz in two volumes which appeared in 1452-6 (siglum a), was printed to meet the growing late medieval demand for lay book possession. Marsden and Matter, *New Cambridge History of the Bible* 2:107.

37. Greenslade, *Cambridge History of the Bible*, 142–43.

38. Norton informs, "Miles Coverdale revised and completed Tyndale's work. Thereafter a series of Bibles revised Tyndale and Coverdale's work until it became the King James Bible (KJB) or Authorised Version of 1611. In turn that became the prime model for later translations. Without Tyndale, the English Bible would have been a different and, very likely, a lesser thing." Norton, "English Bibles," 305.

cluding American versions—are widely available. With the reading of the *Vulgata* in Roman Catholic churches and English Bibles in English-speaking Protestant churches, more people are aware of the idea of salvation through adoption than of υἱοθεσία. Not many people in the Western church had and could read the Greek NT Bible. This situation facilitated the emergence of a new understanding of how an individual could attain salvation from sin and temporal existence.

Adoption in English Bibles and Credo

The literal reading of adoption is popular. A French theologian, clergyman, and Reformer in Geneva gave considerable attention to adoption not long after Luther's 1519 lectures on Galatians. In his commentary on Galatians published in Latin in 1548, Johannes Calvin said: "*ut adoptionem reciperemus*" (the adoption to receive).[39] Notably, Calvin's phrase does not include the term "*filiorum*," which is distinct from the *Vulgata*, which does include it. Calvin, due to his legal expertise, views adoption (not υἱοθεσία) from a legal perspective. This is what I refer to as a preexisting bias. Nevertheless, I concur with Calvin that the concept of υἱοθεσία (or adoption) is a matter of individual responsibility for each member of the triune God.[40]

> Calvin said that predestination is that "by which God adopts some to hope of life, and sentences others to eternal death" (*Inst.* 3:21.6).[41]
>
> Though Calvin relentlessly defended the forensic doctrine of justification, adoption plays such a critical role for him that his theology of redemption has been called the "Gospel of adoption." Howard Griffith affirms its role in Calvin: "*The adoption of believers is the heart of John Calvin's understanding of salvation.*"[42]

If υἱοθεσία is adoption, then the assertion of the "gospel of adoption" should have been recognized as the "gospel of υἱοθεσία," which is the backbone of Paul's soteriology. But if adoption and υἱοθεσία have different meanings, then they represent two distinct soteriological doctrines. Calvin's concept of adoption can be considered unsupported by biblical texts, as

---

39. Calvin, *Commentaries*, 113, 119.
40. Westhead, "Adoption," 102.
41. Helm, "Classical Calvinist Doctrine of God," 19.
42. Garner, *Sons in the Son*, 23. Quoting Griffith, "First Title of the Spirit," 135. Emphasis added.

there appears to be a lack of Greek scriptural verses that explicitly support this doctrine. In addition, I am wondering who is called the Father in the framework of the doctrine of adoption and υἱοθεσία.

English Bibles have existed before the Reformation. John Wycliffe translated the Bible in the 1300s. Let us take an example of a υἱοθεσία phrase in Rom 8:15. Wycliffe, in his late version, renders *"þe spiritt of adopcion of sones"* for *"spiritum adoptionis filiorum"* in the *Vulgata*. This Bible is a very literal translation of the *Vulgata*. During the Reformation, there were different translations—without "sons"—such as *"the sprite of adopcion"* in the Tyndale New Testament of 1526. Similarly, we found *"ye sprete of adopcion"* in the 1535 Coverdale Bible, *"the sprete of adopcion"* in the 1537 Matthew Bible, *"the spirite of adopcion"* in the 1539 Taverner Bible, *"the sprete of adopcyon"* in the 1539 Great Bible, and *"the spirite of adoption"* in the 1568 Bishop's Bible. Note the minuscule "s" in "spirit."

Under the influence of Theodore Beza's Latin text of 1556, William Whittingham and the English Protestants who fled to Geneva from persecution in England produced the 1560 Geneva NT Bible text based on the earlier work of Tyndale and Coverdale.[43] Consider the translation of Rom 8:15. By comparison, John Calvin's Latin translation in his commentary reads, *"Et enim non accepistis spiritum servitutis iterum in terrorem: sed accepistis Spiritum adoptionis, per quem clamamus, Abba, Pater."*[44] The 1560 Reformed Geneva Bible renders, *"For ye haue not receiued the Spirit of bondage, to feare againe: but ye haue receiued the Spirit of adopcion, whereby we crye Abba, Father."* Hence, to this day, many English Bibles render "the Spirit of adoption" with a capital "S" instead of the meaning of "πνεῦμα υἱοθεσίας," which has no article. From 1604 to 1611, the Church of England translated an (Anglican) authorized Bible called the King James Bible. Romans 8:15, in the KJV 1611 edition, reads "the spirit of adoption," with minuscule "s." The Amplified Bible remarks in brackets "the Spirit of adoption as sons [the Spirit producing sonship]." I think the note in brackets should be rewritten as "the spirit that makes sonship."

The Westminster Confession of Faith was probably the first *credo* to express the doctrine of adoption in 1647.[45]

> All those that are *justified* God vouchsafeth, in and for his only Son Jesus Christ, to make partakers of the *grace of adoption*; by which they are taken into the number, and enjoy the liberties and privileges of the children of God; have his name put upon

---

43. Daniell, *Bible in English*, 300.
44. Calvin, *Commentaries*, 295.
45. Trumper, "Theological History of Adoption: I," 1:8.

them; receive the *Spirit of adoption*; have access to the throne of grace with boldness; are enabled to cry, Abba Father; are pitied, protected, provided for, and chastened by him as by a father; yet never cast off, but sealed to the day of redemption, and inherit the promises, as heirs of everlasting salvation.[46]

Its formulation refers to Rom 8:15. Through Latin Bibles and many of the English Bible translations, readers come to know *adoptio*/adoption but do not know υἱοθεσία. Adoption becomes part of the preexisting bias in Bible reading. From time to time, anyone studying υἱοθεσία from the Greek NT Bible will probably read it as "adoption." We also *read* adoption *into* other Bible translations, including Indonesian versions, even though they do not use the word "*adopsi*" explicitly, but instead phrases such as "*menjadikan kamu anak*," "*pengangkatan sebagai anak*," "*diangkat menjadi anak*," or "*diterima menjadi anak*."[47] Because of these translations, many readers assume that the concept of "adoption" originates with Paul and Irenaeus. While numerous commentaries, theological dictionaries, pastoral books, sermons, and arguments support the idea of adoption, references that support υἱοθεσία—which is not the same as adoption—are rarely found or widely overlooked.

The State of Mature Sons

Providentially, the true meaning of υἱοθεσία has never been lost; no human misconception can hide God's word. The Holy Spirit is actively working to restore the true concept of salvation. The biblical context, concept, and meaning of υἱοθεσία keep reappearing. It reveals itself again and again to those who read the Bible attentively. For example, in 1834, Leipzig, Heinrich August Schott wrote in his *Epistola ad Galatas, Caput IV*, "υἱοθεσία *emphatice dic. de transitu ex statu servili qualis* fuerat *puerorum (v.3.) in conditionem filii, qua usum faciat integrum cuiusque iuris et commodi filio competentis*."[48] It says, "υἱοθεσία emphatically says the crossing (or passing) of what had been a slave state (male) child into a state which enjoys the entire right and benefits corresponding to a son." John Brown reiterated in 1970, "'Adoption of sons' is equivalent to 'the state of mature sons as opposed to the state of infants and children.'"[49]

---

46. *Westminster Confession of Faith* ch. 12. Emphasis added.
47. See Rom 8:15, 23; 9:4; Gal 4:5; *Alkitab* (TB²).
48. Schott, *Epistolae Pauli*, 490. Quoted from Brown, *Exposition*, 192.
49. Brown, *Exposition*, 192.

Schott and Brown echo Irenaeus' view of human growth. When Paul compares infants to enslaved people, he uses a simile but does not imply that these children are slaves who can be adopted as sons of another family. However, concerning υἱοθεσία, the ideas of "human development" and "adoption as sons into God's family" coexist in contemporary scholarly discourse.

Owen's Reading

John Owen included an editorial note with his 1849 English translation of Calvin's commentary on the Epistle to the Romans.

> By the Spirit, πνεῦμα, (without article).... The word for adoption, υἱοθεσία, may be rendered sonship, or affiliation, or filiation, as Luther sometimes renders it... so we may translate the two clauses here, "a servile spirit" and "a filial spirit."... —Ed.[50]

According to Owen's notes, an alternative translation of Rom 8:15 can be rendered as, "For you have not received a servile spirit again to fear; but you have received a filial spirit, whereby we cry, *Abba*, Father." I suspect that not many Reformed scholars take Owen's footnote seriously, for numerous English Bibles and scholarly writings support the theology of adoption, or perhaps they consider said Owen's footnote to be less authoritative. Owen's model of translation, where both *pneumas* in this verse are interpreted as human πνεῦμα—rather than "the Holy Spirit"—is supported by Luther, Dodd, Lenski, Meyer, Sanday and Headlam, Moo, and others.[51] I posit that the elevation of humanity by God is contingent upon the presence of the human spirit, emphasizing that without this essential element, divine upliftment cannot occur.

Toga Virilis

Albert Harrill is among the numerous scholars who associate υἱοθεσία with the Roman *toga virilis*.[52] However, it is necessary to consider the other instances of υἱοθεσία in Rom 8:23 and 9:4. Are these verses also related to the *toga virilis*? The two concepts, Paul's υἱοθεσία and the Roman *toga virilis*, share a similar idea but exhibit significant differences. Still, compared to

---

50. Calvin, *Commentary*, 296.
51. Cf., Garner, *Sons in the Son*, 116.
52. Harrill, "Coming of Age."

adoptio, toga virilis is closer in meaning to υἱοθεσία. In Rom 9:4, Paul employs a comparable term, "νομοθεσία," which is typically translated as "law-giving" or "the giving of the law." A comparison can be made between the translations of the terms "υἱοθεσία" (heirship-giving or the giving of *huio-ship*) and "νομοθεσία." Furthermore, it is important to note that the events to which Paul refers in Rom 9:4 occurred before those described in Rom 8:15.

"The Placing as a Son"

In *AMG's Strong's Greek Dictionary of the New Testament*, the Greek word with the number G5206 is defined as follows:

> υἱοθεσία, uihothesia [sic], hwee-oth-es-ee'-ah; from a presumed compound of 5207 and a derivative of 5087; the *placing* as a son, i.e. *adoption* (figuratively, Christian *sonship* in respect to God):—adoption (of children, of sons).[53]

It might be argued that the phrase "placing as a son" is a more accurate translation or interpretation of "υἱοθεσία" than "adoption of sons" or "adoption to sonship." Still, the term "υἱός" has been erroneously interpreted in this AMG's definition as "son." The phrase "to place as a υἱός" offers a new perspective on the context, as "υἱός" encompasses a range of meanings distinct from the conventional understanding of "son." However, this interpretation cannot be universally applied to all instances of the phrase "υἱοθεσία," such as in Rom 9:4, "οἵτινές εἰσιν Ἰσραηλῖται, ὧν ἡ υἱοθεσία . . . (who are Israelites, whose [is] the *huiothesía* . . .)." It is necessary to identify a translation that can be applied consistently to all instances of υἱοθεσία while allowing for slight variations in meaning across different contexts.

SUMMARY

Has the gospel of υἱοθεσία been misinterpreted? The term "υἱοθεσία" has been interpreted and translated in several ways, including "adoption," "adoptive sonship," and "placing as a son" or "placing of a son." Scholars have linked υἱοθεσία with the Roman *toga virilis*. Furthermore, John Brown aligned with Schott's interpretation and attempted to discern the intended context of υἱοθεσία in relation to adoption. As this study does not have access to any of the Latin *Itala*, it can only trace the issue of translating

---

53. Strong et al., *AMG's Strong's Annotated Dictionaries*, 942 (emphasis original); see also McGee in the introduction.

υἱοθεσία back to the *Vulgata*, at least the version quoted by John Calvin in his commentaries. It is also known that Jerome, who edited the *Vulgata* (AD 383–405), employed the *Itala*, except for the Gospels. If Calvin's quotations are consistent with those of Jerome (authorized by the Council of Trent [1546]), then the word "*adoptio*" has been continuously read in the Western church for approximately seventeen centuries or more through the *Vulgata* and most likely also through the *Itala*. It has also been disseminated and read in Protestant English translations with the help of printing machines. The concept of adoption is not easily disassembled, as it is now widely known and supported by a multitude of sources, including theological dictionaries, commentaries, vernacular Bible Versions, modern Bible translations, and numerous writers.

Does any extant translation or definition accurately reflect the biblical concept of υἱοθεσία? If the translations and the teaching that is based on those translations are erroneous, it is possible to envisage the implications for our faith (*fides*), which includes the understanding of the content of our faith (*notitia*); conviction (*assensus*, the assent or acceptance of the intellect to the truth of some proposition); trust and reliance on God (*fiducia*), which is the foundation of our hope (*spes*); and charity (*caritas*). The restoration of the apostle Paul's knowledge of υἱοθεσία requires substantial effort and attention. To gain a full understanding, it is necessary to conduct a comprehensive exegesis of relevant passages from the Greek Bible. In this case, the UBS[5] will be used as the source text.

The objective is to elucidate both the literal definitions and the metaphorical (theological) interpretations of υἱοθεσία that Paul intended. The metaphorical interpretations of υἱοθεσία have significant implications for the theology of salvation beyond its literal meanings. It is thus imperative to engage in theological work in conjunction with biblical work to synthesize the doctrine of υἱοθεσία.

Rather than always thinking the Greek term υἱοθεσία upon each encounter with "adoption as sons," it is imperative to undertake a careful and thorough investigation to identify and employ a more precise translation of υἱοθεσία. I advocate for the replacement of the term "adoption" wherever it appears in translated Bibles. Such an approach will enable readers to engage with the Scriptures more rigorously and contribute novel insights to this ongoing scholarly dialogue.

This work—as disclosure of the truth (ἀλήθεια) of the right gospel of Christ which is suppressed by the Roman idea of *adoptio*—reveals a diverse Christian worldview (*Weltanschauung*). I intend to contribute to the topic of υἱοθεσία/adoption in a way that is accessible to contemporary readers with a knowledge of the contemporary world-picture (*Weltbild*).

BIBLICAL STUDIES OF *HUIOTHESIA*
DECONSTRUCTING THE DOCTRINE
OF ADOPTION

CHAPTER 3

WORDS STUDY AND TEXTUAL CRITICISM

"TRUTH IS EVER TO BE FOUND IN SIMPLICITY, AND NOT IN THE MULTIPLICITY AND CONFUSION OF THINGS." ~ ISAAC NEWTON

OVERVIEW

The following three chapters present a section of the learning process concerning the past, covering Lonergan's dialectical evaluation specialty. It is at the level of "being responsible"; therefore, I will also make decisions or express my opinion in these chapters. My stance serves as the basis for reconstructing the doctrine of υἱοθεσία in the subsequent section.

These three chapters present the findings and address the identified misconceptions and errors. They aim to answer the problem from an authoritative source, from the exegesis of the Greek NT Bible instead of the Latin *Vulgata* and English versions; my interpretations are not limited to a single perspective within the Reformed tradition but rather encompass a broader range of viewpoints.

The exegesis begins with studying a set of words (*words* study) rather than individual words (word study) to determine how these words or phrases interact in Pauline biblical υἱοθεσία (*huiothesía*). A textual criticism work is required for Rom 8:23 due to the presence of two readings, one of which omits the word υἱοθεσία. This provides insight into the circumstances surrounding the case. Subsequently, the term υἱοθεσία is examined in the context of Galatians, Romans, and Ephesians.

WORDS STUDY

This section aims to closely examine select words used by the apostle Paul when teaching υἱοθεσία. With few exceptions, the New Testament was written in Koine Greek. The words used in Greek originate from a non-Christian context but were repurposed by the apostle Paul and other New Testament writers within a Christian framework. John D. Grassmick notes that words can be given new values and meanings, used in new contexts, or modified.[1] However, these human words have never adequately explained the divine and His works.

Grassmick further explains that the area of a word's meaning is defined by its context, including its sentence, paragraph, and the entire state of affairs at the time and place of its occurrence and all that has led up to it. In defining words, the lexicographer aims to specify their meaning.[2] However, this work will not cover the entire spectrum of meaning of the selected words.

The study's purpose is to attain a consistent understanding of the meaning of νήπιος (népios), υἱός (huios), and τέκνον (teknon) in the context of Paul's theological υἱοθεσία. Beyond this context, they may carry different meanings. If we understand the terms in this context, we can grasp the analogy presented regarding ontological transformations of individuals and relationships between created beings and the Godhead, the Father, the Lord Jesus Christ, and the Holy Spirit.

Each discussion of those words will include their transliteration, occurrence in the Greek NT, and reference numbers. I consult definitions in theological dictionaries and other sources. Further discussions of these words are prolonged in the interpretation section.

Népios

The Greek word νήπιος (*népios*) appears fifteen times in the Greek NT, eleven of them used by Paul, and one in Hebrews. It has been numbered N-39 in PBIK, or Strong's G3516; plural, νήπιοι (*népioi*). Sakae Kubo, in Gal 4:3,

---

1. Grassmick, *Principles and Practice of Greek Exegesis*, 147–48.
2. Grassmick, *Principles and Practice of Greek Exegesis*, 145–46.

briefly interprets "νήπιος" as "infant, minor."³ The apostle Paul inscribed, "Now I mean that the heir, as long as he is a minor, is no different from a slave, though he is the owner of everything" (NET). In the context of Gal 4:1, the NASB translates "νήπιος" as a "child" and, in its note, explains it as "minor"; NIV renders it as "underage"; many English Bibles use "child"; YLT interprets it as a "babe." The authorized Indonesian Bible, LAI 1962, translated it as *"lagi kanak-kanak,"* "a baby," "very young child," or "inexperienced." Nevertheless, the 1974 and 2023 versions of LAI have introduced the term *"belum akil balig,"* which denotes a person who is unable to discern between right and wrong, typically below the age of fifteen (before attaining legal adulthood). This term signifies an individual who is not yet equipped with the wisdom and maturity to distinguish between good and evil.

James Strong refers to "νήπιος" as someone who is not yet speaking, such as an *infant*. Figuratively, it can also mean a *simple-minded* person or an *immature* Christian. This term can describe anyone unable to speak, regardless of their age.⁴ Walter Bauer defines "νήπιος," as related to Gal 4:1, as one who is not yet of legal age, a *minor*, not yet at the age of majority. It is a legal *terminus technicus*.⁵

Bertram, as edited by Gerhard Kittel, explains that, in general Greek usage, "νήπιος" refers to a fetus, an infant, a child of five or six, or even a child up to the time of puberty. "Νήπιος" also expresses an inner personal relation between father and son. Bertram further explains that the word's dominant meaning in Greek is "foolish" and "inexperienced." For instance, trusting in fortune is considered folly. Such beliefs illustrate that individuals remain childlike, regardless of their age. However, the world—in this case, the Hellenistic philosophers—asserted that Christians are genuinely νήπιοι.⁶ In the LXX, the term typically refers to children in terms of age, weakness, and vulnerability, especially during war and persecution.⁷

According to Bertram, the use of νήπιος in the New Testament is *not* uniform. Differentiation is necessary between its use in the Gospel tradition, which is based on the Old Testament and is genuinely theological, and its use in Paul and the Epistle to the Hebrews. Paul uses it in various ways. In the first instance, νήπιος is always associated with the idea of a child. If *the state* of νήπιος is something to be left behind in Eph 4:14, it is something that has already been left behind in Gal 4:1, 3. When we were *népioi* (ὅτε

---

3. Kubo, *Reader's Greek-English Lexicon*, 177.
4. Strong at al., *AMG's Strong's Annotated Dictionaries*, 813.
5. BDAG, 671.
6. Bertram, "νήπιος" (*TDNT* 4:912–14).
7. *TDNT* 4:914.

ἦμεν νήπιοι), we were in a state of minority and dependence, similar to a son who requires a guardian appointed by his father in his will to oversee his education and control his income.[8] I can argue that, in the biblical Pauline context of υἱοθεσία, a "νήπιος" is the created child of God in minor state.

There are various instances of this term in the Pauline corpus. The metaphor in 1 Cor 13:11 contrasts the child and the man. Adopting Hellenistic rhetoric, Paul argues that the objective of human development is the τέλειος ἀνήρ (the mature or consummated human).[9] About Gal 4:1, Moisés Silva explains that the apostle Paul uses the term "νήπιος" figuratively to illustrate a theological truth.[10]

Theological words that speak about God and human salvation are symbolic or metaphorical. The discussion about God and human salvation is based on metaphors and symbols. This is because religious language tries to express ideas that are hard for humans to understand, but it has no other way than using the available human words. This way of speaking shows how religious language has two sides. On one side, it talks about God. On the other side, it talks about the human experience. Consequently, religious language is usually a metaphor. This means that it cannot be taken literally. The mix of symbols and reality in these discussions helps us connect with the divine. Human language, while based on our earthly experiences, tries to convey the nature of God and salvation, which cannot be fully described in words. It would be erroneous, therefore, to read such words like the Pauline νήπιος literally. From a theological perspective, protological sarkic-Adamic humans are classified as νήπιοι.

To understand the meaning of the phrase in Gal 4:1, "as long as he is a minor, he is no different from a slave," we might consider in what sense a minor or an infant (νήπιος) is no different from a slave. William Hendriksen comments,

> When a young father dies (several commentators point out that in the illustration here used it is not necessary to assume that the father has died) . . . his minor child will have to wait for the inheritance until he is of age. Though this child is, accordingly, the legal heir and as such "lord," "master" or, as here, "owner" of everything, yet with respect to taking possession of, and exercising control over, the state that has been left to him he is no better off than a slave. Until he attains to the age previously stipulated

---

8. *TDNT* 4:918.
9. *TDNT* 4:919.
10. *NIDNTTE* 3:383.

by the father, he is heir *de jure* (by right) but not as yet *de facto* (in fact).[11]

In the context of Christian salvation as presented by υἱοθεσία, the term "νήπιος" is used to refer to a minor heir who is under the care of his father while the latter is still alive. This also implies that all protological sarkic-Adamic humans are members of the collective family of the One Creator. In Christian theology (in Pauline teaching of υἱοθεσία), becoming a son-heir (υἱός) is considered to be equivalent to achieving salvation. The pivotal issue is whether each individual will be designated as a son-heir by their father; the child does not influence this designation. The decision of whether or not to grant salvation is at the discretion of the Creator God. Thus, how can we be saved?

On the other hand, we should consider the question of what rights a slave (δοῦλος, *doulos*) has. Trevor J. Burke discusses:

> This was carried out by the *paterfamilias* selling off his offspring into civil bondage (*in mancipio*), thereby making him a slave. On the release of his son the latter was still the property of the father and could by right be sold into bondage by him again and again. In order to avoid the son becoming a kind of familial football a law was laid down in the Twelve Table (established by the second Decemvirate c. 450 BC) which stated that when a son was sold three times by his father the latter ceased to have any authority over him.[12]

An enslaved person was bound to someone, or he was a person of servile condition. Its context reflected the Roman culture's perspective on ownership and freedom. An enslaved person was viewed as an object to be owned and traded, which often began with his father's sale. Only a father lacking love would sell his son because he had no other resources. The context of slavery does not fit God because the Creator owns everything. Burke's quoted context does not pertain to or apply to God and His created children.

Galatians 4:1 compares a minor (a son in the *nēpio* state) to an enslaved person without inheritance and freedom. But since it is a metaphor, there is no implication that the minor is a slave. This Pauline context of υἱοθεσία clearly explains that a child has not reached the age of majority, cannot act on their behalf, and does not currently have the right to inherit anything. During the time set by his father, the minor has limited freedom.

---

11. Hendriksen, *New Testament Commentary*, 156.
12. Burke, *Message of Sonship*, 142.

He is continually under the authority of rules and supervision,[13] but unlike an enslaved person, he does not perform lowly work in the household. If ἐπίτροπος (guardian) and οἰκονόμος (household manager) are present, they are assigned to tutor and prepare the child for adulthood. This context is similar to Aristotle's usage of δουλικόν, which refers to a person who cannot live without the support of others.[14] In the context of the Pauline Greek υἱοθεσία, a child who lives according to the flesh must rely on the laws represented by the guardians and household managers as a preparation for becoming a decent mature son (υἱός).

Recall the English Reformation. 1547, following King Henry the Eighth's death, *his son* Edward VI assumed the throne *as a minor* at the age of nine, leading to his advisors wielding actual power. Note that the use of the terms "son" and "minor" provides evidence that the English term "son" does not equate to Pauline υἱός. We cannot write as "his υἱός (adult son-heir)" Edward VI assumed the throne as a "νήπιος (minor, infant)." In King Edward VI's case, these advisors were mainly Protestant in their beliefs. Cranmer, who served as archbishop throughout Edward's reign, implemented overtly Protestant forms of public worship and supported prominent Protestant intellectuals (such as Martin Bucer and Peter Martyr Vermigli) in relocating to England to guide the Reformation theologically.[15] The king was a minor (a νήπιος), so he needed help to be a good king. He was not a slave or a son of another kingdom.

Teknon

The Greek term τέκνον (*teknon*) is listed as PBIK T-38 or Strong's G5043 and appears ninety-nine times in the New Testament; it has a plural form of τέκνα (*tekna*). However, for example, Joseph Henry Thayer's *Greek Lexicon* shows various meanings of the term, but not all are relevant to the context of Rom 8, 9, Gal 4, and Eph 1. Once the usage of the word has been studied, the context of τέκνα Θεοῦ (Rom 8:16) and the concept addressed by Paul in υἱοθεσία passages can be established.

Thayer explains τέκνον in Paul's context as follows.

---

13. In a certain sense, it can be likened to a "ward" in contemporary legal practice. It refers to a person, often a child, who is under the legal protection or care of another individual, court, or government. A similar practice is "conservatorship." In Indonesia, this is referred to as *"perwalian."*

14. See δουλικόν. Rengstorf, "δοῦλος" (*TDNT* 2:263).

15. McGrath, *Historical Theology*, 130.

τέκνα τοῦ Θεοῦ, children of God—in the OT of "the people of Israel" as especially dear to God: Isa. 30:1; Wis. 16:21;—in the NT, in Paul's writings, *all who are animated by the Spirit of God* (Rom. 8:14) and thus are closely related to God: Rom. 8:16f, 21; Eph. 5:1; Phil. 2:15; those to whom, as dearly beloved of God, he has appointed salvation by Christ, Rom. 9:8 . . . [Cf. Westcott . . . "In St. Paul the expressions 'sons of God,' 'children of God,' mostly convey the idea of liberty (see however Phil. 2:15), in St. John of guilelessness and love; in accordance with this distinction St. Paul uses υἱοί as well as τέκνα, St. John τέκνα only" (Lightfoot); Cf. υἱός τοῦ Θεοῦ].[16]

In Liddell-Scott-Jones, τέκνον is explained as a means of address for elders to *their* younger, using phrases such as "my son" or "my child."[17] According to Strong, τέκνον refers to a *child* (as *produced*), a daughter or a son. It also figuratively signifies someone who receives parental affection or demonstrates filial love and respect. It refers to those beloved and cherished by God as a Father.[18] Lenski distinguishes τέκνα from υἱοί:

> "Sons," υἱοί, is the proper word. While it is a close synonym to "children," τέκνα, and is so used here, "sons" agrees with the idea of "adoption," "children" with the idea of the new birth (regeneration), and here Paul wants both. "Sons" is opposed to "slaves" while "children" has the idea of dearness. "Sons" also agrees with conduct, for a son should act the part expected of him in relation to his father; a king's son must act as behooves a prince. "Children" moves in a different sphere, for a child (sometimes it is even made diminutive, "little child") conveys the idea of dependence, even of immaturity. The differences are not immaterial; each word has its own flavor even in English, and the apostle uses them accordingly.[19]

We do not study all the appearances of the word because their meanings are too diverse.

In the context of υἱοθεσία, I suggest that the phrase "τέκνα" be translated as "favored children," "beloved children," "chosen ones," or "the elect." This term represents those individuals who have been chosen from the infant state to be changed (not transferred) to the adult state. The word "τέκνα" cannot be translated "children" because it creates an unintended

---

16. Thayer, *Greek-English Lexicon*, 617–18. Emphasis original.
17. Liddell et al., *Greek-English Lexicon*, 1768.
18. Strong at al., *AMG's Strong's Annotated Dictionaries*, 929.
19. Lenski, *Romans*, 521.

meaning in a sentence like "become the children of God" (John 1:12), as if believers were not already created children of God and now become children. The intended meaning is "[from mere children, νήπιοι] some are chosen to become beloved children of God, the elect." These τέκνα will undergo an ontological transformation within themselves.

Paul discussed τέκνα Israel in Rom 9:8. Please be aware that there are two kinds of "τέκνα" in Paul: τὰ τέκνα τῆς σαρκὸς (Israelites as the descendants of Abraham) and τὰ τέκνα τῆς ἐπαγγελίας (who are τέκνα τοῦ θεοῦ, Christians). See discussions under the heading Rom 9:8 of chapter 5. In addition, after Jesus' resurrection, aside from the specific case of the Israelites, there are τέκνα of the elect gentiles too on the left side (refer to Figure 4) before God's sub-act of υἱοθεσία before they become Christians.

Huios and Son

The Greek term υἱός (*huios*) appears 382 times in the New Testament, where it is labeled U-17 in PBIK or Strong's G5207. The plural form is υἱοί (*huioi*). In previous chapters, we examined the cases of Claudius regarding the giving of the Roman *toga virilis* to his two sons, Nero and Britannicus, and the act of υἱοθεσία of Aemilius, with his two natural sons, Scipio and Fabius. We have a Bible story related to maturity, the parable of the prodigal son in Luke 15:11–32. It states, "There was a man who had two mature sons (υἱούς)." It is about inheritance; thus, it is also about *maturity*, not about *minority*. In addition, it talks about a Father who always welcomes his υἱοί, the assurance of salvation of God's υἱοί. Once the prodigal son becomes a υἱός, he is always a υἱός. A son who has reached the age of majority, who can make a request to his father, cannot be reinstated as a minor (infants, no speaking). In other words, he cannot lose his *huio*-ship. He is a freeman. Salvation cannot be lost.

Theologically, this term υἱός is related to the Messiah, the Christ,[20] or ὁ Υἱός. As I have stated in previous chapters, the Pauline term "υἱός" does not equal the English term "son." According to *Merriam-Webster's Dictionary*, the term "son" refers to

> a male child [who] is considered with reference to either parent or to both parents. Any male descendant. One who occupies the place of a son, as by adoption, marriage, or regard. A person regarded as a native of a particular country or place. A male person who is characterized or influenced by some quality or

---

20. Thayer, *Greek-English Lexicon*, 635.

thing or by a being representing some quality or character: a *son of liberty*; *sons of Belial*.[21]

These definitions show that "son" lacks the idea of *maturity* and inheritance rights that contrast with the *minority*.

Specifically in the context of υἱοθεσία, it is preferable to interpret υἱός as that of a mature son-heir. According to Liddell-Scott-Jones, υἱοὶ θεοῦ refers to sons of God, implying *inheritors of the nature* of God and *participants in the glory* of God.[22] Therefore, translating "υἱός" to "son" results in the loss of its intended meaning and the introduction of unintended meanings. The term "υἱός" as used in the Pauline Epistles is universal in its application and does not discriminate based on gender (male or female), social class (slave or owner), or ethnicity (including tribal religions, such as Judaism or other nations).[23] Even in the gender-insensitive context, Pauline's "υἱός" (*maturity* category) does not align with the English "son" (*irrespective of age*). In the context of υἱοθεσία, a "υἱός" refers to a developed (growth) adult human, or symbolically it refers to the eschatologically consummated Christic human. In the context of theological adoption, "son" refers to someone who was not a son of God's family but was then adopted as a son of God's family. The term "υἱός" agrees with the idea of "υἱο-θεσία."

To be Conformed

The New Testament Greek word "σύμμορφος" (*summorphos*), Strong's G4832, is used in Phil 3:21 and Rom 8:29, where it describes how believers will be *ontologically* transformed to be "conformed" or "like" the glorious body of Jesus Christ. But it is not only the body, but the making of the new being to which the body is the last human constructive element needed to be "conformed" to the image of the Son. Because we are talking about the "body," we are talking about the human being, the human Christ as the model (image), and a physical transformation. The word combines "σύν" (*sun*), meaning "with" or "together," and "μορφή" (*morphē*), meaning "form" or "shape". Thus, in this context, "σύμμορφος" conveys the idea of being conformed to or having the same form as the risen Christ. This is not only about character or morals but about nature or ontic (it deals with what *is*). It highlights the hope of being fully aligned with the human Christ's salvific nature and glorified state.

---

21. *New International Webster's Comprehensive Dictionary*, 1197.
22. Liddell et al., *Greek-English Lexicon*, 1847.
23. Gal 3:26–28.

Summary of Words Study: Foundation

The definitions of Pauline terms "νήπιος," "τέκνα," and "υἱός" challenge the doctrine of adoption. Because a "νήπιος" is not an enslaved person or another family's son to be adopted, but an heir in the infancy of their family. Theologically speaking, our conversation leads us to conclude that νήπιοι have always been the first kind of human members in God's created family. "Τέκνα" refers to a beloved son, a chosen one, the elect. And "υἱός" refers to a mature son (an adult), implying *inheritors of the nature* of God, and *participants in the glory* of God. A υἱός is not an adopted son. Based on these definitions alone, constructing the doctrine of adoption is challenging, but contrarily, it opens up a way to recuperate the doctrine of υἱοθεσία.

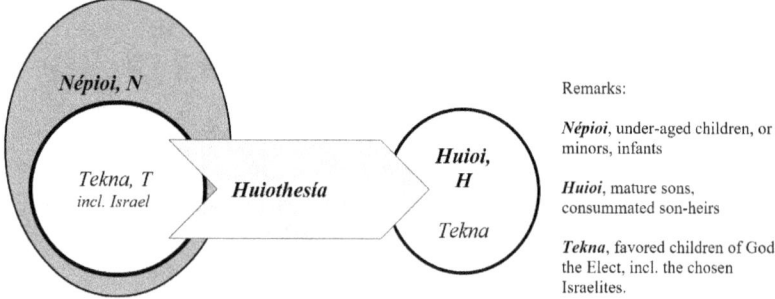

FIGURE 4: Relationship of *Nepios, Teknon,* and *Huios*

Human beings have never been separated from their Creator. All human beings are theologically considered to be created as infants (minors), designated as νήπιοι, protological humans, or sarkic-Adamic humans, and belong to the domain N. On the other hand, Christian believers are classified under domain H. The designations of Νήπιοι (*népioi*) and Υἱοὶ (*huioi*) signify states of being, whereas Τέκνα (*tekna*) is not a state of being but a designation of those who are chosen, the elect, either before or after God's sub-act of υἱοθεσία. Following the υἱοθεσία procedure, these selected individuals may be referred to as υἱοὶ or τέκνα.

In the domain of N, God has τὰ τέκνα τῆς σαρκὸς (Israelites as the descendants of Abraham). Moreover, the elect gentiles, before becoming Christians, can be assigned to this group schematically, not because they come from the descendants of (τοῦ σπέρματος) Abraham, but because they are chosen by God and still in a state of spiritual immaturity—*népio* state (sarkic state). It is truly remarkable to see how God's love extends to all human beings, regardless of their background or origin. After God's sub-act of υἱοθεσία, God has the children of the promise (τὰ τέκνα τῆς ἐπαγγελίας), who are also called the beloved or favored children, belong to God (τέκνα τοῦ θεοῦ). These are the Christians.

The inadvertent obfuscation of the terms "νήπιος," "τέκνα," and "υἱός" can be readily identified, thereby facilitating the discernment of the authentic concept of υἱοθεσία. A genuine understanding of υἱοθεσία, in turn, enables the formulation of a true concept of salvation; it is not about adoption but about conforming to the new nature of the risen Christ—an elevated human nature that cannot be annihilated or decay. A misreading and misconception of the terms "νήπιος," "τέκνα," "υἱός," and "υἱοθεσία" results in a false doctrine of salvation that is incongruent with the teachings of the Bible. This figure above will be referenced frequently in our forthcoming discussions.

TEXTUAL CRITICISM (THE OMISSION OF "*HUIOTHESÍAN*")

The New Testament Greek lemma "υἱοθεσία" (*huiothesía*) appears twice in Rom 8, in vv. 15 and 23. Because the apparatus of UBS[5] shows that there are two readings at v. 23—with or without υἱοθεσία—this needs to be clarified.[24] The number of appearances in Romans chapter 8, once or twice, is significant in Pauline's concept of soteriology. Although the group omitting "υἱοθεσίαν" is small, we must investigate the case to understand what has happened.

Bruce M. Metzger's commentary[25] says nothing about this verse or its variants, perhaps because it is at level {A}. Roger L. Omanson comments:

> Several witnesses, chiefly Western, omit υἱοθεσία, a word that copyists doubtless found to be both clumsy in the context and unnecessary, as well as seeming to contradict v. 15, which says that Christians have already been adopted as children of God. Following the reading in the UBS[4] text, "Paul would then be referring to a phase of adoptive sonship still to be revealed: though we are already children of God, our full status of sonship has not yet been made manifest." . . . The text is translated by NRSV as "we . . . groan inwardly while we wait for adoption,

---

24. When we see *The Greek New Testament*, there are four levels of uncertainty. They are "{A} indicates that the text is certain, {B} indicates that the text is almost certain, {C} indicates that the Committee had difficulty in deciding which variant to place in the text, {D} occurs rarely, indicates that the Committee had great difficulty in arriving at a decision, and for {(")} there is no ranking . . . signifies the highest level of uncertainty." See Aland et al., *Greek New Testament* (UBS[5]).

25. Metzger, *Textual Commentary*, 121.

the redemption of our bodies." NJB, however, follows the shorter text: "we too . . . even we are groaning inside ourselves, waiting with eagerness for our bodies to be set free."[26]

According to Fitzmyer, this second appearance of *huiothesía* in Rom 8 refers to "a phase of adoptive sonship" and "our full status of sonship."[27] We will examine the distribution of the *mss* using data from UBS[5].[28] The tabulated *mss* will help us make evaluations and conclusions to be sure of the text we are working on.

Harold Greenlee has warned us that no Christian doctrine should be based on a questionable text, and the student of the New Testament must be careful not to wish his text to be more orthodox or doctrinally strong than the inspired original.[29] I interpret his point to mean that it is considered inappropriate to add the article "the" to the term "πνεῦμα," as in Rom 8:15, when the context does not require it. Also we cannot develop any concept based on the omission of "υἱοθεσίαν" in the observed verse.

Let us now examine the critical apparatus number 5 23{A}.[30] This apparatus groups the manuscripts that include the word υἱοθεσίαν and those that omit it. Based on this data, I have compiled Table 1 below for further analysis.

TABLE 1: Textual Criticism of Romans 8:23, Apparatus no. 5 23{A}

	Alexandrian		Western		Byzantine		Miscellaneous	
	mss	Era	*mss*	Era	*mss*	Era	*mss*	Era
Reading	υἱοθεσίαν							
Papyrus:	-	-						
Lettered Uncials:	ℵ A B C Ψ	IV V IV V IX/X			K L P	IX IX IX (p)		
Numbered Uncials:								

---

26. Omanson, *Textual Guide*, 304. Note the translation of NJB, a Roman Catholic Bible.
27. Fitzmyer, *Romans*, 511.
28. Aland et al., *Greek New Testament* (UBS[5]), 884–89.
29. Greenlee, *Introduction*, 68.
30. Aland et al., *Greek New Testament* (UBS[5]), 522–23.

Words Study and Textual Criticism

Minuscules:	6 33 81 104 424 1175 1241 1739	XIII IX 1044 c. 1087 XI X XII X	1912	X			256 263 436 459 1319 1506 1573 1852 1881 1962 2127 2200 2464	XI/XII XIII XI/XII c. 1092 XII c. 1320 XII/XII XIII XIV XI/XII XII XIV IX
Versions:	cop^{sa} cop^{bo}	IV IX	vg it^{ar} it^{mon} syr^{p} syr^{h}	IV/V IX X V VII	Lect slav	- IX(?)	it^{b} arm eth geo	VIII/IX c. 1805 VI V
Fathers:	Orig.^{lat}	d. 254	Pelagius Chrysostom Ambrose Augustine	d. 420 d. 407 d. 397 d. 430			Theo.^{lat}	d. 457

Reading	Omit							
Papyrus:	p^{46vid}	c. 200						
Lettered Uncials:			D F G	VI IX IX				
Numbered Uncials:								
Minuscules:								
Versions:			It^{d} It^{f} It^{g} It^{o} It^{t}	V VI IX VII XI				
Fathers:			Ambrosiaster BJ	IV				

Notes:

1. Caesarean or unidentified text types, grouped in Miscellaneous.
2. Roman letters represent centuries, and Arab numbers represent years.
3. "a." active during, "c." circa, "d." death.

Evaluation: Foundation

The critical apparatus provides a list of the manuscripts, and the table, which has been prepared based on the apparatus, illustrates the distribution areas (text types), eras, and characteristics of each manuscript. It demonstrates the relative weight and authority of each reading. The initial step is to evaluate the external evidence.

In the case of the reading containing "υἱοθεσίαν," the lettered uncials provide textual support from manuscripts dating from the fourth, fifth, and eighth/ninth centuries. Additionally, several minuscules and fathers offer corroboration. Moreover, a multitude of vernacular Versions of the New Testament, including *Itala*, *Vulgata*, Syriac, Coptic, Armenian, Ethiopic, Georgian, and Slavic, also provide validation. Furthermore, this reading was utilized by both the early Latin and Syriac fathers.

Among the witnesses that lack this word, the P[46vid] stands out. P[46] is an ancient document from around AD 200. However, the editors add "*vid.*" According to UBS[5], the *vid* is "the most probable reading of a manuscript where the state of its preservation makes complete verification impossible; or the apparent support of a Church Father for the reading cited, where stylistic and contextual factors do not permit complete certainty."[31] Therefore, the papyrus P[46] may have the word "υἱοθεσίαν," or may not. The three lettered uncials (D, F, G) cited are from the sixth and ninth centuries. Only five corrections—beginning in the fifth century and not representing the entire tradition—within a single vernacular Version of the *Vetus Itala* (or *Vetus Latina*) support this omission. Perhaps the unknown father called Ambrosiaster from the fourth century may have influenced them.

In his commentary on the Epistle of St. Paul, c. 366–84, Father Ambrosiaster is presumed to have developed an interpretation of "υἱοθεσία" as parallel to Roman "*adoptio*" instead of "*toga virilis.*" I presume that with the concept of adoption in mind, he then decided not to include the word "υἱοθεσίαν" in Rom 8:23, as it is not possible for the act of adoption to occur twice to a person after the one described in Rom 8:15. It also is not appropriate to the context of "the redemption of our bodies." This assumption

---

31. Aland et al., *Greek New Testament* (UBS[5]), 892.

requires further verification. Ambrosiaster and the *Itala*^{d} of the fifth century later inspired other *Itala* and lettered uncials of Western text types. Consequently, it can be deduced that the concept of adoption is particularly salient during this period in the Latin church. However, it should be noted that the Western text type is generally regarded as less authoritative than the Alexandrian text type.

A review of the internal evidence indicates the presence of a transcription problem. If the hypothesis regarding Ambrosiaster is indeed accurate, then his actions can be classified as intentional changes—an attempt to correct a manuscript error, as he believed. This issue is also referred to as a doctrinal change.[32] If this is indeed the case, it is necessary to reveal the underlying reasons for this doctrinal change. As we read earlier, Omanson has elucidated the intrinsic issue. As the inheritor of this tradition, the 2019 Revised New Jerusalem Bible (RNJB) indicates that it excludes the term "υἱοθεσίαν" in v. 8:23 from its translation. This approach not only excludes the term itself but it also excludes the foundational principles of the apostle Paul's "already/not yet" theology, which, I contend, are rooted in the two occurrences of "υἱοθεσία" in chapter 8 of the Epistle to the Romans.

The following conclusions can be drawn from the evidence presented. The initial reading, "υἱοθεσίαν," is corroborated by both external and internal evidence. Since the transmission of the Bible commenced, there have been instances where an eisegesis interpretation has been applied. In this instance, the omission of a single word was the cause of the discrepancy. The older manuscripts include the word, and they contain a greater number of witnesses with a more extensive distribution. It can therefore be concluded that the autograph also contains this element. Unfortunately, the concept of adoption has persisted into modern times due to its deep embedding in Bible translations. While many Western translations do not omit the one appearance in Rom 8:23, they nevertheless continue to read and translate υἱοθεσία as "adoption." This confusion arises from the conflation of the idea of adoption with that of υἱοθεσία.

Can a Bible translation be produced that avoids importing the concept of Roman *adoptio*?

---

32. See Greenlee, *Introduction*, 66–68.

CHAPTER 4

Galatians: From the Old Being to the New Being

"So that if any one is in Christ, he is a new creature: the old state of things has passed away; a new state of things has come into existence." ~ The Apostle Paul (2 Cor 5:17, Weymouth NT)

OVERVIEW

David B. Garner analyzed the concept of theological adoption (υἱοθεσία) in the Pauline Epistles to the Ephesians, Galatians, and Romans.[1] Tim J. Trumper, inspired by Geerhardus J. Vos, organizes the study of adoption as a "salvation-historical order." He creates an image illustrating the sequence of adoption. The description of the image is as follows: it begins with Eph 1:4–5 on the left, which signifies the protology of adoption; then moves to Rom 9:4, which signifies covenant theology; and then to Gal 4:4–5 (Rom 8:15–16), which signifies soteriology (pneumatology); and finally to Rom 8:22–23, which signifies eschatology.[2] It is evident that Trumper associates Gal 4:4–5 with Rom 8:15–16. I will demonstrate that the initial point

---

1. Garner, *Sons in the Son*, 3–19.
2. Trumper, "Fresh Exposition of Adoption," 62–63.

of departure in the discussion of υἱοθεσία has a determining effect on the outcome.

Because I argue that adoption is not υἱοθεσία, I must first reestablish the context and meaning of υἱοθεσία. To accomplish this, I start with the Letter to the Galatians, where the fundamental definition and context of υἱοθεσία are presented. This approach allows me to derive meaning from its biblical context. Subsequently, I examine the use of υἱοθεσία in the status of Israel as τέκνα in Romans chapter 9 before analyzing the two instances of υἱοθεσία mentioned in Rom 8:15 and 23. Afterwards, I peruse Ephesians chapter 1, which explains the final stage of the development of a fully pneumatic-Christic human being. This hermeneutical study examines the context of υἱοθεσία and demonstrates that the biblical text does not support the idea of adoption. Moreover, it will reveal the true gospel conveyed by Paul's knowledge of υἱοθεσία.

A BRIEF BACKGROUND OF THE EPISTLE TO THE GALATIANS

Galatians is the first epistle written by Paul.[3] Andrew W. Blackwood Jr. said this is an epistle written in love-generated anger.[4] Blackwood continues that the letter discusses the concept of freedom as bestowed upon us by God. The topic is still at the forefront of today's religious debates. The Judaizers had started convincing the Galatian Christians to comply with the law of Moses. The initial Christians were all Jewish and observed the law diligently. The law was not an issue until the church began accepting non-Jewish members.[5]

R. C. H. Lenski informs that the Reformers appreciated Galatians' doctrinal content, its powerful defense of justification by faith alone, and its glorious vindication of *freedom from the law*.[6] Regarding the law, James D. G. Dunn explains that before the faith arrived, we were held in "*protective custody*" under the law (3:23). The law's function in Gal 3:23 is best understood as a protective oversight rather than oppressive and coercive. The law was our "guardian" (Gal 3:24) and has an essentially positive role—to provide instruction in good manners, correct as necessary, and protect as

---

3. NASB dates it 49 or 55. Some argue the First Epistle to the Thessalonians was the first Epistle of Paul, which was written in AD 51, during the year in which Claudius gave *toga virilis* to Nero, his adult stepson and son-in-law too.

4. Blackwood Jr., *Epistles to the Galatians*, 17.

5. Blackwood Jr., *Epistles to the Galatians*, 23–24.

6. Lenski, *Galatians*, 7. Emphasis added.

needed. In Gal 3, Israel is presented as a child growing up in an evil world (cf. 1:4). It needs protection from this evil and discipline to reach the maturity of adulthood safely.[7] There is no sense of legal enslavement and the need for adoption in Paul's intention to the Galatians.

John Kenneth Riches renders, "For Chrysostom, once faith comes, believers are no longer under a tutor but have become sons of God."[8] Thus, this epistle's context is Christian believers' freedom from the provisional *"protective* custody" of the Torah. It has nothing to do with enslavement, adoption, and freedom from another family. Furthermore, the notion of adopting Christians into the family of the God of the Israelites is untenable when one considers that they, the Israelites, must also be adopted.

The following is an outline of Galatians chapter 4. Before the advent of Christ, humanity was subject to the constraints of the Mosaic law, analogous to the status of an heir under the tutelage of a guardian until reaching adulthood (v. 1). However, Christ liberated us from the constraints of the law (v. 5). Consequently, we are no longer subject to its authority (v. 7). Paul recalls the Galatians' benevolence towards him and reciprocates it (v. 14); he demonstrates that Christians are the descendants of Abraham through the freewoman (v. 22).

TEXT

Galatians 4:1–11 has variant readings. In v. 6, there are readings with ἡμῶν (us, we) and ὑμῶν (you). From the UBS[5], we can see there are seven variants at v. 7: διὰ θεοῦ // διὰ θεόν // διὰ Χριστοῦ // θεοῦ // θεοῦ διὰ Χριστοῦ // θεοῦ διὰ Ἰησοῦ Χριστοῦ // μὲν θεοῦ, συγκληρονόμος δὲ Χριστοῦ.[9] The reading of "διά θεοῦ" has been designated as category {A}. It can be stated with confidence that the text under consideration is identical to the Autograph. The following is the text from UBS[5], which is copied from the website of the Academic Bible of *Deutsche Bibelgesellschaft*, with permission.

> 4:1 Λέγω δέ, ἐφ᾽ ὅσον χρόνον ὁ κληρονόμος νήπιός ἐστιν, οὐδὲν διαφέρει δούλου κύριος πάντων ὤν, 2 ἀλλ᾽ ὑπὸ ἐπιτρόπους ἐστὶν καὶ οἰκονόμους ἄχρι τῆς προθεσμίας τοῦ πατρός. 3 οὕτως καὶ ἡμεῖς, ὅτε ἦμεν νήπιοι, ὑπὸ τὰ στοιχεῖα τοῦ κόσμου ἤμεθα δεδουλωμένοι 4 ὅτε δὲ ἦλθεν τὸ πλήρωμα τοῦ χρόνου, ἐξαπέστειλεν ὁ θεὸς τὸν υἱὸν αὐτοῦ, γενόμενον ἐκ γυναικός, γενόμενον ὑπὸ νόμον, 5 ἵνα τοὺς ὑπὸ νόμον ἐξαγοράσῃ, ἵνα τὴν υἱοθεσίαν ἀπολάβωμεν. 6 Ὅτι δέ ἐστε

---

7. Dunn, *Theology of Paul the Apostle*, 140.
8. Riches, *Galatians*, 204.
9. Aland et al., *Greek New Testament* (UBS[5]), 625.

υἱοί, ἐξαπέστειλεν ὁ θεὸς τὸ πνεῦμα τοῦ υἱοῦ αὐτοῦ εἰς τὰς καρδίας ἡμῶν κρᾶζον, Αββα ὁ πατήρ. 7 ὥστε οὐκέτι εἶ δοῦλος ἀλλ᾽ υἱός· εἰ δὲ υἱός, καὶ κληρονόμος διὰ θεοῦ.

8 Ἀλλὰ τότε μὲν οὐκ εἰδότες θεὸν ἐδουλεύσατε τοῖς φύσει μὴ οὖσιν θεοῖς 9 νῦν δὲ γνόντες θεόν, μᾶλλον δὲ γνωσθέντες ὑπὸ θεοῦ, πῶς ἐπιστρέφετε πάλιν ἐπὶ τὰ ἀσθενῆ καὶ πτωχὰ στοιχεῖα οἷς πάλιν ἄνωθεν δουλεύειν θέλετε; 10 ἡμέρας παρατηρεῖσθε καὶ μῆνας καὶ καιροὺς καὶ ἐνιαυτούς, 11 φοβοῦμαι ὑμᾶς μή πως εἰκῇ κεκοπίακα εἰς ὑμᾶς.

GRAMMAR, LEXICAL ANALYSIS, AND PROVISIONAL TRANSLATION

The parsings are taken from the Interlinear Bible of HELPS Ministries and compared with PBIK,[10] Mounce's Interlinear, and Rogers and Rogers' Interlinear. When it comes to grammar, like for the mood, I consult Wallace's *Greek Grammar*. The definitions presented herein are derived from the following dictionaries: Liddell-Scott-Jones, HELPS Word Studies, Thayer's *Lexicon*, BDAG third edition, Gerhard Kittel's *TDNT*, Colin Brown's *NIDNTT*, Moisés Silva's *NIDNTTE*, *BibleWorks10*, and journals.

This provisional translation aims to provide a workable translation for analysis and interpretation, unaffected by previous translations advocating adoption. To engage with the text in a manner akin to reading the original Greek, I have chosen to produce a formally equivalent translation, endeavoring to preserve the syntactic structure of each sentence as faithfully as possible to the source language. Occasionally, additional words are placed in square brackets to interpret the Greek grammar, such as the mood of a verb, or to enhance the flow of the sentence. Other meanings are offered in parentheses. Other translations have been consulted, including the YLT, NET, NASB, ESV, AMP, *Perjanjian Baru Indonesia-Yunani, Alkitab Terjemahan Baru Edisi Kedua*, NIV, David B. Hart's NT translation, and N. T. Wright's contemporary translation.

The following provisional translation will be a starting point for further discussion. Any errors will be corrected during the work of the dialectic specialty.[11] The provisional formal equivalent translations in column 1 will be further discussed and revised in the coming section. While working on this provisional translation, it has become apparent that the translation is

---

10. Sutanto, *Perjanjian Baru Interlinear*.
11. Lonergan, *Method in Theology*, 235–66.

an act of interpretation. For comparison purposes, two additional columns have been included. Column 2 represents the translation of the Peshitta text,[12] while column 3 presents the translation of Coptic text in the southern dialect.[13] In preparing the provisional translations, this work draws on Matt O'Donnell's structural analysis of clause annotation. However, the translation process itself is not included in this publication—only the resulting translations are presented.

TABLE 2: Temporary Translation of Galatians 4:1–7 (ATT)

My Provisional Translation (ATT)	Peshitta	Coptic
4:1 [Now] [with certainty] [I] say moreover, for as long as [in] a particular time [when] the heir is a minor[,] [he] differs nothing [from] a bond-slave [although] [he] [is] lord (owner) [of] all that exist,	4:1 But I say that what time the heir is a child, he differeth not from a servant, though he be lord of all,	4:1 But I say that *as long time as* the *heir* is a little (one) be differeth nothing from a servant, being the lord of every thing.
2 but [he] is under guardians and household managers until the previously appointed time [from] the Father.	2 but is under curators and stewards until the time which his father appointeth.	2 But he is being under *guardians* and *stewards* unto the *term appointed* of the father.
3 So also we, when [we] were minors[,] [we] were brought into (be under) bondage under the elementary religious teachings [of] the world.	3 So we also, while children, under the principles of the world were subjected.	3 Thus we also, at the time (of) being little, we were being under the *elements* of the *world* being servants:
4 Now when it came to the fullness [of] the time, the God [he] sent forth the Son [of] Himself, born out of a woman, born under law (any system of religious thinking),	4 But when the fulness of the time had come, Aloha sent his Son, and made from a woman, and made under the law,	4 but when the completion of the time had come, God sent his Son, having been born out of a woman, he became under the *law*,
5 so that those [who are] under law (any system of religious thinking) he [might] redeem (set free), so that the position (the place) of a son we [might] receive as due.	5 that them who were under the law he might redeem, and we might receive the constitution of sons.	5 that he should buy those who are under the *law*, that we should receive the sonship.

12. Etheridge, "Peschito Syriac."
13. *Coptic Version* 5:163–69.

6 Because now you are sons, God [he] sent forth the Spirit [of] the Son [of] Him into the hearts of ours[,] screaming, *Abba*, the Father.	6 And because you are sons, Aloha hath sent the Spirit of his Son into your hearts, who crieth, Father, our Father.	6 But because ye are the sons of God, he sent the *spirit* of his Son into our hearts, crying out, Abba, Father.
7 So as to no longer you are a bondslave[,] however a son[,] and if a son then an heir through [...] [of] God.	7 Therefore you are not servants, but sons; and if sons, heirs also of Aloha, through Jeshu Meshiha.	7 So that no longer art thou a servant, but thou art a son; but if thou art a son, then thou art an *heir* through the Christ.

The translations of vv. 4:5 (which states, "we might receive the constitution of sons") and 4:7 (which reads "through Jeshu Meshiha" in the Peshitta and "through the Christ" in the Coptic) are available for perusal.

EXEGETICAL ANALYSIS AND TRANSLATION REVISION

The closest co-text of Gal 4, vv. 3:26–29 or the whole chapter 3, should be read first. Gerhard Ebeling sees vv. 3:26—4:11 as a set of ideas and writes, "This focuses attention on the notion of sonship."[14] Though we have many similar conclusions concerning divine sonship, his concept differs. Ebeling states, "We are sons only by adoption, by υἱοθεσία (4:5)."[15] It will be demonstrated that Christians are not sons by adoption; υἱοθεσία is not adoption, and *vice versa*. As discussed in previous chapters, and it will be more apparent in this exegesis of Gal 4:1–7, *unbelievers* are the created sons of God in their minor state (infancy, *nepio*-ship). By contrast, *believers* are the created sons of God in their major state (adults, *huio*-ship).

In his analysis of the incarnation of the Lord Jesus, James Dunn examines the surrounding context. He clarifies that Jesus was sent to experience the state of humankind in all its weaknesses and enslavement so that humanity could be liberated and granted participation in Christ's Sonship. He was commissioned divinely to share the circumstances of (fallen) Adam (= man) so that humanity may partake in His resurrected humanity as the last Adam. Jesus' birth is not the central focus of the act of redemption. Instead, Jesus' prior condition of being born of a woman and under the law enables the act of redemption. The redemption is primarily directed

---

14. Ebeling, *Truth of the Gospel*, 207–8.

15. Ebeling, *Truth of the Gospel*, 210; if one has access to the original book, one can check if it was the translator who had the use of the term "adoption."

towards Jesus' death as the Son rather than the event of His birth.¹⁶ Jesus should experience death as a son of a woman (an ordinary man) for Him to present human resurrection. I submit that the baptism and resurrection of Jesus Christ correlate with the concept of υἱοθεσία. This will become more evident when we discuss the Epistle to the Romans, chapter 8.

This phrase, "you are all son-heirs (υἱοὶ) of God," must refer to the believers as they are beginning to become elevated beings.¹⁷ Although the process of becoming mature sons was still underway, Paul informed both the gentiles and the Judaizers in the Galatians' congregation that they had already been designated as son-heirs (υἱοὶ) and that they were no longer considered infants (νήπιοι).¹⁸ But this problem in the Galatian assembly shows that they are still at the beginning of becoming adults, like those ages thirteen or fifteen, who still show their underage characteristics. In other words, the Christians (υἱοὶ) in Galatia during the time of Paul exhibited characteristics associated with a νήπιοι mentality of tribal (group-oriented) religions.

In the following section, we will examine Gal 4:1–7 verse by verse. My provisional formal equivalent translations (ATT) are provided after the Greek text.

Galatians 4:1

1 Λέγω δέ, ἐφ' ὅσον χρόνον ὁ κληρονόμος νήπιός ἐστιν, οὐδὲν διαφέρει δούλου κύριος πάντων ὤν,

1 [Now] [with certainty] [I] say moreover, for as long as [in] a particular time [when] the heir is a minor[,] [he] differs nothing [from] a bondslave [although] [he] [is] lord (owner) [of] all [that] exist, (ATT)

After arguing the importance of the promise rather than the law, and those who have been baptized are clothed (put on) with Christ, that they are one in Christ, counted as Abraham's descendants, heirs according to

---

16. Dunn, *Christology*, 41–42.

17. Fung explains, "The idea of becoming full-grown sons also mentioned in 3:26 is developed in combination with the idea of being free from slavery, as Paul explains with a human analogy how the Galatians have become full-grown sons and heirs of God." Fung, *Epistle to the Galatians*, para. 3.

18. Fung explains, "But 'a child' (AV, RV, RSV, NASB, NIV)—literally 'an infant' (*népios*); the Greek term 'covers the immaturity of youth as well as the incapacity of childhood' thus denotes 'a minor' in any stage of his minority." Fung, *Epistle to the Galatians*, para. 4.

promise, then Paul inscribes, "Now with certainty I say moreover." The first word of this chapter, λέγω, is in the indicative mood, "the mood of certainty or reality."[19] Paul might want to say, "After laying all of those arguments in Gal 3, looking at that reality with certainty, I conclude." In George S. Duncan's words, "What I mean is this."[20] According to Hans Dieter Betz, Paul illustrates it using an analogy from legal practice.[21] I would like to highlight here that if Paul writes in the chiasm, then the one in the middle of his letter, which he is about to address, is the most crucial message, that is, υἱοθεσία—how God saves humanity. It is the gospel of Jesus Christ.

The phrase "for as long as in a particular time" talks about a period before an inauguration for becoming a son-heir (υἱός).[22] "*The heir is a minor*" clearly states that, as an heir-to-be in his father's house, the minor is not a bondslave nor another son from another family. He is now an underage heir in his age of boyhood, in his life before being inaugurated as an adult son-heir (eschatological human being). He is awaiting his father's decision.[23] This concept is fundamental in refuting the doctrine of adoption.

The minor is part of the family, in the sense of the English term "son," but in the *népio* state of the Pauline Greek term. Before his designation as son-heir (υἱός), the minor is the "master in waiting."[24] It is evident that when Paul addressed this pivotal teaching, he did not contemplate adoption in the sense of transferring a son from one family to another. Consequently, there is no concept of an alien family (a created human family other than

19. Wallace, *Greek Grammar*, 448.
20. Duncan, *Epistle of Paul*, 125.
21. "I tell [you as an ilustration]." Betz, *Galatians*, 202.
22. Rapa writes, "Paul will illustrate the contrast between the age of immaturity, characterized by the supervision of the law, and the age of maturity, which is the age of living by God's Spirit received by means of faith in Jesus Christ. God's people have moved in Christ into a new dynamic with respect to relationships between themselves and God and with one another in Christ. No longer under the tutelage of the Mosaic legislation, which Paul identified as the temporary extension of the Abrahamic covenant, Jewish and Gentile believers who replicate Abraham's faith enter into the age of maturity before the Father." Rapa, "Galatians," 2:603.
23. Luther explains, "The example of the heir who is a minor. . . . Civil laws, says Paul, establish that an heir, although he is lord of all his father's goods, is no different from a servant. He is certain of inheriting; but before he comes to maturity, his teachers hold him in subjection, just as a schoolteacher does with a scholar. They do not let him be in charge of his own possessions but make him serve, so that he is maintained by his own goods like a servant. Therefore, as long as he is under guardians, he is no different from a servant. And this is very good for him, for otherwise, through folly he would soon waste all his goods. His captivity is not permanent, but his father sets a certain time limit." Luther, *Galatians*, 195.
24. See Rapa, "Galatians," 2:604.

God's). The concept of "Latin Pauline adoption" is not familiar to the apostle Paul himself.

"He differs nothing from a servant although he is lord (owner) of all that exist" means a minor is not lawful yet to inherit anything from his father, just like the slaves (servants). Paul does not intend to say that a minor is in a position of servile work, nor is he in bondage like a slave to the Father.[25] A minor born as a freeman can own or do anything without supervision, provided he is a major already.[26] Hence, the minor in waiting is in constant fear, for he worries whether he will be appointed son-heir (υἱός). But unlike the ordinary human families of that time who could sell their minors, God's minors are still wanted and kept by God. In this metaphor, this family signifies this creation, and the father denotes God.

Quoting Jerome, "The infant heir . . . signifies the whole human race up to the advent of Christ, and, to speak more largely, right up to the end of the world."[27] Jerome knows the context of infant heir, but it is unclear why, in his *Vulgata*, he uses the term "*adoptio filiorum.*" However, there is an indication that Jerome does not designate "*adoptio filiorum*" as adoption from another family. Jerome references the concept of "the age of infancy," which reflects his theological perspective on human development.

> People are correctly said to live under tutors and overseers when, having the spirit of fear, they have not yet deserved to receive the spirit of freedom and adoption. For the age of infancy feels dread in relation to sin, fears its custodian and does not believe in its own freedom, even if it is sovereign by nature.[28]

The Epistle to the Galatians is concerned with the concept of "human growth" or "human becoming," rather than "adoption."

---

25. "'A minor'; in N.T. immaturity is always intended by this word." Hogg and Wine, *Epistle to the Galatians*, 179.

26. Duncan renders, "Paul is emphatic that those who are under law are like children who require to be supervised and controlled, and have no more real freedom than the household slaves. . . . His new point is the positive one that even tutelage suggests a future period of emancipation; and in putting His children under restrictive discipline for a period God Himself was looking forward to a time when they should be of age to enter into their inheritance as sons." Duncan, *Epistle of Paul*, 125.

27. Edwards, *Galatians*, 53.

28. Edwards, *Galatians*, 53.

Galatians 4:2

2 ἀλλ' ὑπὸ ἐπιτρόπους ἐστὶν καὶ οἰκονόμους ἄχρι τῆς προθεσμίας τοῦ πατρός.

2 but [he] is under guardians and household managers until the previously appointed time [from] the Father. (ATT)

This analogy portrays an affluent family with a hierarchical order in the household, featuring appointed guardians (ἐπιτρόπους) and managers (οἰκονόμους) responsible for the welfare of the minor. The father strives to be a caring parent who shares everything with his child, including himself entirely. The child is groomed for a momentous destiny; while under the father's roof, the child is protected and monitored until the time determined by the father.[29] The guardians and managers safely prepare the young son for his coming of age.[30] There is no legal enslavement in this context. It should be noted, however, that certain restrictions apply concerning infants (νήπιοι), who are particularly susceptible to falling.

The Father has a predetermined time for His sub-act of υἱοθεσία. If it is about time, then it is about history. I assert that it is essential to examine the relationship between the *ordo salutis* and the *historia salutis*. The former represents a logical priority concerning personal salvation, while the latter pertains to a chronological framework in relation to universal salvation. If one conceptualizes salvation as a process initiated by the resurrection of Christ, which commences at varying times for different individuals but ultimately reaches consummation simultaneously, it can be argued that

---

29. Cf. Ebeling: "We need not analyze in detail the new legal metaphor Paul uses to explain the dramatic change that makes us sons (4:1–2). Whether and where in the ancient world we can demonstrate that the underlying concepts of majority and inheritance were legally in force is irrelevant to Paul's purpose. We can also pass over the minor inconsistency between the metaphor of reaching majority and that of adoption. The former emphasizes the contrast between two stages set apart by a critical date. This leads in turn to the epoch marked by Christ and the increasingly important contrast between slavery and freedom. The latter metaphor serves to interpret sonship itself—not just the right of inheritances—as a gift deriving from the sending of the Son of God. Now when we turn to the state of minority or enslavement, we note that Paul describes it primarily in terms of the pagan past of the Galatians, but also brings the Torah into the discussion, apparently deliberately. There are no concrete references to the earlier religion of the Galatians. Religious syncretism and exposure to a variety of cults are probably in the background." Ebeling, *Truth of the Gospel*, 216.

30. Cf.: "That by law no one is justified before God, that no law was ever given that could impart life, and that the law served only in a preparatory way, namely, as a custodian to bring sinners to Christ." Hendriksen, *Galatians*, 155. Cf. also: "The law functioned as a means to shepherd and protect God's people from the devastation of sinfulness while at the same time showing up sin for all." Rapa, "Galatians," 2:604.

salvation embodies both logical and chronological priorities, as reflected in the distinctions of *ordo salutis* and *historia salutis*.³¹ The apostle Paul describes this in his Letter to the Romans. According to Martin Luther, the period of the law concludes in two ways: through the advent of Christ at the time determined by the Father (Gal 4:4–5) and that same Christ arriving to us, personally, at any time through the Spirit.³² While one element remains constant at a specific point in time (two thousand years ago), the other exhibits variability within each individual. When a person becomes a υἱός (an eschatological everlasting pneumatic-Christic human), the law has no effect.³³ In this fashion, freedom, or liberation, results from a new state of being through the process of υἱοθεσία.

Galatians 4:3

> 3 οὕτως καὶ ἡμεῖς, ὅτε ἦμεν νήπιοι, ὑπὸ τὰ στοιχεῖα τοῦ κόσμου ἤμεθα δεδουλωμένοι
>
> 3 So also we, when [we] were minors[,] [we] were brought into (be under) bondage under the elementary religious teachings [of] the world. (ATT)

This letter has two audiences: Judaizers and gentile Christians. Therefore, it is essential to know to which group a passage was addressed: Judaizers, gentiles, or both. One of the critical questions is, what are "ἡμεῖς" (we) in this passage? According to Lenski, the term "we" refers to Jews only.³⁴

---

31. Rapa renders, "In salvation history, as in the human realm, it is the Father who determines the timing of the consummation of his set purpose. . . . As was true of the Son, the Spirit is 'sent' by the Father into the life of the believer, implying the redemptive-historical significance of the presence of the Spirit in one's life." Rapa, "Galatians," 2:605–6.

32. Luther, *Galatians*, 196.

33. Lenski writes, "Much more important for Paul's illustration is this mention of the father. It is he who made the testament, he who designated the heir, he from whom the inheritance comes. Thus it is he who in one way or in another fixes the time when his heir is to enter upon control of the inheritance. The heir is no more of an heir after this date than he was before it as the participle used in v. 1 indicates; but after this date the heir is, indeed, no longer under anybody as he was before. This is the *tertium*, the essential point: once *under*, then *no longer under* according to the testamentary provision of the heir's own father." Lenski, *Galatians*, 194. Emphasis original.

34. Lenski explains, "By 'we were minors' he means 'we Jews' just as he does in 3:23–25. Before Christ came, we were nothing but minor heirs. The distinction between believing and unbelieving Jews during the period before Christ is not stressed in this 'we'; if we desire to stress it, we shall, of course, have to say that only believing Jews could be included. Yet 'we' refers also to Paul himself as well as to all Jews who came to

Still, Heinrich August Wilhelm Meyer,[35] Gerhard Ebeling,[36] and Betz,[37] for example, opined that "we" refers to the Jewish and gentile Christians. The definition of "we" here is fundamental because it affects the whole context. The subject is minors. "When we were minors" suggests a stage when we were in an underdeveloped spiritual life,[38] in the age of immaturity,[39] or before we believed in Christ. The clause "[we] were brought into (be under) bondage" in this context should have something to do with regulated or "*protective* custody." This is the context of "we were enslaved." We, both the Judaizers and gentile Christians, were νήπιοι under the bondage of laws, but now we are not. See the discussion of Rom 9:4.

There are two distinct contours of religious life. The Law (Torah) was given to the nation of Israel, while the elementary religious teachings (τὰ στοιχεῖα)[40] were given to the gentiles, to all other nations, and all humankind. The Law and all religious teachings are inherently unsatisfactory because they demand absolute conformity to their tenets, which are incapable of being fully satisfied by any individual throughout their lifetime. The actions of any individual, regardless of their age, are either positive or negative. However, unless that individual's spirit has been awakened, their actions will always be following the flesh (κατὰ σάρκα).

---

faith after Christ came. So it is best to take 'we' in this broader sense. God intended the inheritance for all Jews, treated all of them as minor heirs before Christ came." Lenski, *Galatians*, 194–95.

35. Meyer comments, "Ἡμεῖς] . . . In favour of this view we may decisively urge, firstly, the sense of στοιχεῖα τοῦ κόσμου; secondly Gal 4:5, where the first ἵνα applies to the Jewish Christians, but the second, reverting to the first person, applies to Christians generally, because the address to the readers which follows in Gal 4:6 represents these as a whole, and not merely the Jewish Christians among them, as included in the preceding ἵνα τὴν υἱοθεσίαν ἀπολάβωμεν; lastly, thirdly that the οὐκέτι and τότε, said of the Galatians in Gal 4:7–8, point back to the state of slavery of the ἡμεῖς in Gal 4:3. Therefore ἡμεῖς is not to be understood as referring either merely to the Jewish Christians (Chrysostom and most expositors, including Grotius, Estius, Morus, Flatt, Usteri, Schott, Baumgarten-Crusius, de Wette, Wieseler); or—as Hofmann in consistency with his erroneous reference of Gal 3:29 to the Gentile readers holds—to 'the Old Testament church of God, which has now passed over into the New Testament church;' or to the Jewish Christians pre-eminently (Koppe, Rückert, Matthies, Olshausen); or, lastly, even to the Gentile Christians alone (Augustine)." Meyer, *Epistle to the Galatians* 7:216–17.

36. Ebeling, *Truth of the Gospel*, 217.

37. Betz, *Galatians*, 204.

38. "Underdeveloped spiritual life," after Bundrick, "*Ta Stoicheia Tou Kosmou* (Gal 4:3)," 355.

39. After Rapa, "Galatians," 2:605.

40. According to Luther, "Paul is referring to written laws and traditions." Luther, *Galatians*, 196; note the plurals, "laws" and "traditions."

The Law serves to protect individuals from further moral decline; however, it is insufficient to facilitate a pneumatic union with the Creator. The purpose of the Law and the elementary religious teachings was only to give temporary direction to those living κατὰ σάρκα, in the absence of their πνεῦμα. Martin Luther writes, "The Law gives nothing living, healthy, divine, or heavenly, but only worldly things. That is why Paul aptly calls the laws *the basic principles of the world*."[41] Laws (τὰ στοιχεῖα, including the Torah) make their adherents focus on how to suppress their desires of the flesh, or for those who think they have overcome them, to be so proud of it. But laws will never be able to free people from the will of the flesh (the source of the problem) that characterizes their mortal existence. The nature of the "coming αἰών (*aiôn*)" will be spiritual and atemporal.[42] Therefore, the nature of human beings must become spiritual if they are to enter the coming αἰών; consequently, the necessity for these laws will be obviated by the extinction of the source of the human beings' carnal desires.

Let us now return to the phrase "we, the Jewish and gentile Christians together, were minors" (νήπιοι). This clause implies that although the τέκνα Israelites are children of the promise, these individual Israelites were still in the *népio* state before the υἱοθεσία took place for each individual.[43] See the left side of Figure 4 in the Words Study. Thus, before the coming of the Son (before the appointed time), the rest of God's created children, including the Israelites (the chosen ones), were minors.

Galatians 4:4

> 4 ὅτε δὲ ἦλθεν τὸ πλήρωμα τοῦ χρόνου, ἐξαπέστειλεν ὁ θεὸς τὸν υἱὸν αὐτοῦ, γενόμενον ἐκ γυναικός, γενόμενον ὑπὸ νόμον,
>
> 4 Now when it came [to] the fullness [of] the time, the God [he] sent forth the Son [of] Himself, born out of a woman, born under law (any system of religious thinking), (ATT)

---

41. Luther, *Galatians*, 197; bold in the original replaced with italic. *Ta stoicheia* is the generic term for all written laws and traditions, including the one for Israel.

42. Meyer, *Epistle to the Galatians* 7:221–2.

43. Hogg and Wine explain, "While the law was in force the Jews were in a state corresponding to the state of childhood, or minority, among men; cp. 'infant,' used of a minor in English law." Hogg and Wine, *Epistle to the Galatians*, 181.

After a long and desperate wait for the son of a woman, the time has come.[44] Following Dunn,[45] I agree to render "born of woman" rather than "born out of a woman." According to Betz, "It is a definition of human life."[46] This incarnate *Son*, born of woman, theologically was born as an *infant* (νήπιος) under the Jewish Torah. The clause, "now when it came to the fullness of the time," should be seen from the standpoint of the Old Testament, beginning with Gen 3:15. This "time" was when the state of being of this creation began to change from the human's side.[47] This event was when the human being's consciousness of his salvation matured, and he could no longer stand.[48] It is when humans want to escape their present human situation. This incarnation of the Son is an event that breaks out in time, in history.[49]

44. For Luther, "The law of Moses gives nothing but worldly things; it merely shows, civilly and spiritually, the evils that are in the world. However, if it is used properly, it drives the conscience to seek and thirst after God's promise and to look to Christ. But in order to do so, you need the aid of the Holy Spirit, who may say in your heart, 'It is not God's will that, after the law has done its work in you, you should merely be terrified and killed. When the law has brought you to know your misery and damnation, God does not want you to despair but to believe in Christ, who is "the end of the law so that there may be righteousness tor everyone who believes" (Romans 10:4).'" Luther, *Galatians*, 198.

45. Dunn explains, "'Born of woman' was a familiar phrase in Jewish ears to denote simply 'man' (Job 14.1; 15:14, 25:4; IQS 11:20f., IQH 13:14, 18:12f., 16, Matt. 11:11)—man is by definition 'one who is/has been born of woman.' So the reference is simply to Jesus' ordinary humanness, not to his birth." Dunn, *Christology*, 40.

46. Betz, *Galatians*, 207.

47. Rapa renders, "When God the Father had determined that Israel and all humanity were prepared to enter into *maturity* through the person and work of Christ. In *salvation history*, as in the human realm, it is the Father who determines the timing of the consummation of his set purpose." Rapa, "Galatians," 2:605. Emphasis added.

48. Vos argues, "For redemption is a divine procedure taking place in the form of time, in the form of history. Therefore, as such, it cannot be thought of without the implied idea of a terminus, a point of arrival. If an uncorrupted world already stretches itself out toward some goal of consummation, how much more will a creation fallen into sin and corruption. All the abnormalities, the uncomfortableness, the frictions and attrition of sin cry out for it. Paul has very strikingly described that state of mind by the figure of 'groaning' (Rom. 8:22). Owing to the primordial sin of man, the whole creation groans, hoping to find deliverance from the bondage in which it is compelled to live as a result of the fall." Vos, *Eschatology*, 6.

49. According to Tillich, "It is as far from right to call history purely God-abandoned as to call it simply God's revelation. Indeed, when speaking of revelation, one must say that history is always equipped with revelation because it always contains divine answers and human questions. Thus there can be a 'fullness of time,' a moment in history when history by means of preliminary procedures has become capable of realizing the ultimate—a moment when history has become ripe for the event, which does not originate from history and also is not injected into it as a foreign substance, but breaks out within it and is capable of being received in history. Liberalism speaks

From that point forward, it is more reasonable to understand humanity as progressing toward its consummation, having entered the second phase of its ontological constitution—an "improved state of being" shaped under the structure of the Son, an elevated form of humanity. If this visitation of the Son had not taken place, humankind would have inconceivably deteriorated to the point of ultimate despair and total extinction because humans are created in temporality.

Notice the phrase "under law" rather than "under the law," for there is no Greek definite article "τὸν." What is ὑπὸ νόμον with no article? Wallace rationalizes that a noun does not need an article to be definite. However, a noun with the article *cannot* be indefinite. Therefore, a noun *may* be definite without the article but *must* be definite when it has it.[50] For Kenneth S. Wuest, law in general is referred to here. Paul considered the gentiles to possess divine law, as he spoke about the law written in their hearts (Rom 2:14–15). However, this law should not be turned into a legalistic system. "Those who are under [the] law" refers to anyone living under a system of legalism, whether Jew or gentile.[51] This lifestyle is not just a past issue. Such phenomena can be observed in the religious communities of Indonesia.

This question should be resolved not only based on grammar but also on context. It is closely related to "we" in v. 4:3, "the Jewish and gentile Christians together." Jesus Christ, a *Nazarenus*, a born νήπιος, like everyone else, regardless of race, was "made subject to law." Thus, the human condition does not refer only to those under the Torah but to all people under any tribal (group-oriented) law.

The phrase "the God, he sent forth the Son of Himself, born of woman, born under law" refers to the most critical event in the history of salvation (*historia salutis*). The eternal preexistent Son entered the finite creation as a temporal, earthly human, and in Him, these two natures cannot be separated; they are mysteriously interwoven. Infinite Being (Creator) and finite being (creation) are united for the first time through the pneumatic fellowship facilitated by the unitive Being (the Holy Spirit) in the person of Jesus Christ. Salvation occurs (commences) for the first time at this "meeting point," as God saves humanity through the incarnation of God the Son, who unites divinity and humanity in Himself.[52] This spiritual unity opens

---

of this as an event arising out of history, and supernaturalism calls it a foreign injection into history. In his radical opposition to the possibility affirmed by the liberals, Barth has made his decision in favor of the supernatural rather than the dialectical interpretation. This is his limitation." Tillich, "What Is Wrong," 33.

50. Wallace, *Greek Grammar*, 243.
51. Wuest, *Wuest's Word Studies* 1:115.
52. Macquarrie, *Principles*, 294.

the opportunity for human beings to be saved. Following this visit, elevated individuals possess new potentialities, possibilities, and facticity.

Since all human beings were minors, God's reconciling work[53] has been ongoing for eternity, and the incarnation is the event that allows human beings to begin to observe it. God constantly loves humans. His common and special grace started when we were still minors. He applies special grace to the elect (τέκνα).

Galatians 4:5

> 5 ἵνα τοὺς ὑπὸ νόμον ἐξαγοράσῃ, ἵνα τὴν υἱοθεσίαν ἀπολάβωμεν.
>
> 5 so that those [who] under law (any system of religious thinking) he [might] redeem, so that the position as son we [might] receive as due. (ATT)

As discussed in v. 4:4, Wuest explains that "νόμον" refers to law in general, which includes the Torah and "τὰ στοιχεῖα." Our inquiry concerns the definition of "redeem" in the context of the law. What does "ἐξαγοράζω" mean? Büchsel explains,

> The LXX does not use ἐξαγοράζω for "redeem." . . . In the NT the word is used of the redeeming and *liberating* act of Christ (Gal. 3:13; 4:5). . . . The purchase does not transfer to the possession of God or Christ, but to *freedom*. . . . It speaks of an action of God towards us in the history of salvation.[54]

These νήπιοι are God's created children under the possession of God, who live in God's created family. The act of purchase does not result in the transfer of a νήπιος to the custody of God, as they are already under God's custody. Consequently, the concept of "redeem" cannot be equated with the concept of adoption. According to Donald Macleod, redemption means liberation from punishment liability in the Galatian context. God is

---

53. Macquarrie states, "The people may break a covenant and slip back into idolatry, but God is represented as continually seeking to restore and renew the relationship with himself; and this is at the same time a restoration and renewal of the people in their very being. . . . The New Testament claims that this climax of God's reconciling work did come with the historical revelation in Jesus Christ. 'When the time had fully come, God sent forth his son' . . . is seen as a critical moment of history when God's reconciling work moves out into the open and takes a new and decisive leap forward toward building up that commonwealth of beings which would realize the potentialities of the creations." Macquarrie, *Principles*, 271.

54. Büchsel, ἐξαγοράζω (*TDNT* 1:126–27).

the Lawgiver, and He is the one who has declared a curse on sin: "Cursed is everyone who does not continue to do everything written in the Book of the Law (v. 3:10)."[55] The focus of "redeem" is not on the payment or the transfer but on the liberation of God's created children. In this verse, Paul describes the process of liberating the Galatians from the perceived curse of the law. This implies that even in the absence of specific laws, such as circumcision and kosher food, they can still maintain a state of peace with the giver of the law. This phrase can also be interpreted as "so that he may set free those under law."

Yet again, the term "νόμος" (*nómos*) pertains to law in general, including "τὰ στοιχεῖα." Therefore, the phrase "those who under law" encompasses all tribes, including non-Jewish Galatians, without exception. It is essential to free the "τέκνα" (favored children) from these religious laws (temporal guardians). The word "might" is inserted to indicate the subjunctive mood, as the verb "ἐξαγοράσῃ" is in the aorist subjunctive active form, third-person singular of the lemma "ἐξαγοράζω." The subjunctive mood implies uncertainty but a likelihood of the action taking place.[56] Therefore, we can infer from this phrase that not every νήπιος (Adamic human) will be chosen to enter the eternal reality, but only the τέκνα. If all the νήπιοι will be chosen, then Paul may not be required to have the term "τέκνα" (beloved children).

Believers are redeemed and liberated from all legalistic practices of religions. Liberation is not about doing the Torah but about ontologically transforming the person. The ἐξαγοράζω (liberation) takes place through the transformation of minors (νήπιοι) into mature son-heirs (υἱοί). Salvation does not involve adoption or payment to Satan or God. Instead, the Father grants a quickened spirit to the minors through υἱοθεσία (we will discuss this in Rom 8:15). Because the main idea is not about literal "νήπιος becomes υἱός" but a transformation from an old state of being into a new elevated state of being, and because a state of being is not simply about a position, therefore, the phrase "the position as a son" in our draft translation can be replaced with "the constitution of a [mature] son" where the phrase "a mature son" refers to an exalted being. Later, we will see that human exaltation brings freedom from Adamic facticity (sin and temporality) which, in turn, results in liberation from the temporal law.

In "ἵνα τὴν υἱοθεσίαν," there should be no idea of adoption from another family at all. H. A. Ironside gives a historical background:

---

55. Macleod, *Christ Crucified*, 223.
56. Wallace, *Greek Grammar*, 461.

> In that day, minor children were not recognized as the father's heirs until, when they came of age, he took them down to the forum, answering to our court-house, and there officially adopted them as sons. From that time on they were no longer considered as minor children, but recognized as heirs.[57]
>
> Adoption has a meaning different from that of our contemporary society.... However, the Roman custom in Paul's day was to adopt one's own son. That, you recall, was what was done in the *toga virilis* ceremony. Adoption (the Greek word is *huiothesía*) means to place as a son. A believer is placed in the family of God as a full-grown son, capable of understanding divine truth.[58]

We have seen that, according to Ironside, biblical "adoption" has a different meaning from that of our contemporary society. In English, adoption can be "to approve formally or accept."[59] However, I must respectfully disagree with the following definitions. According to John M. Frame, "In adoption, God places us in his family. . . . What this means ultimately is a new family. Believers become sons and daughters of God, not of Satan. . . . Adoption describes admission to a family that we were *not* born into."[60] Murray states, "Adoption, as the term clearly implies, is *an act of transfer from an alien family into the family of God himself*. This is surely the apex of grace and privileges."[61]

None of the definitions presented aligns with the Pauline concept of υἱοθεσία. The term "adoption" can lead to various interpretations and does not fully encapsulate the meaning of υἱοθεσία. Therefore, it would be more appropriate to discontinue its use and consider alternative translations.

What does ἀπολάβωμεν (ἀπολαμβάνω) say? Liddell-Scott-Jones (LSJ) define it in part I as "*take or receive from* another . . . *receive what is one's due*," and in part II, "*regain, recover*."[62] In line with the definition in LSJ part II, Frederic Rendall writes, "Accordingly it describes the adoption in Christ as a *restoration* of the original birthright."[63] The concepts of adoption

---

57. Ironside, *Expository Messages*, 59.
58. McGee, *Galatians*, 69–70.
59. Summers, *Longman Dictionary*, 14.
60. Frame, *Systematic Theology*, 975, 976, 977. Emphasis original.
61. Murray, *Redemption*, 134. Emphasis added.
62. Liddell et al., *Greek-English Lexicon*, 205. Italics original.
63. Rendall comments, "ἵνα . . . ἵνα. These two final clauses couple together two gracious purposes of God in the scheme of redemption, firstly, the obliteration of a guilty past, secondly, divine adoption with the blessings which sonship entails. The description under Law includes Gentiles as well as Jews: for though they had not the Law, they were not without Law to God (Cf. Rom. 2:14 . . .): they have indeed been

and restoration cannot be harmonized. If it is restoration, why does it need adoption, and *vice versa*? Restoration, in its true sense, brings humanity to a pre-fall state, while adoption brings humanity to a new legal status. Advocates of adoption seek to establish adoption as a necessary part of salvation.

In contrast to Rendall, Heinrich A. W. Meyer states,

> For before Christ men never possessed the υἱοθεσία here referred to (although the old theocratic adoption of the Jews was never lost, Rom. 9:4): hence Augustine and others are in error when they look back to the sonship that was lost in Adam.[64]

What Meyer said is that each individual has never experienced God's sub-act of υἱοθεσία. What about the nation of Israel? The nation has experienced a unique υἱοθεσία no other nation has experienced. The nation becomes the elect, described as τὰ τέκνα τῆς σαρκός—elected children, but still sarkic. It is one of the milestones of God's sub-acts of υἱοθεσία to facilitate the incarnation of God's Son into the world.

Paul discussed this in Rom 9, especially v. 8. Here, we should begin to see that υἱοθεσία is a process of building up mature sons or a process of forming consummated eschatological human beings. If this is the case, then "we [might] get back" is inappropriate. There is a sense of building up mature sonship, step by step, and the teaching of υἱοθεσία represents each step of the process. The exegesis of Rom 9:8 will make this clear.

---

expressly specified in Gal. 3:14 as included in the redemption from the curse of the Law.—ἀπολάβωμεν. This verb denotes receiving back, as ἀποδιδόναι does giving back (Cf. Luke 19:8): accordingly it describes the adoption in Christ as a *restoration* of the original birthright, withheld throughout many generations for the sake of necessary discipline." Rendall, *Epistle to the Galatians* 3:176. Emphasis added.

64. According to Meyer, "ἀπολάβ.] not: that we might again receive, as is the meaning of ἀπολαμβ. very often in Greek authors (see esp. Dem. 78.3; 162.17), and in Luke 15:27; for before Christ men never possessed the υἱοθεσία here referred to (although the old theocratic adoption of the Jews was never lost, Rom. 9:4): hence Augustine and others are in error when they look back to the sonship that was lost in Adam. Nor must we assume with Chrysostom, Theophylact, Bengel, and others, including Baumgarten-Crusius, Hofmann, and Reithmayr, that, because the υἱοθεσία is promised, it is denoted by ἀπολάβ. as ὀφειλομένη,—a sense which is often conveyed by the context in Greek authors and also in the N.T. (Luke 6:34; Luke 23:41; Rom. 1:27; Col. 3:24; 2 John 1:8), but not here, because it is not the υἱοθεσία expressly, but the κληρονομία (Gal. 3:29, Gal. 4:7), which is the object of the promise. As little can we say, with Rückert and Schott, that the sonship is designated as fruit (ἀπο = inde) of the work of redemption, or, with Wieseler, as fruit of the death of Jesus apprehended by faith: for while it certainly is so in point of fact, the verb could not lead to it without some more precise indication in the text than that given by the mere ἐξαγορ. On the contrary, ἀπολάβ. simply denotes: to take at the hands of any one, to receive, as Luke 16:25 . . . and very frequently in Greek authors." Meyer, *Epistle to the Galatians* 7:226–27. Edited.

Once again, Meyer is correct: no sonship (*huio*-ship) was lost in Adam; therefore, neither restoration nor adoption is required. Consequently, these questions surface: Was Adam a υἱός, a τέκνον, or a νήπιος? Adam was created physically as an adult with a spouse, but metaphorically (theologically), represents all the νήπιοι (infants, protological humans). Macquarrie states, "Man is unfinished and incomplete."[65] The process of creation has commenced but has not yet reached its conclusion. This prompts the question of whether there is a correlation between the fall and the sonship (*huio*-ship), or whether the fall represents a transition from a state of perfection to one of imperfection. All humans classified as νήπιοι (protological humans) are susceptible to falling. Every νήπιος falls, except for one human figure—Jesus of Nazareth. Without God's sub-act of υἱοθεσία, all human beings are protological humans; thus, they fall. Only God's υἱοί (new beings, eschatological consummated humans) are exempt from falling. God is actively engaged in the process of perfecting humanity to fulfill the intended nature of human beings within His divine plan.

The Coptic Bible, in literal English translation, renders Gal 4:5 "that he should buy those who are under the *law*, that we should receive the sonship."[66] Etheridge's English translation of Peshitta reads "that them who were under the law he might redeem, and we might receive the constitution of sons."[67] Following these, then our translation of the last phrase can be alternatively rendered in singular form, "and we might receive the constitution (forming, making up)[68] of a consummated son," or "and we might receive the position of an adult son." Luther renders it "that we might receive the full rights of sons."[69] I rewrite Gal 4:5 "so that those [who] under law (any system of religious thinking) he [might] liberate, so that the constitution of a [mature] son we [might] receive as due." Please be aware that "the-constitution-of-a-mature-son" (τὴν υἱοθεσίαν) is in the singular form.

Galatians 4:6

6 Ὅτι δέ ἐστε υἱοί, ἐξαπέστειλεν ὁ θεὸς τὸ πνεῦμα τοῦ υἱοῦ αὐτοῦ εἰς τὰς καρδίας ἡμῶν κρᾶζον, Αββα ὁ πατήρ.

---

65. Macquarrie, *Existentialism*, 72.
66. *Coptic Version* 5:165.
67. Etheridge, "Peschito Syriac."
68. "Constitution, from *constitute*, [L not in progressive forms] means to form or make up"; Summers, *Longman Dictionary*, 271.
69. Luther, *Galatians*, 203.

> 6 Because now you are sons, God [he] sent forth the Spirit [of] the Son [of] Him into the hearts of ours[,] screaming, *Abba* [to] the Father. (ATT)

One can only become an elevated pneumatic being, υἱός, through υἱοθεσία. It transfers human beings from death to life and makes them death-proof. The determiner is a quickened human spirit (Rom 8:15). To be in spiritual fellowship, humans and God must have an interface (mediator). We can compare it to this: we need an adapter to plug an Indonesian *stekker* (power plug) into a UK electrical power outlet. The God-human is like the adapter, which can connect to both sides—one side to the Godhead and the human being—for both sides are "wired" in him. Human beings should be compatible with the human side of the God-human. Once they have a compatible interface, they can communicate with each other. Only the individual with quickened spirits[70] can establish a spiritual fellowship with the [human] spirit of the consummated son and the [divine] Spirit of the Son. Therefore, receiving the quickened spirit is a prerequisite before a person can enter spiritual communion.[71] A υἱός has a vivified spirit.

The verb "κρᾶζον" is neuter, and "the Spirit" (τὸ πνεῦμα) is the only other neuter noun and article in this verse. We can recognize who is crying out or screaming: "the Spirit [of] the Son [of] Him,"[72] not the new sons' spirits, that address the anxious longing. Here, "κρᾶζον" means "screaming" and "calling" because the Son's Spirit knows of the long-suffering emotions in human beings' hearts that cannot be contained anymore.

As a result of the union, the mature children (υἱοί) are counted as part of ὁ Υἱός (Messiah). The *huio*-ship (mistakenly rendered as "sonship") of the υἱοί (mature sons) depends on the *huio*-ship of the mature Son (ὁ

---

70. To be repeated here: human spirit differs from human soul. Human spirit is a faculty of human soul. If they are the same then it is difficult to read 1 Thess 5:23 (NET), "May your spirit and soul and body be kept entirely blameless at the coming of our Lord Jesus Christ." For it makes no sense if we render "may your *soul* and soul and body."

71. Cf. Rapa: "The relationship between believers' being children of God and the reception of the Spirit is a difficult issue; in chapter 3, Paul has seemingly argued from the Galatians' reception of the Spirit to demonstrate they are children of God (3:2–5, 26); this is the same order he presents in Romans 8:15–17. Here the argument seems to be that God sent his Spirit into the lives of the Galatians 'because [the Galatians] are sons.' The argument over which is the proper order has a long history..... However, it is likely that Paul conceives of the two as being so 'intimately related' that he 'can speak of them in either order ... with only the circumstances of a particular audience, the issue being confronted, or the discussion that precedes determining the order to be used.'" Rapa, "Galatians," 2:607.

72. Cf. Betz: "It is the Spirit which 'cries out' (κρᾶζον)." Betz, *Galatians*, 210.

Υἱός).⁷³ That's why He asked, "Abide in me." There is no *huio*-ship outside of Him. The *huio*-ship of believers is not in a direct relationship with the Father, because they lack the divine nature, but through the divine Son whose Spirit screams with a little sound, a faint groan, "*Abba*," to the Father.

The concept of adoption, particularly in a theological context, is fundamentally flawed. Legal adoption does not establish a genuine spiritual relationship, as adopted individuals remain in a state of infancy (νήπιοι), lacking an ontological transformation of their being. In the theology surrounding adoption, if a son reaches adulthood prior to the adoption, that adulthood is acquired within a different familial context, which does not correlate with a transformation into a pneumatic existence. The adopted son simply has a legal relationship with the adopter—a very weak relationship. Human beings that are non-pneumatic are categorized as νήπιοι, representing protological humanity with the inability to partake in a pneumatic union.

This perspective highlights the distinction between legal and spiritual familial relationships, emphasizing that true ontological change is necessary for an integration into the triune God. The implications of this understanding challenge conventional notions of adoption by asserting that without such ontological transformation, the adopted individual cannot fully embody the identity and privileges associated with being a pneumatic eschatological human (an adult child of God).

Νήπιοι (sarkic protological humans) are not υἱοί (pneumatic eschatological humans), and they have no capability to partake in the pneumatic fellowship (the fellowship of the pneumatic beings) provided by the Holy Spirit. The person of Jesus Christ—who has two natures—participates in the human pneumatic fellowship so that believers may be grafted into the person of Jesus Christ. Remember the vine and the branches (John 15:1–15), "I am the true vine . . . remain in me." In this creation, God is always the Father of all created beings, but Christian believers (υἱοί) exclusively call the Father "*Abba*"—a distinct terminology—after the Christ (ὁ Υἱός).⁷⁴

---

73. For Campbell, "Faith ἐν Χριστῷ is the means through which people attain divine sonship. The Fatherhood of God is extended to human beings by nature of the relationship between the Father and Son, 'as he is God's Son inherently, so in him they become God's sons and daughters.'" Campbell, *Paul and Union with Christ*, 134.

74. Cf. Stott: "This sonship of God is 'in Christ'; it is not in ourselves. . . . God is indeed the universal Creator, having brought all things into existence, and the universal King, ruling and sustaining all that He has made. But *He is the Father only of our Lord Jesus Christ and of those whom He adopts into His family through Christ*. If we would be the sons of God, then we must be 'in Christ Jesus . . . through faith' (v. 26), which is a better rendering than the familiar 'by faith in Christ Jesus' (AV). It is through faith that we are in Christ, and through being in Christ that we are sons of God." Stott, *Message of Galatians*, 99. Emphasis added.

[Father] is the word of communion.... Into this life of communion with the Father and the Son the sons of God are introduced by the Holy Spirit... "that they may be one even as We are One," John 17:11, 22.[75]

At the parousia, all [consummated] sons (οἱ υἱοὶ) will be one in spirit, one in Christ, and Christ in the Triune. We will further discuss the *Abba* call in Rom 8:15.

Galatians 4:7

7 ὥστε οὐκέτι εἶ δοῦλος ἀλλ' υἱός· εἰ δὲ υἱός, καὶ κληρονόμος διὰ θεοῦ.

7 So as to no longer you are a servant[,] however a son[,] and if a son then an heir through [...] [of] God. (ATT)

This passage discusses the themes of existence, being, and becoming rather than legal status, familial membership, office, or attribution. According to Hogg and Wine, the argument comprises two parts: first, the assertion that their minority had come to an end, and second, the empirical evidence that they had received the Spirit.[76] It is about an ontological transformation from an Adamic old being (portrayed as a νήπιος, a minor) who is a servant (δοῦλος) under the guidance of law to become an exalted Christic being (a υἱός, a mature son) after receiving a vivified spirit. The change is not literally a transition from slave to son but figuratively from being a minor (a sarkic protological human) to a mature son (a pneumatic eschatological human), as depicted in Rom 8:15. The term "slave" only refers to minors (infants) enslaved by the law.

Regarding this verse, Robert K. Rapa states, "Believers are no longer slaves but have the redemptive-historical status of sons and heirs."[77] As interpreted by Hogg and Wine, any laws no longer bind a son.[78] It agrees with Luther: "This bondage no longer continues."[79] It was noted in v. 3:28 (ESV)

---

75. Hogg and Wine, *Epistle to the Galatians*, 194–95.
76. Hogg and Wine, *Epistle to the Galatians*, 195.
77. Rapa, "Galatians," 2:606.
78. Hogg and Wine explain that "not merely a child of God, though that certainly, but a child come to the full consciousness of his relationship with his Father through the operation of the Spirit"; Hogg and Wine, *Epistle to the Galatians*, 196.
79. For Luther, "Paul uses the word *slave* in a different sense here than he did in v. 3:28 where he said there is *neither... slave nor free.*... Being a servant... means being guilty and captive under the law, under the wrath of God and death—to see God not

that "there is neither Jew nor Greek, there is neither slave nor free, there is no male and female, for you are all one in Christ Jesus." Despite the presence of Jews and non-Jews, enslaved people and freemen, males, and females in congregations, all were considered equal in Christ—as "mature sons" in its symbolic sense. It is intriguing to understand the connotation of the word "slave" from the viewpoint of an actual enslaved person like Onesimus as they hear vv. 3:28 and 4:7. Here, we have the literal and figurative meanings at the same time. Onesimus embodies a faithful enslaved person. At the same time, Philemon is an enslaver, yet v. 4:7 allegorically states they are no longer "slaves" as they are both redeemed as mature sons of Christ. The term "slave" has disparate connotations. Conversely, the child in question is not enslaved but in a living state with no freedom and rights. This state of being necessitates transformation, as the child's rights should be recognized.

Is there any missing word before the *genitive* θεοῦ in this verse? What does "an heir through [. . .] [*of*] God" mean? The Cambridge Bible gives something worth perusing: "The expression 'through God' has the same sense as in Galatians 1:1. It stands in antithesis to all human effort or merit, by the appointment and grace of God." It provides a variant, "of God through Christ."[80] AMP inserts "[the gracious act of] God [through Christ]."[81] The Coptic Bible in literal English renders the last phrase, "but if thou art a son, then thou art an *heir* through the Christ."[82] The Peshitta English Aramaic has "inheritors of Elohim by Y'shua the Mashiyach."[83] A Christian is an heir through the Christ. Thus, I submit that the verse can rendered as, "So as to no longer you are a servant [of laws] but a mature son (υἱός)[,] and if a mature son (υἱός)[,] then an heir through [the Messiah] [of] God."

---

as a merciful Father but as a tormentor, an enemy, and a tyrant. This is indeed to be kept in slavery and cruelly tormented in it. The Law does not set us free from sin and death but reveals and increases sin and engenders wrath. This bondage (as Paul describes it in Rom. 3:20 and 4:15) no longer continues; it does not oppress us or make us burdened anymore. . . . So you are without the law, without sin, without death; that is to say, you are saved and are now quite delivered from all evils. . . . Anyone who is a son must also be an heir, for his birth makes him worthy of being an heir." Luther, *Galatians*, 210–11. Bolts in original have been replaced with italics.

80. Biblehub, "Cambridge Bible."
81. *Amplified Holy Bible*, 756.
82. *Coptic Version* 5:167.
83. Roth, אשידק אבתכ, 597.

AN ALTERNATIVE TRANSLATION OF GALATIANS 4:1–7 (AHT)

Several adjustments have been made as a result of this discussion. My translation (AHT) of the passage is summarized here.

> 4:1 Now with certainty I say moreover, for as long as in a particular time when the heir is a minor (νήπιος), he differs nothing from a bondslave although he is lord (owner) of all that exist, 2 but he is under guardians and household managers until the previously appointed time from the Father. 3 So also we, when we were minors (νήπιοι), we were brought into (be under) bondage under the elementary religious teachings of the world. 4 Now when it came to the fullness of the time, the God, he sent forth the [eternal preexistent] Son (τὸν Υἱὸν) of Himself, born of woman (become a human being), born under law (a minor under any system of religious thinking), 5 so that those who under law (so that those minors) he might liberate, so that the constitution of a [mature] son (τὴν υἱοθεσίαν) we might receive as due. 6 Because now you are [mature] sons (υἱοί), God, he sent forth the Spirit of the Son (τὸ πνεῦμα τοῦ Υἱοῦ) of Him into the hearts of ours, screaming, *Abba*, [to] *ho Pater*. 7 So as to no longer you are a servant [of laws] but a mature son (υἱός), and if now a mature son (υἱός), then an heir through [the Messiah] [of] God.

SUMMARY: FOUNDATION

According to Gal 4:1–7, a minor, as a prospective heir, is no different from an enslaved person during his minorship. In this sense, a minor is not a slave; he is an underage freeman, but in some ways, he is identical to an enslaved person. The Torah has provisional "protective custody" of a minor. The context of this passage has nothing to do with slavery and adoption. Human deliverance from the enslavement of the Torah is the product of υἱοθεσία—an ontological transformation of being.

Israelites are τέκνα (beloved children) of God, but before they have faith in the Messiah, individually, they are still in νήπιο-state. Following the time determined by the Father, there are τέκνα among the gentiles, and God's sub-act of υἱοθεσία begins to transform those τέκνα from νήπιο-state (old sarkic-Adamic being) into υἱο-state (new pneumatic-Christic being).

My theological analysis of this passage posits that the christological portrait in this passage affirms both the full humanity and full divinity of the person of Jesus Christ. As articulated in Chalcedonian orthodoxy, Christ exists as one person (ὑπόστασις) with two distinct, unconfused natures—divine and human—united without separation or alteration. The text underscores Jesus' genuine humanity through His birth (born of [a] woman), and status as νήπιος (born under law), that is, a human infant subject to legal and developmental constraints, while simultaneously affirming His preexistent divinity as written "God sent His [preexistent] Son."

This duality necessitates a soteriological trajectory: Jesus' maturation from νήπιος to υἱός under the Mosaic covenant marks His fulfillment of the law's demands, thereby inaugurating his role as πρωτότοκος (firstborn) among many brethren (Rom 8:29). As the "last Adam" (1 Cor 15:45), Christ's perfected natures as both Son of Man and Son of God establishes a paradigmatic sequence—His ontological transition from subordinate νήπιος to glorified υἱός models the transformative journey for created children of God. The hypostatic union ensures that this human experience, while finite and developmental, remains inseparable from His eternal divine Sonship, thereby enabling His unique mediatorial function. There must have been a time when Jesus was declared a human υἱός who was freed from the law. The events mark Him as the first [mature] Son of Man, and as the first [mature] [human] Son of God, or *the* Christ (ὁ Υἱός), becomes the pattern for other of God's created children to follow His human ontological transformation experience.

CHAPTER 5

ROMANS: THE CREATION OF PNEUMATIC BEINGS

"THE SOUL'S TRUE TRANSFORMATION IS NOT A SUPERFICIAL AL-
TERATION BUT A REBIRTH INTO A NEW MODE OF EXISTENCE." ~ ST.
GREGORY OF NYSSA

OVERVIEW

This chapter examines the messages of St. Paul to the people of Christ gathered in the synagogues and house churches of Rome. Our discussion begins with vv. 9:4 and 8, then 8:14–23, for chronologically, the nation of Israel experienced the *huiothesía* (υἱοθεσία) before the Christians. We will read this passage along with our previous exegesis of Galatians, for there are many related thoughts.

This exegesis will focus on the translation of πνεῦμα. This word can refer to either the Spirit of God or the human spirit. To begin with, we must assume the possible existence of the human spirit. In the words of Paul, "For God is my witness, whom I serve with my spirit in the gospel of his Son, that without ceasing I mention you" (Rom 1:9 ESV). The human spirit is essential to human redemption because it links the infinite and the finite, allowing access for God to change the protological Adamic human ontologically. Any concept that denies the existence of the human spirit will be unable to grasp Paul's explanation of salvation. A refusal to incorporate the human spirit into the Christian's notion of salvation will lead to misinterpretation and the formation of a different gospel.

Romans 8 speaks of "making man whole" through "the constitution of a sarkic-Adamic being to become a *pneumatic*-Christic being." The process in itself involves two substages. It begins with the vivification of the humans' sleeping spirit; it is called the resurrection of the spirit, which takes place at the beginning of individual υἱοθεσία (Rom 8:15). The resurrection (regeneration, renewal) of his body (the consummation of υἱοθεσία) will perfect this son of man (Rom 8:23). In this discussion, I argue that a person can achieve a *pneumatic* authentic being only after the parousia. Before all this can happen, another preliminary stage should be established, τὰ τέκνα τῆς σαρκὸς nation.

A BRIEF BACKGROUND OF THE EPISTLE TO THE ROMANS, CHAPTERS 8 AND 9

In this section of the epistle, we explore how the promise that once belonged to the nation of Israel has now become a universal blessing to all peoples. Israel, as a community, is considered the τέκνα of God, but in terms of individual *huio*-ship, the individual gentiles surpass Israel (Rom 11). It is reminiscent of the parable of the landowner and his one-denarius wages for all of his workers (Matt 20:1–16), where "the last shall be first, and the first last." Among the congregation in Rome, there are Judaizers and unbelieving Israelites. Many are still considered first Christian believers and have passed down their old traditions within the new Christian sect.

In Rom 8:2, Paul identifies the dual regulative principles (νόμος). They are: "the regulative principle of the Spirit of life in Christ Jesus" and "the regulative principle of sin *and* death." I assert that human sin and death, as described in Rom 5:12, are not merely sequential phenomena but represent embedded aspects of humanity's protological state of being.

This interpretation situates υἱοθεσία within a broader Pauline framework, where the Spirit's transformative work liberates believers from the dominion of sin and death. The "Spirit of life" operates as the antithesis to the law of sin and death, signifying a transition from humanity's inherent mortality and moral failure to eschatological life in Christ, free from sin and temporality. My analysis underscores that υἱοθεσία is not a legal declaration but an ontological reconfiguration, wherein believers are conformed to the image of *the* Christ (Rom 8:29) through the Spirit's regenerative power.

By framing sin and death as intrinsic to humanity's original (protological) condition, I challenge traditional theological paradigms that treat these elements as external impositions. Instead, I highlight their pervasive influence on Adamic human existence and their ultimate defeat through Christ's redemptive work. This perspective deepens the understanding of υἱοθεσία as a transformative process that transcends the protological state, enabling believers to fully participate in divine communion.

THE STRUCTURE OF THE EPISTLE TO THE ROMANS

Ben Witherington holds that, in this letter, Paul addresses Jews in chapters 1 to 4 and 9 to 11 and gentiles in 5 to 8 and 12 to 15.[1] I found that Romans chapter 8 talks about the salvation of every individual human being—Jews and gentiles. Romans 9 carries up complex issues, such as the doctrine of election.

For the topic of υἱοθεσία, we will discuss Rom 9:4 and 8, which are about the status of the nation of Israel, before vv. 8:14-23, which discuss the two stages of *huiothesía* for all individuals. To have this discussion, I prepared a textual criticism work for Rom 8:23, as there is one variant that does not have the word "υἱοθεσίαν."

TEXT

The following text is an excerpt from the Epistle to the Romans, taken from the United Bible Societies Greek New Testament 5 (UBS⁵) Bible text, which is copied from the Academic Bible of *Deutsche Bibelgesellschaft*, with permission.

> 8:14 ὅσοι γὰρ πνεύματι θεοῦ ἄγονται, οὗτοι υἱοὶ θεοῦ εἰσιν. 15 οὐ γὰρ ἐλάβετε πνεῦμα δουλείας πάλιν εἰς φόβον ἀλλ' ἐλάβετε πνεῦμα υἱοθεσίας ἐν ᾧ κράζομεν, Αββα ὁ πατήρ. 16 αὐτὸ τὸ πνεῦμα συμμαρτυρεῖ τῷ πνεύματι ἡμῶν ὅτι ἐσμὲν τέκνα θεοῦ. 17 εἰ δὲ τέκνα, καὶ κληρονόμοι· κληρονόμοι μὲν θεοῦ, συγκληρονόμοι δὲ Χριστοῦ, εἴπερ συμπάσχομεν ἵνα καὶ συνδοξασθῶμεν.
> 18 Λογίζομαι γὰρ ὅτι οὐκ ἄξια τὰ παθήματα τοῦ νῦν καιροῦ πρὸς τὴν μέλλουσαν δόξαν ἀποκαλυφθῆναι εἰς ἡμᾶς. 19 ἡ γὰρ ἀποκαραδοκία τῆς κτίσεως τὴν ἀποκάλυψιν τῶν υἱῶν τοῦ θεοῦ ἀπεκδέχεται. 20 τῇ γὰρ ματαιότητι ἡ κτίσις ὑπετάγη, οὐχ ἑκοῦσα ἀλλὰ διὰ τὸν ὑποτάξαντα, ἐφ' ἑλπίδι 21 ὅτι καὶ αὐτὴ ἡ κτίσις ἐλευθερωθήσεται ἀπὸ τῆς δουλείας τῆς φθορᾶς εἰς τὴν ἐλευθερίαν τῆς δόξης τῶν τέκνων τοῦ θεοῦ. 22 οἴδαμεν γὰρ ὅτι πᾶσα ἡ κτίσις

---

1. Witherington and Hyatt, *Paul's Letter to the Romans*, 20. (Note: Paul uses the term "Israelites" when highlighting their national and historical identity.)

συστενάζει καὶ συνωδίνει ἄχρι τοῦ νῦν 23 οὐ μόνον δέ, ἀλλὰ καὶ αὐτοὶ τὴν ἀπαρχὴν τοῦ πνεύματος ἔχοντες, ἡμεῖς καὶ αὐτοὶ ἐν ἑαυτοῖς στενάζομεν υἱοθεσίαν ἀπεκδεχόμενοι, τὴν ἀπολύτρωσιν τοῦ σώματος ἡμῶν. . . .

9:4 οἵτινές εἰσιν Ἰσραηλῖται, ὧν ἡ υἱοθεσία καὶ ἡ δόξα καὶ αἱ διαθῆκαι καὶ ἡ νομοθεσία καὶ ἡ λατρεία καὶ αἱ ἐπαγγελίαι . . . 8 τοῦτ' ἔστιν, οὐ τὰ τέκνα τῆς σαρκὸς ταῦτα τέκνα τοῦ θεοῦ ἀλλὰ τὰ τέκνα τῆς ἐπαγγελίας λογίζεται εἰς σπέρμα.

GRAMMAR, LEXICAL ANALYSIS, AND PROVISIONAL TRANSLATION

The following translations are the result of a provisional, formal-equivalent approach. While the translation process itself is not included in this chapter, it was informed by the structural analysis method developed by Matt O'Donnell and partners. His original clause annotations are not reproduced here, but his analytical framework contributed meaningfully to the shaping of the tentative text. This translation will be revised during the discussion in the next section. For comparison purposes, I include translations in column 2 from the Peshitta[2] and in column 3 from Coptic in the southern dialect.[3]

TABLE 3: Temporary Translations of Romans 8:14-23 and 9:4-8 (ATT)

My Provisional Translation (ATT)	Peshitta	Coptic
8:14 Indeed[,] as many as are led [by] spirit [from] God, they are sons [of] God.	8:14 For they who by the Spirit of Aloha are led, they are the sons of Aloha.	8:14 For those who walk in the *spirit* of God, these are the sons of God.
15 Indeed not [you] received [a] spirit [of] bondage again into fear[,] but [you] received [a] spirit [of] placing (anointing) as a son in (by) that we scream aloud, abba the father.	15 For we have not received the spirit of servitude again unto fear, but we have received the Spirit of the adoption[A] of sons, by whom we cry, Father, our Father!	15 For ye received not a *spirit* of servitude unto a fear again; but ye received a *spirit* of sonship, this in which we cry out, Abba, Father.

2. Etheridge, "Peschito Syriac."
3. *Coptic Version* 4:83–95.

16 The Spirit himself [he] testifies together in support of the spirit [of] ours that we are favored children [of] God.	16 And the Spirit himself witnesseth with our spirit, that we are the sons of Aloha.	16 The *spirit* himself beareth witness with our *spirit*, that we are the children of God.
17 Subsequently if favored children[,] then heirs—truly heirs [of] God, consequently joint-heirs [of] Christ—if indeed [we] suffer together with [Christ][,] so that also [we] [might] [be] glorified together with [Christ].	17 And if sons, heirs also; heirs of Aloha, and the sons of the inheritance of Jeshu Meshiha. For if we suffer with him, with him also shall we be glorified.	17 If we are the children, then we are the *heirs*, the *heirs indeed* of God, but the fellow-*heirs* of the Christ; if we suffer with him, that we should be glorified also with him.
18 Indeed [I] [now] reckon (reason, conclude) that not comparable the undergoing sufferings [of] the present time towards the glory (splendor) [that] [is] about to [be] revealed into us.	18 For I consider that the sufferings of this time are not equal to that glory which is to be revealed in us.	18 For I think that the sufferings of this present time (are not) worthy of the glory which will be revealed unto us.
19 For the eager expectation [of] the creation[,] the revealing [of] the sons [of] God[,] [it] waits eagerly.	19 For the whole creation hopeth and waiteth for the manifestation of the sons of Aloha.	19 For the expectation of the creation expecteth the revelation of the sons of God.
20 For [to] the vanity the creation [was] subjected, not voluntarily but because of the [. . .] subjected [it] to, on the basis of trust	20 For the creation hath been subjected to vanity, not willingly,[B] but on account of him who subjected her, upon the hope	20 For the creation was humbled to the vanity, not of its will, but because of him who humbled it in (lit. upon) *hope*,
21 and because the creation itself will be made free away [from] the bondage [of] the decay (destruction) into the state of freedom [of] the splendor [of] the favored children [of] God.	21 that the creation herself also shall be made free from the servitude of corruption into the liberty of the glory of the sons of Aloha.	21 because the creation itself also will be made free out of the servitude of the corruption unto the freedom of the glory of the sons of God.
22 For [we] know that the whole creation [it] groans together and [it] travails together until even now	22 For we know that all creatures groan and travail until this day;	22 For we know that all the creation groaneth with us and travaileth even until now.

23 and not merely [it], but even [we] ourselves having the firstfruits [of] the Spirit, we even [we] ourselves in ourselves [we] groan await eagerly [the] position as a son, [of] the deliverance [of] the body [of] ours.	23 and not only they, but we also who have in us the first-fruit of the Spirit, groan within ourselves, and wait for the adoption, the redemption of our bodies.	23 But not it alone, but we ourselves also, having received the *firstfruit* of the *spirit*, we groan in ourselves, expecting the sonship, the redemption of our *body*.
...	...	...
9:4 whosoever are Israelites[,] [from] whom are the position as a son[,] and the splendor[,] and the testaments[,] and the law giving[,] and the worship[,] and the promises,	9:4 who are the sons of Israel, and whose was the adoption of sons, and the glory, and the covenants, and the law, and the ministry, and the promises,	9:4 who are these, Israelites; these, whose is the sonship, and the glory, and the *covenant*, and the *legislation*, and the service, and the promises.
...	...	...
8 It is not the favored children [generated of] the flesh [are] these favored children [of] God[,] but the favored children [of] the promise[,] reckoned into (among) descendant.	8 but that is, the children of the flesh are not the children of Aloha, but the children of the promise are reckoned the seed. *A Rucho da-simath benayo*: The Spirit of the constituting of sons. B Or, not with her will.	8 That is, that not the children of the *flesh*, these are the children of God; but the children of the promise (are) those who will be reckoned the *seed*.

Peruse the notes provided by Peshitta.

EXEGETICAL ANALYSIS AND TRANSLATION REVISION

Romans 9:4

4 οἵτινές εἰσιν Ἰσραηλῖται, ὧν ἡ υἱοθεσία καὶ ἡ δόξα καὶ αἱ διαθῆκαι καὶ ἡ νομοθεσία καὶ ἡ λατρεία καὶ αἱ ἐπαγγελίαι,

4 whosoever are Israelites[,] [from] whom are (namely) the position as a son[,] and the splendor[,] and the testaments[,] and the law giving[,] and the worship[,] and the promises, (ATT)

The word Ἰσραηλῖται, the plural form of Ἰσραηλίτης, refers to the theocratic national name of Israelites.[4] Paul lists the advantages of the theocratic

> 4. Cf. Harrison and Hagner: "When Paul uses 'people of Israel' rather than 'Jews,'

nation Israelites[5] over gentiles. Those on the list are the privileges of God's *chosen* people. Each individual of the *sarkic* beloved children of the nation Israel (τὰ τέκνα τῆς σαρκὸς) is only one step away from becoming a son-heir (υἱός) by believing in *Yeshua HaMashiach*. Human salvation is personal.[6] In the context of salvation, the recipient should be an individual because an existence (*existenz*) is individual and bodily, not an abstract object like a nation, a tribe, a family, a congregation, or a church denomination.

The unbelieving Israelites are τὰ τέκνα τῆς σαρκὸς, or "beloved children of the flesh." They are in νήπιο-state (minors) under the law, not υἱοί (son-heirs) yet, as God has not initiated them before the coming of God the Son incarnate. Referring to our discussion in Gal 4:5, we have replaced the phrase "the position as a son" with "the constitution of a [mature] son." The underlying rationale is as follows: Israelites were still in νήπιο-state before the *individual* υἱοθεσία took place, so they did not have the individual position of an adult son yet. They were in the process of "constituting." Let us look back at Figure 4 at the end of chapter 3. At the domain named "*Népioi*" (Νήπιοι), there is a sub-domain called "*Tekna*" (Τέκνα). Each domain has members (elements). The elements are the individuals. The figure depicts that before God's sub-act of υἱοθεσία to individuals begins, every element is a νήπιος.

To save God's created infants, God made a promise: Eve's seed, *a* son.[7] God has accomplished his purpose of the τέκνα nation Israel, for out of them, there came "her seed" who became ὁ υἱὸς τοῦ ἀνθρώπου (literally, "the mature son of the human" or traditionally, "the son of man"), dwelled among τὰ τέκνα τῆς σαρκὸς (the beloved children of the flesh) of the νήπιοι (created protological children) of God. That is the good news for every

---

he apparently wants to emphasize that they are the covenantal people of God different from every other people on earth." Harrison and Hagner, *Romans*, 147.

5. Cf. Wolter: "By contrast, Paul himself uses the term 'Israel' with much more differentiation. We can distinguish four ways of utilizing it: (a) . . . as a collective name for *non-Christian* Judaism. . . . (b) . . . Paul designates not only non-Christian Jews but also Jewish Christians (or Christian Jews). 'Israel' is the collective name for all Jews, and one who confesses Jesus does not cease to belong to Israel. . . . (c) . . . The term 'Israel' refers in a historicizing way to the people of God of the times of Elijah or Moses. (d) . . . The restrictive designations 'Israel *according to the flesh.*'" Wolter, *Paul*, 401–2. Emphasis original.

6. "The subject is not one about nations, but about individuals, not one about ethnic supremacy or leadership, but about personal salvation." Stifler, *Epistle to the Romans*, 164.

7. "I will put enmity between you and the woman, and between your offspring and her offspring; he shall bruise your head, and you shall bruise his heel." Gen 3:15 (ESV). *zarʿāh* (her seed, Noun—masculine singular construct :: third person feminine singular).

individual of all nations. The gospel, εμμανουηλ (*emmanouêl*), has come through the tribe of Israel. In this congregation, God raised a mature son of God, and this event can be referred to as the making of the Messiah, the *first* consummated Son and the only one before the parousia. Thus, from this perspective, we can rewrite this verse as "whosoever are Israelites[,] [from] whom (started from them) are (namely) the constitution of the [primogenetic] [mature] Son (the making of ὁ Υἱός, the Messiah)[,] and the splendor [,] and the testaments[,] and the law giving[,] and the worship[,] and the promises." The ablative "from" denotes "source," that all these things are *from* the Israelites, not the gentiles; still, all these things are not only concerning or possessed (genitive case) by the Israelites alone. This is why I chose to engage the ablative sense of the genitive case (from the eight-case system: *from*) to clarify the meaning.

God favored Israel but could not affect their individual ontological change before the resurrection of Jesus of Nazareth, as the prototypical pattern of how a νήπιος can become a υἱός was not yet available. Unfortunately, after his resurrection, many of the Israelites remained in their νήπιο-state because they had no faith in their Messiah. Faith in *the* Christ is essential for ontological transformation and full participation in divine pneumatic union. We will discuss this further in Rom 8.

Romans 9:8

> 8 τοῦτ' ἔστιν, οὐ τὰ τέκνα τῆς σαρκὸς ταῦτα τέκνα τοῦ θεοῦ ἀλλὰ τὰ τέκνα τῆς ἐπαγγελίας λογίζεται εἰς σπέρμα.
>
> 8 It is not the favored children [generated from] the flesh [are] these favored children [of] God[,] but the favored children [of] the promise[,] reckoned into (among) descendants. (ATT)

Please refer again to Figure 4 for further clarification. There is a group of Νήπιοι on the left of the process of υἱοθεσία and a group of Υἱοὶ on the right. Also, there are subgroups of Τέκνα on the left (who are in νήπιο state) and on the right (who are in *vio* state). Every τέκνον (favored child [generated from] the flesh) in the left category must be transformed to the right side to become the favored children [of (relating to)] the promise—those who *believe* in the promised Son. Israelites on the left of the equation are the descendants of Abraham;[8] thus, they are still τὰ τέκνα τῆς σαρκὸς, or the fa-

---

8. Cf. Cranfield: "The natural explanation would seem to be that, whereas the adoption referred to in v. 4 is one of the privileges of the Jewish nation as a whole (so that the possibility of a comprehensive use of 'children of God' or 'sons of God with regard to

vored children [generated from] the flesh. Those who are transformed into the favored children [of (relating to)] the promise are the favored children [of (belongs to)] God; they are οἱ υἱοί. During this in-between time, not every τέκνον has been saved, let alone the unchosen νήπιοι. Still, τὰ τέκνα τῆς σαρκὸς (the chosen people of Israelites on the left side of Figure 4) have a better standing (opportunity) than the unchosen νήπιοι.

The Israelites are a distinct people, set apart from other nations. The term "favored children" (τέκνα) indicates a discrimination of love, whereby a select few, or certain νήπιοι, are distinguished from the larger group. Abraham fathered Ishmael with Hagar, Isaac with Sarah, and six other sons with Keturah. However, only those of the lineage of Isaac and Jacob (Israel), who are referred to as the "children generated from the flesh (τὰ τέκνα τῆς σαρκὸς)," are of the select lineage that originated from Abraham. From the beginning, with the first humans, God initiated the process of transforming sarkic protological humans into pneumatic eschatological beings. This divine work represents a trajectory of pneumatic ontological change, culminating in a new phase of development with the advent of Jesus the Messiah, the Son. His coming marks a pivotal moment in this transformative process, offering humanity the opportunity to transcend their original state through faith and participation in Christ's redemptive work.

Although the path to salvation prepared by God may appear lengthy, it is certain to reach its fulfillment. At the second coming of the Messiah, a greater number of the τέκνα Israelites will be personally convinced and come to believe in their Messiah. This shift in belief arises from the fact that it is easier for the τέκνα to recognize the glorified Messiah during His second coming than it was during His first coming, when He appeared as the humble son of Joseph and Mary who died on the cross like a criminal.

Romans 8:14

14 ὅσοι γὰρ πνεύματι θεοῦ ἄγονται, οὗτοι υἱοὶ θεοῦ εἰσιν.

14 Indeed[,] as many as are led [by] spirit [from] God,[9] they are sons [of] God. (ATT)

---

all Jews is probably implied), the phrase 'children of God' is here used with a selective connotation, of those who are what we have termed the Israel within Israel.'... It was because of the promise... that he was Abraham's seed in the special, selective sense, the one who (rather than Ishmael) should be the father of those who should be recognized as Abraham's descendants." Cranfield, *Critical and Exegetical Commentary* 2:475–76.

9. πνεύματι, [by] the Spirit, or [in] the Spirit. It is also possible with the human spirit: "Indeed as many as are led [by] [the] spirit [from] God." Here I choose "from,"

In conjunction with v. 8:15, the following interpretation is more plausible: "Indeed as many as are led by the [human] spirit from God, they are [mature] sons of God." The text is concerned with the concept of a mature son-heir, whose sarkic or pneumatic faculties may exert influence. The soul of a person listens to the Spirit through the person's spirit that is involved in a spiritual relationship. A person's actions and character display the person's true mode of existence—sarkic or pneumatic. Jesus, as in Luke 6:43-45, teaches about phenomenological ontology when he explains that the quality of a tree can be discerned by its fruits. Similarly, the spiritual maturity of an individual can be identified by their alignment with the Spirit, which results in the constituting of their spiritual essence. In this state, they are symbolically referred to as "mature sons" (υἱοὶ) of God. This is the state of being in which humans can discover their authentic selves.

John R. W. Stott comments on the previous v. 8:13:

> Such is the solemn alternative of verse 13. "If you let the flesh live," Paul says, "allowing it to prosper and flourish, *the real you* will die. But if you kill the deeds of the body, mortifying them or putting them to death, *the real you* will live." And each of us has to *choose* between this way of life and this way of death. But Paul's point is that *our choice* is not really in doubt. "We are debtors"; under obligation *to make the right choice*. If the Spirit has given life to *our spirits*, then we *must* put the deeds of the body to death, so that we may continue to live the life which the Spirit has given us.[10]

He says there are two kinds of people: those in the flesh (the unregenerate) and those in the Spirit (the regenerate).[11] This is not a matter of membership in an unknown versus a divine family. The concept pertains to the true self, which is central to authentic existence. The verse concerns the concept of transformed beings and their new existence.

If we interpret v. 8:14 using the conventional English interpretation of the word "sons" rather than the original Greek text, "υἱοί," we run the risk of committing the same interpretive error as James M. Boice did in his comprehensive analysis of this verse. This would result in the assumption that there are two fathers and two families.[12] Boice cites John 8:31-47 as

---

that is the ablative case which denotes separation instead of the genitive case "of" which denotes possession.

10. Stott, *Men Made New*, 90. Emphasis added.

11. Stott, *Men Made New*, 91.

12. Boice, *Romans* 2:829-36. "Paul is talking about assurance of salvation and is arguing that one basis for this is our new relationship to God, which is a family

evidence to support his argument. However, Rom 8:14 refers to two distinct modes of existence among the two categories of God's children: those who possess a spiritual mode of existence (υἱοί), which have the possibility to be led by the Spirit of God, and those who solely have a sarkic mode of existence (νήπιοι), who can only be directed by fleshly will and do not have the possibility to be led by the Spirit of God. These two categories of children are members of God's family.

Let us see how Rom 8:14 relates to Gal 4:6 (AHT): "Because now you are [mature] sons (υἱοί), God, he sent forth the Spirit of the Son of Him into the hearts of ours, screaming *Abba*, to the Father." Those two verses are not in contrast. As to the Galatians, Paul explains, because now you have received a quickened spirit that makes you υἱοί, then you can partake in the fellowship of spirits with the Spirit. Therefore, God has sent forth the Spirit of the Son to have the said fellowship, and in that fellowship with Him, you can follow Him to call the Creator as he calls Him, "*Abba!*" Whereas to the Romans, Paul says "those who the Spirit leads" (or their human spirits lead) proved that they had been made υἱοί, or, in other words, had received a quickened spirit. Spirit can only lead υἱοί (pneumatic sons) through their human spirit;[13] νήπιοι can only follow their σάρξ (*sarx*), for they have a sleeping spirit which has no guidance from the Spirit. The following verses make this context more apparent.[14]

Romans 8:15

> 15 οὐ γὰρ ἐλάβετε πνεῦμα δουλείας πάλιν εἰς φόβον ἀλλ' ἐλάβετε πνεῦμα υἱοθεσίας ἐν ᾧ κράζομεν, Αββα ὁ πατήρ.
> 15 Indeed not [you][15] received [a] spirit [of] bondage again into fear[,] but [you][16] received [a] spirit [of] constitution of a son in (by) that we scream aloud, *Abba* the father.[17] (ATT)

relationship." He has a subheading, "Two Fathers, Two Families" that leads to adoption.

13. Lenski explains, "From what our own spirit does and is to do the apostle advances to God's Spirit who enables our spirit to do the Spirit's will; for when we kill the doings of the body with our spirit, God's Spirit is leading us." Lenski, *Romans*, 519–20.

14. Some of the dialogues here are similar to the one of Gal 4, but because this is an exegesis work, we have to do it again to see if there are similarities or differences in its context. There will be found some repeating ideas here.

15. Second person plural.

16. Second person plural.

17. "In that we scream aloud" or "by that we scream aloud."

When has the Spirit given life to *our spirits*? The NET Bible translates this verse, "For you did not receive the spirit of slavery leading again to fear, but you received the Spirit of adoption, by whom we cry, 'Abba, Father.'" Its Greek text has no article before πνεῦμα. This raises the question of how we might determine whether the two spirits in question—πνεῦμα δουλείας and πνεῦμα υἱοθεσίας—refer respectively to the human spirit (or another spirit) in the former case, and to the Holy Spirit in the latter. The YLT renders, "For ye did not receive a spirit of bondage again for fear, but ye did receive a spirit of adoption in which we cry, 'Abba—Father.'" This problem is a classic of translating Pauline πνεῦμα, a difficult one to determine whether it is a human spirit or God's Spirit.

Lenski explains why πνεῦμα here cannot be the Holy Spirit. Born of the Spirit is "spirit." It is inconsistent to contrast the Holy Spirit, the Third Person of the divine Trinity, with "the flesh" that remains in us or our body as the instrument or medium through which the power of sin operates. The dative πνεύματι (of v. 8:14, ed.) indicates means, and the rule cannot be violated that we never employ God's Spirit as a means. He engages us as a means, and we do not use Him as a means. It is our "spirit" by which we put to death the evil deeds that sin would like to produce by misusing our eyes, ears, hands, feet, etc., and all the desires in our old nature that require the body and are associated with bodily movements and functions in a sinful, tempting world.[18]

I submit that πνεῦμα δουλείας and πνεῦμα υἱοθεσίας refer to different states of the human spirit. God must vivify the human spirit (v. 8:15) and replace the elect's old body (v. 8:23) to constitute a complete spiritual human being for a new existence. Lenski explains, "The deduction is also unwarranted that 'adoption' is not to be understood as resting on a declaration of God's will concerning us but is an operation of God *in us* which *alters us inwardly*."[19] This operation is called υἱοθεσία. The purpose is to transform a sarkic being (νήπιος) into a pneumatic being (υἱός), like *the* Christ (ὁ Υἱός). This is the essentialist philosophy aspect of Christian theology.

This verse is similar in structure and parallel in meaning to 2 Tim 1:7, "For God did not give us *a spirit*[20] of fear but of power and love and self-control." Having the spirit of power, love, and self-control leads a person to an authentic existence. The Holy Spirit can live within us only when we have received a vivified spirit. Thus, it is not about receiving the Holy Spirit. The Holy Spirit is the one who acts here. The Holy Spirit does not give himself

---

18. Lenski, *Romans*, 518–19.
19. Lenski, *Romans*, 522. Emphasis added.
20. See Technical Note J. *NET Bible*, 2276.

to us but vivifies (enlivens, ignites) our spirit. Romans 8:15 explains that a believer receives a quickened spirit (the regenerated spirit) that can cause one to become a mature son (υἱός).²¹ When one gets a spirit that makes him a mature son (υἱός), it theologically (symbolically) means one begins to become a new pneumatic being in this present time (τοῦ νῦν καιροῦ, temporality).

Even though my opinion differs from Ernst Käsemann's in terms of the spirit/ Spirit, it is in line with his idea of the κατά formulation. He inscribes, "'In the flesh' and 'in the Spirit' now replace the κατά formulations. . . . In the end-time, it will be revealed that the powers which rule the world fight for each person to make him their representative on earth."²² Let us see what Macquarrie says from the perspective of philosophical theology (existentialist theology) on how lives κατὰ σάρκα are associated with one who loses himself in the world.

> Man is always in the world, and yet he is quite distinct from it in his way of being. But in his intimate concern with the world, claims Heidegger, "*Dasein* can lose himself to the being that meets him in the world, and be taken over by it." Because he has a relation to himself, man can become an object to himself, and can understand himself as one object among the other objects in his world. This is what is meant by an inauthentic existence—man becomes merged in the world. He exists authentically when, instead of being enslaved to the world, he is free for his world, in Heidegger's phrase. In that case he resolves to be himself in the face of a world the being of which is alien to his own being. These fundamental possibilities of authenticity and inauthenticity may be expressed in another way by saying that man can either gain himself or lose himself.²³

Humans must be free from this fleshly, temporal world. In one's protological state of being as an underdeveloped (unconstituted) being, one can only live κατὰ σάρκα. To be authentic in this situation, one can only choose to live from the realm of σάρκα, the unconsummated (unspiritualized) human nature. It is the kind of natural authenticity living in temporality. In

---

21. Brown renders, "The word translated 'adoption' (υἱοθεσία) is, in signification, quite equivalent to sonship. 'The spirit of adoption' is the spirit with which dutiful children regard their father, and the employments he is pleased to assign to them—a spirit of love and confidence, producing tranquillity of mind, and cheerful obedience and submission." Brown, *Analytical Exposition*, 214.

22. Käsemann, *Commentary on Romans*, 219–20.

23. Macquarrie, *Existentialist Theology*, 39.

their picture, there is no God nor afterlife; therefore, all will vanish. Humans themselves should create their own existence.[24]

I observe that through the explanation of Rom 8:15, God introduces a further dimension (another level) of authentic existence that transcends the former self, a transformation made possible through God's sub-act of υἱοθεσία. As individuals are elevated, they acquire new facticity, potentiality, and possibility, thereby entering into a fundamentally new mode of existence. The newly elevated beings can live either κατὰ πνεῦμα, κατὰ σάρκα, or the combination of the two, in their being-in-the-world;[25] see vv. 8:8 and 9. That is why, as Christians, we are still capable of sinning and must continually learn to choose what is right.

The degree of the spiritual authenticity of the regenerated beings, though they are still *in temporality*, is designed by God to differ from their old, unregenerated being. God designed it because humans cannot make themselves new beings. This concept of authenticity is fundamentally distinct from the understanding found in atheistic existentialism. Only after one becomes a new being can one choose to live κατὰ πνεῦμα. However, as human beings, not God, we can only know someone's essence (nature) through his existence. A person who can live κατὰ πνεῦμα is a υἱός who has the possibility to live beyond this temporal reality, too. God works on the human essence through God's sub-act of υἱοθεσία and leads the new beings to produce a certain attitude (existence).

The contrast between life κατὰ σάρκα and life κατὰ πνεῦμα is introduced in Rom 8:1–9, then v. 8:10 says, "Yet *your spirit* is alive," and v. 8:11 says "will also give life to *your mortal bodies* through his Spirit, who lives in you." Those arguments lead to vv. 8:15 and 8:23, which talk about the two steps of υἱοθεσία that an elect child of God must undergo. The whole context is about the gradual formation (constitution) of a human being to become a consummated human being. The process commenced by the quickening

24. For Sartre, "what is meant here by saying that existence precedes essence? It means that, first of all, man exists, turns up, appears on the scene, and, only afterwards, defines himself. If man, as the existentialist conceives him, is indefinable, it is because at first he is nothing. Only afterward will he be something, and he himself will have made what he will be. Thus, there is no human nature, since there is no God to conceive it. Not only is man what he conceives himself to be, but he is also only what he wills himself to be after this thrust toward existence." Sartre, *Existentialism*, 18.

25. Macquarrie explains, "Bultmann suggests, because he had become so acutely aware of the split within the self in a sinful existence that his thought assumes a dualistic form—or at least appears to come very close to it. When the body has fallen completely into sin it becomes 'the body of death' from which man must be rescued—but this means deliverance from the σάρξ, the evil possibilities of somatic existence, and not from the body as such, the possibilities of which maybe either good or bad." Macquarrie, *Existentialist Theology*, 42.

of one's spirit (8:10 and 15), then will be finalized by the replacing of one's mortal body (8:11 and 23)—which at the consummation makes him free from the mortal flesh;[26] consequently, the individual is exempt from the influence of the flesh, which is prone to sin and deterioration (temporality).

These discrete stages of the *human constitution* (the making of everlasting humans in stages) are the key message of these Epistles to the Romans and the Galatians. It is the teaching that Paul reminded Timothy of and also discussed with the Corinthians. A νήπιος is a living soul.[27] The good news is that a human being will be reformed because their current initial created state of being is unsuitable for everlasting communion with God. God wants humans to exist everlastingly with him to share love. That is God's purpose in creating humankind in God's image. The first υἱοθεσία amends a decaying earthly human being in their life in τοῦ νῦν καιροῦ so that they can foretaste the communion with the Spirit, which is the first fruit only. It leads to the second υἱοθεσία that will make them consummated pneumatic beings to everlastingly enter the eternal pneumatic reality, which will bring even more new possibilities.

Paul borrows the idea from Diodorus Siculus, who describes the mythical story of Heracles and Hera. According to this story, Hera "rebirthed" Heracles by mimicking the natural birth process.[28] Thus, the heart of this mythical story is that υἱοθεσία implies a rebirth from a god. Siculus did not write the term "adoption" but "υἱοθεσίαν." Υἱοθεσία is not adoption that

---

26. Stott renders, "But it is also that 'the flesh,' our fallen sinful nature, dwells in our mortal bodies, 'sin which dwells within me' (7:17, 20)." Stott, *Men Made New*, 96.

27. 2 Tim 1:7 ESV, "For God gave us *a spirit* not of fear but of power and love and self-control." Emphasis added. 1 Cor 15:45–49 ESV, "Thus it is written, 'The first man Adam became a living being' [Gk, a living soul]'; the last Adam became a life-giving spirit. But it is not the spiritual that is first but *the natural, and then the spiritual*. The first man was from the earth, a man of dust; the second man is from heaven. As was the man of dust, so also are those who are of the dust, and as is the man of heaven, so also are those who are of heaven. Just as we have borne the image of the man of dust, we shall also bear the image of the man of heaven." Emphasis added. Note the phrase "life-giving spirits" for the sons, and the steps of creation, "natural, then spiritual" human beings. Adam, a νήπιος, was not a spiritual son of God.

28. W. V. Martitz writes, "In Greek there are *no* instances of adoption in the transf. sense (Wenger-Oepke). Even when the ruler cult made its way into the Gk. world (→ 336, 26 ff.) the divinity of the ruler was viewed in terms of *descent rather than adoption*. For this reason the use of adoption terminology in a myth in Diod. S., 4, 39, 2 is all the more noteworthy. After the deifying (ἀποθέωσις) of Heracles Zeus persuaded his spouse Hera to adopt him (υἱοποιήσασθαι); to this end Hera took him to her body and let him slip down to earth under her robes. She imitated the process of natural birth (μιμουμένη τὴν ἀληθινὴν γένεσιν). The pt. of this remarkable rite was to confer legitimacy on the son of Zeus (→ 336, 13 ff.), this being regarded as necessary in addition to apotheosis." *TDNT* 8:398. Emphasis added.

transfers a person from one family to another, but transforms (re-births) the person from an old to a new being. It reminds us of the apostle John's concept of γεννηθῇ ἄνωθεν (be born from above, John 3:3).

I offer a nuanced perspective on the transformative work of the Lord Jesus the Christ. While Michael Wolter emphasizes that Christians are *transferred* into a new state of being through Jesus' salvific death,[29] I argue that it is the resurrection of Jesus that marks the pivotal ontological *transformation*. Specifically, this resurrection elevates Jesus' human *nepio*-ship (childlike state) to *huio*-ship (mature sonship), setting a model for the transformation of all created children of God. Furthermore, I highlight that the person of Jesus Christ unites believers into the fellowship of the Spirit, creating an everlasting union that preserves them from decay. This transformation and unity reflect the collaborative work of the Holy Trinity in shaping human identity and destiny.

This elevation can also be seen as freedom from the tribal laws of the Jews and gentiles to enter a *spiritual* brotherhood of humans in Christ through spiritual fellowship (the fellowship of the pneumatic υἱοί). The believers' father is not Abraham but the Universal Creator, the Godhead. Human salvation is not based on blood (tribal, human family), or earthly Christian family, but on the spiritual fellowship with the Son. Salvation is subject to the ontological change. Adoption has no such significance.

I highlight that,[30] according to BDAG, "*Abba*" is an Aramaic term used in prayer and the family context, and the Greek-speaking Christians adopted that as a liturgical expression.[31] Some scholars contend that "*pater*" is the Greek equivalent of "*Abba.*"[32] However, Moisés Silva points out that "*Abba*" was a common word for *adult* children to address their fathers and even a respectful title for scholars, akin to the "*rabbi.*"[33] Silva further argues

---

29. Wolter renders, "Paul expresses the diachronic boundary either by the temporal antithesis 'no longer-but' as in 2 Corinthians 5:15, 16, 17 ('the old has passed away, see things are new') and Galatians 2:20; 4:5/7, or he construes the temporal succession of *two different states* of affairs with the concept that the Christians were transferred *from one to the other state* by Jesus' salvific death: from one relationship of possession to the other (1 Cor. 6:18–29, 7:22–23); redeemed from the 'curse' of the law or enslavement through the law (Gal. 3:13; 4:5/7) and transferred to the status of 'adoption as children' (Gal. 4:5: υἱοθεσία); 'set free' from this world (Gal. 1:4); from sin to righteousness (Rom. 3:21–26; 8.3–4; 2 Cor. 5:21)." Wolter, *Paul*, 111–12. Emphasis and brackets added.

30. Tan, "Call of 'Abba.'"

31. BDAG, 1.

32. Cf. Lenski: "The appositional nominative *ho Pater* is quite regular after the vocative *Abba*; it is the doubling of the Aramaic and the Greek terms for Father that is so exceptional." Lenski, *Romans*, 524.

33. *NIDNTTE* 1:85. Emphasis added.

that "*Abba*" does not have a childish connotation. Robert Hamerton-Kelly supports this idea.[34] This argument implies that νήπιοι might have used different words to refer to their fathers (gods). The [mature] Son of God (ὁ Υἱός τοῦ Θεοῦ) employed this term to call God. Believers follow Jesus' example and call God "*Abba*," for they share a similar status with him, as υἱοί.

In Greek usage, "*pater*" referred to "the supreme deity, who is responsible for the origin and care of all that exists, Father, Parent."[35] This concept aligns with the portrayal of God in Gen 1. Therefore, "*Abba*" (the term used exclusively by adults) and "*ho pater*" (a term designating the Creator) are not synonymous. This distinction suggests that "*ho pater*" is not a translation or equivalent of "*Abba*." I propose that the phrase "*Abba*, [to] *ho pater*" may plausibly include the proposition "to," emphasizing that Christians—as mature children—invoke the Universal Creator as *Abba*.

Romans 8:15 centers on the creation of a pneumatic-Christic human being, rather than addressing the concept of legal adoption. This verse reflects the transformative work of the Spirit in shaping individuals into beings aligned with Christ's pneumatic nature, highlighting the spiritual elevation inherent in this process. This interpretation challenges traditional readings that associate the verse primarily with the idea of adoption into God's family. It can be translated and amplified as follows: "Indeed not [you] received [a] spirit [of] bondage again into fear[,] but [you] received [a] spirit [of] constitution of a [mature] son like (ὁ Υἱός) in (by) that we scream aloud, *Abba*, [to] *ho Pater* (the Creator, the Father of all beings)."

The designation "[mature]" in the phrase "constitution of a [mature] son" is intentionally employed to underscore its contrast with the "adoption of a son." In this context, "mature" refers to a pneumatic mode of existence, associated with the human spirit and the Spirit, in contrast to sarkic, which denotes a fleshly or carnal state rooted in materiality and protological human nature. This distinction describes the possible nature of humans as the human Christ is described as having both a sarkic (fleshly) and a pneumatic (spiritual) aspect: he is "having been put to death in [the] flesh, having been made alive however in [the] spirit" (1 Pet 3:18, cf. 1 Cor 15; Rom 1:3-4).

---

34. Cf. Hamerton-Kelly: "The Lord's Prayer reveals God the Father to be the one who moves history towards true humanity. He gives us a foretaste of that humanity in the experience of forgiveness and reconciliation, and in the sustenance that comes in times of temptation. Most of all, however, the prayer reveals Jesus to be the human face of God, for 'Abba' is an address of deepest intimacy which only the son could use. In giving his disciples this prayer Jesus admitted them to the privilege of divine sonship and daughter-hood, the right to call God 'Abba' (Cf. Rom. 8.15–16), and thereby bestowed on them the true humanity of the Kingdom of God." Hamerton-Kelly, *God the Father*, 77.

35. BDAG, 787.

The contrast thus highlights a theological progression from a state defined by the flesh (sarkic) to one constituted by the spirit (pneumatic), reflecting early Christian understandings of ontological transformation and mature sonship in relation to Christ's resurrection and the believer's participation in the divine life.

Notice in my translation that the word υἱοθεσία, so far, has two diverse readings. Unlike the case of the τέκνα Israelites that we discussed earlier, in this verse, the individual νήπιος is transformed into a υἱός. From here, we can see that biblical υἱοθεσία has equivocal meanings that differ from the univocal *adoptio* or *toga virilis*.

This translation allows us to interpret the following verse more coherently, as it introduces the concept of the human spirit in the context of the passage, rather than having "the spirit of ours" appear abruptly in v. 8:16, as in other translations.

Romans 8:16

> 16 αὐτὸ τὸ πνεῦμα συμμαρτυρεῖ τῷ πνεύματι ἡμῶν ὅτι ἐσμὲν τέκνα θεοῦ.
>
> 16 The Spirit himself [he] testifies together (bears witness to our spirits) in support of the spirit [of] ours that we are favored children [of] God. (ATT)

After human beings receive a spirit of the constitution of a [mature] son (v. 8:15), the divine Spirit proceeds to make fellowship with them. It works on their will and emotions to surrender their whole life to the [mature] Son of Man and believe in him, his birth, life, deeds, death, and resurrection. According to Rudolf Bultmann, they

> receive the gift of "God's righteousness," and in which the divine deed of salvation accomplishes itself with [them]. . . . The acceptance of the message in faith takes the form of an act of obedience . . . the genuine obedience which God's Law had indeed demanded, but which had been refused by the Jews by their misuse of it to establish "their own righteousness," using it as a means for "boasting."[36]

He adds, "[Faith] is not . . . salvation itself. Rather—as genuine obedience—it is the condition for receiving salvation."[37] This raises the question:

---

36. Bultmann, *Theology of the New Testament* 1:314–15.
37. Bultmann, *Theology of the New Testament* 1:316.

What constitutes the means by which this condition is attained? Within this framework, the elect is first endowed with a resurrected spirit (v. 8:15). Following this initial impartation, she receives the Spirit's message, which catalyzes the emergence and growth of her faith in the person and the redemptive work of Christ. Cf. Phil 1:29; Eph 2:8–9.

Discussions on "quickened human spirits" inherently involve the divine Spirit (the unitive Being). The Spirit himself[38] testifies together with,[39] even bears witness to, our spirits that *we* are favored children of God.[40] This way, we have two witnesses.[41] Then the inaugurated sons, led by the Spirit, come to the Father through prayer as they imitate the Lord Jesus, calling God "*Abba!*"[42] Each of these human spirits is surprised with the new consciousness that they are τέκνα of God, but more than the nation τέκνα Israelites, for they have become υἱοί in ὁ Υἱός, *the* Christ, the Anointed One. A believer's conviction comes after this *spiritual* revelatory experience.

At that point, a υἱός has faith generated from his new spiritual state of being.[43] Think of when Peter confessed to the Lord Jesus and the Lord answered, "For flesh and blood has not revealed this to you, but my Father who is in heaven" (Matt 16:17). Macquarrie states:

> This is a revelatory experience . . . it is a way of knowing in which, so to speak, that which is known seizes hold of us and makes itself known to us, or, in the language that Heidegger uses in connection with primordial thinking, this is the occurrence of Being in us. It is true that revelation involves God in all his aspects, primordial, expressive, and unitive, but our apprehension of the revelation we rightly associate in a special way with

---

38. *Himself*, after Rogers Jr. and Rogers III, *New Linguistic and Exegetical Key*, 330. Here, the use of "himself" serves to make the point explicit.

39. συμμαρτυρέω, "witness together." Kubo, *Reader's Greek-English Lexicon*, 139.

40. "Beareth witness to our spirits." Brown, *Analytical Exposition*, 216.

41. For Shedd, "it is as if, when the believer says: 'I am a child of God,' then the Holy Spirit made answer, 'Thou art indeed a child.'" Shedd, *Critical and Doctrinal Commentary*, 248. He refers to John 8:17–18, "It is written in your law that the testimony of two men is true. I testify about myself and the Father who sent me testifies about me." This is possible too.

42. Cf. Mounce: "Not only does the Spirit guide the believer, but he initiates the action as well." Mounce, *Romans*, 27:182.

43. Cf. López: "As noted, the notion that faith must be given by God before a person is regenerated poses several theological problems. Instead, the Scriptures present the view that people can exercise faith to receive God's offer of salvation. In His convicting work the Holy Spirit draws sinners to Himself and waits for their simple response of faith. God then imparts eternal life to them the moment they believe. As Paul and Silas told the Philippian jailer,—Believe on the Lord Jesus Christ, and you will be saved (Acts 16:31)." López, "Is Faith a Gift," 276.

the work of the Holy Spirit (unitive being). . . . The Holy Spirit then is God's coming to man in an inward way to enlighten and strengthen him; it is the awakening in man of the realization of his kinship with Being, an awakening brought about by Being itself that is already immanent in man.[44]

For believers are now son-heirs (υἱοί) through the fellowship with the Christ; it makes them have faith[45] in the Christ (Christ-faith) and want to submit and trust their lives to Him and stay in Him[46] to grow in faith in Him when facing life's problems—as "*abide* in Me, and I in you."[47] Karl Barth explains,

> Knowledge of God is a knowledge completely effected and determined from the side of its object, from the side of God. But for that very reason it is genuine knowledge; for that very reason it is in the deepest sense free knowledge. Of course it remains a relative knowledge, a knowledge imprisoned within the limits of the creaturely. Of course it is especially true here that we are

---

44. Macquarrie, *Principles*, 332–33.

45. Wolter writes, "Is faith a 'free act of obedience' (and indeed 'free' in the sense that it could also be refused), a 'decision' that therefore is also a 'condition for receiving salvation? (Bultmann, *Theology*, 316). Or does it have to do, in this way of seeing things, with 'a synergistic understanding of faith' . . . that makes faith a 'human achievement' and a 'human work,' although it can always be only a 'gift' that 'cannot be given to oneself'? . . . Does faith therefore 'have to be understood in strict exclusivity as *creatura verbi* . . . or does 'the proclamation merely' open 'the possibility of faith?' . . . Can the hearers of Paul's proclamation accept or reject the gospel 'in a free decision of the will' . . . or did Paul reply to the question about the reasons for the acceptance and rejection of the gospel in a 'predestinarian' way?" Wolter, *Paul*, 78.

46. Wolter explains, "In Galatians 5:6, with the expression 'in Christ,' Paul describes the new reality of God according to 6:15 as a symbolic universe that is differentiated from other symbolic universes in that it is faith that determines the true identity of a person. To put it another way, the essence of 'Christ-faith' consists in the fact that it interprets the symbolic universe that exists 'in Christ' as God's 'new creation.' According to Paul's understanding, the assurance of faith that God has thereby revealed salvation in Jesus Christ also implies the certainty that God has thus created a new reality. This new reality still stands over against the existing reality of the 'flesh' and of the 'world,' and in it those who believe receive a new identity. This new identity has nothing to do with the identities that were ascribed to them outside of the scope of reality according to God." Wolter, *Paul*, 86–87.

47. We read from John 15:4 (NASB), "Abide in Me, as I in you. As the branch cannot bear fruit of itself unless it abides in the vine, so neither can you unless you abide in Me." Believers possess new life only insofar as they are in Christ. To expand Ludwig Feuerbach's dictum, "Where there is no 'thou' there is no 'I,'" the believer's new existence is essentially communal in Christ: without him as the thou (the object of faith), there can be no "I" as a believer. See Feuerbach, *Essence of Christianity*, 92.

carrying heavenly treasures in earthen vessels. Our concepts are not adequate to grasp this treasure.[48]

By creating such a situation—granting a τέκνα a new state of being, which awakens in him a new awareness as a υἱός in a new life[49]—he would be unable to say "No!" even if he had the freedom to do so. It is how God reveals himself to his τέκνα.

Denney notices, "τέκνα θεοῦ, not υἱοί, is used with strict propriety here, as it is the reality of the filial nature, not the legitimacy of the filial position, which is being proved."[50] They are addressed as the *beloved* children. The Christian understanding of God is not based on one's legal status as an adopted son, but rather on the spiritual union with the divine. Once a believer has entered into this union, they will remain in that fellowship indefinitely. This is the indubitable certainty of Christian salvation. Those who are God's υἱοί are also God's τέκνα. However, not all who are God's τέκνα are necessarily God's υἱοί already. This is because there are instances where the process of υἱοθεσία has not yet occurred to them. In regard to the various types of τέκνα, one may find pertinent information in our discussion of Rom 9:8.

Bruce Demarest posits that the initial three benefits of the *ordo salutis* in covenant Reformed theology are calling, regeneration, and faith.[51] Notwithstanding my divergence from Demarest's definitions, my interpretation of the order is consistent with the first three benefits. In the initial stage, God selects and calls a τέκνον from the group of νήπιοι, imparting upon him a quickened spirit that has been regenerated from his slept spirit. This τέκνον, who has been designated a υἱός, surrenders himself completely and has faith that the person of Jesus Christ can save him. An individual's adherence to Christ is subsequent to their ordination as a υἱός. Human salvation is contingent upon God's sub-act of υἱοθεσία, which cultivates Christ-faith as a consequence of the new spiritual state of being.

---

48. Barth, *Dogmatics in Outline*, 24.

49. Fee renders, "Just as the Son himself was sent into the world to effect redemption, so also the Spirit of the Son has been sent into the hearts of believers to effect the experienced realization of that redemption." Fee, *Pauline Christology*, 549.

50. Denney, *Expositor's Greek Testament* 2:648.

51. Demarest, *Cross and Salvation*, 38–39.

Romans 8:17

> 17 εἰ δὲ τέκνα, καὶ κληρονόμοι· κληρονόμοι μὲν θεοῦ, συγκληρονόμοι δὲ Χριστοῦ, εἴπερ συμπάσχομεν ἵνα καὶ συνδοξασθῶμεν.
>
> 17 Subsequently if favored children[,] then heirs—truly heirs [of] God, consequently joint heirs [of] Christ—if indeed [we] suffer together with [Christ][,] so that also [we] [might] [be] glorified together with [Christ]. (ATT)

Becoming υἱοί is not the destiny of all νήπιοι, but only of those who are τέκνα. The salvation of the τέκνα depends on their state of being as mature sons (υἱοί), and because they are adults, they are also heirs. Every being in this creation is suffering (the subhuman creations, in their sufferings, are also groaning), but the particular sufferings as the coheir with Christ are the effects of being υἱοί[52] (being in the same state of being with the Messiah).

What is the inheritance? A new possible existence that transcends the old natural facticity has been given to Christians. Godhead's internal pneumatic fellowship (union) has been prolonged (protracted) to these new beings, and more than that, another status as coheir with the Heir.[53] Shedd explained,

> Heirship follows sonship. θεοῦ] God is regarded not as the deceased testator, but the living dispenser of his wealth. Compare Luke xv.12. . . . Christ being their elder brother (verse 29), they have a share in the kingdom of God with him. According to the

---

52. Brown renders, "It seems to be this: that we shall be heirs of God, and joint-heirs with Christ Jesus, if we so suffer with Christ Jesus as to be ultimately glorified together with Him. But, from the first clause of the verse, it is obvious that the apostle suspends the security of our heirship, or fixed relation, not on contingent circumstances—not on our suffering in a particular temper or cause, but on our being sons." Brown, *Analytical Exposition*, 221.

53. Moore compares, "The advantages and benefits of earthly life are bound up in mediocrity. But genuine religion has an inverse relationship to the finite. Its aim is to raise human beings up so as to transcend what is earthly. It is a matter of either/or. Either prime quality, or no quality at all; either with all your heart, all your mind, and all your strength, or not at all. Either all of God and all of you, or nothing at all! We clever humans, however, prefer to treat faith as if it were something finite, as if it were something for the betterment and enjoyment of temporal life. It is supposed to bring us meaning and fulfillment, happiness and direction. This kind of religion is nothing but a deception. If you were honest and if you would look at it more closely, you would see that this really is contempt for religion, a dangerous and culpable irreligion. True faith insists on being an either/or. To treat it as if it were like drink and food is fundamentally to scorn it. But this is precisely the way of mediocrity." Moore, *Provocations*, 18.

Roman law, the inheritance of the first-born is no greater than that of the other children; according to the Hebrew law, it was double.[54]

The preexistent Son is infinite. I concur with Wolfhart Pannenberg's assertion that the "inheritance" is the everlasting new life with the [human] [consummated] Son.[55] It is inaccurate to equate the term "everlasting" with "eternal." Human everlasting existence is contingent upon the divine Son's eternal existence. It is possible that Raimundo Panikkar's term "tempiternal" may be a more appropriate description.[56] Christ provides the structure through which the love of the Father can be delivered to the created sons in a manner that is not temporal, as was the case with Adam. Those who believe are referred to as "brothers" of Christ due to their shared relationship with the Father, which is symbolized by the *Abba* call. The notion of sharing the creation is not applicable in this context, as believers are still creatures who are owned by the Creator.

The future everlasting inheritance contrasts with the temporal suffering in the flesh, and when the body is replaced with a *pneumatic* one, the issue of the flesh should be gone. First Peter 3:13—4:11 is about the suffering of believers; v. 4:1 says, "Christ suffered in the flesh." What is the suffering of the Christ? He bears the cause of the sin by becoming a full human to enter the sin-filled world full of craving. Like a King thrown into an unknown desert, He was alone.

His sufferings started when He emptied Himself (to make void), followed by assuming human life in the flesh; the cross ended it. It does not underrate the cross, but to say that Christ's passion is too enormous, and the cross is only a part of it. When the eternal, infinite Creator enters the

---

54. Shedd, *Critical and Doctrinal Commentary*, 249.

55. Pannenberg renders, "Faith links believers to Jesus Christ as they rely on him and on the promise of salvation that is given in his message and history. But fellowship with Jesus Christ includes participation in his relation as Son to the Father. This is the 'divine sonship' that grants believers assurance of the future 'inheritance,' the new life manifested already in Jesus Christ." Pannenberg, *Systematic Theology* 3:211. Brackets added.

56. According to Panikkar, "Time seems to be intrinsic to Becoming and eternity to Being. If Being and Becoming belong together in an *advaitic* relationship, this entails that time and eternity are the two faces, as it were, of what I call *tempiternity*.... From the side of the creature, creation is contemporal and coextensive with the creator because time and space are created in the very act of creation. Or rather time and space are not created, they are not creatures; rather it is the creatures that are temporal and spatial. From the side of God, so to speak, creation is coeternal, continuous with (*continere*, "hang together") and contiguous to (*con-tingere*, "contact on all sides") God. This would be another way to introduce the notion of *tempiternity*." Panikkar, *Rhythm of Being*, 98, 286. Emphasis original.

temporality of finite created existence, how many of Him should be emptied during His human life? It is the real suffering, not only a moment on the cross, but by becoming a fully created existence that experiences human anxiety.[57] He comes from the closed fellowship of the triune God into an *I-It* relationship with the people of sin whom He loves. With eyes and hearts full of hate, these people treated Him as an object to be killed—the *It* of the primary word *I-It*. Christ is the enemy, the unwanted object of the craved, corrupted world. He experiences the hate of those He loves. Absurdly, the purpose of His coming is to make them the *Thou* of the *I-Thou*.[58] That is the price He pays because sin has entered the creation. No other human being endures it, only the Son of Man. He dies unnaturally, not because of disease or old age, but because He is killed, like many of His brothers, on the cross, like thousands of other unwanted human beings. So, the real passion of the Lord Jesus is His finite existence in this temporal world. God-in-the-world suffers *more* than human-in-the-world.

The suffering that Christ endured on the cross forms an integral part of the broader experience of suffering that marked His life in the world. His passion and crucifixion are not isolated events but are deeply connected to His entire earthly journey, wherein He bore both physical and spiritual anguish for the sake of humanity. The cross is the culmination of Christ's solidarity with human suffering throughout His life.

Believers suffer together with Him as the *It* of the *I-It*. There are manipulations addressed to *It*. *It* becomes an object of others or themselves by living in the flesh. Those in their personal life who have experienced life as "*It*" probably know the suffering. R. H. Mounce explains,

> Obviously we do not share the redemptive suffering of Christ, but we do share the consequences in terms of opposition from the world he came to save (cf. Phil. 3:10; 1 Pet. 4:13). As a member of the same family we share in the trials of life as well as the benefits.[59]

We share only a small part of Jesus' existence as a new being in the old *aeon*, and we share in the trials of life. The old beings are facing different

---

57. Since, then, the Son knows the problem of his created νήπιοι, he knows their struggles. That's why the Spirit cries. That's why he wants to bring as many as people given to him by the Father.

58. The primary word *I-Thou* is about relationship. Herberg explains, "Primary words do not signify things, but they intimate relations. Primary words do not describe something that might exist independently of them, but being spoken they bring about existence." Herberg, *Writings of Martin Buber*, 43.

59. Mounce, *Romans*, 183.

trials in their life of κατὰ σάρκα. During this time, both old and new beings are distressed.

Romans 8:18

18 Λογίζομαι γὰρ ὅτι οὐκ ἄξια τὰ παθήματα τοῦ νῦν καιροῦ πρὸς τὴν μέλλουσαν δόξαν ἀποκαλυφθῆναι εἰς ἡμᾶς.

18 Indeed [I] [now] reckon (reason, conclude) that not comparable the undergoing sufferings [of] the present time towards the glory (splendor) [that] [is] about to [be] revealed into us. (ATT)

The anxiety and hope of human beings and subhuman creation are discussed in this passage. "Us" refers to the believers, who are expected to live κατὰ πνεῦμα, seeking perfection while in their flesh, training themselves in choosing what is right. Those believers had been released from the anxiety of a perishable life (ontological finitude, being-unto-death) when they had faith. Christians are being transformed, but the world is still the same. The world will be changed only after the Christians are fully transformed. At this moment, Christians entered another anxiety as the semi-mature sons of God in the current unperfected world, awaiting the splendor of everlasting life. Paul can sense the anxiety of the church members as he experiences it, and he wants to give them hope. Paul uses γὰρ (indeed) here as a conjunction of his argument in v. 8:17 regarding the sufferings.

Still, when it talks about glorification alongside Christ, it goes up to v. 8:14, especially v. 8:15, where the two spirits are compared. It follows with the usage of two word pairs: "λογίζομαι . . . ὅτι" ([I] [now] reckon (reason, conclude) that). "λογίζομαι" is a financial term, that is, when someone makes a calculation, compares profit and loss carefully, and then arrives at a definite and confident conclusion. It is a mature calculation based on his experience when he met the Messiah, not speculations, and is carried out by himself instead of following other people's opinions. Paul addresses his belief, reflected in the indicative mood of λογίζομαι, "the mood of assertion, or *presentation* of certainty."[60] Cranfield states that it is a firm conviction reached by rational thought based on the gospel.[61] What is the gospel that he refers to? It should be v. 8:15, "[you] received [a] spirit [of] constitution of a [mature] son[,]."

Dunn advises translating the pair "λογίζομαι . . . ὅτι" as

60. Wallace, *Greek Grammar*, 448. Emphasis original.
61. Cranfield, *Critical and Exegetical Commentary* 1:408.

"I am firmly of the opinion that," "It is my settled conviction that." It should be noted that the conviction is not merely the product of "rational thought on the basis of the gospel" (Cranfield), but even more prominently here of the experience of the Spirit (cf. 5:3–5; 8:23).[62]

What does it mean by "the experience of the Spirit?" It is the work of the Spirit that quickens a believer's human spirit. If the divine Spirit enters the human spirit, it does not remain there but drives the human spirit out of itself. It is still the human spirit; it is what it is, but it also goes out of itself under the influence of the divine Spirit.[63] This experience makes believers realize what they are, their potential in everlasting life, and their ability to enter into the pneumatic fellowship with the loving Father. From old human beings, they are becoming exalted human beings.

Within the Christian journey, salvation is understood as a process that has already begun through faith in Jesus Christ but awaits its ultimate fulfillment. During this period—between the initial experience of salvation (justification) and its final consummation (glorification)—believers continue to endure suffering and hardship as part of their earthly existence. This ongoing experience reflects the "already-but-not-yet" nature of Christian salvation: while deliverance from sin has commenced, its complete realization remains in the future. It aligns with Bultmann, who argues that "the Cross of Christ is an ever-present reality."[64] Being an unfinished υἱοὶ does

62. Dunn, *Romans 1–8*, 468.

63. How can a human spirit be quickened? Tillich explains this: "The question of the relation between Spirit and spirit is usually answered by the metaphorical statement that the Divine Spirit dwells and works in the human spirit. . . . If the Divine Spirit breaks into the human spirit, this does not mean that it rests there, but it drives the human spirit out of itself. . . . It is still the human spirit; it remains what it is, but at the same time, it goes out of itself under the impact of the Divine Spirit. 'Ecstasy' is the classical term for this state of being grasped by the Spiritual Presence." Tillich, *Systematic Theology* 3:111–2.

64. Bultmann explains, "The cross becomes a present reality first of all in the sacraments. In baptism men and women are baptized into Christ's death (Rom. 6:3) and crucified with him (Rom. 6:6). At every celebration of the Lord's Supper the death of Christ is proclaimed (1 Cor. 11.26). The communicants thereby partake of his crucified body and his blood outpoured (1 Cor. 10:16). Again, the cross of Christ is an ever-present reality in the everyday life of the Christians. "They that are of Christ Jesus have crucified the flesh with the passions and the lusts thereof" (Gal. 5:24). That is why St. Paul can speak of "the cross of our Lord Jesus Christ, through which the world hath been crucified unto me, and I unto the world" (Gal. 6:14). That is why he seeks to know "the fellowship of his sufferings," as one who is "conformed to his death" (Phil. 3:10). The crucifying of the affections and lusts includes the overcoming of our natural dread of suffering and the perfection of our detachment from the world. Hence the willing acceptance of sufferings in which death is already at work in man means: "always bearing

not stop our suffering. Dunn informs that οὐκ ἄξια . . . πρὸς "would be familiar to Greek speakers—'not of like value, not worth as much as'—though Paul is probably as much or more influenced by Semitic usage."[65] Käsemann supports it by saying that ἄξια . . . πρὸς "links up with rabbinic school language; it occurs especially in discussions of the problem of the sufferings of the pious. ἄξιος means 'of equal weight,' then 'of value,' and in acclamation, 'worthy.' πρός means 'with regard to.'"[66] I render this phrase "not comparable . . . towards the glory (splendor)."

τὰ παθήματα indicates multiple sufferings, plural, not just one, one after another, or happening simultaneously, or unceasingly in sufferings. The sufferings here include everything that happens to human and subhuman creation due to the corruption of the unfinished creation itself. I agree with Wuest but disagree with Vincent's statement that "mere suffering does not fulfill the condition. It is suffering with Christ."[67] I interpret it differently. It includes all human sufferings. I concur with Stott, who argues

> the sufferings and the glory are married; they cannot be divorced. . . . The sufferings and the glory characterize the two ages or aeon . . . the sufferings include not only the opposition of the world, but all our human frailty as well, both physical and moral, which is due to our provisional, half-saved condition.[68]

Moo renders "are not only those 'trials' that are endured directly because of confession of Christ—for instance persecution—but encompass the whole gamut of sufferings, including things such as illness, bereavement, hunger, financial reverses, and death itself."[69] For Liddon, "this suffering was a necessary preliminary to a share in Christ's glory (εἴπερ): because it is a mark of real union with Christ suffering and glorified, of true incorporation with His Body Mystical; cf. Act.ix.4 τί με διώκεις."[70] I conclude that τὰ παθήματα should include all sufferings resulting from being in the

about in our body the dying of Jesus" and "always being delivered unto death for Jesus' sake" (2 Cor. 4:10ff.). Thus *the cross and passion are ever-present realities.*" Bultmann, *Kerygma and Myth*, 36–37. Emphasis added.

65. Dunn, *Romans 1–8*, 468.

66. Käsemann, *Commentary on Romans*, 232.

67. Wuest, *Wuest's Word Studies* 1:136.

68. Stott, *Message of Romans*, 237. The term "half-saved" can be misunderstood. Believers have been transferred from the domain of sin to the domain of the Spirit; they have been justified, but are still in the process of sanctification, and have not been consummated at parousia.

69. Moo, *Epistle to the Romans*, 511.

70. Liddon, *Explanatory Analysis*, 134. Acts 9:4: "Saul, Saul, why are you persecuting me?"

protological (unconsummated) world that has not been healed (completed). Believers are suffering in the realm of σάρξ and πνεῦμα. Because the believers are still in sanctification, they are making mistakes that cause suffering, too. In addition, physically, their bodies are degrading and weak.

τοῦ νῦν καιροῦ—Stott translates it as "of the now time."[71] Cranfield renders, "They are characteristic of the period of time which began with the gospel events and will be terminated by the parousia."[72] Dunn calls it "between time." It has "the unique character for believers of being a period of overlap between 'this evil age' and the age of resurrection life already shared 'in Christ.'"[73] It is the period between the two υἱοθεσία where the making of pneumatic sons (υἱοί) has started but is unfinished yet.

καιροῦ (noun—genitive masculine singular) is a limited period, which is the time of a particular season, the time that is going on, not long; a temporality. A καιρός is not an αἰών.[74] Glorification will be taking place at parousia; it is the time to end the current αιών (*aiôn*) and καιρός (*kairós*), and believers enter "the coming αιών (*aiôn*),"[75] that is, human life in its wholeness and complete knowledge of God.

The focus of "reckon" must be towards the glory (splendor) that is about to be revealed to us, for it is the constant target, and the present sufferings are in between the two υἱοθεσία only. τὴν . . . δόξαν will be revealed to believers in the αιών to come when they are partaking of the glory of Christ.

> Cranfield, following Chrysostom in deducing that for Paul the glory was already present and possessed, only concealed, confuses glory with adoption/sonship. The glory is future, something hoped for and waited for in hope (5:2; 8:24–25); it belongs to the transition to heaven (hence "to us," as well as "of us" implied in v. 21), the final transformation of this bodily existence into the bodily existence of heaven (Phil. 3:21).[76]

---

71. Stott, *Message of Romans*, 237.

72. Cranfield, *Critical and Exegetical Commentary* 1:409.

73. Dunn, *Romans 1–8*, 468.

74. For Καιρός (G2540), and αἰών (G165) see Strong at al., *AMG's Strong's Annotated Dictionaries*, 749, 545.

75. Keizer explains, "Discerning as I do in the (extra-biblical) meaning of *aiōn* three notions, I have described the first as 'life,' the second as 'time,' and the third variously as 'whole,' 'completeness,' 'totality,' or 'entirety.' The third notion distinguishes *aiōn* when used as a word for 'life' from the other words *zōē* and *bios*, and when *aiōn* is used as a word for 'time' this notion adheres to its meaning no less. *Aiōn* is the 'entirety' of time; 'eternity' is too much an 'anachronistic,' misleading or unclear rendering." Keizer, "'Eternity' Revisited," 53–71.

76. Dunn, *Romans 1–8*, 468

The process of glorification is underway now, but has not been achieved yet. Human beings live between two υἱοθεσία. Tragically, those who have not experienced the first υἱοθεσία have no hope of sharing in the coming glory.

There are some considerations in translating the pair of μέλλουσαν . . . ἀποκαλυφθῆναι, which has temporarily been translated to "that is about to be revealed." We see μέλλουσαν is a verb of the *present tense* of μέλλω where its semantic meanings are: "to be about to," "to be intended to," "to be a delay to," "to linger to." On the other hand, ἀποκαλυφθῆναι is a verb of the *aorist tense* of ἀποκαλύπτω where its semantic meanings are: "to be uncovered," "to be revealed," "to be brought to light." The present tense[77] of μέλλουσαν is categorized under "Specific Uses," for it is related to an aorist tense of ἀποκαλυφθῆναι. This particular use of the present tense is a "Historical Present (Dramatic Present)." Quoting Wallace,

> The reason for the use of the historical present is normally to portray an event *vividly*, as though the reader were in the midst of the scene as it unfolds. . . . If intentional, then it is probably used to show the prominence of the events following. If unintentional, then it is probably used for vividness, as if the author were reliving the experience. . . . The historical present has suppressed its aspect, but not its time. But the time element is rhetorical rather than real.[78]

Thomas R. Schreiner says, "The word μέλλουσαν (*mellousan*, about to) . . . or whether the emphasis is on *certainty* or the *imminence* of the glory, it is future, in either case."[79] Like Schreiner, but unlike Dunn, I think "μέλλουσαν" is about certainty. It purposely shows the importance of the event.

What is δόξαν? Murray describes it as the glory of the resurrection and the age to come. It is said to be "the glory which shall be revealed to us-ward. The phrase indicates the certainty of future revelation."[80] Murray translates

---

77. Wallace, *Greek Grammar*, 516–39 and 554–65.

78. Wallace, *Greek Grammar*, 526–27. Emphasis original.

79. Schreiner, *Romans*, 434. Emphasis added. Schreiner notes, "Dunn . . . says both. It is the former in my opinion, for Paul does not give any clues that the glory is imminent." Screiner refers to Dunn, *Romans 1–8*, 468.

80. Murray, *Epistle to the Romans*, 300–1.

εἰς ἡμᾶς to *"to us-ward,"* Beza, and NIV, *"in us,"* Denney, *"toward us and upon us,"*[81] while AMP Bible, *"to us and in us."*[82] Colin G. Kruse writes:

> Our future glory will include a glorious resurrection body: the present mortal body will die, sown, as it were, in dishonor to be raised in glory (1 Cor. 15:43), for when Christ appears he will "transform our lowly bodies so that they will be like glorious body" (Phil. 3:21).[83]

There are two kinds of bodies, the mortal body and the glorious body. There are arguments about what kind of body we will receive.[84]

At the parousia, it is anticipated that we will be endowed with a glorified, pneumatic body—one that is entirely disentangled from sarkic desires and possesses the capacity for everlasting existence. The resurrection body should be a kind that can everlast in the coming αἰών. Barth writes, "For this glory *shall be revealed to us-ward.—Shall be*. This future is our misery and our infinitely greater hope. The *Futurum resurrectionis* reminds us that we have been speaking of God and *not* of some human *possibility*."[85] It is not the old human possibility, for human resurrection was not an option for protological Adamic human beings. God has unlocked the human potential for regeneration through the work of Christ. He brings human beings from the possibilities in the current reality to another. After the resurrection of the spirit (υἱοθεσία, the beginning), then follows the potential renewal of the body (υἱοθεσία, the consummation). As *coheirs* of the Heir, humans will have more possibilities, but also, at the same time, they still have facticity as created beings.

Perhaps some congregations in Rome were considering leaving the faith because of their sufferings. Paul was attempting to convince them about the coming glorification. They should not compare their current temporal struggles to future everlasting glorification. A believer will remain steadfast by focusing on the glory of the Son. Due to this awareness, many people can choose to keep their faith during difficult times. The verse reveals to

---

81. The opinion of Beza and Denney are quoted from Wuest, *Wuest's Word Studies* 1:137.

82. *Amplified Holy Bible*, 730.

83. Kruse, *Paul's Letter to the Romans*, 341–2.

84. Shedd renders, "It is natural that he should speak of the alteration in this material world which is to occur, according to many scripture passages, at that time. As the body of the believer was made subject to death on account of sin, but is to be raised in glory; as, the outward would in which the believer's body resides was cursed (Gen. iii.17–19), but is to be repristinated as a suitable dwelling-place for it . . . deliverance from the 'bondage of corruption.'" Shedd, *Critical and Doctrinal Commentary*, 251–52.

85. Barth, *Epistle to the Romans*, 306. Emphasis added.

Roman believers that splendor does not belong to Nero alone.[86] The wonder of Christ, which amazed the apostle Paul when he fell on the pavement in Damascus, transcends all glory that originates from this world.

I rewrite this verse as follows: "Indeed I now reckon (reason, conclude) that not comparable the undergoing sufferings of the present time towards the glory (splendor) that is about to be revealed to us-ward and in us." The glory of the Son (ὁ Υἱός) is manifested *to* us, while the glory of our full *huio*-ship is manifested *in* us.

Romans 8:19

19 ἡ γὰρ ἀποκαραδοκία τῆς κτίσεως τὴν ἀποκάλυψιν τῶν υἱῶν τοῦ θεοῦ ἀπεκδέχεται.

19 For the eager expectation [of] the creation[,] the revealing [of] the sons [of] God[,] [it] waits eagerly. (ATT)

The subject is ἀποκαραδοκία, and literally, it means "lengthening the neck, lurking with a stretched neck, waiting enthusiastically, or longing. καρα or 'head,' and the ἀπο- signifies the intensity of the act."[87] The NIV translates "eager expectation," the ESV "eager longing," and the NET "eagerly waits." It signifies an impatient wait.

The term "creation"[88] in this verse excludes believers, for they are mentioned separately in vv. 8:19, 21, and 23, and excludes angels. Humans (believers and unbelievers) and angels cannot be subjected to futility, not unwillingly, οὐχ ἑκοῦσα (8:20).[89] The unbelievers are not likely to think that they will wait eagerly. For this reason, the word "creation" does not include them. Others argue that angels should not be counted in the creation who wait eagerly, for angels will not be set free from the bondage of corruption (8:21). They are not waiting eagerly for the revealing of the sons of God and not participating in the glory of the beloved children, τῆς δόξης τῶν τέκνων (8:21).[90] There are no Israelites and non-Israelites in the context nor believers and unbelievers, for creation, in this context, refers to nonhuman.

---

86. During this period, Nero occupied the throne, under whose rule civilians—including his own mother and members of the nobility—were subjected to bullying, humiliation, and persecution.

87. End, *Surat Roma* 7:437.

88. For Käsemann, "the main emphasis today is rightly put on non-human creation, and the phrase πᾶσα ἡ κτίσις in v. 22 supports this. The contrast with v. 23ff. achieves added sharpness in this manner." Käsemann, *Commentary on Romans*, 232–33.

89. Schreiner, *Romans*, 435.

90. See Cranfield, *Critical and Exegetical Commentary* 1:411–12.

I think it is *Vorhandenheit* in Heidegger's and Macquarrie's ontological category; ontic beings that are simply there without self-awareness or relation (let alone fellowship) to Being-Itself.

The creation referenced in vv. 8:19–22 is not the object of the disclosure of the promise. Rather, the object is the sons of God. The creation becomes the object of discussion in v. 8:21, where Paul discusses its participation in eschatological freedom. The freedom of nonhuman creation referenced here is understood as liberation from the dominion of temporality (annihilation or decay), which is intrinsic to the nature of finite ontic beings. Indeed, the creation will participate in the promises given to the people of God. God will renew them to suit the everlasting eschatological existence of God's υἱοί. Without the nonhuman creation (new world), the eschatological humans (υἱοί) have no place to exist. Thus, both parties are mutually dependent upon one another, in the protological and eschatological realms.

The personification of this κτίσις (here, subhuman creation) anticipates God for revealing of the mature sons in the future. It eagerly longs for this revelation, which is the initial step towards restoring the whole κτίσις. The certainty of salvation of the κτίσις rests on the existence of God's pneumatic sons (υἱοί). For this revelation, Paul utilizes the term "ἀποκάλυψιν" or "disclosure" to reveal something that was previously hidden. It is akin to the unveiling or removal of the believers' hoods. Their splendor already emanates when they are transformed into beloved children of God (8:15, 17), but it is not yet fully revealed, still obscured, and will be consummated in the parousia.

ἀπεκδέχεται is a verb—present indicative middle or passive—third-person singular. To translate it, I have added the middle voice [itself] and [now] to show the present. The lemma ἀπεκδέχομαι means "to wait earnestly." This word can be translated as "[it] [itself] awaits earnestly," waiting eagerly. The whole verse is rendered, "For the eager expectation of the creation for the revealing of the sons (τῶν υἱῶν) of God itself awaits eagerly now." Verse 8:19 pictures the *anxiety* and *hope* of the creation.

Romans 8:20

20 τῇ γὰρ ματαιότητι ἡ κτίσις ὑπετάγη, οὐχ ἑκοῦσα ἀλλὰ διὰ τὸν ὑποτάξαντα, ἐφ' ἐλπίδι

20 For [to] the vanity the creation [was] subjected, not voluntarily but because of the [. . .] subjected [it] to, based on trust (ATT)

There are some discussions about whether the words "ἐφ' ἐλπίδι" should be included in this verse or the next. Another problem in this verse is the absence of a *noun* following the article "τὸν." For the NET, the noun is "God," and for the NIV, the "one." Many people read this verse along with Gen 2 and 3, where God gives humans dominion over the creation, and when Adam sinned, carrying consequences that extended to the whole realm intended originally for his dominion.[91] How do we interpret it if there is no historical Adam, no historical fall, and the implications to the creation?

The term "space-time" explains that all of the creations in space-time, human and subhuman, are spatial and temporal (created and finite). Shedd says,

> In this place, it denotes the tendency to deterioration and dissolution characteristic of material nature: its equivalent, φθορά, in verse 21, proves this. The material creation, in the midst of which the "sons of God" are now placed, has no permanency. The instant anything begins to exist here upon earth, it begins to die. Such an environment is unsuited to the sinless spirit and the celestial body of the risen believer.[92]

Hence, everything in this *spatiotemporal* creation has an end if it does not proceed into everlastingness. To exist, the sons of God have their existential worlds in a physical world. If a person (*Dasein*, characterized by being-in-the-world) is not in this physical world, then he does not exist. *Dasein* is always in a world of relationships, tools, people, and concerns. Still, there is the argument that the physical world is in one's existential world.[93] Even though the existential world is bigger than the spatial world, the two are still related; if there is no physical world, then there is no "*existent* in the world."

In space-time, time will not end if there is space; the two cannot be separated. If there is space, then there is time. If there is an everlasting space, then there is an everlasting time. In Gen 1, we learn that God first created

---

91. Denney, *Expositor's Greek Testament* 2:649.
92. Shedd, *Critical and Doctrinal Commentary*, 253.
93. This is a physical space-time: the whole three dimensional space plus the fourth dimension of time. Existentialists see space and time in reference to the existent. Cf. Macquarrie: "Heidegger seems to be explicitly differentiating his own position from Kant's when he writes: 'Space is not to be found in the subject, nor does the subject observe the world "as if" that world were in a space; but the "subject" [*Dasein*], if well understood ontologically, is spatial.' On the other hand, Heidegger prefers to say that space is in the world, rather than that the world is in space.... Existentialists do not speak of 'space-time'; thus we have to discuss space and time separately." Macquarrie, *Existentialism*, 96–97.

space (the heavens and earth). There will be no spatial body without space. Spatial human beings need this creation. God has prepared the subhuman creation for human beings. The survival of the subhuman creation was subject to the survival of human beings. If human beings perished, the subhuman creation would serve no purpose to have existed. That is why this personified creation eagerly awaits and *hopes* for the revealing of the sons of God—the consummated beings (8:19). Thus, the creation is also eager to enter everlastingness.

A finite temporal creation has risks, and it can fail.[94] It fails due to its facticity (givenness). The literary Adam and Eve fall at their perfect initial (protological) stage of becoming consummated humans. They are not eschatologically perfect humans yet. At the final stage, consummated pneumatic humans will not fall anymore. Carl Gustav Jung states, "The biblical fall of man presents the *dawn* of consciousness."[95] The historical fall of unhistorical literary human parents (Adam and Eve) does not occur. However, rather than being the result of original sin, the fall is ingrained in every aspect of the finite temporal creation as an innate sin (inherent sinful nature of humanity).[96]

There are crucial risks if God creates an infinite creation that can fall because it can fall everlastingly. God is the archetypal Project Manager. God manages the risks. God divides the life of this creation into two stages. If the first stage fails, it fails in spatial temporality (perishability), which leaves no risk to God. In that case, Being-Itself returns to the state before there were other beings. The creation does fall, and we probably think another creation will replace it, but this is not the plan. God planned a perfect creation at the end of the creation process. God oversees the project of creation, from Eden to the parousia, from its initiation to its completion. God also prepared the cost that will be incurred for this creation, God's only Son.

A construction (creation) begins after a design has been approved. Re-creation (elevation of beings) is not a reaction to the fall of the creation, but

---

94. Cf. Macquarrie: "Creation involves risk, and this risk in turn issues in sin and evil which threaten the creatures with dissolution and distortion." Macquarrie, *Principles*, 268.

95. Cf. Jung: "This necessity is a psychic fact of such importance that it constitutes one of the essential symbolic teachings of the Christian religion. It is the sacrifice of the merely natural man—of the unconscious, ingenuous being whose tragic career began with the eating of the apple in Paradise. *The biblical fall of man presents the dawn of consciousness* as a curse. And as a matter of fact it is in this light that we first look upon every problem that forces us to greater consciousness and separates us even further from the paradise of unconscious childhood." Jung, *Modern Man*, 96. Emphasis added.

96. "Each one shall be put to death for his own sin." Deut 24:16 (ESV); repeats in 2 Kgs 14:6; Jer 31:30; Ezek 2:4, 20.

both creation and re-creation are in one umbrella concept design.⁹⁷ God has an entire *program* of creation from Alpha to Omega, not a separate project of six-day creation and re-creation from the fall.⁹⁸ The initial step of the act of creation was generated due to the divine's love, and thus, the exaltation is also the result of this same love until the completion of the act of creation at the parousia. All planning, execution, control, evaluation, and rectification of both stages are carried out and brought to completion from the outside of time. The exaltation prepares the created things for the coming everlasting spiritual *aeon*—Christ's age.

For intelligent beings, God first created the protological sarkic-Adamic humans for temporal existence. God is now improving them to become the planned eschatological pneumatic-Christic human beings for everlasting existence. Thus, with or without the fall, the Son was to be incarnated, for only the Son could bring this finite creation to its second stage, in which human beings can participate in spiritual communion with Being-Itself. This union (first manifested in the person of Jesus Christ, the God-human) is the only means that brings humans to everlasting life.

Protological humans (νήπιοι), by their own will and imperfection, bring evil and sin into creation (they displace it from the goal). Creation is now entangled with sinful human beings, whom it was created to serve. Creation has no choice but to obey, for it cannot do anything even if it is unwilling, οὐχ ἑκοῦσα (not voluntary). Often this little phrase goes unnoticed, but here the creature waits for the revelation of God's sons, ἐφ' ἐλπίδι (based on trust). When God liberates God's elect (τῶν τέκνων τοῦ θεοῦ), it brings freedom to the subhuman creation, for they will enter a new reality. When their Master is glorified, it is time for them to be free from dissolution and distortion. They were created in temporality and will enter everlastingness to serve humanity.

What is the missing noun "[. . .]?" I assume that it should be the Creator. This allegorical verse can be rendered, "For to the vanity the creation was subjected, not voluntarily but because of the [*Creator*] who put it into subjection, based on hope (trust)" that God will make υἱοί out of νήπιοι. In temporality, it is vanity when everything vanishes. Regarding humans, the Preacher said, "and the dust returns to the earth as it was, and the spirit returns to God who gave it. Vanity of vanities . . . all is vanity" (Eccl 12:7–8 ESV). Everything is futile, still, the creation can escape vanity when it proceeds to the coming everlasting *aeon*, and humans can return to God

---

97. For Ward, "the whole universe from beginning to end has to spring from God in one timeless act." Ward, *God*, 142.

98. In construction project management, a program is a group of projects that are related which are coordinated as a group instead of as independent projects.

as whole spiritual beings (beings with quickened spirit, spiritual soul, and spiritual body) which have a new extended possible existence.

Romans 8:21

> 21 ὅτι καὶ αὐτὴ ἡ κτίσις ἐλευθερωθήσεται ἀπὸ τῆς δουλείας τῆς φθορᾶς εἰς τὴν ἐλευθερίαν τῆς δόξης τῶν τέκνων τοῦ θεοῦ.
>
> 21 and because the creation itself will be made free away [from] the bondage [of] the decay (destruction) into the state of freedom [of] the splendor [of] the favored children [of] God. (ATT)

There is a variant reading in v. 8:21 that is ὅτι // διότι under category {A}, which indicates that the text is certain. "ἀπὸ τῆς δουλείας τῆς φθορᾶς" has been translated here into "away from the bondage of the decay (destruction)." How is it possible? δουλείας is connected to ὑπετάγη (it was subjected, v. 8:20). Dunn writers, "Creation itself must be redeemed in order that redeemed man may have a fitting environment. . . . It recalls the talk of liberation from sin (6:18, 22) and from the law (7:3; 8:2) and . . . of the age of Adam."[99] In the context of salvation, "redeem" signifies both the payment of a price and the granting of freedom to the one who is redeemed. Redemption, therefore, involves securing liberation through a sacrificial payment as exemplified in the biblical narratives (Eph 1:7, 1 Pet 1:18–19, and Gal 3:13).

The resurrection frees us from death, sin, and the law. And to live everlastingly, humans need the everlasting creation as well.

Romans 8:22

> 22 οἴδαμεν γὰρ ὅτι πᾶσα ἡ κτίσις συστενάζει καὶ συνωδίνει ἄχρι τοῦ νῦν
>
> 22 For [we] know that the whole creation [it] groans together and [it] travails together until even now (ATT)

The creation is personified like a mother who is in pain and joy for giving birth. What is delivered is described in v. 8:23, the new bodily appearance that the creation can see. These verses, 8:19–22, should be comprehended along with the event in Gen 3:8–19. Collin G. Kruse explains that it is as if Paul is stating that "we," the source of creation's groaning, "right up to the present moment," recognize this reality and look forward to its release when God's protological children are brought into "their freedom

---

99. Dunn, *Romans 1-8*, 471.

and glory."[100] All wait and travail until now. R. C. H. Lenski explains, "Travail, i.e. pains that end by bringing forth something, they are like a woman giving birth to a child. . . . The groaning is not to end by subsiding when death sets in but to end when a new condition comes out of it."[101] It is our existential condition; only a new human (including subhumans) condition can solve our protological situation.

This explanation reminds us of the narrative of liberation, which begins with the grieving complaint of Israel in Egypt, as in Exod 2:23–25. Their case was a family liberation from the bondage of slavery in another land. Still, now the case is a liberation of all humankind from the bondage of laws and finiteness in their temporality. They are decaying and facing the end of their existence. Subject to the transformation of the humans' state of being, all the creation will be freed from the bondage of decay. Thus, the whole creation is dependent on the liberation of humankind first.

Romans 8:23

> 23 οὐ μόνον δέ, ἀλλὰ καὶ αὐτοὶ τὴν ἀπαρχὴν τοῦ πνεύματος ἔχοντες, ἡμεῖς καὶ αὐτοὶ ἐν ἑαυτοῖς στενάζομεν υἱοθεσίαν ἀπεκδεχόμενοι, τὴν ἀπολύτρωσιν τοῦ σώματος ἡμῶν.

> 23 and not merely [it], but even [we] ourselves having the firstfruits [of] the Spirit, we even [we] ourselves in ourselves [we] groan await eagerly [the] position as a son (the final constitution of a son), [of] the deliverance [of] the body [of] ours. (ATT)

The Lord described the situation as both pain and joy.[102] The opening phrase, οὐ μόνον δέ (and not merely it), shows very clearly that Paul distinguishes between believers and subhuman creation. The clause ἀλλὰ καὶ αὐτοὶ τὴν ἀπαρχὴν τοῦ πνεύματος ἔχοντες (but even we ourselves having the firstfruits of the Spirit) has many interpretations.[103] The whole gift is given in stages. God resolves the incompatibility problem, starting from the human spirit, soul, and bodily existence, and then makes a new world. The believers have received an activated spirit as "the initial stage of *the work* of the Holy Spirit"[104] through the first υἱοθεσία (v. 8:15) where

---

100. Kruse, *Paul's Letter to the Romans*, 344.
101. Lenski, *Romans*, 539–40.
102. See John 16:20b–22.
103. See End, *Surat Roma* 7:444–45.
104. Genitive [of] has been emphasized here. There are two possible meanings: "firstfruits which is the Spirit" (Dunn), and "referring to the Spirit works in us" (Fitzmyer, Cranfield), where Kruse chooses the first option. Kruse, *Paul's Letter to the*

believers are the first party to participate in the incomplete salvation in the present world; God recognizes God's τέκνα as His υἱοὶ in their sin-filled body of their half-elevated being, in the sin-filled creation that also has not been renewed.[105] The next stage will be the harvest season.

ἡμεῖς καὶ αὐτοὶ ἐν ἑαυτοῖς στενάζομεν (we, even we ourselves by ourselves, we groan in ourselves) remarks that not only is creation still subjected to vanity, which is now groaning, but God's beloved children are also groaning in their waiting for their completion of the constitution of pneumatic sons. In agreement with Murray, Cranfield, and Dunn, but *contra* Käsemann, Moo explains,

> These groans are not verbal utterances but inward, nonverbal "sighs," inactive of a certain attitude. This attitude does not involve anxiety whether we will finally experience the deliverance God has promised . . . but frustration at the remaining moral and physical infirmities that are inevitably a part of this period between justification and glorification (see 2 Cor. 5:2–4) and longing for the end of this state of "weakness."[106]

Dunn clarifies, "But the inward sense of frustration of individual believers (as a whole) at the eschatological tension of living in the overlap of the ages seems the most obvious reference."[107] Therefore, groaning relates to the believer's existence, who has been saved but not entirely freed from the flesh and sufferings. Those who have faith in Jesus Christ are proleptic υἱοὶ. As a half-saved human being (half νήπιος and half υἱός) Christians need

---

Romans, 349. I argue based on the genitive case of πνεύματος that "[of] the Holy Spirit" is not Himself.

105. Wolter comments, "This dissonance explains why Paul can speak about the present possession of the Spirit only as ἀπαρχή ('first fruits') and ἀρραβών ('down payment') (Rom. 8:23; 2 Cor. 1:22, 5:5) and why he gives such a great weight to the transformation of human corporeality that is still pending. It is because of the frailty and weakness of their corporeal existence that Christians in the present are still separated from complete solidarity with the risen and exalted Lord. In 2 Corinthians 5:6–8, Paul makes the point of this matter with ample clarity (see also 1 Cor. 15:50). That for which Christians ought to hope in distinction from the 'others' (1 Thes. 4:13) is the integration of even their corporeality in the experience of God's eschatic salvation. In this, it is of great significance that Paul understood this hope never as the redemption 'from the body,' but always only as the 'redemption of the body,' as he writes in Romans 8:23, and in fact from the disastrous consequences of sin that caused it to turn out to be in 'slavery to decay' (v. 21)." Wolter, *Paul*, 208–9. See his discussion on the "already now—not yet," at p. 191.

106. Moo, *Epistle to the Romans*, 519.

107. Dunn, *Romans 1–8*, 474.

the law to control their sarkic will, but their salvation is determined by the state of new beings brought through God's sub-act of *huiothesía* (υἱοθεσία).

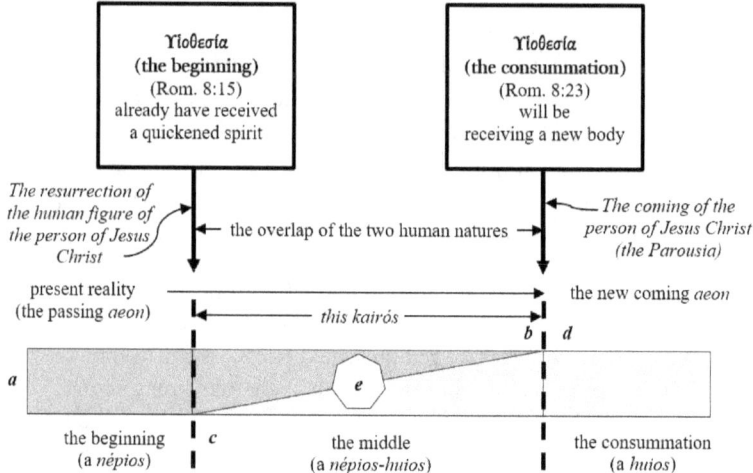

The making of everlasting pneumatic exalted human beings
a. the beginning of the Adamic human life,
b. the conclusion of the Adamic human mode of being,
c. the beginning of the Christic human mode of being,
d. the beginning of the fully Christic human life;
e. Christian believers are in between the two υἱοθεσία; they are proleptic υἱοί.

FIGURE 5: *Huiothesía* **(the Beginning) and** *Huiothesía* **(the Consummation)**

Υἱοθεσίαν ἀπεκδεχόμενοι (await eagerly for the position of a son)[108] is the peak (consummation) of the constitution of a pneumatic son—the making of eschatological humanity for the new world. With the new pneumatic body,[109] the wholly pneumatic humans are ready to enter the everlast-

---

108. Lenski saw these v. 8:15 and 23 like in the Pauline concept of "already/not yet." "Paul leaves no doubt on this score, for he adds: 'waiting out adoption, (namely) the ransoming of our body.' The participle is temporal: 'while waiting out' (this verb occurs also in v. 19). What the anarthrous 'adoption' means is shown by its apposition 'the ransoming of our body.' To wait out adoption (ἔχ in the verb) does not mean to receive it for the first time (v. 15 speaks of this reception); it means to wait until its full consummation arrives; and the apposition shows what this consummation is. When a child is adopted it does not at once possess and enjoy all that adoption assures; as an adopted child it waits until these things arrive in due course. Thus adoption, for instance, makes the child an heir, but it must wait out the time to have the inheritance turned over to it (v. 17)." Lenski, *Interpretation of St. Paul's Epistle*, 541–42.

109. For Stott, "our future glory is defined in two ways. First, it is 'the redemption of our bodies,' because we are going to be given new bodies on the last day, set free from their double burden, their frailty and their 'flesh.' Our resurrection bodies will have

ing pneumatic reality as elevated beings in their new existence with new pneumatic facticity and possibilities as the coheir of the Creator God. τὴν ἀπολύτρωσιν τοῦ σώματος ἡμῶν (the deliverance of the body of ours) is the final inauguration of υἱοθεσία (*huiothesía*).

To the Corinthians, Paul explained the old clothes and the new clothes. Through God's sub-act of υἱοθεσία, human is clothed with "adult garments." This event is the final stage mentioned in v. 8:18 about the glory that must have begun to be revealed to us. In this future existence, the exalted individuals are together in the Logos structure, and those outside it will cease to exist as human beings. In the absence of divine intervention, the inevitability of mortality precludes the possibility of human transcendence. The phenomenon of decay represents the ultimate reality of this condition.[110]

At the parousia, believers will recall the words of the apostle Paul as he wrote to the Corinthians,[111] which he quoted from the book of Hosea, 13:14: "Where, O death, is your victory? Where, O death, is your sting?" Rahner refers to this as the ultimate salvation, encompassing the body and the soul.[112] Humans become spiritual beings, thereby becoming free from the protological corporeal facticity that defines them. The clause of Rom 8:23, "the position as a consummated pneumatic son (state of being as a fully υἱός), of the deliverance of the body of ours," marks the conclusion of the *ordo salutis* and *historia salutis* altogether.

At the eschatological consummation, the glorification of the creation will occur. At this time, Christian believers will receive deliverance of their bodies. The former creation shall undergo the final transformation into a new state, and the temporal realm will neither reach a conclusion nor terminate, but rather transition into a state of perpetual existence (everlastingness).[113]

---

new, undreamed-of powers, and no indwelling sin." Stott, *Men Made New*, 91.

110. Barth explains, "Death is the end of all present possibilities of life. Dying means exhausting the last of the possibilities given to us." Barth, *Dogmatics in Outline*, 117.

111. "Where, O death, is your victory? Where, O death, is your sting? The sting of death is sin, and the power of sin is the law. But thanks be to God, who gives us the victory through our Lord Jesus Christ!" 1 Cor 15:55–57 NET.

112. For Rahner, "Of course one should not conceive of this resurrection as a return to the limits of a life restricted by space and time and the facts of biology. One should rather think of it as the ultimate salvation of the one complete person, body and soul, in God. . . . Christianity is thus simplicity itself because it embraces the totality of human existence and leaves all the details to the free responsibility of the human person, without providing an exact recipe for them. All the same time it is the hardest thing of all, a grace offered to all that can be and is received, even when unconditional hope has not yet discovered its seal in Jesus of Nazareth." Rahner, *Content of Faith*, 64–65.

113. Cf. Eph 1:13–14.

AN ALTERNATIVE TRANSLATION OF ROMANS 8:14–23 AND 9:4, 8 (AHT)

The summary of our revised translations (AHT) is as follows.

> 8:14 Indeed, as many as those who are led by the spirit from God,[114] they are mature sons of God (υἱοὶ θεοῦ). 15 Indeed not you received a spirit of bondage again into fear, but you received a spirit of constitution of a mature son (like ὁ Υἱός) in (by) that we scream aloud, *Abba*, [to] *ho Pater* (the Creator, the Father of all beings). 16 The Spirit himself, He testifies together in support of the spirit of ours that we are favored children of God (τέκνα θεοῦ). 17 Subsequently, if favored children (τέκνα), then heirs—truly heirs of God, consequently joint heirs of Christ—if indeed we suffer together with Christ so that we might also be glorified together with Christ.
>
> 18 Indeed, I now reckon (reason, conclude) that not comparable the undergoing sufferings of the present time towards the glory (splendor) that is about to be revealed to us-ward and in us. 19 For the eager expectation of the creation for the revealing of the sons of God (τῶν υἱῶν τοῦ θεοῦ) itself awaits eagerly now. 20 For to the vanity the creation was subjected, not voluntarily but because of the *Creator* who put it into subjection, based on hope (trust) 21 and because the creation itself will be made free away from the bondage of the decay (destruction) into the state of freedom of the splendor of the favored children of God (τῶν τέκνων τοῦ θεοῦ). 22 For we know that the whole creation it groans together and it travails together until even now 23 and not merely it, but even we ourselves having the firstfruits of the Spirit, we even we ourselves in ourselves we groan await eagerly for the position as a consummated pneumatic son (the state of being as a fully υἱός), of the deliverance of the body of ours.
>
> 9:4 whosoever are Israelites, from whom (started from them) are (namely) the constitution of the primogenetic mature Son (the making of ὁ Υἱός [the Messiah]), and the splendor, and the testaments, and the law giving, and the worship, and the promises, (...)
>
> 8 It is not the favored children generated from the flesh (τὰ τέκνα τῆς σαρκὸς) are these favored children of (belongs to) God (ταῦτα τέκνα τοῦ θεοῦ), but the favored children of (relating to)

---

114. The term "the spirit from God" (not "the spirit/Spirit of God") implies that God sends the spirit as a gift or anointing for a specific work, vivification of the soul, or supernatural (divine) intervention.

the promise (τὰ τέκνα τῆς ἐπαγγελίας) who are reckoned into (among) descendants.

SUMMARY: FOUNDATION

Before the making of a υἱός can happen, another necessary stage should be prepared: a τέκνα nation (a nation of the *elect* νήπιοι). Israel has been chosen, and there was a promise that all nations would be blessed through them (Gen 3:12; 18:18; 22:18). From this nation, a child who assumed human nature became the first pneumatic son (υἱός) to establish a pattern (image) for other human beings. The first formation of a pneumatic Son (the making of ὁ Υἱός) took place in this tribe of Israel. Jesus of Nazareth, born of woman, who was born under the Torah (born as a νήπιος like us), becomes ὁ Υἱός, *HaMashiach*, our Lord, through His baptism and resurrection. The human Christ is the consummated human figure of the person of God the Son.

Following the model of ὁ Υἱός, Adamic humans (νήπιοι) are being transformed into pneumatic sons (υἱοί). The first stage of this transformation takes place in the person's spirit, in what is referred to as the first υἱοθεσία (Rom 8:15). In this stage, a νήπιος receives a spirit of the constitution of a pneumatic son. This vivified spirit (a mode in contrast to the dormant spirit) transforms him into a half υἱός, in the pattern of ὁ Υἱός. The divine intervention in that person's existence begins here. The second stage involves removing the source of carnal desire by granting a spiritual body in the second υἱοθεσία (Rom 8:23). This new body prepares a wholly pneumatic son (υἱός) to enter spiritual existence in the everlasting creation. Therefore, the temporally created world must be transformed into an everlasting world. This new world serves no purpose without the eschatological pneumatic sons (οἱ υἱοί); conversely, οἱ υἱοί (new beings) require an endless world for their new everlasting existence.

In the everlasting future, the renewal of human beings will facilitate the unlocking of new pneumatic possibilities. The souls of these individuals will possess self-control derived from their vivified spirit and will be liberated from the constraints of this protological world due to their new pneumatic form. Moreover, the sinful world will no longer exist because the new beings will be pneumatic. Under this condition, the Spirit can effectively guide believers to live in a manner that aligns with their true, planned nature, leading to an ultimate pneumatic authentic existence that is influenced by the divine. In the realm of τὰ ἄνω (things above—heavenly, eternal, pneumatical, eschatological), the human soul will no longer be subject to the influence of the sarkic desire of the physical created world, but rather to the influence of the Spirit. As a result, the possibility of the soul being lost within the physical world (i.e., of sinning) will no longer exist. Consequently, the necessity for the Torah and τὰ στοιχεῖα τοῦ κόσμου (the basic principles of the world) is fully obviated.

The book of Romans (and the whole Greek New Testament) does not address the topic of adoption, but *huiothesía* (υἱοθεσία)—the liberation from temporality and sarkic corporeality.

CONSTRUCTIVE THEOLOGY
RECONSTRUCTING (UNCONCEALING) PAUL'S KNOWLEDGE OF *HUIOTHESIA*

CHAPTER 6

The Person of Jesus Christ and the Holy Spirit

"Humanity is formed after the likeness of God, and moulded by His hands, that is, by the Son and Holy Spirit." ~ Irenaeus

OVERVIEW

In this chapter, we will learn the role of the person of Jesus Christ and the Holy Spirit in laying down the foundation of υἱοθεσία (*huio*-fication). Colin E. Gunton refers to Irenaeus' concept of the two hands of God, asserts,

> If God works among us through his two hands, it is argued, then the Son and the Spirit belong intrinsically to his *eternal* being. In some way, therefore, God must be Father, Son and Spirit always, to the heart of his being.[1]

Like the Holy Spirit, the Son is always an eternal being. How do we, Christians, explain the work of the human *Yeshua HaMashiach*, the "Anointed One" who is the created human figure of the divine preexistent Son? The Jewish Messiah is a human figure, just like us, but Christians see Jesus as the

---

1. Gunton, *Father, Son, and the Holy Spirit*, 12. Emphasis added.

Messiah differently than Jews do.² The divine figure acts to create, sustain, and improve the world,³ but he requires a human figure to operate from the side of created beings and be made a patron as a human archetype. God will remake the whole of humankind based on this image—the human Ἰησοῦς ὁ Χριστός (*Iēsoús ho Christós*). God's creative act is initiated in Eden and reaches its zenith in the creation of fully consummated pneumatic humans.

Ted Peter writes, "God is in the process of self-relating through relating to the world he loves and redeems. God is constituting himself as a God in relationship with what is other than God."⁴ In order to accomplish this purpose, the infinite, eternal God first creates finite temporal humans, and second, God makes them capable of having a pneumatic communion with him everlastingly. These are the two episodes called diversification and homogenization. Since "the other than God" takes place in temporality, God has set *times* for the two episodes: the protological creation of sarkic-Adamic humans and their elevation to become the eschatological pneumatic-Christic humans.⁵ How do humans move from one episode to another? Entering the homogenization episode requires pneumatic compatibility. The Pauline Greek biblical concept of υἱοθεσία explains how God ontologically transforms the protological sarkic creatures into consummated eschatological pneumatic creatures.

In this chapter, we will examine how υἱοθεσία begins. God's sub-act of υἱοθεσία is founded on the ontological transformation experienced by the human figure of Jesus of Nazareth. In Brian Arnold's podcast, while

---

2. Dahl explains, "It has been assumed that *ho Christos* is used in the sense of 'the Messiah' in Ephesians (and Colossians), thus differing from the other Pauline epistles.... But there is at least one passage, Romans 9:5, where the result is unambiguous. Anyone who knows the original meaning of the name understands that the Christ belongs to Israel precisely as Messiah. There are other places as well where the careful reader would detect messianic connotations. In most of these cases, though not in all, the definite article is used with *Christos*. Paul speaks most clearly of the messiahship of Jesus in Romans 1:2–4, but it is still questionable whether *Christos* is to be especially stressed in the expression 'Jesus Christ our Lord.' The result appears to be slight but does signify something. The name 'Christ' does not receive its content through a previously fixed conception of messiahship but rather from the person and work of Jesus Christ.... The name 'Christ' has content: it connotes more of the nature and significance of Jesus. This is not, however, to distinguish between the person and the office. Everything that Jesus is and does, he is and does as the Christ." Dahl, *Jesus the Christ*, 17

3. For O'Collins, "nothing exists unless God constantly keeps it in existence and does not let it slip back into nothingness." O'Collins, *Jesus Our Redeemer*, 27.

4. Peters, *God as Trinity*, 145; quoted from Gunton, *Father, Son, and the Holy Spirit*, 23.

5. Gunton writes, "So Christ, by becoming human, not only corrects what was wrong, but brings to perfection what was begun in the creation." Gunton, *Father, Son, and the Holy Spirit*, 29.

discussing his book entitled *God the Son Incarnate*, Stephen Wellum explains that God's unchanging *nature* cannot incorporate another nature. Still, the *person of the Son* can add to himself a human nature. Accordingly, the person of Jesus Christ, the *Creator-creature*, has two natures—divine and human. The divine nature of the Son does not add another nature; instead, it is the *person* of the Son who combines the two natures. Thus, the incarnation is not about a divine person with a divine nature becoming a human person with a human nature,[6] but a divine person with a divine nature becoming *a divine person with divine* plus *human natures*. Because now God the Son has human nature, he can live a human life, act like a human, and serve as our Savior, obeying, dying, and being resurrected for humanity—this way, he elevated humanity from decaying creatures to everlasting creatures. When the one individual—God the Son incarnate—preserves the two distinct natures, it retains the idea that God remains unchanging even as God the Son acquires human nature.[7] This idea helps us to understand that there are two sonships (*huio*-ships) of the person of the Son (the Being-becoming).

Robert W. Jenson uses the terms "*logos asarkos*."[8] Jenson, following some debates, explains, "I continue to regard *Logos asarkos*, used for something 'before' the incarnation on any sort of line, as a *Vorstellung* (concept) in futile search of a *Begriff* (definition)."[9] It seems that Jenson misreads the terms "God's Son" and "the Son of God" when he refers to Rom 1:3-4. He renders:

> Paul introduces his gospel to the Roman Christians by identifying the object of his faith. This is "Jesus Christ," whom Paul specifies, on the one side of a parallel construction, as "originated from David's seed, according to flesh," and, on the other side of the construction, as "determined God's Son . . . according to Holy Spirit, from resurrection of the dead." We must carefully observe the parallels and their shifts. As creature, Christ has an origin; as Son of God, he does not have an origin, but rather a determination. Parallel to David's seed as that "from" which he originates as creature is resurrection as that "from" which his

---

6. Cf. Augustine: "In order to make gods of those who *were* merely human, one who was God made himself human [*Deos facturus qui homines erant, homo factus est, qui deus erat*]. . . . Without forfeiting what he was, he wished to become what he himself had made. He himself made what he would become, because what he did was add man to God, not lose God in man." Quoted in Meconi, *One Christ*, 92.

7. See Arnold, "Why Did God Become Man?"

8. Jenson, *Systematic Theology* 1:141

9. Jenson, "Once More the *Logos Asarkos*." Parentheses added.

being God's Son is "determined." And parallel to his reality as creature is "Holy Spirit."[10]

The two verses, especially v. 4, have no parallel shift. Paul talks about the human Christ. Paul explained that the gospel concerns "the Son of Him, who was descended from David according to the flesh (temporal human figure) and *was declared to be* υἱοῦ θεοῦ in power κατὰ πνεῦμα ἁγιωσύνης by his resurrection from the death, Jesus Christ our Lord." The words "flesh," "death," and "resurrection" must refer to the finite, temporal, corporeal human figure of Jesus,[11] not to the eternal divine figure. The *human figure* was an assumed nature of the *person* of God the Son incarnate (God-human). The eternal divine figure of God-human cannot fall and cannot be changed, or die. It was the human figure (the "becoming" nature) of God-human who starts in the flesh, which was later declared to be υἱοῦ θεοῦ ([mature] son of God), a consummated human being—the planned fully developed human being.

Regarding the human nature[12] of Jesus, the Messiah, John Macquarie explains:

> As existent, man is always incomplete and on his way, so that if it is proper to talk of him having a "nature," this must be conceived as open-ended. . . . Christ has a complete human "nature" . . . at the furthest point along the road toward fulfilling or unfolding this "nature" (existence), he manifests divine Being.[13]

Jesus has achieved the highest existential state humans can reach. It is our existential interest to study Christology from below. We will focus more on the human sonship of Jesus of Nazareth because it takes place in temporality to solve the problem of human facticity. That is the basis of the Christian teaching of salvation. The humanhood of Jesus is the center of attraction, as all other humans want to be like him—having the ability to escape death.[14]

With references to Gal 4:4–5, James A. Waddell highlights:

---

10. Jenson, *Systematic Theology* 1:142.

11. Fee renders "Jesus as descended from David 'according to the flesh' meaning . . . 'according to ordinary human descent.' . . . 'Flesh' for him denotes humanity . . . in its fallen creatureliness." Fee, *Paul*, 129.

12. For the definitions of "nature," see Macquarrie, *Principles*, 297.

13. Macquarrie, *Principles*, 297–98.

14. Cf. Gunton: "That any doctrine of the Trinity which loses its hold on that particular historical human being no longer represents the historic faith of the Church." Gunton, *Father, Son, and the Holy Spirit*, 26.

According to Paul, the divine figure presented, or "put forward," the messiah figure to be crucified. The divine figure redeemed those who were under the law by sending his son (Gal. 4:4–5). According to Paul, the divine figure willed the death of the messiah figure.[15]

It is worth noting that the text references the "divine figure" and "the death of the messiah figure." I am consistent with the view that the Messiah is a human figure and that the person of God-human can be understood as having two figures, thus two *huio*-ships.

THE TWO SONSHIPS OF THE SON VERSUS THE TWO *HUIO*-SHIPS OF *HO HUIOS*

Our study on the doctrine of adoption shows that Robert A. Webb has discussed the issue of sonships, which is not *huio*-ships. According to Webb, restoring the sinner to paternal favor and filial life must be solved by the mediatorial act of Christ as the Son of God.[16] Does his term "the Son of God" refer to the person of the Son, the divine figure of the Son, or the human figure of the Son? Webb explains, "Atonement by a servant for a servant."[17]

Before we continue, it is essential to be reminded again that Webb's term "son" and all appearances of "son" in the doctrine of adoption do not necessarily refer to Pauline "υἱός," primarily when it refers to human *huio*-ship (*mature son*-ship).

Webb pointed out that our Scriptures throughout liberally style the Savior as "the Son of God;" for example, his incarnation, baptism, temptation, sufferings and death, resurrection and ascension, and the session in glory are all predicates of "the Son of God."[18] He asks, in what sense is Jesus "the Son of God?" Webb gives three possibilities: it refers to the Trinitarian Son of God, the mediatorial Son of God, or He is both, the theanthropic Son of God.[19] I submit that it is necessary to clarify whether baptism, temptation, suffering, and death are exclusive to human nature and whether "Son of God" refers to the human *huio*-ship of Jesus, born of woman—a human like us.

---

15. Waddell, *Messiah*, 113–14.
16. Webb, *Reformed Doctrine of Adoption*, 93.
17. Webb, *Reformed Doctrine of Adoption*, 93.
18. Webb, *Reformed Doctrine of Adoption*, 93.
19. Webb, *Reformed Doctrine of Adoption*, 94.

In contrast to Webb, I posit that the terms "mediatorial" and "theanthropic" are essentially synonymous in this regard, involving the two natures of the *person* of God the Son incarnate. Furthermore, the Son can only assume the role of mediator because a mediator between God and humans must be a God-human (*theanthropos*). Consequently, it is inappropriate to refer to his *huio*-ships as "mediatorial sonship" (singular), but rather as "mediatorial *huio*-ships" (plural). Webb also argues,

> If, however, Jesus possesses a dual sonship—one monogenetic and one theanthropic—it will be possible for sinners, through him, to be made partakers of the one without their being made partakers of the other; He can be the Elder Brother in the family of the redeemed without the family of the redeemed being incorporated into the Trinity.[20]

What are monogenetic sonship and theanthropic sonship, according to Webb? He asks, "Jesus was 'the only-begotten (monogenetic) Son of God.' ... In what sense is He the only child of His Father?"[21] In one of his arguments, he says, "And now, Father, glorify me in your own presence with the glory that I had with you before the world existed" (John 17:5), showing that the person of Jesus Christ addresses the First Person of the Godhead instead of the Trinity.[22] In line with it, Rodney A. Whitacre says that Jesus "is praying from the realm of eternity."[23] Webb renders, "The designation, Son of God, so often given to him, imports far more than His messiahship."[24] In contrast to Webb, I contend that it is reasonable to posit that the phrase "Son of God" is intended to refer to the human Messiah.[25] Consequently, it would be preferable to refer to the Son in His divine nature as "God the Son," "the preexistent Son," or "the Logos."

In his opening statement regarding the mediatorial Sonship, Webb asserts, "In the fullness of time ... 'the Son of God' became 'the Son of Man.'"[26] If the word "son" refers to Pauline "υἱός," then the statement is ambiguous or wrong, for, in the fullness of time, God the Son (the Logos) assumed the human nature in its minor state (νήπιος); for, literally and theologically (symbolically), Jesus of Nazareth was born into temporality as a νήπιος. But then Jesus grew in wisdom, stature, and favor with God and

---

20. Webb, *Reformed Doctrine of Adoption*, 94.
21. Webb, *Reformed Doctrine of Adoption*, 95.
22. Webb, *Reformed Doctrine of Adoption*, 97. The verse has been replaced with ESV.
23. Whitacre, *John*, 402.
24. Webb, *Reformed Doctrine of Adoption*, 99.
25. Webb, *Reformed Doctrine of Adoption*, 105.
26. Webb, *Reformed Doctrine of Adoption*, 99.

humans (Luke 2:52). Therefore, it can be posited that Webb's assertion may indeed be accurate when the phrase "the fullness of time" is interpreted not as a reference to Jesus' nativity, but rather to the moment when Jesus had already attained the fullness of his humanity through the resurrection—the *Nepios* of Man became the *Huios* of Man. Nevertheless, this "the Son of God became the Son of Man" is not reflected in the Gospel narrative. It is a mistaken theological construct. The two phrases refer to the same *huio*-ship of the human Christ. It is crucial that we examine the initial statements made by the church fathers regarding this topic.

Webb says:

> The whole significance of the incarnation was, therefore, mediatorial and redemptive. He was born in order that He might die; He died in order that He might redeem. Consequently, had there been no sinner there would have been no incarnate Savior.[27]

The birth of Jesus of Nazareth was predestined to result in His demise; His subsequent passing was intended to pave the way for His resurrection and triumph over death. If death is no longer a threat, then the sting of death (sin)[28] will have no power, and the law has no purpose, too. The necessity for the incarnation of the preexistent Son is not derived from sin; instead, it is the human protological state of being, which inherently entails the potential for transgression and decay.

JESUS GREW FROM AN INFANT OF GOD TO THE [MATURE] SON OF GOD

In his humanity, the Christ was born as an infant (νήπιος, Adamic being) under the law.[29] From Luke 1:35, we learn that the angel said, "The holy one being born *will* be called the Son of God (υἱὸς θεοῦ)." He was not born as the Son of God (ὁ Υἱός τοῦ Θεοῦ), but he will be called so. Webb stated that messianic sonship "was *constituted* in time that the world of sinners might

---

27. Webb, *Reformed Doctrine of Adoption*, 100.

28. "'O death, where is your victory? O death, where is your sting?' The sting of death is sin, and the power of sin is the law. But thanks be to God, who gives us victory through our Lord Jesus Christ." 1 Cor 15:55–57 ESV.

29. Irenaeus argued, "God had power at the beginning to grant perfection to man; but as the latter was only recently created, he could not possibly have received it. . . . It was for this reason that the Son of God, although He was perfect, passed through the state of infancy in common with the rest of mankind, partaking of it thus not for His own benefit, but for that of the infantile stage of man's existence, in order that man might be able to receive Him." *ANF* 1:521.

have a Redeemer."[30] He also noted that Trinitarian sonship was established for eternity.[31] But then he added, "In the one, the Son was only divine in nature; in the other, the Son was *both* human and divine in His nature."[32] There are categorical issues in Webb's statements that we must examine and make corrections.

In the incarnation, the Second Person of the Holy Trinity becomes a theanthropic being, or God-human (*Theos-anthropos*). The designation "God-human" expresses the two natures united in the hypostatic union of the person of Jesus Christ, who, having entered temporality, assumed a human form. Following the resurrection, the *person* of the Son possesses two forms of mature sonship (*huio*-ship): the divine sonship, which is monogenetic and unique to him, and the acquired (constituted) human messianic mature sonship, which is primogenetic, as He is the first human to attain it. The person of Jesus Christ (referring to a proper noun), as the theanthropic (God-human) person, possesses an eternal divine spirit, a human spirit, a human soul, and a human body—making His personhood far more profound and complex than that of an ordinary human, who has only a human spirit, soul, and body (trichotomic).

Webb explains, "'Christ' and 'Son of God' are interchangeable. . . . 'Christ' of course means Messiah, the Anointed One, who was theanthropic in His constitution, and is never a synonym of the Logos or Second Person in the Trinity: it always imports a divine-human being."[33] We agree with Webb about the *person* of Jesus Christ, but we must be careful when deciding the kinds of his two mature sonships (*huio*-ships). He sees it as divine sets against divine-human (theanthropic); he applies the term "theanthropic sonship"[34]—God-human sonship—to distinguish it from the eternal Trinitarian sonship. His concept is quite ambiguous because he slightly differs from it when he says in another part, "Two classes of attributes are ascribed to Him—the one class is infinite, and the other class is finite."[35] Still, the term "theanthropic" relates to the *person* of the Son who has two combined *natures* and *huio-ships*; thus, it specifically shows the combined natures rather than emphasizing the distinct *natures* of the person of Jesus Christ. I repeat here: mediatorial mature sonships (*huio*-ships) consist of divine *huio*-ship and acquired human (messianic) *huio*-ship. To

30. Webb, *Reformed Doctrine of Adoption*, 103. Emphasis added.
31. Webb, *Reformed Doctrine of Adoption*, 103.
32. Webb, *Reformed Doctrine of Adoption*, 103. Emphasis added.
33. Webb, *Reformed Doctrine of Adoption*, 105.
34. Webb, *Reformed Doctrine of Adoption*, 106.
35. Webb, *Reformed Doctrine of Adoption*, 107.

avoid confusion regarding the Lord Jesus Christ, the distinguishing terms here are "the person," "the human figure," and "the divine figure."

What is the path to a messianic *huio*-ship? John writes, "And the Word became *flesh* and dwelt among us, and we have seen his glory, glory as of the only Son from the Father, full of grace and truth."[36] It shows the person of the Son (the divine figure) and His newly acquired human nature. Besides our discussion in Gal 4:4, the word "flesh" in this verse indicates that Jesus was born as a νήπιος (a mere human like us).

When did Jesus, the Son of Mary, who was a mere human like us, become ὁ Υἱός (the mature Son)? Wolfhart Pannenberg renders:

> In *his resurrection from the dead*, Jesus Christ has been instituted into authority as the Son (Rom. 1:4). With the reception of the Spirit at his baptism by John came also a declaration of his divine sonship (Mark 1:10f. par.).[37]

But Pannenberg added an explanation: "In the power of the Spirit, he was the Son of God already *from his birth*."[38] Richard N. Longenecker, in his criticism of J. A. T. Robinson, who does not address when this messianic ordination has been or will be revealed, argues that

> *Jesus has not as yet entered into messiahship* but that honor has been reserved for him in the counsels of God *for the future*. Presently, of course, Jesus is "Messiah-designate" awaiting the future *Parousia* of the Son of Man; and then he shall be Messiah in fact.[39]

Thus, for Pannenberg, Jesus was the Son of God (the Messiah) from His birth. In contrast, according to Longenecker, Jesus (the Messiah-designate) will become the Son of Man (the Messiah in fact) at the parousia. Longenecker further argues that the fact that God raised Jesus from the grave, however, was essential in establishing Jesus as Messiah in the minds of the earliest Christians. While acknowledging heavenly attestation during His earthly ministry, Peter is reported to have focused his attention on the fact that God "raised Him up," with the conclusion: "God has *made* (ἐποίησεν) Him both Lord and Christ." The concept of God's "Son," or the "Son of God," is closely related to that of the human Messiah.

The *huio*-ship of Jesus is announced as having been "declared" by the resurrection from the dead in Acts 13:33–37, quoting specifically Ps 2:7. In

---

36. John 1:14 ESV. Emphasis added.
37. Pannenberg, *Systematic Theology* 2:317. Emphasis added.
38. Pannenberg, *Systematic Theology* 2:317. Emphasis added.
39. Longenecker, *Christology*, 78. Emphasis added.

the pre-Pauline portion of Rom 1:3–4, "the sonship of Jesus is proclaimed as having been 'declared' by the resurrection from the dead, which, because of this association of concepts, has an obvious bearing on the theme of the messiahship of Jesus."[40] Based on those verses, we understood that Jesus' *huio*-ship (messiahship, Christ-ship) was completed at his resurrection. If it is incomplete, God cannot start making other *Christic* sons (υἱοὶ), for there is no complete image of the mature Son (new being) yet. The phrase "τοῦ ὁρισθέντος Υἱοῦ Θεοῦ (having been declared the consummated son-heir of God)" in Rom 1:4 refers to the human figure of the person of the Son, and it represents the first human being to experience complete growth (elevation/exaltation).

We have learned that the messiahship (Christ-ship) is associated with the *huio*-ship of the human figure of Jesus. Each Pannenberg and Longenecker sees an *event* where Jesus of Nazareth becomes the Messiah (the Christ), but the path to messiahship is a *process*. Becoming a Messiah (a Christ) has its beginning and consummation; two events—his baptism (Matt 3:17) and his resurrection (Rom 1:3–4)—mark the milestones of the process. The method and the steps applied to the human figure of Jesus of Nazareth for becoming a Messiah set the foundation and the function of υἱοθεσία that every Christian has to experience. It is the process of making a mature son or the process of constituting an eschatological everlasting pneumatic-Christic being. The making of the Messiah in Galilea shows us the process of "human becoming," or becoming a consummated eschatological being in the whole *ktisis* (universe).

THE IMAGE OF THE *ADIPUTRA* (THE FIRST CONSUMMATED SON)

In the following, I shall occasionally depict Jesus in His consummated human nature as *Adiputra*. "*Adiputra*" is an Indonesian loanword from Sanskrit. "*Adi*" has a range of significance: "the first, the primary, the best." "*Putra*" is a word that signifies "the son of a king."[41] The *Adiputra*—the Principal Son, the Preeminent Son, or the First Son of God the King—represents a complete picture of the Messiah rather than merely "Son." The transformed life of the *Adiputra* demonstrates the possible reality that Adamic human beings can transcendentally move upward, to live everlastingly, out from their protological human facticity—their transience.

---

40. Longenecker, *Christology*, 80.
41. Translated from "Kamus Besar Bahasa Indonesia."

The Pauline concept of *népio*-ship and *huio*-ship relates to image and likeness. It relates to the fellowship of the Godhead and the fellowship of human beings with the Godhead. *Népio*-ship, *huio*-ship, likeness, and fellowship also correspond to the ontological aspect of human beings. Let us start with the source of the image: the Godhead. The finite dimensions of created space-time dwell *in* the incomprehensible infiniteness of the I Am That I Am.[42] Paul Tillich calls It "being-itself."[43] Being-Itself cannot be contained in any definition. Definitions stop Being-Itself from being the Infinite, thus preventing It from being God. Transient minds cannot conceive of the eternal Infinite. Raimundo Panikkar repeats Hilary, Irenaeus, and others: "Only God knows God."[44] Human minds and languages are not sufficient for describing Being-Itself.[45] We should look for a concept other than "human beings are created as a copy (created in the image) of an indeterminate being."[46] How can a copy be made based on an *indeterminate* being? An *indeterminate* being cannot be defined as an anthropomorphic god. If there is no anthropomorphic god, there is no such anthropomorphic image. God has no form. The image is also not the moral values we project onto the indeterminate being and then reflect on ourselves.

---

42. See Exod 3:14 NET.

43. Discussion on Being and the Question of God can refer to Tillich, *Systematic Theology* 1:163–210. By using lowercase, Tillich avoids treating "being-itself" as a personal name or a particular entity; instead, he highlights that God transcends all categories and distinctions we use for finite beings.

44. Panikkar renders, "The early christians [sic] (Hilary, Irenaeus, and others), who stood at the confluence of the hebrew [sic] notion of Yahweh and a Hellenic idea of *theos*, saw rightly that only God knows God. As I have already stressed, only in and through God can we know about God." Panikkar, *Rhythm of Being*, 129.

45. Ellicott described that God cannot be declared in words, cannot be conceived of by human thought. "I AM THAT I AM. It is generally assumed that this is given to Moses as the full name of God. But perhaps it is rather a deep and mysterious statement of His nature. 'I am that which I am.' My nature, i.e., cannot be declared in words, cannot be conceived of by human thought. I exist in such sort that my whole inscrutable nature is implied in my existence, I exist, as nothing else does—necessarily, eternally, really. If I am to give myself a name expressive of my nature, so far as language can be, let me be called 'I AM.' Tell them I AM hath sent me unto you.—I AM, assumed as a name, implies: first, an existence different from all other existence. 'I am, and there is none beside me' (Isa. 45:6); second, an existence out of time, with which time has nothing to do (John 8:58); third, an existence that is real, all other being shadowy; fourth, an independent and unconditioned existence, from which all other is derived, and on which it is dependent." Ellicott, *Ellicott's Commentary* 1:200.

46. For the discussion of Robert C. Neville's term "indeterminate being" in Bahasa Indonesia please refer to Adiprasetya, *Berteologi*, 67–74. I would like to add an alternative Indonesian translation to the phrase "the indeterminate being," that is, *"yang Ada namun tidak dapat ditentukan."*

The two words "image" and "likeness" have different meanings. According to Pannenberg, the image was still in the process of emerging.[47] The image source is the internal, eternal, and indivisible fellowship of the persons of the Godhead; it is called the *imago Trinitatis*, the image of the Trinity. The person of Jesus Christ, as the symbol of Being, expresses the ultimate image to humankind. It is characterized by His participation in the inner communion of the triune God and His ability to prolong (protrude) the fellowship of the spirits to the created beings. The Spirit and the Logos (the two hands of God) each have unseparated roles here. Please note that there are two images in this discussion.

In His human nature, Jesus of Nazareth is the first human figure to experience both the episode of diversification and the episode of homogenization. Matthew C. Steenberg asserts:

> This Christ, as the perfect image of the Father, the "visible of the invisible" who declared that "he who has seen me has seen the Father" (John 14.9), is the living paradigm for an anthropology of the image. It is not Adam, as too many scriptural commentators assume. Adam is, in point of fact, prohibited from being the full example of the image and likeness, for, as Irenaeus makes clear in the last lines of the *Refutation*, the perfected image is an *eschatological*, not a protological reality. It is known and realized only in the Incarnate One who stands as the full human "*adult*," whereas Adam had been a "child," however we may understand that analogy.[48]

Accordingly, there are two images: the protological Adamic and eschatological Christic images.[49] The latter is *built* based on the former; it is not a restoration of the protological image, but a constitution of the eschatological image. Jesus, born under the law, acquired the first image like every

---

47. Pannenberg explains, "Humans are according to God's image, but not to the same degree. In the early days of humanity, the likeness was perhaps still imperfect. Through sin, there was then increasing distortion in individuals. Only in Jesus, as Christian anthropology sees it, did the image of God appear with full clarity. . . . In the story of the human race, then, the image of God was not achieved fully at the outset. It was still in process. This is true not only of the likeness but of the image itself. But since the likeness is essential to an image, our creation in the image of God stands implicitly related to full similarity. This full actualization is our destiny, one that was historically achieved with Jesus Christ and in which others may participate by transformation into the image of Christ." Pannenberg, *Systematic Theology* 2:216–17.

48. Steenberg, *Of God and Man*, 33. Emphasis added.

49. *Contra* Genderen and Velema: "Sanctification restores the image of God." Genderen and Velema, *Concise Reformed Dogmatics*, 645. Sanctification relates to new mode of being and new existence.

other Adamic human to live in decaying temporal reality.⁵⁰ At this stage, the person of the Son is God-infant (*Theos-népios*) or God-natural protological human.

Jesus of Nazareth was born as an Adamic being under the law, which makes Him mortal and has innate sin (has the potential to sin but not necessarily must sin). This is evidenced by His subsequent temptation in the desert following His baptism. He can fulfill the law; thus, He does not sin. He is also mortal. Hence, after his baptism (the quickening of his human spirit), like no other protological human being, Jesus transcends the death inherent in bodily existence. He died but was then resurrected, which makes Him the first human υἱός (the First Mature Son). At this point, the person of Jesus Christ became *Theos-huios*. This ontological transformation is His work in terms of putting together the two natures in Himself. Because of the close union of the combination of *Theos-anthropos*, He does not sin (He lives authentically as a spiritual being) under the guidance of the Spirit, and He can transform His Adamic being into a new being (Christic being). It is the work of the Spirit that quickens Jesus' human spirit and provides a means called the fellowship of the spirit for human spirits to have a spiritual union with a divine spirit. This new being becomes a patron (model, image) for making other human υἱοί (which is also υἱοί of God, or mature sons of God).

A being that resurrects from death is something new that differs from the old natural beings. In 1 Cor 15:44, Paul talks about the natural and spiritual body. With a quickened spirit (an enlivened or believing spirit) received at baptism and a spiritual body established at the resurrection, Jesus becomes the first natural being fully transformed into a spiritual being. Jesus of Nazareth produces an elevated human essence that makes Him a pneumatic human being compatible with God, who is Spirit.

Jesus was born a human νήπιος, and at His resurrection became a human υἱός or the [mature] Son of God, the Messiah, the Christ. Catherine Mowry LaCugna writes,

> As a result of the work of Christ, all are *restored* to communion with God and human nature is elevated (divinized). The economy is the whole plan of God realized through Christ since the beginning of the world, up to its final consummation.⁵¹

In contrast, I do not subscribe to the idea of salvation as restoration or reinstatement to a prior condition or state of being. Rather, human salvation

---

50. Even after the fall, the Bible says, "God has made humankind in God's image" (Gen 9:6).

51. LaCugna, *God for Us*, 26. Emphasis added.

is the elevation of the old into new beings through ontological transformation. The elevated pneumatic human nature produces the ability to partake in communion with God, which humans did not have during their protological nature. This new pneumatic communion makes them free from fall and decay. The *Theos-huios* communion is unseparated. The created figure is tied to the Source of Life. This way, the resurrected Jesus, in His humanity, sets a new image for humanity: a new being (a υἱός, a *spiritual* being) that can conquer death.

Because the Logos and the Spirit can work to make a natural figure become a spiritual figure that saves the natural figure from decay (temporality), They can do the same to other Adamic beings. Jesus conquers death because of the communion of His *spiritual* human nature with the divine, not because of His superior moral conduct. "If Christ has not been raised . . . you are still in your sin" (1 Cor 15:17).

Entities in a pre-redemptive state (old beings) may achieve morally upright conduct under the law (resisting sin, the sting of death), yet this cannot liberate them from the ontological condition of human facticity. Characterized by decay and being-toward-death (*Sein-zum-Tode*), such beings ultimately succumb to mortality. Everlasting salvation—contrary to merit-based soteriology—is attainable not through moral performance, but exclusively via ontological renewal into a new creation (Gal 2:16; Rom 11:6; Eph 2:8–10; 2 Cor 5:17–18; Titus 3:4–7). To be saved, we need to be ontologically like the Christ.[52] Only the resurrection (that completes the *huio*-fication) can free humans from sin and decay.[53] Because of His resurrection, the human *figure* of the Christ can partake in the *personhood* of Jesus Christ forever.

After His resurrection,[54] Jesus enters the episode of homogenization. The *Theos-huios*, or God-consummated pneumatic human, is bound by an

---

52. Cf. Leloup: "But there is also a consciousness that arises directly from knowledge of ourselves, of the 'Living One' within us. It is toward this consciousness, this *gnosis*, that Yeshua invites us in the Gospel of Thomas, not in order to become 'good Christians,' but to become *christs*—in other words, gnostics, or awakened human beings." Leloup, *Gospel of Thomas*, 4. Emphasis added.

53. Cf. Zizioulas: "This is why salvific grace can consist only in transforming perverted creaturely existence—perverted insofar as it individualizes human beings—into creaturely existence expressing their being as persons and their communal nature. This transpired paradigmatically in the incarnation." Volf, *After Our Likeness*, 83.

54. Cf. Leloup: "The Gospel of Philip says: 'Those who say that the Lord died and then was resurrected are wrong; for he was first resurrected and then died.' Yeshua had awakened to the Eternal Life within him." Leloup, *Gospel of Thomas*, 145. In his baptism, the human spirit of the human νήπιος Jesus of Nazareth awakens, and his human *nature* starts to be transformed.

unseparated and eternal pneumatic union of the Spirit (the unitive Being). Even when the consummated Son, the *Adiputra*, is a *created temporal being*, He can *everlastingly* live because He partakes in the *atemporal* communion. It appears that there is no purpose in God's plan for sinless temporal humans, as He intends to share His love everlastingly. It can therefore be surmised that the intention was to create everlasting humans who would be incapable of sinning.

The above explanation agrees with Jürgen Moltmann when he said, "Jesus' personhood does not exist in isolation, *per se*; nor is it determined and fixed from eternity."[55] The person of Jesus Christ is the Being-becoming. But, the rest of Adamic humans are characterized by a singular nature. Their situation differs somewhat from that of Jesus Christ, who is said to possess two natures but is similar to His nature as a fully human being. In their baptism, the *individual* protological human beings (νήπιοι) are constituted into the eschatological pneumatic human beings (υἱοί) in the same way as the Christ, the Living One, the Awakened One.[56]

From the perspective of ontology of being, Jesus of Nazareth did not become the Messiah through His moral actions but through the ontological transformation of His being when he was baptized as a human νήπιος to begin His journey towards becoming a υἱός and achieving full status as a consummated υἱός (Messiah) in His resurrection.[57] His perfect moral conduct under the law does not free Him from death on the cross.[58] The sarkic temporal nature that the person of Jesus assumed at His birth has been fully transformed to become a pneumatic everlasting nature following His resurrection and transformation.[59] Only in this renewed nature can a person conquer death and the sting of death (sin).

55. Moltmann, *Way of Jesus Christ*, 136.

56. "The Living One, the Awakened One," after Leloup, *Gospel of Thomas*, 60.

57. Cf. Moltmann: "The words and ministry of the earthly Jesus, and his fellowship with other people, are therefore presented in wholly messianic terms. But Jesus is as yet only *the messiah on the way* and *the messiah in his becoming*, led by God's Spirit and sustained by what he has experienced with other people through his energies and his words. That is why he responds to the question whether he is the one 'who is to come' by pointing to the 'signs and wonders' which take place in his presence (Matt. 11.5). Jesus does not possess the messiahship; he grows into it, as it were, since he is moulded by the events of the messianic time which he experiences. These events find their completion in him through the sufferings of the new Servant of God and the birth pangs of the new creation." Moltmann, *Way of Jesus Christ*, 139. Emphasis original.

58. LaCugna renders, "The Logos suffers in his humanity (*kat' oikonomian*), not his divinity (*kata theologian*)." LaCugna, *God for Us*, 42.

59. For Moltmann, "in Israel's messianic promises the one who is anointed with God's Spirit is also called 'Son of God' (Ps. 2.7). . . . If Jesus of Nazareth is declared Son of God on the basis of his experience of the Spirit at his baptism, this initially means

The new being (ὁ Υἱός, the Christ) and His works cannot be separated. His new being makes Him capable of doing the works of salvation; in return, the works determine His existence as the Savior of the world. Therefore, human salvation lies in the person and the work of Jesus Christ. He made Himself the image of a consummated human; since then, He has been helping His brothers and sisters become consummated humans like Him. John Macquarrie renders,

> The relation between the manhood of Christ and the existential dimension of christology is to be seen both in the recognition that Christ is the goal or limit toward which human existence tends (he is "Lord"), and also . . . in the fact of his historicity, which makes this limiting case a "factical" one and therefore one that can seriously engage our existential interest, as a merely ideal or imaginary figure could not do.[60]

He adds, "At the limit of human existence (in this sense, that is to say, of the goal of human fulfillment) Christ manifests divine Being so that in him humanity and deity come together."[61] Torrance writes, "The unity of God and man in Jesus Christ means that true unimpaired humanity does not vanish like smoke in the presence of eternal majesty. *Nec tamen consumebatur!*"[62] Macquarrie, quoting Karl Rahner:

> Human being is a reality absolutely open upwards; a reality which reaches its highest (though indeed "unexacted") perfection, the realization of the highest possibility of man's being, when in it the Logos himself becomes existent in the world.[63]

Rahner, when discussing imitation of Christ, writes,

---

the messianic sonship. It does not yet signify a metaphysical identity of essence with God. Jesus is chosen by God, or 'adopted,' to take the word used in modern so-called 'adoptionist' christology. . . . But at the same time, Jesus' relationship to God as Son, like the sonship and daughterhood of later believers, is defined entirely and wholly pneumatologically (cf. Rom. 8:14, 16). Yahweh's *ruach*/God's Spirit creates the reciprocal relationship in which Jesus calls God 'Abba' and understands himself as 'child' of this Father." Moltmann, *Way of Jesus Christ*, 142.

60. Macquarrie, *Principles*, 295.

61. Macquarrie, *Principles*, 296.

62. Torrance, *Incarnation*, 8–9. The Latin phrase "*Nec tamen consumebatur*" translates as "Yet it was not consumed." It alludes to Exod 3:2, which describes the flaming bush that Moses observed while herding sheep. Despite the flames, the bush was not consumed, symbolizing God's presence and power."

63. Macquarrie, *Principles*, 298–30.

The human person's opportunity and obligation to imitate Christ, established by the incarnation, is . . . an imitation in the acceptance of *human existence*. . . . In regard to this imitation of Christ, it must be remembered that this humanity as it exists in Christ, in the actual shape of that life's destiny, is also *the existential of our own life*. We are not simply projected and sustained by the Logos who has assumed an abstract human nature, but by the Logos who willed and accomplished this human life in fact as his revelation and self-utterance in the finite world. That is why everything concrete about this human life tells us what is really intended with us. The Christ-conformation of existence is not merely the result of the abstract assumption of human nature by the Logos, but comes about through the actual shape of existence. That is why we meditate on the life of Christ, why we say we will imitate our Lord in his poverty, why we say that our life is a participation in the death and in the cross of Christ.[64]

God is transforming believers into υἱοὶ like the *Adiputra*, the ideal Υἱός. Old beings are saved (have permanency) when they become new beings like Him. They must, however, imitate the Son's way of life in this fallen world to authentically exist like Him.

THE PREEXISTENT SON BORN UNDER THE LAW

The eternal God wants an everlasting *ktisis* as God's permanent object of love. God did not plan for a temporal creation but must begin with a temporal one, which differs from Godself, who is eternal. Again, a child born of a woman and under the law is a human νήπιος like Adam.[65] Θεός is eternal and pneumatic, but νήπιος is temporal and sarkic. How can we explain the likelihood of a *Theos-népios* relationship in the person of Jesus Christ before His baptism? Unlike the external relationship between God and Adam, the *Theos-népios* relationship existed entirely within the person of God the Son, who would become *the* Christ. However, *how* do these two aspects coexist?

This heading, "The Preexistent Son Born Under the Law," may be read as "The Eternal Adult Son-Heir Becomes a Temporal Human Infant." It seems contradictory in itself. The Logos, the divine Son, can help humanity to transcend from a state of human infant to a state of human adult son. Therefore, He becomes like us to make us *similar* (but *not the same*) to Him

---

64. Rahner, *Content of Faith*, 347–49. Emphasis added. "The separated is reunited" shall include God and renewed men, and the whole creation.

65. Cf. Dunn, *Theology of Paul the Apostle*, 203.

in His human nature. During His incarnation, God transformed the Son of Mary from His primordial (basic, unconsummated) *népio* state of being to His consummated being. It can be done because there is no such thing as historical or original sin. After all, there is no historical Adam. Indeed, everyone falls when they are in a protological state of being. Still, when Jesus took on the protological human nature (born of [a] woman and born under the law), He did not inherit original or historical sin, but innate sin. We desire to be like Him and to follow His path to salvation because He is truly human *népios*, like us. If He were not, then salvation would be out of reach for us. If He is fundamentally different from us, then a different way of salvation would be required—one that truly applies to us.

There will be no human Messiah if there is a historical or inherited sin. Sin is the result of a harmful human innate desire. Unlike the other Adamic beings, Jesus' life was without sin, even when He had an innate desire. He is the only person who has no guilt whatsoever. Although He was in the Adamic state with the protological condition, He did not lose himself in the world (He did not sin). He was a mere human figure without blemish. From the case of Jesus, we can see that humans in the protological state can fall like Adam, but do not necessarily have to fall or be in a fallen state. In this state, because He has no sin, His divine and human natures can coexist and have the potential to be elevated.

Only Jesus of Nazareth has the potential to become ὁ Υἱός, *HaMashiach*, the Christ. God the Father, in communion with God the Son and God the Spirit,[66] transformed Jesus' natural figure through the process of υἱοθεσία. Specifically, in Rom 8:11, according to Paul, "it is the Spirit of the [One] (v. 8:9: the Spirit of Christ) that raised Jesus from the dead." Still, it may appear perplexing how Jesus might be said to have raised Himself. Again, the *person* of Jesus has two figures. Jesus was more than just a mortal man who died; He was the eternal God the Son. Thus, the resurrection is intrinsically linked to the divine Spirit of the person of Jesus Christ, whereby the vivification of His humanity is effected through the life-giving power of the Holy Spirit, affirming the Trinitarian unity in the redemptive act.

He (the person of Jesus Christ) lays down His human natural body only to take it up again (John 10:17–18). The preexistent Son, whose unique abilities make Him the only one capable of fulfilling this task. Such a calling

---

66. All three Persons of the triune God were present at the human Jesus' resurrection. Galatians 1:1 writes that the Father raised Jesus from the dead. First Peter 3:18 writes that the Spirit raised Jesus from the grave (see also Rom 1:4, and note that Rom 8:11 states that God will revive believers "through His Spirit"). In addition, in John 2:19, Jesus predicts that He would rise from the grave (see also John 10:18). So, the triune God (the Father, Son, and Holy Spirit) raised Jesus from the dead.

cannot be accomplished by a mere human prophet. This uniqueness makes the salvation that is taught in Christianity irreplaceable and incomparable.

There was a scenario to prevent Jesus from becoming the Savior. The temptation in the wilderness is a significant moment for humanity and the triune God. If Jesus had sinned, there would be no God-human because sinful human nature cannot dwell in His personhood. The communion of God-human will stop (the case of the prodigal son is dissimilar, for his fellowship with the father is based on the extended fellowship from the God-human). Without the union of God's nature and human nature in Him, He would not have been raised from death and would not have been the Christ (the Anointed); in such a case, there would be no such mediatorial *huio*-ship*s*, no such Savior, and no such human salvation. It is inconceivable if Jesus sinned; if He was a sinner, the incarnation failed; there will be no hope, no human *huio*-ship, and no other way to save humankind from corruption and decay. For this reason, *the* Messiah must be highly exalted as the Lord. It is the most cunning scheme when Satan plans to undermine God's purpose. What a catastrophe if the human Jesus sinned, for there is no iteration for the incarnation; once failed, it is failed. What a celebration when a human can be called *HaMashiach*, the Anointed One. That is why we celebrate Jesus' resurrection weekly.

The person of Jesus Christ is the only way to salvation (free from temporality because of the everlasting communion with the Source of Life). What can human prophets do to save humankind without the union of God-human? What sets Jesus apart?[67] Adamic individuals possess a created form of personhood that is of a lower degree than the personhood of God the Son (the Logos). Humans can only have one nature, whereas the Son is capable of having multiple natures. These various natures are united in His personhood. Thus, the "glue" or "the bridge" is the *person* of Jesus, who introduces the New Being. He reconciled and harmoniously merged the two sides—the Creator and the conscious creatures.[68] He alone possesses this quality; He can hold the two natures together by reconciling them *inside*

---

67. Cf. "The Definitiveness of Jesus." Macquarrie, *Principles*, 303–5.

68. Tillich explains, "Being reconciled—that is the first mark of the New Reality. And being reunited is its second mark. Reconciliation makes reunion possible. The New Creation is the reality in which the separated is reunited. The New Being is manifest in the Christ because in Him the separation never overcame the unity between Him and God, between Him and mankind, between Him and Himself. This gives His picture in the Gospels its overwhelming and inexhaustible power. In Him we look at a human life that maintained the union in spite of everything that drove Him into separation. He represents and mediates the power of the New Being because He represents and mediates the power of an undisrupted union." Tillich, *New Being*, 22.

himself, making Him irreplaceable. Jesus can do it to himself and to the other human beings who have been given to Him.

As Jesus Christ possesses both divine and human natures, He should have both divine and human spirits, allowing for inseparable pneumatic communion. When a person becomes a υἱός of God, the spirit of Christ dwells within them, leading to fellowship with the Son and the communion of spirits. Union with the Son, made possible by the Spirit (unitive Being), provides access to extended external participation in the internal fellowship of the triune God. This ability is unique to Jesus Christ and the Spirit alone.

The human figure of the Son is the firstborn *of the eschatological members of* God's created family.[69] This Son gives way to all other humans so that their possibility of a relationship with the Father may be actualized through Him. This mysterious communion of this consummated human, the Lord Jesus Christ, with the triune God is the only source of image and structure. His being and fellowship with the Father—as an image—should be imitated by all human beings, even in different degrees of perfection. This imitation makes its recipients become *like* the Son in His humanity. He took Adamic humanity and elevated it to a new level,[70] setting the goal for all human beings to reach. God now constitutes the elect according to the elevated nature of the resurrected Christ.

METAXÚ

The figure below illustrates that the finite can only exist inside the Infinite. It takes something else to place the finite and Infinite, turning the Infinite into *a being* if the finite is outside the Infinite. It is only possible when God makes room for physical reality by contracting (emptying) Godself[71]

---

69. Cf. Dunn: "On the contrary Gal. 4:4 can be understood quite adequately and comprehensively as a version of the familiar Pauline association between Jesus' sonship and His redemptive death—Jesus as the Son of God sent by God as one born of woman born under the law to redeem (by His death) those likewise under the law and bring those likewise born of woman to share in the relation of sonship which He had himself enjoyed during His ministry and now could 'dispense' to others as *the first born of the eschatological family of God*." Dunn, *Christology*, 44. Emphasis added.

70. According to Nellas, "If man, for whom all the material creation was brought into being, rose last of all creatures from the earth, it is surely logical that Christ, who is the goal of the whole of the material and spiritual creation, should be later than Adam, since all things are led from imperfection to perfection. Christ, as the highest realization of man, naturally constitutes the goal of mankind's upward journey, the beginning but also the end of history." Nellas, *Deification in Christ*, 37.

71. Nancy tells, "There is a very beautiful story in religion, in what is called a mystical form of the Jewish religion known as Kabbalah. It says that god created the world

through expansion. Like in the phrase "the empty room," "empty" does not imply "void," "nothing," or "nihil" (Gen 1:1–2). The "empty" has dimensions to it. These are how the creatures can continue to exist. In my understanding, "God empties Godself" means that part of God's infinite dimensions are reduced to a finite. This finite dimension is still more than the fifth dimensions that humans can perceive, such as electromagnetism and gravity, or the fourth dimensions of time and temperature.

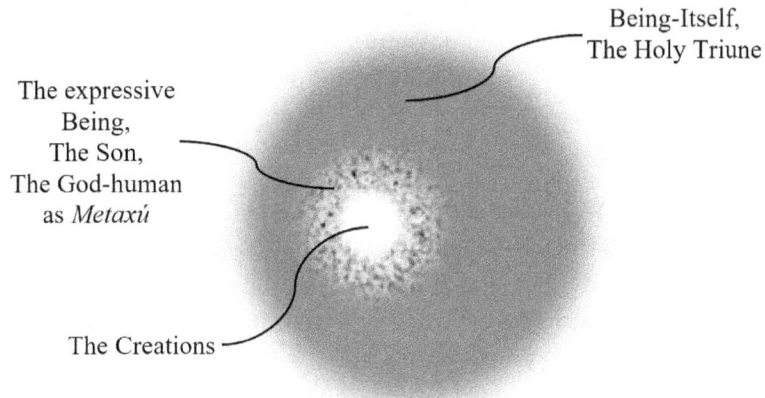

FIGURE 6: Panentheism, with the God-human as *Metaxú*

The "empty" space, *tsim-tsum*, is not, however, a complete void; unless there is nothing to "support" the finite creation, certain dimensions of God—closer to finiteness—remain. This is where the *person* of Jesus Christ, who has two natures, appears. Simone Weil describes *metaxú* (μεταξύ, in-between, in the midst, among) as the wall in the following analogy: two prisoners whose cells are adjacent communicate by knocking on the wall. The wall separates them, but it also serves as a way of communication for them. The same is true for us and God. Every break is a link.[72]

However, I have a different opinion regarding the role of the Son as the *metaxú* (metaxy). In His function as the mediator, Jesus is not like a wall *separating* the Creator and the creatures. From a schematic perspective, I consider Him more like a doughnut (granite textured in Figure 6) than a circumferential line of a fence or wall, with the Son's infinite essence interacting with the triune God on the outside and His finite nature meeting the Creation on the inside (color-coded white). The gray circular area

not at all by making something but by withdrawing, by breathing himself in, by emptying himself. By hollowing himself out, god opens the void in which the world can take its place. This is called the tsim-tsum in Kabbalah." Nancy, *Noli Me Tangere*, 92.

72. Weil, *Gravity and Grace*, 145.

in Figure 6 represents Being-Itself. For Being-Itself, there is no such thing as "outside" like in the expression "outside the football field." Everything exists inside God. "For in God we live, and move, and have our being" (Acts 17:28).

The interfaces to the finite and Infinite are represented by the two "surfaces" of the mediator. He is the Infinite-finite rather than "standing" between the finite and the Infinite. He is not a third substance, but He presents himself in the two substances. He adds human nature to His divine nature. While His one "face" deals with temporality, the other deals with eternity. I perceive Raimundo Panikkar's term "tempiternal"[73] in this way, where temporality is surrounded by eternity. Thus, the communion of the spirits is extended "inwardly" to the created humans. The figure illustrates that the finite can only exist inside the Infinite. The temporal was made possible by the Eternity. The *Metaxú*, which unites the temporal and the eternal, embodies the temporal reality. Despite the ontological distinction between God and creation, it is coherent to conceive of them as a single temporally heterogeneous entity. However, this unity attains homogeneity when considering the union of God with pneumatic new beings, a union theologically articulated as communion with God.

The person of Jesus Christ *unites* the two sides in Himself with no wall between—they are intertwined. As we have discussed earlier in Gal 4:6, by another analogy, we need an adapter to plug the Indonesian *stekker* (power plug) into the UK socket (wall power outlet). The God-human is like an adapter that can connect to both sides—one to the Deity and one to the human being. He is compatible with the human side and also with the God side. The person of Jesus Christ is not the dash (-) in the expression of "God-human," but rather the merger of the two natures as expressed in "God-human." He is not a line or a wall between the two sides, but rather a domain (an area) where the two sides are present in Him. Hence, the assembly (the union) is in Him.

The person of Jesus Christ is fully God and fully human. He is the divine preexistent Υἱός and the temporal υἱός of God, born of a woman as a νήπιος. The two natures in Christ are not merged as equals but are united in the eternal hypostasis of the divine Logos, which assumes human nature. The divine nature precedes and grounds the hypostatic union; the Logos is eternal, infinite, uncreated, self-subsistent (*aseitas*, originating entirely from Himself), and necessary, existing before the assumption of finite, contingent, and created human nature. This asymmetry between the natures safeguards both the unity of Christ's person and the immutability of

---

73. Panikkar, *Rhythm of Being*, 286.

the divine essence, preventing any reduction of the incarnation to a merely anthropological or symmetrical union. Thus, the hypostatic union does not create a new person; rather, Christ's personhood is properly understood as the person of the eternal Son, who assumes human nature without confusion, change, division, or separation. His divine nature holds His human nature.

His function as the mediator begins after the resurrection of His human figure when He became ὁ υἱός of Man, which is also ὁ υἱός of God. So, after His resurrection, the person of Jesus Christ, the divine preexistent Υἱός, has the elevated nature of ὁ υἱός of Man (ὁ υἱός of God), which makes Him ready to become the *Metaxú*. Only when the human figure of Jesus becomes the Christ—both ὁ υἱός of Man and ὁ υἱός of God—do His intertwined divine and human natures, united with the preexistent Υἱός, become inseparable forever through the pneumatic union of the two natures. This union, sustained by the Holy Spirit, ensures that Christ's divinity and humanity remain eternally undivided, transcending mere coexistence to form a singular, inseparable reality.

If following His baptism (the beginning of His *huio*-ship), Jesus fails during the temptation in the desert, the two natures will be separated forever; the human figure of Him will die with no resurrection and therefore no human Messiah, thus, no *Metaxú*. The highlight is this: the *person* of Jesus Christ becomes the mediator not only because He has the two natures but because in each of both natures, He has the position of a υἱός who can partake in the fellowship of spirits.

So, the first conciliation (not reconciliation) was not between fallen humans and God, but Jesus first conciliated the two natures (divine and human)—He took on the Adamic nature, not the Adamic sin, which has the potential to fall or grow—in Himself before He could make the Adamic humans become Christic humans and then mediate between the One and the Many. Recall that "Christic" relates to the resurrection. The human Christ provides the image of what the human mature son is, and the *person* (*Theos-huios*) becomes the mediator of the Christians (οἱ υἱοί) only. Joas Adiprasetya said that the position of the *Metaxú* (the *In-between*) becomes significant precisely because of the problem of the One and the Many.[74] On the one hand, the *In-between* cannot simply be part of the One but must also be part of the Many because only in that way can He be the *In-between* among the Many. I see the Many here as only οἱ υἱοί (pneumatic humans), so only οἱ υἱοί pray in the name of Jesus Christ. And God recognizes these

---

74. Adiprasetya, *Berteologi*, 156.

God's created pneumatic children because they call Him "*Abba*" or "*Papa*" in their prayers.

Still, the Father, the paradigmatic Existence, and the unitive Being are working to make υἱοί from νήπιοι who do not pray (speak) to the Father of the Son. The mediation provided by the *Metaxú* through the fellowship of spirits is exclusive to Christians (the pneumatic human being) only. These νήπιοι are not mediated yet. The first step prior to mediating Adamic human to the Father is its elevation through *huio*-fication.

THE ROLE OF THE HOLY SPIRIT

The extended everlasting relationship between humans and God is established through spiritual fellowship. The Holy Spirit, the Third Person of the Godhead, draws out the potentiality of humankind for becoming a wholly spiritual existent; therefore, a person can avoid the tension between the *sarx* (σάρξ) and the *pneuma* (πνεῦμα).

> The Spirit's role seems to be not so much *creation ex nihilo* as the drawing out of the potentialities of creation at all levels. For this reason, therefore, we have called the Spirit "unitive Being," for the Spirit that has proceeded into the creation labors there to build it up into a harmonious whole, at one in itself and with God.[75]

During the temporality, it is true to say that before the quickening of a person's spirit, a person is fully sarkic (in the *nēpio* state of being) but has the potential to be pneumatic (to be in the *huio* state of being). Jesus' human figure was born as a νήπιος, but He was not drawn into the distorted sarkic way of being. After the Spirit quickened His human spirit during baptism, His human figure began the process of becoming a wholly pneumatic being. He lived in the tension of sarkic and pneumatic poles. Satan tested Him in the desert, but His human spirit, which is in union with His divine Spirit and the triune God, won His inner battle. He rejected all the offers.

The Holy Spirit, or the unitive Being, facilitates pneumatic fellowship to unite new beings. He provides the medium of fellowship. Look at 2 Cor 13:14. Notice the genitive case of the article "τοῦ" before "ἁγίου πνεύματος," which denotes possession.[76] So the phrase "ἡ κοινωνία τοῦ ἁγίου πνεύματος" can be translated as "the fellowship that belongs to the Holy Spirit," or "the Spirit's fellowship." It is the fellowship where the pneumatic

---

75. Macquarrie, *Principles*, 329.
76. Mounce, *Basics*, 43.

υἱοὶ participate, too. Without the unitive Being, there will be no fellowship of God, who is Spirit, with the created beings; no union with the person of Jesus Christ. Consequently, no salvation.

Regarding Paul's usages of the Spirit of God and the Spirit of Christ, Gordon D. Fee suggests

> that Paul uses these "of God/Christ" qualifiers to indicate relationship or identification. That is, the Spirit to whom Paul is referring is the Spirit who is to be understood in terms of his relationship either with God or with Christ. "God" and "Christ" in each case give identity to the Spirit, in terms of what relationship Paul is referring to.[77]

In this chapter, I previously argued that if the person of Jesus is fully God and human, He also has the human spirit in His humanity. In the case of humans' relation to the person of Jesus Christ, the believers' human spirits are in union with Jesus' human spirit and divine Spirit. Hence, through the pneumatic fellowship provided by the unitive Being, these human spirits are connected to other human spirits, including the human spirit of Christ and the divine Spirit of Christ.[78] This union is what we call the "mystical body of Christ." It serves as the only way for humans to participate, as external partakers, in the internal communion of the holy triune God.

Macquarrie renders:

> The Holy Spirit then is God's coming to man in an inward way to enlighten and strengthen him; it is the awakening in man of the realization of his kinship with Being, an awakening brought about by Being itself that is already immanent in man.[79]

The unitive Being works from the "inside" of a νήπιος by quickening the human spirit (Rom 8:15). He partakes in transforming *sarkic* into *pneumatic* conscious beings and acts as the provider of *pneumatic* communion. After the day of Pentecost, the Holy Spirit initiates God's sub-act of υἱοθεσία among all nations. He is also the one who helps us to have Christ-faith. "The Spirit Himself He testifies together in support of the spirit of ours that we are favored children of God (ὅτι ἐσμὲν τέκνα θεοῦ)" (Rom 8:16). God gives us the Spirit to dwell with us. Fee states, "The Spirit is the way God

---

77. Fee, *Paul*, 31.

78. Cf. Fee: "Paul's doctrine of the Spirit is Christ-centered, in the sense that Christ and His work help define the Spirit and His work in the Christian life" Fee, *Paul*, 32. Fee does not recognize human spirit.

79. Macquarrie, *Principles*, 333.

is now present."[80] The Spirit, who quickened the human spirit, determines whether a person belongs to Christ. He leads and enables people to be able to live κατὰ πνεῦμα, to exist in their pneumatic mode of being. Thus, salvation (free from human facticity including temporality and sarkic desire) is not determined by obtaining *bar mitzvah* (by becoming the son of the Torah), *adoptio*, and the like status, but by possessing the ability to live in a pneumatic mode of being. During the time in between the two *huiothesía* (Rom 8:15, 23), with the two modes of being—sarkic and pneumatic—an eschatological existent (a being that exists independently) has freedom and responsibility for his actions; the Spirit guides but is not responsible for human actions.[81]

SUMMARY

We learned from the translation of Rom 9:4 in chapter 5 of this work:

> whosoever are Israelites, from whom (started from them) are (namely) the constitution of a [primogenetic] son (the making of ὁ Υἱός [the Messiah]), . . .

And from the translation of Gal 4:4–5 in chapter 4:

> Now when it came to the fullness of the time, the God, he sent forth the [eternal preexistent] Son (τὸν Υἱὸν) of Himself, born of woman (become a human being), born under law (a minor under any system of religious thinking), so that those who under law (so that those minors) he might liberate, so that the constitution of a [mature] son (τὴν υἱοθεσίαν) we might receive as due. (AHT)

God's economy of salvation requires the establishment of a time program within the world's temporality, dependent upon the physical, earthly presence of God the Son. This presence is vital for fulfilling God the Father's salvation mission. The person of Jesus Christ embodies the idea of God-human, possessing a unique dual nature as both divine and human. The infinite God the Son assumed human nature as a mere νήπιος under the law, making him a *Theos-népios*. Subsequently, He transformed into a *Theos-huios*, indicating His infinite and finite natures. To quickly grasp this idea, it is necessary to differentiate between the Son's divine and human *huio*-ships (mature sonships). The Son's divine nature coexists with the preexisting

---

80. Fee, *God's Empowering Presence*, 7.
81. Macquarrie, *Principles*, 335.

Son, while the transient human nature was assumed at birth to fulfill the role of the promised Savior (Messiah, or ὁ Υἱός).

The person of Jesus Christ has two different natures that cannot be combined to form a third nature. Therefore, theanthropic sonship does not exist. He has the status of *huio*-ship in each nature. Jesus of Nazareth (the human figure) was born as a human infant with an unfinished protological nature. He is the agent through whom this creation will attain its enduring nature. After His baptism and resurrection, this divine-human assumes the human identity of the Son of Man (ὁ Υἱός του ανθρώπου) and signifying His position as the Son of God (ὁ Υἱός του Θεού). Both titles, "ὁ Υἱός," represent the same pneumatic state of being, denoted as *huio*-ship. His journey towards complete humanity as Μεσσίας (Messiah) or Χριστός (*Christós*) laid the foundation for the Pauline Greek teachings on υἱοθεσία (misread as adoption). His role as Messiah pertains only to His humanity, not His theanthropic dual natures. It allows believers to follow in Jesus' path towards becoming perfect humans. However, humans cannot attain the theanthropic status as no one can replace the irreplaceable position of the *person* of Jesus Christ. The Son and the Holy Spirit make us *huioi* whose characteristics are similar to, but not the same as, the human Messiah.

The titles "the Son of Man" (ὁ Υἱός του ανθρώπου) and "the Son of God" (ὁ Υἱός του Θεού) refer to the same pneumatic state of being of the human Messiah, or His Lordship.[82] Jesus' baptism and resurrection resulted in a two-step ontological transformation of His human nature, which the Logos assumed at His birth. He is the ideal of what humanity can be, a new possibility—this is a kind of "impossible possibility."[83] This ontological change of Jesus' human figure also causes the overall ontological shift of Jesus' personhood. These terms, the Son of Man, the Son of God, the human Messiah, the Christ, and the Lord, relate to the risen human figure of Jesus of Nazareth.

---

82. Cf. Bacon: "The history of the doctrine of Jesus as Lord indicates then that . . . the belief rested upon a great experience, the occurrence of a single, definite day, an occurrence which all Christians from that time forward regarded as 'a designation with power of Jesus as the Son of God,' a day ever memorable as the coronation-day of the risen Jesus. . . . It was the day when 'God made him both Lord and Christ.'" Bacon, "Jesus as Lord," 215–16. See also p. 228.

83. Tillich explains, "The paradox of the 'impossible possibility' is an impossibility from the standpoint of men but is a possibility from the standpoint of God." Tillich, "What Is Wrong," 32.

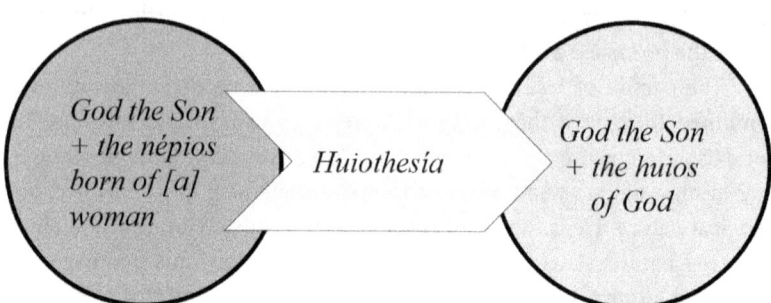

FIGURE 7: God the Son (Infinite Divine) and the Son of God (Finite Human)

The terminology "the Son" (ὁ Υἱός) holds an ontological meaning distinct from that of a νήπιος. In the context of Pauline υἱοθεσία (which is not adoption), a υἱός (an adult) is an elevated position of a νήπιος (an infant) where both terms refer to the same person in his different stages of life in the same family. At His birth, Jesus was a νήπιος; at His baptism, Jesus started to become a υἱός, and at His resurrection, Jesus was declared to be υἱοῦ θεοῦ (Son of God), a consummated human being, the Messiah. Jesus referred to himself as the Son of Man, as He is the only divine being deserving of such a title and the first and only human to achieve that state of being, in full, before the parousia. Any human person who becomes a human υἱός is a (created) υἱός of God.

The designation "the Christ" or "the Messiah" pertains specifically to the human office assumed by Jesus, rather than to His eternal divine essence. The anointing by the Holy Spirit served to empower and equip His humanity for the work of redemption. In contrast, His divinity remains unchanging, eternal, and inherently unanointed, as it does not require such consecration. This crucial distinction addresses and resolves the theological paradox often encountered in christological discourse: while the title "the Christ" acknowledges and honors the dual nature of Jesus as both fully human and fully divine, the anointing itself applies solely to His human nature. Thus, the office of "the Christ" underscores the unique role of Jesus' humanity in the economy of salvation, while preserving the transcendence and immutability of His divine nature.

The Christ sets the pattern of salvation, the new state of humankind, and the way to God. Adamic humans who become like Christ in His humanity are called Christic humans. Still, these Christic humans need to commune with the divine Son—just like the human Christ of Nazareth—to be externally attached to the internal fellowship of the triune God. Remember when Jesus stated, "I am the way, the truth, and the life" (John 14:6). To achieve salvation (permanency of human authentic existence), all other beings must follow His path, become τέκνα (beloved children, or the chosen) of God who will be made a υἱός like Him at their resurrections and engage in everlasting spiritual fellowship with the divine—the Source of Life.[84] Salvation can only be accomplished by becoming ontologically *like* the Christ.

Many religious leaders can teach about religious laws (τὰ στοιχεῖα τοῦ κόσμου, Gal 4:3), but only the Lord Jesus Christ (κύριον Ἰησοῦν Χριστόν), along with the Holy Spirit, can *ontologically* transform those who are νήπιοι into υἱοὶ (Phil 3:20–21), and teach the mature sons and daughters of God. The Lord Jesus Christ alone is the Savior of the world (ὁ σωτὴρ τοῦ κόσμου, John 4:42).

The person of the Lord Jesus Christ and the Holy Spirit are the two hands of God who work for our salvation. As the unitive Being, the Spirit provides the pneumatic union that makes the everlasting pneumatic communion of the Creator and the created beings possible. The Spirit also initiates the transformation of the protological, temporal, sarkic humans into the eschatological, eternal, pneumatic humans by vivifying human spirits. The quickening of the human spirit of Jesus of Nazareth during His baptism marks the beginning of the eschatological pneumatic era, which is the threshold into a new spiritual everlasting *aeon*. His baptism and the descent of the Spirit open the new *aeon*. Human beings can only have a kinship with the Son in their elevated being.

---

84. Cf. Meconi: "The humanity of Christ establishes a new relationship between divine and created persons. The Son has become one with humanity so as to establish a new bond between the Father and created persons." Meconi, *One Christ*, 94.

CHAPTER 7

THE PNEUMATIC-CHRISTIC BEINGS

"BE NOT ANXIOUS ABOUT WHAT YOU HAVE, BUT ABOUT WHAT YOU ARE." ~ GREGORY OF NYSSA

OVERVIEW

The translation of Rom 8:14–16 in chapter 5 revealed that humans possess spirits. The state of one's spirit—whether dormant or enlivened by the Holy Spirit—determines one's state of being, which may be considered to be either "infant" or "adult." Adamic humans (νήπιοι)—evidenced by the absence of faith in the Lord Jesus Christ among them—are in a state of infancy or a protological sarkic state or the state of estrangement with the Godhead due to the dormant nature of their spirits. In contrast, Christic humans (υἱοί) are entering the state of adulthood or an eschatological pneumatic state or the state of participation with the Godhead as a result of the vivification of their spirits.

> Indeed, as many as those who are led by the spirit from God,[1] they are mature sons of God (υἱοὶ θεοῦ). Indeed not you received a spirit of bondage again into fear, but you received a spirit of constitution of a mature son (like ὁ Υἱός) in (by) that we scream

---

1. The term "the spirit from God" (not "the spirit/Spirit of God") implies that God has given the awakened human spirit as a gift or anointing for a specific work, vivification of the soul, or supernatural (divine) intervention.

aloud, *Abba*, [to] *ho Pater* (the Creator, the Father of all beings). The Spirit himself, he, testifies together in support of the spirit of ours that we are favored children of God (τέκνα θεοῦ). Rom 8:14–16 (AHT)

The phrase "the constitution of a mature son" represents the establishment of humanity from its physical temporal state to its pneumatical everlasting state, or the elevation of protological Adamic beings to become eschatological Christic beings. Because the υἱοὶ (adult sons) of God have their spirits quickened (enlivened), they can participate in the eternal pneumatic union of the Spirit. The pneumatic union is *eternal*, but humans fundamentally are temporal entities by nature since they exist within the framework of space-time and have a definite origin. Those who are saved from temporality can live *everlastingly* (not eternally); therefore, they can also participate in the eternal pneumatic union of the triune God everlastingly.

Because of this spiritual union, which transcends physical presence, the Spirit of Christ can guide Christic humans through their spirits even when the Christ is not physically present in the world. However, this is not the case for those with dormant spirits who cannot even participate in that eternal pneumatic union because they are in a minor or old state of being with sarkic mode of being only—the problem of essence and existence. The Holy Spirit guides the pneumatic sons (υἱοὶ, who are already in their new state of being) to have a new mode of being that offers a new possible alternative to their existence—a spiritual existence.

To describe their new state of being, which has two modes of being from the vestige of old nature (remnant) and the new nature, Paul uses the "*kata*" formulas: κατὰ σάρκα and κατὰ πνεῦμα. In Gal 6:8, Paul showed the new believers (υἱοὶ) the consequences of each way of being.

> For what things a man shall sow, those also shall he reap. For he that soweth in his flesh of the flesh also shall reap corruption. But he that soweth in the spirit of the spirit shall reap life everlasting. (Gal 6:8 DRC)

It discusses the individual human being (*Dasein*)[2] undergoing an ontological transformation, which can only be understood from the perspective

---

2. Macquarrie explains, "Heidegger prefers to speak not of man but of *Dasein*, a term which he thinks expresses man's peculiar way of being man considered ontologically. *Dasein* means literally 'being-there.' . . . *Dasein* is said to exist, and it is important that we should be clear about the meaning of this basic term, existence (*Existenz*). It does not merely mean to be extant, the traditional sense of *existentia*. For that way of being, Heidegger uses the term *Vorhandenheit*. An inanimate object, such as a stone,

of Christian existentialism. In contrast, they are entering the *huio* (adult) state of being while still retaining their previously owned sarkic mode of being, alongside their newly acquired pneumatic mode. This concept is fascinating and thought-provoking, as it highlights the complexity of human nature and the potential for growth and change. It is vital to acknowledge our past and present selves as we continue to evolve by reducing (putting to death) the old and developing the new. The transformation has not been consummated yet.

Each mode has its respective consequences. If a person's soul chooses the will of his spirit (his true spiritual self), who is in union with the eternal Spirit of the Son, the person is said to be in his *pneumatic* authentic existence. On the other hand, if he follows his *sarkic* desire, he is inauthentic, for he loses himself in the world. Luke describes this idea in his parable of the prodigal son (Luke 15:11–31). The parable can be retitled "The Reckless Believers" (plural). It teaches us that both new and seasoned believers may become lost in the world and live inauthentically. It is important to note that this discussion of pneumatic authentic existence differs from atheistic existentialism,[3] which posits that authentic existence can be achieved even in a sarkic-Adamic way of being.

In the preceding chapter, we saw the role of the Messiah and the Holy Spirit in laying down the way for human salvation. In this chapter, we will discuss several ideas concerning υἱοθεσία in its application to the personal salvation of Adamic beings. In this part, we will also discuss some existentialist and essentialist theologies' ideas.

THE PAULINE GREEK *HUIOTHESÍA* IS A METAPHOR, NOT A LEGAL LITERAL TERM

Before Paul, we learn that Diodorus Siculus had used the word "υἱοθεσία" to describe something very similar to the Roman *toga virilis* or Jewish *bar mitzvah*. We had discussed this topic in the introduction to this work when we learned that Diodorus recorded the story of Aemilius and his two birth sons, Scipio and Fabius, and the giving of υἱοθεσία. It reads, "When Aemilius, *his real father*, died and left his property *to him and to Fabius*, the

---

is extant, it occurs, but it does not exist in the sense in which Heidegger uses the term. What, then, are the distinctive characteristics of existence?" Macquarrie, *Existentialist Theology*, 32.

3. The atheistic existentialism rejects the idea of a preset human essence bestowed by God and focuses on individual freedom, choice, and responsibility.

sons he had given in υἱοθεσίαν."[4] It is evident in this usage that υἱοθεσία is not about "adoption" because Scipio and Fabius were the natural sons of Aemilius. On the other hand, W. v. Martitz, under the topic of υἱοθεσία as religious presuppositions in *TDNT*, quoted Wenger-Oepke, stating that in Greek, there are *no* examples of adoption in the transferred sense. It is about a rebirth—Martitz, who also refers to *Diod. S.*, 4, 39, 2, continues that this rite (υἱοποιήσασθαι, *huiopoiēsasthai*) is to legitimize Heracles as the son of Zeus, which is regarded as necessary in addition to elevating him to divine status (ἀποθέωσις, *apotheōsis*).[5]

The apostle Paul employs the Greek term υἱοθεσία—the formation of a mature son (υἱός) from an infant (νήπιος)—and Christianizes it to metaphorically[6] (theologically) describe the process of making a new eschatological Christic being (υἱός) from an old protological Adamic being (νήπιος). The metaphorical use of Paul's υἱοθεσία is not limited to the context of Diodorus' work. However, it is essential to note that Paul's υἱοθεσία also carries the connotation of "the maturity of human nature." As we learned from chapter 2, the biblical meaning of υἱοθεσία has been interpreted in many ways. Again, we have to be aware that the Pauline *Greek* theological concept of υἱοθεσία has nothing to do with the translated Pauline *Latin* [legal] *adoptio*, the Roman *toga virilis* or Jewish *bar mitzvah*. Pauline *Greek* theological concept of υἱοθεσία denotes a divine sub-act of elevation, redefining humanity's ontological relationship to God.

The Latin translation of Pauline υἱοθεσία to "*adoptio*" and the English "adoption" have created different meanings. Υἱοθεσία is not concerned with the transfer of an enslaved person from a foreign family (Satan's family or no family) to God's family. The new status is a result of the ontological transformation of the person. An Adamic human with a new legal status who has not undergone the ontological transformation cannot be considered a new being. The transformation into a new being must occur before

---

4. Diodorus, *Diodorus of Sicily* 11:385. Emphasis added.

5. *TDNT* 8:389. Emphasis added.

6. Searle renders, "The existence of such utterances—utterances in which the speaker means metaphorically something different from what the sentence means literally—poses a series of questions for any theory of language and communication: What is metaphor, and how does it differ from both literal and other forms of figurative utterances? . . . It conveys its truth conditions by way of another semantic content, whose truth conditions are not part of the truth conditions of the utterance. The expressive power that we feel is part of good metaphors is largely a matter of two features. The hearer has to figure out what the speaker means—he has to contribute more to the communication than just passive uptake—and he has to do that by going through another and related semantic content from the one which is communicated." Searle, "Metaphor," 83–111.

a new status is attained. The Pauline Greek concept of υἱοθεσία cannot be approached from a legal perspective in the same way as the Latin *adoptio*.

We must highlight that the ontological concepts of being, becoming, and categories are fundamentally important within the framework of biblical υἱοθεσία.

HUIOTHESÍA DESCRIBES AN ONTOLOGICAL TRANSFORMATION

I found that Carlo Collodi's Pinocchio metaphor can help us understand the underlying concept of υἱοθεσία. Pinocchio's journey with the family of his creator and *papa* from a puppet to a human being illustrates the idea of human ontological transformation within the created family of God, from a sarkic, temporal, protological Adamic being to a pneumatic, everlasting, eschatological, Christic human being. It is called christification: a process of human exaltation to be like the human Christ.

This tale of the Adamic human condition is depicted as a puppet's condition. The narrative opens with a piece of enchanted wood. Master Cherry bestowed a piece of timber to Geppetto, who crafted it into a wooden puppet.[7] This puppet-to-be displayed its inherent mischief in its features. Despite its incomplete hands, they seized Geppetto's wig.[8] When Geppetto completed crafting the feet, he suddenly endured a sharp kick to the tip of his nose. Subsequently, the puppet leapt into the street and ran away.[9]

In his journey, Pinocchio encountered the Talking Cricket who cautioned him that those boys who rebel against their parents and flee capriciously from home will never achieve anything good in the world. They will have to regret it severely sooner or later.[10] Having learned from his experiences, Pinocchio aspired to be a decent boy and enjoyed growing up after his ordeal. But the Fairy said,

> But you cannot grow, because puppets never grow. They are born puppets, live puppets, and die puppets.[11]

This puppet condition describes our Adamic human condition, where we cannot escape our facticity as fleshly, temporal, protological decaying creatures. We are born fleshly, live fleshly, and die as fleshly humans. During

7. Collodi, *Pinocchio*, 9.
8. Collodi, *Pinocchio*, 16–17.
9. Collodi, *Pinocchio*, 18.
10. Collodi, *Pinocchio*, 22.
11. Collodi, *Pinocchio*, 114–15.

our primordial perfection, we are anxious about the future—either we will have the consummated perfection like the Lord or corruption (decay). We want to quit this current primordial situation. Like Pinocchio, we want to be perfect people; as the puppet said, "I promise you. I will become a good little boy, and I will be the consolation of my papa."[12] To Pinocchio's wish, the Blue-Haired Fairy replied:

> I know it, and it is on that account that I have forgiven you. I saw from the sincerity of your grief that you had a good heart; and when boys have good hearts, even if they are scamps and have got bad habits, there is always something to hope for: that is, there is always hope that they will turn to better ways. That is why I came to look for you here. I will be your mamma.[13]

Unfortunately, we are powerless to help ourselves. Nevertheless, there is still hope. Our Creator knows our longing because it is His longing, too.

The repentance was momentary. Pinocchio got into a fight with his friends, which led to his detention. When he returned to the Fairy's home, she said, "I will pardon you once more, but woe to you if you behave badly a third time! . . . Tomorrow, your wish shall be gratified. Tomorrow, you shall cease to be a wooden puppet and become a boy."[14] The naughty puppet broke his promise again and went to the "Land of Boobies," also known as the "Land of Cocagne." Pinocchio grew donkey ears and became a little donkey.[15] Subsequent immersion in water transformed him back into a puppet.[16] He eventually came across Geppetto. The puppet worked 'til midnight after their reunion before falling asleep: "Upon awakening, he discovered that he was no longer a wooden puppet, but that he had become instead a boy, like all other boys."[17]

He has been freed from the puppet's facticity (givenness), the puppet condition.

Pinocchio serves as a relatable symbol for us. An individual with an Adamic nature will invariably produce Adamic things, including both Adamic inauthentic and authentic existence, as described by Jean-Paul Sartre. Still, salvation (human permanency) is more than authentic or inauthentic temporal Adamic existence. It is about everlasting spiritual beings who can live authentically before their Creator. I want to address this point: the

---

12. Collodi, *Pinocchio*, 115.
13. Collodi, *Pinocchio*, 116.
14. Collodi, *Pinocchio*, 141.
15. Collodi, *Pinocchio*, 148–69.
16. Collodi, *Pinocchio*, 170.
17. Collodi, *Pinocchio*, 190–91.

focus must be on transforming the being and its nature rather than solely on the resulting moral actions. Through divine intervention, temporal Adamic beings and their nature can be transformed into everlasting Christic beings with a new nature, enabling them to perform "Christic things."

As we have observed, Pinocchio undergoes two distinct transformations: he can become a donkey—a degradation of being resulting from his own choices—or he can be transformed into a human son, an elevation of being effected by the intervention of the Fairy within her home. Atheistic existentialism operates within the former scenario, where humans exercise control. The former signifies the self-destructive consequences of his actions, while the latter represents his aspirational state, attainable only through the Fairy's agency. This narrative underscores the notion that humans are capable of morally degrading themselves but incapable of independently altering their fundamental nature to attain perfection; rather, they require a Savior.

Early in Pinocchio's narrative, we discover that "this puppet-to-be displayed its inherent mischief in its features." Thus, its traits (characters) are found in the wood (essence). Does this contradict the existentialist belief that "existence precedes essence" and the "dynamic process of self-creation?"[18] I see here the importance of discussing human essence (nature). For atheistic existentialism, Adamic humans exist in the protological realm only because they recognize only one human category, referring to the protological Adamic being. They find their authentic selves here.

Christians are different. In this work, we perceive two categories of human beings: the protological Adamic being with the fundamental essence (nature) and the eschatological Christic being with the elevated essence (nature). As an Adamic being, in their sarkic state of being, a person can be authentic or inauthentic. In a person's new state of being as a Christic being, she can still be authentic or inauthentic. However, the degree of pneumatic-authentic existence is higher than that of somatic sarkic one. According

---

18. Aho explains, "What this statement suggests is that there is no pre-given or essential nature that determines us, which means that we are always *other than* ourselves, that we do not fully coincide with who we are. We exist *for ourselves* as self-making or self-defining beings, and we are always in the process of making or defining ourselves through the situated choices we make as our lives unfold. This is, according to Sartre, 'the first principle of existentialism,' and it 'means, first, that man exists, turns up, appears on the scene, and, only afterwards, defines himself.' ... The point here is that there can be no complete or definitive account of being human because there is nothing that grounds or secures our existence. Existence is fundamentally unsettled and incomplete because we are always projecting forward into possibilities, 'hurling ourselves toward a future' as we imagine and re-imagine who we will be. Existence, then, is not a static thing; it is a dynamic process of self-making." Aho, "Existentialism." Emphasis original.

to Paul, even if a pneumatic person exists inauthentically, they will still be saved but it will be like through fire.[19]

FROM CORRUPTIBLE TO INCORRUPTIBLE HUMAN BEINGS

Corporeal sarkic human beings can find their true selves in their Adamic stage of existence, but cannot progress toward God, who is Spirit; only the Creator can draw humans to Itself. Only the Creator may initiate the process of human ontological transformation, resulting in an elevated being. God's goal for humanity is not to maintain a temporal, blemish-free Adamic existence, but to bring about an ultimate, everlasting pneumatic-Christic being capable of living pneumatically, sinlessly, and everlastingly. For this purpose, God sends the Messiah to inaugurate this new state of being.

For Paul Tillich, Christianity's primary message is the New Creation, the New Being, and the New Reality. Tillich writes, "For it is the Christ who brings the New Being, who saves men from the old being, that is, from existential estrangement and its self-destructive consequences."[20]

God must free us, humans, from our *transient* primordial nature that is *sinful*. When there are no more protological humans, human sin will vanish. The law can limit our ability to sin, but it does not solve the issue of temporality and the source of our fleshly desire. Remember, the apostle Paul himself wrote:

> So I find it to be a law that when I want to do right, evil lies close at hand. For I delight in the law of God, in my inner being, but I see in my members another law waging war against the law of my mind and making me captive to the law of sin that dwells in my members. Wretched man that I am! Who will deliver me from this body of death? Thanks be to God through Jesus Christ our Lord! So then, I myself serve the law of God with my mind, but with my flesh I serve the law of sin. (Rom 7:21–25 ESV)

All religious procedures, such as circumcision practiced by Jews, sacrifices observed by pagans, or baptism observed by Christians, are irrelevant; only a New Creation matters.[21] Tillich further explains

---

19. The apostle Paul wrote, "If the work that anyone has built on the foundation survives, he will receive a reward. If anyone's work is burned up, he will suffer loss, though he himself will be saved, but only as through fire." 2 Cor 3:14–15 ESV.

20. Tillich, *Systematic Theology* 2:150.

21. Tillich, *New Being*, 15–16; "if anyone is in Christ, he is a new creature." 2 Cor 5:17.

the New Creation is the reality in which the separated is reunited. The New Being is manifest in the Christ because in Him the separation never overcame the unity between Him and God, between Him and mankind, between Him and Himself.[22]

Only through union with the eternal Creator can the creature be saved from decay; however, this requires that humans attain a new state of being. How, then, can one become a new being? Tillich writes, "Resurrection happens now, or it does not happen at all."[23] I submit that the human ontological transformation begins with the resurrection of the human spirit (Rom 8:15) before it proceeds to the resurrection of the body (8:23),[24] resulting in a fully consummated person, with a vivified spirit, ascended soul, and a pneumatic body.

Irenaeus teaches that humans grow,

> and in this respect God differs from man, that God indeed makes, but man is made; and truly, He who makes is always the same; but that which is made must receive both beginning, and middle, and addition, and increase.[25]

> Now it was necessary that man should in the first instance be created; and having been created, should receive growth; and having received growth, should be strengthened; and having been strengthened, should abound; and having abounded, should recover [from the disease of sin]; and having recovered, should be glorified; and being glorified, should see his Lord.[26]

In creating humans, God had the image of Christ in mind. Thus, the life promised to the new beings differs from the life of Adam in his prelapsarian state of being. Salvation is not about restoring life to its original pristine condition before the fall but becoming a new humankind that

---

22. Tillich, *New Being*, 22.

23. Tillich, *New Being*, 24.

24. Tillich renders, "But Paul realizes—better than the Apostles' Creed—the difficulty of this symbol, the danger that it may be understood in the sense of a participation of 'flesh and blood' in the Kingdom of God: He insists that they cannot 'inherit' it. And against this 'materialistic' danger he calls the resurrection body 'Spiritual.' Spirit—this central concept of Paul's theology—is God present to man's spirit, invading it, transforming and elevating it beyond itself. A Spiritual body then is a body which expresses the Spiritually transformed total personality of man. One can speak about the symbol 'Spiritual body' up to this point; concepts cannot go beyond this, but poetic and artistic imagination can." Tillich, *Systematic Theology* 3:412.

25. *ANF* 1:474.

26. *ANF* 1:522.

cannot fall, decay, or be annihilated.²⁷ A truly pristine life will emerge, but it is not a state humans have previously attained.

With this in mind, we do not need to teach the historical fall and the *historical* Adam. We can accept the progressing scientific discoveries of human origins and still believe that the Bible teaches about the *literary* Adam and Eve (humans) who fall. The story in Eden describes and acknowledges that every protological human (genus *Homo*, not only species *sapiens*, including *transhuman*—humans with augmented capabilities) falls. Everyone falls, and humans cannot come to God in their fallenness. They cannot "talk and walk with God" as the protological literary human Adam did in Eden. Lacking the guidance of the Spirit, humans require laws for direction. Only one historical Adamic being (read: figure) did not sin—Jesus of Nazareth.

There are different modalities of life. John Behr explains,

> It is similarly mistaken to equate the pre-lapsarian life of Adam with the life of the Spirit manifested by Christ. That they should be regarded as different modalities of life is demanded by, first, Genesis 2:7, which speaks only of the first man becoming a "living soul" (ψυχὴν ζῶσαν); second, the apostle Paul, who specifies that it is the last Adam who became a life-creating Spirit (πνεῦμα ζωοποιοῦν), in contrast to the first Adam who was a "living soul" (1 Cor. 15:45–6); third, the whole movement of Irenaeus's theology of the economy, which moves from "animation" to "vivification": as Adam was animated by the breath of life, so Christ was vivified by the Spirit, as also will be those who, as adopted sons in him, presently have the pledge of the Spirit.²⁸

A person comprises body, soul, and spirit. Those who think the soul is the spirit and the spirit is the soul will face difficulties reading those verses. I view the human spirit, either dormant or vivified, as a faculty of his soul. Paul refers to Adam as a "living soul" because Adam was in a *nēpio* state of being (infant, minor) whose spirit is still dormant. Verlyn D. Verbrugge writes, "He is the representative of those who are animated by the human soul."²⁹ In such a condition, Adam's spirit must not be active yet.

Even though Verbrugge does not comment on the following clause, "the last Adam became a life-giving spirit" (1 Cor 15:45), still, in parallel,

---

27. For comparison's sake, Julia S. Konstantinovsky writes, "All pre-modern Christian thinkers (notably Irenaeus, Athanasius, Basil, Gregory the Theologian, Augustine, and Maximus), as well as early modern theologians such as Calvin and Luther, contrast the fallen condition of creation (characterized by the presence of evil and mortality) with the original pristine one." Hays et al., *When the Son*, 125.

28. Behr, *Asceticism*, 95.

29. Verbrugge, "1 Corinthians," 11:402.

we can interpret the last Adam as the representative of those enlivened by the human spirit (the human infinite element); it is only possible if the human Christ (the last Adam) and those whom he represents have their spirit vivified.[30] If Adam, led by his soul, could fall, then sarkic-Adamic humans need to be elevated (by augmenting their state of being) so that the presence of their spirit can make it possible for them to be led by the counsel of the Spirit of Christ. Again, Adamic humans can live an authentic life, but it is temporal (finite), ending in existential despair.

In 1 Cor 15:46, the apostle Paul says, "But it is not the spiritual that is first but the natural, and then the spiritual." It signifies the gradual creation of humankind. Adamic humans are born in temporality and die, but God has put in them the potentiality to escape from this condition. Macquarrie writes, quoting Irenaeus,

> On the contrary, "created things must be inferior to him who created them . . . they come short of the perfect. Man could not receive this perfection, being as yet an infant." The image of God, in other words, was given as a potentiality, into the realization of which man might grow—though equally, through sin, he might slip back from it. Mistaking the parallelism of "image" and "likeness" in the Hebrew for two distinct concepts, Irenaeus seems to have supposed that man's original endowment was the potentiality for growing towards God (this was the "image"), and that the goal would be the glory of closeness to God, the realization of the potentiality (this was the "likeness"). So actual human life is the progression, though it may be interrupted, from the potency of the image to the fulfillment of the likeness.[31]

Origen also has a similar opinion about the "image" and the "likeness," but for him, the "likeness" is achieved through human efforts.[32] Therefore, it is something that we have not achieved yet. On the contrary, Claudia Welz, referring to the work of Niels Jørgen Cappelørn, writes:

---

30. Cf. Leloup: "In some gnostic texts we encounter the theme of the Savior who must be saved. According to this theme, Yeshua the Christ can be totally free only when all his sparks of divinity, now dispersed in matter, are reunited. This spark of Spirit in us, which is his, must be awakened in order to reascend to the Father." Leloup, *Gospel of Thomas*, 203.

31. Macquarrie, *In Search of Humanity*, 33.

32. Blosser explains, "This is so that human beings would work to acquire it by their own industrious efforts to imitate God; for in the beginning only the possibility of perfection is given them by the dignity of the 'image,' while in the end they are to acquire for themselves the perfect 'likeness' by the carrying out of works." Blosser, *Become Like the Angels*, 230.

This means that Irenaeus's distinction between *imago* and *similitudo Dei*, where the image of God (*imago*) in the soul is not lost, but the likeness to God (*similitudo*) in the spirit has been lost because of the Fall of man, can also be found in Kierkegaard.[33]

I'm afraid I have to disagree with Irenaeus and Kierkegaard in this section. I discovered that human *growth* is incompatible with the line "the likeness to God (*similitudo*) in the spirit has been lost because of the Fall of man." This line posits the necessity of human restoration instead of elevation.

I base my objection on my reading of Pauline υἱοθεσία (not adoption), especially Rom 8:15, which brings the idea of the elevation of human nature that begins from the human spirit, which does not connect with the idea of human restoration to a prelapsarian state of being.[34] If the literary Adam began with his self-consciousness,[35] then the υἱοθεσία in Rom 8:15 elevates the Adamic humans so they can have Christ-consciousness. I understand that υἱοθεσία is about the elevation of humans from the infancy category to the adult category, which symbolically (theologically) means the elevation of human original nature to its consummated nature that can ignite a *spiritual* relationship with the Creator. Here, I cannot entirely agree with Herman Bavinck on the account that grace was seen as *restoring* and *healing* the created character from sin and its consequences; however, I agree with the "Roman views" on the exaltation of human nature.[36]

---

33. Welz, *Humanity*, 123.

34. *Contra* Bavinck: "Grace was not regarded as elevating and perfecting nature beyond its created character but as restoring and healing it from sin and its consequences. The Reformation opposed the Roman conception of nature and grace as a matter of fundamental principle. . . . Reformed theologians thus avoided significant errors that set grace against nature rather than sin." Bavinck, *Reformed Dogmatics*, 323.

35. See our discussion of Rom 8:20 in our biblical studies where Carl Gustav Jung explains about the first appearance (the dawn) of human consciousness.

36. Cf. Bavinck: "Flesh by its very nature is here opposed to the spirit. Hence, according to Rome, grace is a supernatural gift as such and not incidentally a divine response to sin. Sin does not in any way change the nature of grace; both before and after the fall it was an *elevation* of humanity *above nature*. As a religion of redemption, Christianity is not a *reparation* but an *elevation* of nature; it elevates nature above itself, it divinizes humanity. Speaking strictly and logically, the incarnation was necessary before the fall and apart from sin; in order that man might become like God, God had to become man. Atonement is subordinated to incarnation; the point of gravity does not lie in satisfaction for sin and the forgiveness of sin, but in the humanization of God and the divinization of humanity. The Reformation took its stand against this Neoplatonic Areopagite philosophy because Scripture knows no such contrast between the natural and the supernatural; it knows only one idea of humanness, one moral law, one final destiny, and one priesthood, which is the portion of all believers." Bavinck, *Reformed*

I submit that, based on Pauline υἱοθεσία, grace is understood as the elevation and perfection of human nature beyond its original protological character; in its final state, due to the pneumatic union with the Creator (the Source of Life), pneumatic elevated humans will be free from decay, and because of the absence of sarkic desire then they will be free from sin and its consequences. Bavinck's rejection overlooks valuable insights within what he labels as Neoplatonic Areopagite philosophy, when in fact it is the gospel that teaches about the elevation of humans beyond their initial state. This is akin to "throwing the baby out with the bathwater." Unfortunately, the endorsement of the doctrine of adoption, in place of υἱοθεσία, obscures this truth, rendering the theme of the exaltation of human *nature* (the gospel of the Christ) absent from Reformed teaching.

The "*similitudo*" was first given to the Adamic creatures as a potentiality and cannot be lost. The potentiality of Adamic humans is contingent upon the retention of this quality. It is recommended that this be viewed in the following manner: Every human being is created in the image of God, who is capable of participating in a relationship. However, as infants, they can only participate in a carnal relationship initially because they do not yet possess a spiritual likeness to God. They sin because they are created with the material of the world, and they have an inherent carnal desire. However, during their creation, Adamic humans are also designed with the potential to free them from their original state of being, thus enabling them to attain a renewed, elevated state of being. The capacity to engage in a sarkic relationship can be elevated to an ability to participate in a pneumatic relationship, analogous to (but not to the same extent as) the fellowship of the triune God.

Believers—who were of created νήπιοι—will never earn divine sonship[37] because they do not have a direct relationship with the transcendent Father in any form of sonship (*huio*-ship); they are not divine in any way, so

---

Dogmatics, 322–23. Emphasis original.

37. Ebeling writes, "The association with Jesus Christ is meant to indicate a double relationship. First, our sonship corresponds to his sonship, because it is brought about by his sonship. On the other hand, however, for this very reason our sonship differs from his. What it means to say that *we are God's sons* is defined in terms of Jesus Christ. In addition to 4:4–5, other Christological formulas in Galatians also provide important evidence (1:4; 2:20; 3:13). Here *all human fantasies about the meaning of divine sonship are scattered to the winds*. But there is also an indirect warning against weakening the unprecedented statement that *we are God's sons* through a terminological distinction, to the effect that *we are children of God*, in contrast to the only Son of God. This could result in a failure to observe the internal relationship between the two expressions." Ebeling, *Truth of the Gospel*, 209. Emphasis added. Even though we reach the similar conclusion, we do so with different concepts.

human beings will never participate in such a divine family; in other words, there is no such adoption into a divine family. Like Jesus the νήπιος became Jesus the υἱός (Jesus the Christ), in the same way His believers experience the same path to become christic beings, but Christians are not becoming like the person of the divine Logos.[38] The potentiality (the image) is actualized through conformity (the likeness) to the image of the [mature] Son (Rom 8:29).

Under the subtitle "The divine Likeness in the OT," Gerhard von Rad states in *TDNT* that "the OT says nothing about the divine likeness being lost."[39] If the likeness is the "destination" (conform to the Mature Son's image), Adam did not lose the divine likeness, for he did not have it yet when he ate the fruit. "Just as we have borne the image of the man of dust, we shall also bear the image of the man of heaven" (1 Cor 15:49). Clearly, there are two images: one is built on top of the other.

The new image does not replace the first but brings an elevated human essence (nature). As a physical being, Adam's likeness in spirit primordially existed before the advent of faith.[40] His spirit was dormant (latent, existing but not functioning), not as a consequence of the fall, but because it had not been vivified.[41] This condition resulted in the individual experiencing only carnal desires. If his spirit were functioning properly (or if Adam were created as a υἱός), he would not have fallen.

In his primordial state, Adam could not exist spiritually and could not participate in the spiritual fellowship (the fellowship of the pneumatic υἱοί)

---

38. *Contra* Schweizer: "The fact that Christ, as Logos, is God's image underlies the possibility that believers will be fashioned in His likeness and can thus return to the world of God. But once again this background has been completely reconstructed in terms of apocalyptic thinking. Believers already live as a new creation. This is the work of the Son of God who in His Spirit (Gal. 4:6) embraces a whole world and brings into being a new creation. Man is set in this at baptism and therewith becomes God's son." *TDNT* 8:392.

39. *TDNT* 2:391–92.

40. Cf., "Now before faith came, we were held captive under the law, imprisoned until the coming faith would be revealed." Gal 3:23; even in prelapsarian life, there was law in Gen 2:16.

41. Cf. Heard: "The pneuma is that part of man which is made in the image of God—it is the conscience, or faculty of God-consciousness which has been depraved by the fall, and which is dormant, though not quite dead. The pneuma in the psychical or natural man has some little sense of the law of God, but no real love for Himself, and therefore it drives man from God, instead of drawing him to God. . . . The pneuma would direct the psyche, and the psyche our carnal appetites. There would not be a single motion of sinful desire. . . . But such is not the state which man is in at present. He begins life with a dormant pneuma, and therefore with desires which have become exorbitant, and with a reason unable to control them." Heard, *Tripartite Nature of Man*, ix–x, 212.

with the Son of God. Even if Adam (a νήπιος who represents all humankind) did not sin, he was still temporal and corruptible, for he had no participation in the New Being due to no fellowship with the Son yet. God's primary purpose is to have incorruptible beings so God can share love unceasingly. The process of human ontological transformation is initiated with the baptism of the human figure of Jesus. This event represents the rebirth of humanity.

According to Tillich, "Faith, justifying faith, is not a human act, although it happens in man; faith is the work of the divine Spirit, the power which creates the New Being, in the Christ, in individuals, in the church."[42] I deduce this act as giving faith to the quickened human spirit. Welz penned imperative sentences.

> The spirit is the location of faith or unfaith, belief or disbelief. . . . The spirit decides how the powers of body and soul are used. For this reason, the spirit becomes the core of the self. It is here, in the spirit, that the spiritual relation to God is determined and consummated.[43]

In Adam's case, *if* a spirit in its dormant state *were* functioning, why could not the Spirit commune with it? Human salvation requires the human figure of Jesus Christ to take effect. The salvation of humanity is not contingent upon the efficacy of teaching or laws; instead, it is a result of the transformation of Yeshua into ὁ Υἱός and His actions. I maintain that a protological being has a [dormant] spirit with no faith in the incarnate Son yet.[44] Such a spirit does not function yet as it should; it is inactive but has the potential to be enlivened.[45] Only a quickened human spirit can have Christ-faith.

The Holy Spirit transforms human potentiality into actuality. Paul explains the work of the divine Spirit in Rom 8. His two usages of the term υἱοθεσία in that chapter lay the foundation of "already/not yet" (the process of human salvation has already started but not finished yet) theology.

---

42. Tillich, *Systematic Theology* 2:178.

43. Welz, *Humanity*, 126.

44. *Contra*, Irenaeus' anthropological teaching in *Against Heresies*. Ben C. Blackwell abridges, "In *ah* 5.6.1, those that are 'carnal' and 'imperfect' consist of only a body and soul, and they possess the image of God but not his likeness. In contrast, those who are 'spiritual' and 'perfect' 'partake in the Spirit of God,' have God's Spirit in addition to the body and soul, and therefore are in the image and likeness of God (cf. *ah* 3.22.1)." Blackwell, *Christosis*, 40. *ah*, added.

45. Existing but not yet developed. Cf., "And I will give you a new heart, and a new spirit I will put within you. And I will remove the heart of stone from your flesh and give you a heart of flesh. And I will put my Spirit within you, and cause you to walk in my statutes and be careful to obey my rules." Ezek 36:26–27 (ESV).

Verse 8:15 explains how the process starts, while v. 8:23 is related to its consummation. Paul described this idea as the making of a [mature] son, which theologically means the making of a new spiritual being.

> Indeed not you received a spirit of bondage again into fear, but you received a spirit of constitution of a [mature] son (like ὁ Υἱός) in (by) that we scream aloud, *Abba*, [to] *ho Pater* (the Creator, the Father of all beings). (Rom 8:15)

This allegory portrays a scene in which the Holy Spirit is working on the human spirit that He took out from the people and has successfully "added" faith to it. Thus, He did not give back the unbelieving spirit, which causes fear of death; instead, He gave the spirit with justifying faith. In return, this human vivified spirit (the believing spirit) reciprocates with the Son's Spirit and makes a union (fellowship). It is the reason why humankind must be in expectation of the coming of the Messiah. To be saved, humans must have the Son (the Bridegroom) as their "partner" in a spiritual fellowship culminating in the parousia (Rev 19:7). We call this a new kind of fellowship (the fellowship of the pneumatic υἱοί), the mystical body of Christ, or church.[46]

A υἱός symbolizes a person who has received faith in his spirit.

> Because now you are [mature] sons (υἱοί), God, he sent forth the Spirit of the Son (τὸ πνεῦμα τοῦ Υἱοῦ) of Him into the hearts of ours, screaming, *Abba*, [to] *ho Pater*. (Gal 4:6)[47]

As a result of this union with the [mature] Son, the Spirit resides within and guides the [mature] sons (1 Cor 3:16). In the absence of spiritual compatibility and the pneumatic fellowship provided by the unitive Being, there is no means of union with the sarkic corporeal beings. The guidance provided by the Spirit to the spirits of Christians facilitates the sanctification of their souls.[48]

---

46. Tillich renders, "The Spiritual Community is not a group existing beside other groups but rather a power and a structure inherent and effective in such groups, that is, in religious communities. If they are consciously based on the appearance of the New Being in Jesus as the Christ, these groups are called churches." Tillich, *Systematic Theology* 3:162.

47. *Contra* Fowler: "Paul is not advocating a cause and effect sequence whereby in becoming a Christian one first becomes a 'son of God' and then receives the Spirit of Christ. These spiritual realities are concomitant rather than consequential." Fowler, *Commentary*, 148.

48. For Tillich, "the multidimensional unity of life means that the impact of the Spiritual Presence on the human spirit is *at the same time*, an impact on the *psyche*, the cells, and the physical elements which constitute man. . . . The Spirit grasps the spirit

Still, the rising soul is under the influence of the flesh. Christians have savored the new state of things but have not yet reached its final form, which is culminating at parousia. At the same time, Christians have not fully left the old state of things. Behr writes, "The followers of Christ do not receive the fullness of the promise until the resurrection."[49] The "redemption of our body" will happen at once at the coming υἱοθεσία as portrayed in Rom 8:23.[50] Having the spiritual body dissolves the domination of the flesh and makes the soul (ψυχή, *psūkhē*) entirely led by the spirit. It finalizes the ontological transformation of sarkic beings. These two milestones of the processes of υἱοθεσία renew individual beings to become new, incorruptible human beings. Thus, υἱοὶ (sons) assume the pneumatic incorruptible bodies to enter the coming αἰών, everlastingness in eternity—no death in the new reality.[51]

THE CROSS, THE RESURRECTION, AND THE ULTIMATE EVERLASTING SALVATION

The concept of justification involves two exciting elements: pardon and imputed righteousness.[52] As we learned from Green and Baker, "In this case, sins might be forgiven, but are we any less likely not to engage in disobedience tomorrow?"[53] The cross deals with the problem of sin in temporal existence. This salvation is only a predecessor to the *ultimate everlasting* salvation. To save Adamic humans from *sin* and *decay*, God not only forgives sins and imputes righteousness but also transforms human nature from a state of being capable of sinning and decaying to a state of being incapable of sinning and decaying. It is truly remarkable how the Lord's sacrifice pardoned human sins, but more than that, His baptism and resurrection set the pattern for the ontological transformation of God's τέκνα. Justification requires the cross; it does not require Jesus' resurrection, but the transformation of being does. Only through spiritual and bodily resurrections can

---

and only indirectly and in a limited way the *psyche* and the *physis*." Tillich, *Systematic Theology* 3:276. Emphasis original.

49. Behr, *Asceticism*, 80.

50. A spiritual self needs a spiritual body. Welz writes, "On the one hand, God's image cannot be read off a person's physiognomy, but, on the other hand, the spiritual cannot show itself without embodiment." Welz, *Humanity*, 256.

51. Cf. "With what kind of body will they come?," 1 Cor 15:35; "heavenly bodies," v. 15:40.

52. *Westminster Confession of Faith* 11.33.

53. Green and Baker, *Recovering the Scandal of the Cross*, 202.

a person begin a new life with a new human nature. Its perfection will take place at the parousia.

Thus, human glorification is achieved when they decay no more.[54] There is no glory in the sinless dead persons. Accordingly, the ultimate everlasting salvation is not merely about forgiveness but a substantial change. Through this ontological transformation, God elevates the constitutive elements of human beings, making them fully pneumatic beings with everlasting pneumatic lives and the inability to sin. The forgiveness of sins is only required during this καιρός between the two υἱοθεσία (Figure 4).

The salvation of human beings is not solely based on the cross of Christ but on the whole of Christ's event. Salvation is not only legal-forensic, but more than that; it is essential-existential.

DEIFICATION, *HUIO*-FICATION, *HUIOPOESIS*, AND *HUIOSIS*

The Human Soul

As one of the essential components of the human being, the human soul plays a significant role in elevating the human nature. I posit that it is the sole element that remains constant yet serves to determine the entirety of a person's existence. When B. P. Blosser discusses *Become Like the Angels: Origen's Doctrine of the Soul* in his book's introduction, he writes, "A theological anthropology was at the core of the *kerygma* proclaimed by the early Christians—a message about what *kind of being* man is, and what are his *origin* and *destiny*."[55] For Origen, "the soul constitutes the heart of the human person."[56] It is the human soul that determines human existence. But I submit that the human *pneuma* (the divine gift, the human infinite

---

54. Cf. Sproul: "And those who are justified are immediately glorified in the sense of being adopted as children of God." Sproul, "Order of Salvation."

55. Blosser, *Become Like the Angels*, 2. Emphasis added.

56. Blosser argues, "Because neither the body nor the human spirit (*pneuma*), in Origen's view, is particularly central to the human person as such: the body is a part of the sensible cosmos that is shared by all embodied beings, and the human spirit is a divine gift that remains extraneous to the human personality. The soul, on the other hand, constitutes the very heart of the human person. It is the soul that defines the person, both morally and ontologically, and it is the soul that determines his destiny. Delicately balanced between the carnal influence of the body and the enlivening power of the spirit, the soul is the locus of freedom and self-determination." Blosser, *Become Like the Angels*, 3–4.

element) is the starting point of human ontological transformation and that its spiritual influence transforms the soul. Thus, God works first on the human spirit (Rom 8:15), then on the human soul during the two υἱοθεσία, and finally on the human body (Rom 8:23).

Origen also spoke of human divinization.[57] Origen (as translated by Thomas P. Scheck) wrote in his commentary on Romans,

> For the Spirit is in the law, he is in the Gospels, he is always with the Father and the Son; and he always is, was, and shall be, just like the Father and the Son. Consequently, he is not new, but he renews those who believe when he leads them from the old evils to the new life and *the new observance* of the religion of Christ, and when *he makes spiritual men out of carnal ones*.[58]

It is difficult to detect Origen's "human spirit" in this translation of Scheck because of the use of "the Spirit of adoption," "the Spirit of adoption of sons" (p. 63), or "the Spirit of sons" (p. 64). Notice the use of the capital "S." Still, I suspect they are referring to Origen's Greek, which relates to Paul's "πνεῦμα υἱοθεσίας." The book writes:

> The starting point of serving God [as a slave] is being filled by the spirit of fear, while one is still called a child. . . . That is to say, we have not become children and beginners again, but as those who are perfect we now receive the Spirit of adoption once and for all, "by which" Spirit "we cry: *Abba*, Father!" For no one but a son cries out to a father.[59]

We find that Origen explained the true meaning of Pauline υἱοθεσία. Notice his line, "he makes spiritual men out of carnal ones," and "we have not become children and beginners *again*, but as those who are perfect, we now receive the Spirit of adoption." His words symbolically teach about the elevation of human nature. Also, Origen commented, "He [Paul] has

---

57. Blosser continues, "'Gods' he calls those who by grace and participation in God are given the name of gods. . . . And yet although these are capable of being God and seem to be given this name by grace, none of them is found to be like God in power or nature. . . . For example if we say that a portrait is like the one whose image is seen expressed in the portrait, the similarity is due to the quality of the expression—grace—while in substance the two remain quite different. . . . Therefore no one is 'like the Lord among the gods' . . . except the Father with the Son and the Holy Spirit." Blosser, *Become Like the Angels*, 231.

58. Origen, *Commentary*, 29. Emphasis added.

59. Origen, *Commentary*, 63.

admirably said that the Spirit of God bears witness not with the soul but with the spirit, which is the human being's better part, the central part of a person."[60]

Thus, Origen has a trichotomous view of man and perceives that the human spirit is the better part of man, the central part of a person. The human spirit is the light of the soul when it is enlivened. The vivified human spirit leads the person who has it to a spiritual, ultimate, authentic penumatic existence.

Earlier in this chapter of Blosser, we learned that for Origen, the "likeness" is achieved by human effort.[61] I still maintain that the "likeness" can only be attained at the parousia (Rom 8:23) and is God's grace.[62] According to Wolfhart Pannenberg, "Paul described Jesus Christ as *the eschatological form of humanity* that in contrast to the previous Adamic humanity, *obeys God* and *overcomes mortality*."[63]

Before υἱοθεσία in Rom 8:15, a sarkic-Adamic person can only live according to the flesh, which is why he needs the law as a guardian to give him direction. During the time between υἱοθεσία in Rom 8:15 (the vivification of an infant's spirit) and υἱοθεσία in 8:23 (the final constitution of a υἱός), the souls of Christians must make an effort to choose whether to live according to the fleshly or the spiritual desires. During this period, they must learn how to listen to their spirits. Only after the day of perfection (the final constitution of a υἱός) will Christians no longer have to choose between the two, for they have become fully spiritual, and can only live according to the will of their spirits that are in union with Christ's Spirit, obeying God and overcoming mortality. It is only possible by *imitatio Christi*, by making Adamic humans be like Christ's humanity and then imitating His way of being. The latter is the result of human action, while the former is the result of God's action—the actualization of the potentiality that God has given to His created infants.

I contend that God exerts a profound impact on forming an individual's identity, but God does not negate the intrinsic nature bestowed upon

60. Origen, *Commentary*, 64. Brackets added.

61. Blosser, *Become Like the Angels*, 230. (*On First Principles* 3, 6, 1.)

62. Cf. Tillich: "Hence all naturalistic theology signifies in the last analysis a tendency toward the deification of man. This danger is concealed especially in teaching about the possibility of man's likeness to God. Barth holds that the likeness of God in man is a thing to be sought, a goal of salvation and perfection, but is nothing given, no natural equipment by whose help one can attain any knowledge of God. We can attain knowledge of God only by means of God himself, that is, through his spirit which is in us but not of us. The spirit alone makes possible man's likeness to God." Tillich, "What Is Wrong," 26.

63. Pannenberg, *Systematic Theology* 2:297. Emphasis added.

humans at the time of their creation. Instead, He enhances this nature, enabling humans to transcend their temporal physical bodies and carnal desires. In this way, God saves God's created children, who were initially created as somatic sarkic beings. The *ontological* transformation of a believer shaped by God through υἱοθεσία denotes an elevation in her being rather than a complete replacement of the protological being. As a result of this transformation, a new being emerges in a novel mode of existence. This shift is made possible by the fact that protological humans were endowed with the potential for growth in the form of a dormant spirit (analogous to seed) as a gift from the divine. When this potential is actualized, it begins to shape the eschatological humans.

The Human Body

In the context of human redemption, the human body plays a pivotal role in ensuring the continued existence of humans. The transformation it undergoes encompasses the entire span of human existence, from its creation as Adamic humans to its ultimate planned existence as Christic humans. The human body is a fundamental aspect of defining human identity. It is not merely a vehicle for the soul and spirit; it is an essential component of what it means to be human.

The human body is essential to human nature, for God created humanity as embodied souls from the beginning (Gen 2:7). The significance of the body is further affirmed in the incarnation and resurrection of the Lord Jesus. Without the body, human existence remains incomplete. The body is not a prison, but the vessel through which the soul lives, acts, and is redeemed. It is through the body that we experience mortality, limitation, and dependence—what Scripture calls our "lowliness" (Phil 3:21). In this way, the body grounds both our facticity and the human condition.

The incarnation, life, death, and resurrection of Jesus Christ represent the total transformation of humanity, including a transformation of the body. The final aspect of humanity to be changed is the body itself, which will be transformed at the parousia. Christ's resurrection serves as a model of this future bodily resurrection for believers. In Christ, the transition from the corruptible *sarkic* body to the incorruptible *pneumatic* body has already been accomplished, inaugurating what will one day be fulfilled in all believers. As an inaugural manifestation of the new creation, *the* Christ exemplifies the glorified state that awaits those who are united with Him.

As a result of this ontological transformation that advances through successive stages, believers will become incorruptible and immortal, no longer subject to sin, and fully capable of participating in the divine life. Irenaeus rendered,

> The flesh, therefore, when destitute of the Spirit of God, is dead, not having life, and cannot possess the kingdom of God: [it is as] irrational blood, like water poured out upon the ground. And therefore he says, "As is the earthy, such are they that are earthy." But where the Spirit of the Father is, there is a living man; [there is] the rational blood preserved by God for the avenging [of those that shed it]; [there is] the flesh possessed by the Spirit, forgetful indeed of what belongs to it, and adopting the quality of the Spirit, being made conformable to the Word of God.[64]

This conformity to the Son is more than just symbolic; it entails a profound spiritual and relational transformation—the pneumatic union—that culminates in an everlasting life with God. That communion occurs in the spirits through the unitive Being. Consequently, it is not the entirety of the Christian's body, soul, and spirit (the totality of their being) that will be in union with the Creator; rather, it is only their spirits. This is to ensure their particularity. However, humans cannot exist in the pneumatic realm without pneumatic bodies.

Deification Through Adoption

A significant number of scholars interpret the teachings of the apostle Paul on υἱοθεσία through the lens of adoption.[65] Notable among these are Eusebius Sophronius Hieronymus (Jerome) and Aurelius Augustinus Hipponensis (Augustine of Hippo). David Vincent Meconi summarizes Augustine's teaching on salvation as follows.

> We then begin to see how Augustine's account of salvation can be described as an account of deification. So, at times he will explain deification in terms of divine adoption, at other times as "becoming gods," while elsewhere in terms of the Son's exchanging his humanity for our divinity.[66]

---

64. *ANF* 1:535.

65. Hays renders, "Thus, there was a program of perfection, the Creator's plan A for the world—in the words of Paul Blowers, 'the overarching divine plan (λόγος; βουλή)'—which God traced especially upon the human creation: humans were to become his own sons and daughters, and gods (cf. Ps. 82:6: 'I said you are gods'), not by nature, but by the grace of adoption." Hays et al., *When the Son*, 126.

66. Meconi, *One Christ*, 80.

Meconi reveals four different paradigms pivotal to Augustine's theology.

> The first paradigm is what I will refer to as a recapitulative model. Unlike the Gnostic separation between a deity who creates and another who liberates, the same God who creates for Augustine is clearly the same God who deifies. The second paradigm explains humanity's becoming gods by way of the Pauline concept of divine adoption. Through grace the Son extends his filiation to human persons, thereby giving them a share in the divine nature. The third paradigm is seen in the "great exchange" of natures. Here Augustine relies on and continues a standard patristic insight: God becomes human so humans can become divine. The fourth paradigm illustrates how deification effects ethical and physical changes in the human person. The deified are endowed with the mind and eyes of Christ himself, called to love and to see and to understand as he does.[67]

I disagree with the idea of "great exchange" of natures—namely, that "God becomes human so humans can become divine." I argue that this is theologically problematic for two reasons. First, such an exchange implies a change of nature that results in entirely different beings, leaving no room for the salvation of the original human nature (the old being). Second, if humans were to become gods, then there will be no longer be any place for ὁ Υἱὸς τοῦ ἀνθρώπου.

From the correct perspective of υἱοθεσία we can see that God who creates human beings in the *népio* state is the same God who causes them to become human beings in *huio* state. The Pauline υἱοθεσία (not adoption) teaches about the Creator God, who elevates protological sarkic-Adamic humans to a higher level of humanity. There is no such exchange of natures between the divine nature of Jesus and our human nature, but elevation. What happened was that the person of Jesus Christ, who has a divine nature (D), added to Himself the human nature of the *népio* state (Hn) to elevate it to the human nature of the *huio* state (Hh). It is this elevated human nature that He introduces to the Adamic humans. Thus, in mathematical expression, D becomes $D+Hn$, and $D+Hn$ becomes $D+Hh$ so that Hn can become Hh.

Again, there is no such exchange of divine and human natures. Human beings will be elevated to the highest degree that created beings can attain—*huio*-ship. With this new exalted nature, humans can be united with the Christ. Only through the pneumatic communion of the mature Son (ὁ

---

67. Meconi, *One Christ*, 89.

Υἱός) with the mature sons (οἱ υἱοὶ) can the extension of the Son's filiation to human persons take place, and it can be seen as the extension of the inner communion of the triune God to the created beings. With this extension of the internal eternal pneumatic fellowship of the triune God to the υἱοὶ, the διάστημα (*diastema*, extension) structure of existence[68] can be everlastingly maintained. And through this extension, God shares God's *self*.

Jerome disregarded the distinction between *pneuma* and the human *psyche*. According to Vit Hušek, despite Jerome's extensive knowledge of Greek literature, his love of analyzing Hebrew and Greek terms, and his love of comparing Greek and Latin translations, Jerome never used Greek terminology for deification.[69] Jerome's deification is based on *adoptio*.[70] Still, according to Hušek, to become adopted sons of God, we must first "receive faith in and knowledge of his Son Jesus Christ." We were predestined; when we trusted the Son of God, we received the spirit of adoption.[71] No, Paul did not state that Christians would become God's *adopted* sons, but he unambiguously explained that God's infants would become God's *mature* sons.

Regarding Ps 81:6, Jerome adjusts his vocabulary, stating that we are referred to not only as "sons of God" but also as "gods." He clarifies that we are "gods" not by nature but by grace.[72] However, his sentence, "We are gods by grace," explains the *how* rather than the *what*. So Jerome does not mean "gods" here as "essence." In contrast, the context of υἱοθεσία can provide answers to what we are and what we are becoming: elevated creatures with elevated essences, new beings in the New Being. Tillich renders,

> New Being is an essential being under the conditions of existence, conquering the gap between *essence* and *existence*. For this same idea, Paul used the expression "new creature," calling those who are "in" Christ "new creatures." "In" is the preposition of participation; he who participates in the *newness of being* which is in Christ has become a new creature.[73]

---

68. Julia S. Konstantinovsky writes, "As created, we belong within the structures of existence that ancient Christians term *diastema* (διάστημα), 'extension.' In contrast to divine non-extended (*adiastemic*) life, creatures *by definition* belong within the created 'extension' and are, thus, 'extended' beings. That is to say, they are subject to the limitedness of the 'extended' spatio-temporal continuum, which is radically *unlike* the 'non-extended' divine eternity." Konstantinovsky, "Negating the Fall," in Hays et al., *When the Son*, 121.

69. Hušek, "Rebirth into a New Man," 153.

70. Hušek, "Rebirth into a New Man," 154.

71. Hušek, "Rebirth into a New Man," 155. Emphasis added.

72. Hušek, "Rebirth into a New Man," 155.

73. Tillich, *Systematic Theology* 2:118–19. Emphasis added.

Hušek has noted that Jerome uses the term "gods" figuratively to describe individuals who have abandoned human vices and embraced divine thinking. However, he is reluctant to apply this term to saints and ideal Christians, emphasizing that they remain human and that God and man do not share the same nature.[74] Are there terms other than "gods" that could convey this concept?

Proposed Terminologies

In the doctrine of adoption, when *sons* of an unknown family are adopted into God's family, they become God's adopted *sons*. There is no ontological change in their being, only the old being with a new legal position. In contrast to it, the true Pauline υἱοθεσία outlines the process of human development. The Latin term "*adoptio*" and its English equivalent "adoption" do not fully capture the essence of biblical υἱοθεσία. The actual meaning of the term "υἱοθεσία" is "*mature son-making (to make a mature son)*." However, since the English word "son" does not convey the Pauline meaning of υἱός, I prefer "υἱό-making" or "*huio-fication*" over "son-making" or "sonification." In linguistics, a noun that has the suffix "-fication" added to it frequently denotes the act of creating something or transforming something into the concept of the noun—in this case, υἱός. The development of a new term to translate Pauline υἱοθεσία is necessary to raise awareness that the term does not refer to "adoption."

The elevated beings are still human. In connection with the idea of exaltation through υἱοθεσία, I prefer the "υἱο" to the "θεο" in the Greek terms of deification[75] like the term "υἱοποίησις"[76] (*huiopoiesis, das zum Sohne machen,*[77] to make that into a [mature] son) as an alternative for "θεοποίησις" (*theopoiesis*) to preserve the creatureliness of the new beings. Υἱοποίησις is the process of transfiguration into a υἱός, which allows the υἱός to merge or establish a personal connection with ὁ Υἱός. We may also consider whether υἱοσις (*huiosis*) is a better alternative to θεοσις (*theosis*). By "deification," it means that a person should be like the resurrected human Christ, the [mature] Son (ὁ Υἱός), who was transformed (Matt 17:1–9;

---

74. Hušek, "Rebirth into a New Man," 156.

75. Cf. Russell, *Doctrine of Deification*, 342–44.

76. There is an online encyclopedia written in the Russian Cyrillic alphabet that contains "(υἱότης, υἱοθεσία, υἱοποίησις)." Н. В. Герасименко, "АФАНАСИЙ I ВЕЛИКИЙ [Греч. Ἀθανάσιος ὁ Μέγας]. Translated by ChatGPT: N. V. Gerasimenko, Athanasius I the Great [Gr. Athanásios ho Mégas].

77. Academic, "Υἱοποίησις." Brackets added.

Mark 9:2–8; Luke 9:28–36) and ascended (Mark 16:19; Luke 24:50–53; Acts 1:9–11) into heaven. Thus, the limit of "human becoming" becomes clear. Through God's sub-act of υἱοθεσία (*huio*-fication), a person ontologically experiences christification (the making of human messiah).

These terms are to be used exclusively in an academic context. We may start to include the term "*huio*-fication" in academic Bible translations presented as a footnote or other remark in brackets.

SUMMARY

Being is becoming. According to Raimundo Panikkar, every being is in a constant state of becoming, not becoming another being, but becoming what it is because Being is Becoming. Creation is the constant Becoming of Being.[78] But what are we, human beings, becoming? We learned through the events of Jesus Christ that a temporal being who typically decays can be resurrected from death. In Paul's terminologies, a νήπιος became a υἱός, which are observable phenomena for the first witnesses who tell the story and come to us in the form of biblical narratives. The Gospels record the birth of Jesus, His life, death, and resurrection, and His return to the Father. These serve as a typical example of the Christic life.

John Macquarrie explains that in Christ, as the Paradigmatic Existence, we receive a renewed understanding of ourselves that amounts to a

---

78. Panikkar explains, "In other words, Becoming belongs to the very essence of Being. An entity is not an entity because it persists 'in' Being. Becoming is the very act of Being, and Being is only Being when it becomes (Being). *Being has no inertia*. It has energy, ἐνέργεια, Aristotle would say: Being is act. An entity is an entity insofar as it *is* Being. If an entity is, it is. This *is*, the *is* of Being and Becoming is neither merely temporal nor solely eternal; it is *termpiternal*. Time seems to be intrinsic to Becoming and eternity to Being. If Being and Becoming belong together in an *advaitic* relationship, this entails that time and eternity are the two faces, as it were, of what I call *tempiternity*. At present, suffice to say that were an entity not to become what it is each moment that it is, it would cease to be. The entity exists and this existence is its Becoming. When the scholastics, Descartes, Malebranche, Spinoza, and others wrote about continuous creation, *creation continua*, this was their latent problem. Every being is becoming; not becoming another being, but becoming what it is, because Being is Becoming. If the creation, in this hypothesis, happened *in illo tempore* (once upon a time), it is still continually happening. Creation did not happen in time, but brought about time along with it. Creation is not a temporal event. It is the very event of time. It has nothing to do with any 'Big Bang' at the beginning of time. Creation is Becoming, the continuous Becoming of the creature. In such a perspective, if God created once, he has to 'go on' creating constantly. Creation is neither a temporal act, nor is it a gigantic work of an all-powerful Engineer. Creation is the constant Becoming of Being." Panikkar, *Rhythm of Being*, 98–99. Emphasis original.

new possibility of existence.[79] Humans were created as physical beings, but the ultimate goal is for them to become spiritual beings like the Christ, the Son (ὁ Υἱός). The old way of being is limited to the physical realm. At the same time, the new being, who has undergone God's sub-act of υἱοθεσία (*huio*-fication), has access to a broader range of experiences in both the physical and spiritual realms. The old way of being is part of one's vestige, which is expected to be entirely nonfunctional at the end of one's proto-logical existence, which marks the beginning of one's new eschatological existence in a new world.

On the way to becoming like the Christ (a pneumatic being), sanctification is necessary for all believers. It is a learning process to consistently choose spiritual guidance over personal sarkic desires by following the leading of the Spirit of God through the Christian's fellowship with the Spirit of Christ. (Rom 8:9). Christians' authentic selves are spiritual. This concept is still consistent with George Ivanovich Gurdjieff's explanation of human essence, clarifying the choice to follow one's innate pattern or deviate from it. Gurdjieff believes that embracing one's authentic self and connecting it with the pattern of one's latent potential is what he refers to as our essence.[80] In our case, God's endowment of Adamic beings with dormant spirits provides the potential for them to become Christic beings, but only God can awaken these spirits—this is part of God's work. Christians with an awakened spiritual essence may choose a spiritual life that conforms to their spiritual nature, which is the purpose of the human creation.

A new υἱός (a new Christlike being) is a proleptic being. The term "proleptic" describes a believer's state of being in which his present participation in the benefits of salvation through his union with the Messiah is still incomplete, awaiting the complete fulfillment of being fully υἱός in the parousia. There is a dynamic tension in the life of a new υἱός until he reaches

---

79. Macquarrie, *Principles*, 272. "The Paradigmatic Existence" shows the possible existence that humankind can have.

80. Cf. Bennett: "The presence of two possibilities is still only a very limited form of consciousness. The whole situation has much more in it than that. My existence has much more in it than just the choice of yes and no at a given moment. When the pattern of my existence begins to be present to me, my consciousness is transformed. That is the second great transition. It is the entry into the third state of consciousness, which Gurdjieff calls true self-consciousness. It is called self-consciousness because it is the presence of the possibilities that are in oneself. My choice then changes; it is no longer a choice only between two different directions in my functional activity but the choice of conforming to my pattern or not; of being what I am or not. That being what I am, *the pattern of my possibilities*, is what Gurdjieff calls our Essence. Essence-consciousness, the presence of the pattern of one's own being, is the condition for a real direction of life." Bennett, *Making a Soul*, 37, 40. Emphasis added.

his completion as a υἱός (τέλειος ἀνήρ, the mature or consummated human) in the future.

Paul advises about the renewal of the mind (Rom 12:2). In his guidance to the Philippians, he wrote, "Finally, brothers, whatever is true, whatever is honorable, whatever is just, whatever is pure, whatever is lovely, whatever is commendable, if there is any excellence, if there is anything worthy of praise, think about these things" (Phil 4:8 ESV). During this transitional καιρός (*kairós*), Christians must consider that to be authentic, one must not follow one's desires just because it is the strongest, but one must decide which desires to let go of and which to pursue. It includes choosing whether to focus on the memory of positive or negative past life experiences and determining which future aspirations to pursue.

Those who identify as Christians may find themselves becoming inauthentic or part of the crowd (the herd) if they act on their strongest urges without first considering whether or not they should act on them. Freedom is not synonymous with the capacity to act in any manner one chooses; instead, it is freedom from a single mode of being, namely the sarkic mode. It is because a [mature] son (a υἱός) has both a sarkic and pneumatic mode of being, representing two distinct alternatives. If an individual is capable of enslaving himself, it may be necessary for him to be protected by the law.

Jesus initially liberates individuals from the sting of death (sin) by making the death itself have no power over a person like Him, thereby enabling humans to transcend the constraints of the law. New potentiality arises; instead of becoming protological humans with no sin, humans can become spiritual beings. Then, the Spirit progressively makes Christic beings capable of refusing their sarkic desire until they become entirely spiritual at the parousia. Still, suppose sarkic desire continues to exert a dominant influence over an individual's life. In that case, it is questionable whether that person has truly been liberated from the constraints of the flesh. In any case, Christians must learn to control their actions and decisions. It is called the sanctification of the soul. It is not always the case that natural cravings result in wrongdoing. Indeed, while we are here in this body, the desires of the flesh are embedded in this physical body and cannot be killed—only abandoned.

When tempted during his wilderness experience, the Paradigmatic Existence—the baptized Jesus as a human model—set *an example* by resolutely rejecting the offers. Accordingly, since renewed people have the option of living κατὰ σάρκα or κατὰ πνεῦμα, they are not puppets. The human soul has to choose between the two. A person is said to have a spiritually authentic existence in his world if he constantly decides to follow his spirit's guidance. The Paradigmatic Existence also sets an even more important example: a υἱός rises from the dead.

At the final stage of *huio*-fication, *ontically*, a person—with the awakened spirit, the new spiritual body, and the "upper soul" (the "unicameral" soul that has been closer to God)—will become an entirely spiritual being through God's sub-act of υἱοθεσία and enter the eternal spiritual realm to live a wholly spiritual existence.

What about the salvation of those who lived before the incarnation, from the beginning of creation and throughout the Old Testament, including those who dwell behind the wall of religious persecution and have never heard of the historical Christ? Without other human efforts, the Spirit can now quicken the spirits of those with no physical bodies. They believed in the undisclosed "seed of woman," and He appeared to them in spirit. The dead do not have bodies, but they will when the Messiah returns. No "wall" can prevent Jesus from meeting His loved ones, including the oppressed and persecuted ones.

He who conforms to the Son's image (he who experiences υἱοποίησις) does not become like Him as the divine God the Son but rather acquires His consummated human image (the Christ), which allows them to participate in the Spirit's spiritual fellowship. The clause "we are the sons of God" should not imply an idea of divinization, and that we are not entering into a divine relationship between God the Son and God the Father, but rather an expanded relationship through God the Son. The true sonship is not to be found in us, the sons, but in the Son. In the pneumatic union, the created [mature] sons are not members of the uncreated triune God, as the Second Person of the divine Trinity is, but rather are tied to and subordinate to God the Son incarnate in the fellowship of the pneumatic sons (οἱ υἱοί)—the church. In this instance, the person of Jesus Christ (God the Son and the Son of God) is incorporated under the designation of *Metaxú* in the communion of the Godhead and the sons of God.

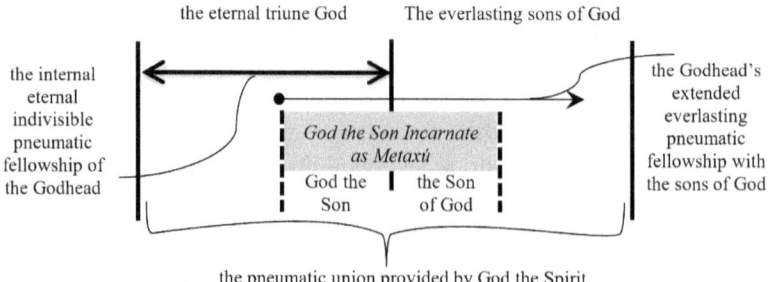

FIGURE 8: The Extended Participation of the Sons in the Godhead

CHAPTER 8

METHODUS SALUTIS DEI

"The 'old man' and 'new man' are not primarily to be understood in the sense of the *ordo salutis* but rather in the context of the *historia salutis*." ~ Herman Ridderbos, *Paul*, 297 (paraphrased)

OVERVIEW

Some Reformed scholars place adoption—which for them is the translation of υἱοθεσία—as a benefit in the *ordo salutis*.[1] For instance, John Murray says, "Adoption is never separable from justification and regeneration."[2] For Beeke, adoption differs from regeneration, justification, or sanctification.[3] Trumper renders:

> In any case, issues germane to the construction of an *ordo salutis* have typically taken precedence over the panoramic perspective of the *historia salutis*. A survey of the volumes of systematic theology dealing with adoption will reveal that the focus is often

---

1. The *ordo salutis* explains the "how" of the salvation not in terms of temporal sequence but of logical dependency, since these benefits can in fact occur simultaneously.
2. Murray, *Redemption*, 132–33.
3. Beeke, *Heirs with Christ*, 25–34.

very much on its connections to regeneration, justification and sanctification.[4]

But adoption is not υἱοθεσία, and *vice versa*, and I perceive that the panoramic perspective of the *historia salutis* precedes the *ordo salutis*.

It is clear from Paul's discussion in Rom 8:15, 23, 29–30 that υἱοθεσία—conformed to the image of the Son of Him—is part of his order of salvation.

> For those whom he foreknew he also predestined to be conformed to the image of his Son, in order that he might be the firstborn among many brothers. And those whom he predestined he also called, and those whom he called he also justified, and those whom he justified he also glorified (Rom 8:29–30 ESV).

I schematize the above-mentioned Paul's *ordo salutis* as follows: foreknew → predestined to be conformed to the image of the Son of Him → called → justified → glorified (as His υἱοί). It is the logical process of becoming a consummated son (υἱός). However, several interpretations of the order exist because each person experiences a unique process of salvation. Now, what about the significance of υἱοθεσία in its other appearances?

HUIO-FICATION AS *METHODUS SALUTIS DEI*

As we discussed earlier in this work, I want to propose an alternative viewpoint. Paul's υἱοθεσία has no univocal meaning like adoption. Υἱοθεσία has several meanings (equivocal) that open to more than one interpretation within its context. From its five appearances in the Pauline corpus, each has a unique significance. Υἱοθεσία is not only a benefit in the order of salvation. Paul uses the word when he discusses the nation of Israel and its function in the history of salvation (Rom 9:4–8), which the church does not replace (the church is not the new Israel; both have distinct functions). We can see from Gal 4:1–7 that υἱοθεσία is historical because it refers to the historical coming of Jesus of Nazareth, who became the object of faith. Υἱοθεσία in Eph 1:5 will close the history.

The purpose of God's sub-act of υἱο-θεσία (*huio*-fication) is to create human υἱοί, which includes the *creation* of ὁ Υἱὸς τοῦ Θεοῦ (the Son of God), the Christ. The history of salvation commences with the narrative of human creation and the subsequent fall. This etiological account talks symbolically about the emergence of conscious beings like Adam (meaning "man"

---

4. Trumper, "Fresh Exposition of Adoption," 62.

or "human") in many places of the cosmos. I perceive the word "Adam" as parallel with the term "*Homo*" in biological taxonomy and anthropology to relate my and all humans' lives with the biblical account. This way, I put the authority and the relevancy of Scripture into my life as a member of the genus *Homo*. If Adam is a historical Mediterranean person, other people like me have no connection with him and his fall.

The etiology also shows that every human being sins from the beginning of their existence in the world. No one is righteous (Rom 3:9–12). The history of salvation began with the divine selection of Abraham as the patriarch of a great nation. Abraham's exceptional faith and unwavering obedience paved the way for the special relationship that would develop between the Israelites and the future Messiah (ὁ Υἱός). Abraham's willingness to sacrifice Isaac foreshadowed the divine sacrifice of God's Son on the cross. Abraham's children become a new nation.

This new nation plays some roles. They were called to dedicate themselves to God completely. This was central to their function. As a result, God and His chosen people formed a one-of-a-kind covenant, fostering unprecedented intimacy. The people of this nation became the τέκνα (plural) even when they were still living according to their *sarx*. Paul, in Rom 9:8, classifies this nation as τὰ τέκνα τῆς σαρκὸς. However, the Israelites' commitment and decency made them the principal channel of divine grace for humanity. Their constant commitment to God resulted in blessings, eventually leading to the coming of the Redeemer, who would bring salvation to all. God shows His plan through this nation. Their past journey foreshadowed events in redemptive history. They provide a "place" where the Messiah-to-be can enter the created world through a woman of virtue as the vehicle through which God became man.

The Torah, given to Moses on Mount Sinai, revealed God's ideals to humanity. As carriers of this divine law, the Israelites were critical in preparing humanity for a higher moral standard. However, a high moral standard can prevent them from sinning, but it does not deliver them from human facticity, such as temporal corporeal existence. Humans still require the prophesied Son of Man (the Messiah) to free them from temporality so they will not decay. The Blessed Virgin Mary embodies the pinnacle of Jewish virtue and piety. Her role as the Mother of the Redeemer marked the apex of the Israelites' spiritual preparation for the Messiah. Expressions of devotion and adoration, such as David's psalms,[5] demonstrate the Israelites' expectation and reverence for the Messiah before His arrival. They were tasked

---

5. For instance, "Because you will not abandon me to the realm of the dead, nor will you let your faithful one see decay" (Ps 16:10 NIV). "I will proclaim the Lord's decree: He said to me, 'You are my son; today I have become your father'" (Ps 2:7 NIV).

with providing a temporary home for the Messiah when He arrived. Their responsibility included sharing the great news of His coming to the nations.

This journey, marked by faith, commitment, and prophecy fulfillment, exemplifies God's specific purpose for redemptive history through His chosen people, the Israelites. Their various tasks and responsibilities were essential components of the divine plan, culminating in the incarnation when the Son added human nature to His personhood to bring salvation to humanity.

Given the universal inclination toward sin within temporal reality and the consequent disqualification of all humanity from fulfilling the messianic role, it follows that divine intervention became a soteriological necessity. This demand required the eternal God to dispatch a singular emissary from beyond the bounds of temporality into the material cosmos to redeem creation. The preexistent Υἱός, eternally co-substantial with the Godhead, emerged as the uniquely qualified agent for this salvific mission. Within His person, the ontological divide between the temporal and eternal was decisively reconciled, effecting a cosmic restoration through His incarnational mission.

The Son's entry into the created order was providentially mediated through the nation of Israel, which served as the conduit for this redemptive historiography. This intricate divine economy demanded meticulous preparation across generations: the cultivation of theological frameworks within the covenantal community, the systematic eradication of heterodox conceptions, the formation of a people disciplined in eschatological expectation, and the establishment of sociocultural structures capable of propagating the messianic message globally. Such preparations, orchestrated through divine sovereignty, ensured the eventual fulfillment of the Messiah's advent—a convergence of celestial purpose and terrestrial readiness that enabled the proclamation of redemption to permeate human history.[6]

God revealed Himself in the flesh. The Lord Jesus Christ experienced υἱοθεσία, transforming His human figure into a complete son of humanity—ὁ Υἱὸς τοῦ ἀνθρώπου. The same trend applies to human beings. After the arrival of the Son, everyone who is foreknown will be predestined to be conformed to the image of the Son of Him, which is the objective of *huio*-fication (υἱοθεσία, υἱοποίησις). These persons are called, justified, and later will be fully exalted as God's υἱοί.

The doctrine of υἱοθεσία explains the history of redemption (*historia salutis*) and how it affects each individual (*ordo salutis*). Historia salutis

---

6. These materials are inspired by the work of Schoeman, *Salvation Is from the Jews*, 15–23.

illustrates God's steps in creating and improving His creation, which has gradually been disclosed. God operates throughout history. The incarnation of the divine Son is a significant event in salvation history. The Son of Man emerges on earth after many years of waiting. After His resurrection, human sons follow in His footsteps. But these sons are like under a veil. "Conformed to the image of the Son of Him (τοῦ υἱοῦ αὐτοῦ)" is the basic thought of Rom 8:29–30; all other aorists explain the *ordo salutis*. This conformity can only happen at the end of history. It is a two-step process that transforms an old being into an exalted new being. The words "old" and "new" incorporate time, which is more than just a logical priority of how a person can be saved. *Huio*-fication (υἱοθεσία, υἱοποίησις) explains God's way of salvation.

SUMMARY

The apostle Paul's *huio*-fication (υἱοθεσία, υἱοποίησις) describes the path to salvation. The *historia salutis* describes how God prepares and finishes God's sub-act of υἱοθεσία in human history, whereas the *ordo salutis* discusses how υἱοθεσία applies to individual believers. These conclusions are schematized in Figure 9. The historical aspect of Pauline υἱοθεσία is presented in steps one through seven, and the order in which a person experiences it is described in step six.

Figures 5 and 9 show that Christians have begun to experience salvation, but not all of their salvation has been revealed. At the time of the Son's return, when the unification of beings with their Creator begins, the ultimate salvation will occur with the final revelation. Through this eternal pneumatic union that the Holy Spirit provides, Christians will finally be forever delivered from *sin* and *decay*, and they will be able to know the Father (1 Cor 13:12).

The pneumatic union, the unity of the holy triune God, is *eternal*. Still, human participation in it is only everlasting because human beings begin in temporality. Hence, their participation is also temporal but will not end because the Lord Jesus Christ, a partaker of the divine eternal union, sustains this participation. God plans to have a pneumatic homogeneous union with humans. Yet, God must begin with a temporal, pneumatic-sarkic, heterogeneous relationship before both sides can enter the everlasting homogenous pneumatic union.

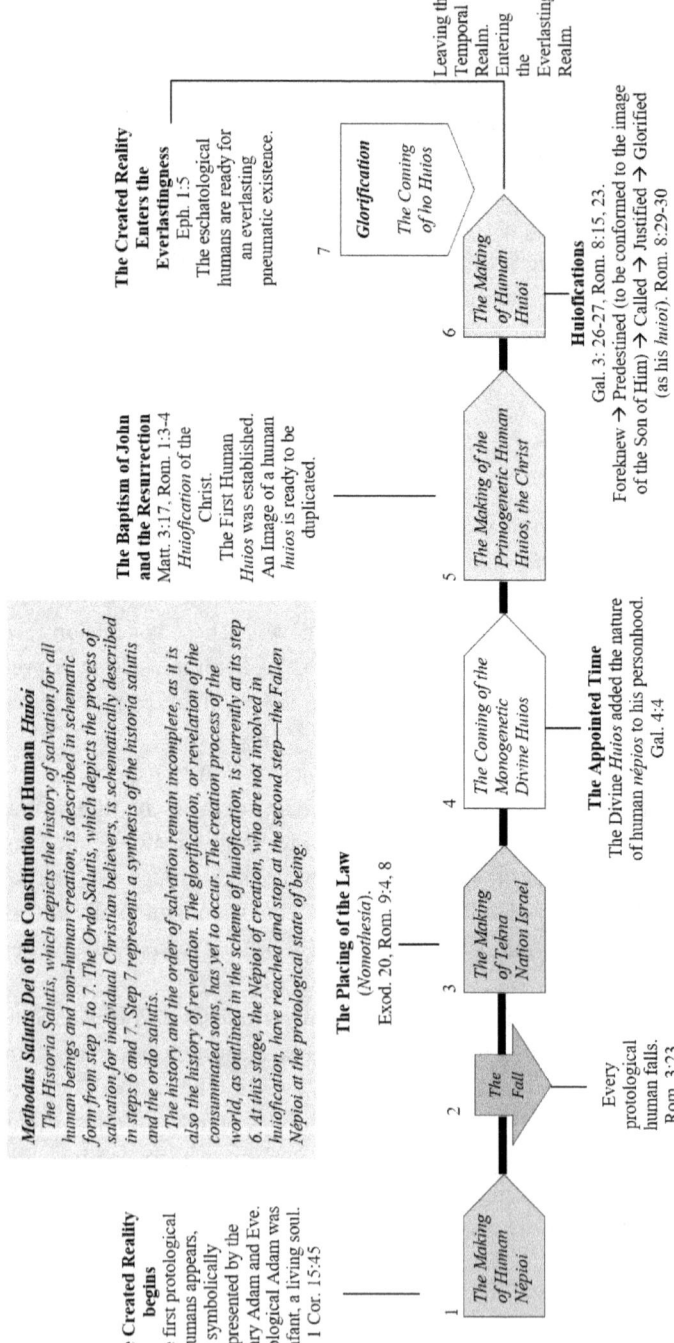

FIGURE 9: *Methodus Salutis Dei* (The Historical and Order of Salvation)

Final Reflections

"The truth is not hidden but concealed, and it is revealed to those who seek with a pure heart." ~ St. Athanasius of Alexandria

OVERVIEW

This scholarly endeavor was initially conceived as an attempt to address a specific theological problem. However, it ultimately culminates in a confession of a deeper reality. At the core of the apostle Paul's doctrine of *huiothesía* (υἱοθεσία) resides a profound mystery of how human beings can be saved (how life can be permanent without sin), yet it also demands faithful and thoughtful articulation of how we should live our lives. Thus, this work concludes not merely as an academic exercise but as reflections and ideas for continual exploration and faithful proclamation of our Christian faith.

PASTORAL APPLICATIONS

Lonergan's final specialty, communication, which deals with practical theology, is explored here. The following text is not intended to be a sermon but rather an introduction to the fundamental concepts of υἱοθεσία.

Essentialism and Existentialism

Essentialism and existentialism are inextricably linked. The concepts of protological Adamic sarkic humans and eschatological Christic pneumatic humans are examples of essentialism elements in this work. The former are people with natural bodies and latent spirits, whereas the latter are people with vivified spirits who will also eventually take on pneumatic bodies. Thus, categories and universals are present here. The protological beings' fundamental characteristics are temporal—they will ultimately decay—and sarkic, meaning they are susceptible to futility and sin. Consummated pneumatic creatures are incapable of sinning and are endowed with the fundamental attribute of perpetual (unending) existence, which allows them to continue to participate everlastingly in the eternal fellowship of the spirit. God must start with the creation of the protological humans and share God's love with them, even though it is finite. The protological humans serve as a precursor to the creation of eschatological humans. The latter aims to establish a continuous union with God the Creator, enabling the Creator to bestow eternal love upon these everlasting creatures. (Cf. 2 Tim 1:9; before the creation, God had prepared to save us.)

However, the substance of these two human categories is invisible to humans. All we can do is observe the individual (or our own) existence and way of life—live κατὰ σάρκα or κατὰ πνεῦμα. A person can live authentically or inauthentically, even if they fall into the first category. Furthermore, a member of the latter group may live a life of *ultimate* pneumatic authenticity.

A Tree Is Known by Its Fruit

The apostle Paul's teaching of υἱοθεσία relates to human ontological transformation, that is, the change of human nature from a protological state of sarkic-Adamic being to an eschatological state of pneumatic-Christic being. The words "protological," "sarkic," "Adamic," "eschatological," "pneumatic," and "Christic" are significant here. To the "sarkic," we can add "somatic" because both terms are closely related. An ontological transformation meant by Pauline υἱοθεσία relates to transformations—not a replacement—of human *nature* (from protological Adam-like to eschatological Christlike being), its *existence* (sarkic to pneumatic) and *reality* (temporal to everlasting).

Luke recorded what the Lord Jesus Christ tells us about a tree and its fruit. A good tree yields good fruit, but a wrong tree produces bad fruit. Trees are identified by their fruit. A decent person acts from a good heart, whereas an evil person acts from a dark heart. The actions express the essence[1] (Luke 6:44–45). It is an example of what we call phenomenologi-

---

1. John Macquarrie explained that for Heidegger, "the essence (*Wesen*) of *Dasein* lies in its existence ... that *Dasein's* essence is constituted not by properties but by possible way of being." Macquarrie, *Existentialism*, 67.

cal ontology. From one's existence, we know one's essence. But how do we understand Jean-Paul Sartre's words, "Existence precedes essence?" Unlike a tree, which we can sometimes recognize even without its fruit, or an ax, which we can recognize even when it is not in use, humans (*Dasein*) can only be recognized by other humans through their actions. The tree's nature (essence) enables it to produce certain fruits (existence). Sarkic humans can produce sarkic existence, and pneumatic humans can produce pneumatic existence. However, we can only determine whether someone is sarkic or pneumatic by observing their existence. However, humans grow from sarkic beings to pneumatic beings. This does not mean that humans have two natures; rather, humans have one nature that can develop into a higher nature, from sarkic to pneumatic.

Those who espouse atheistic existentialism are said to reside in their Adamic essence, regardless of whether this is an authentic or inauthentic state of being. In contrast to atheists, who adhere to a protological essence and existence, Christians occupy a position between the two poles of protology and eschatology. In the life of a Christian, there is a conflict between the old carnal desires and the new spiritual desires. Consequently, depending on the soul's decisions, Christians may experience a sarkic existence and/or a pneumatic existence as they transform from an old Adamic being (former essence) to a new Christic being (elevated essence). An individual with an old being can only engage in sarkic actions and behaviors. Accordingly, authentic existence is attained by atheistic existentialists within their sarkic being.

In contrast, Christians can only achieve their ultimate authentic existence in their consummated pneumatic being. However, during the interim period between the first and second υἱοθεσία, Christians who are still in a state of being a half υἱός also engage in sinful actions. This situation is what I refer to as the Christian state.

The Prodigal Sons

In his Gospel, Luke tells of God saving the believers, as described in the parable of the lost sheep (15:1–7) and the parable of the lost coin (15:7–11). He describes the lives of a recently ordained υἱός (adult son) and his elder brother in vv. 11–31; therefore, the parable of "the prodigal sons" is about two Christians. It begins, "There was a man who had δύο υἱούς (two adult sons)." It is about God with His two υἱοί. The newly inaugurated υἱός cannot resist the temptation of his fleshly desires. This younger υἱός chooses to leave God to follow his old "self," pursuing what he thinks is his authentic existence. His sarkic desire still dominates his newly activated pneumatic desires.

The older υἱός is in his sarkic-pneumatic existence as well because even though he does not leave God, he is still jealous when his younger brother comes home. This story is about Christians who take turns sometimes being the newly appointed υἱός and sometimes being his older brother. Christians are not perfect yet; none of them are fully υἱοὶ yet. Unconsummated υἱοὶ can engage in sinful behavior. In Christian existentialist words, sin is about "losing oneself *into* the world." A son-heir (υἱός) is a son-heir in imperishability,[2] as this designation is the result of divine intervention named God's sub-act of *huiothesía* (υἱοθεσία). God initiates the process of becoming a son-heir (υἱός) and cannot be undone by any other being, including Christian elders and preachers.

The elders, preachers, and congregants, including new believers, are unified in their way of becoming new beings; they are the created *huioi* in progress (unfinished *huioi*). It is important to note that, in this context, the terms "elders" and "preachers" are used rather than "priests." It is because they have not yet achieved the state of being fully coheirs with Christ, a state that all Christians do not yet share. It is not yet accurate to describe Christians in this present time (τοῦ νῦν καιροῦ) as "consummated sons of God." Except for the Christ, all those initiated into the faith are still in the process of becoming fully *huioi*. In this context, Christ is the sole priest, serving as the mediator between humanity and God. All Christians may be considered to be either younger or elder prodigal sons.

"I Will Be a Father to You"

The context of 2 Cor 6:16–18 is regarding intermarriage, being an unequal partner with unbelievers. Verse 16, "I will walk among you and be your God, and you shall be my people," was initially addressed to the Israelites during the giving of the commandments. This sentence does not mean that God was not the God of the Israelites before the commandments were issued. Instead, it describes the type of relationship between God and the Israelites. Verse 17 explains the separation of Israelites from the gentiles, which was intended to sanctify the nation and create a suitable environment for the future Messiah's birth and upbringing. This separation was necessary to fulfill God's plan for His people.

In verse 18, Paul wrote that "the Lord Almighty will be a Father to you, and they shall be His sons and daughters (υἱοὺς καὶ θυγατέρας)." The term

---

2. Cf. 1 Pet 1:3–9. "Begotten us again to a living hope" is not a restoration.

"you" is ὑμῖν, which is the second-person plural and refers to the Corinthian Christians. It is essential to highlight that in this verse, Paul mentions both daughters (θυγατέρας) and sons (υἱός), underscoring both parties in the marriage who are in the *huio* state.[3] It is central to acknowledge that for God to be regarded as the spiritual Father of a marriage, both partners must adhere to the same religious beliefs. This assertion underscores the significance of shared Christian faith in a marriage. In this context, it is not intended to imply that God becomes the Father of believers.

Again, the term "father-son" describes the type of relationship between God and individual Christians, where they are in the *huio* state. It is not the same kind of relationship that infants (νήπιος, who cannot speak) have with the Father. Therefore, if an unbeliever becomes a partner of a believer, he/she may not be able to communicate with God the Father in the same way as Christians. This is because the person has no spiritual fellowship with God the Son incarnate through the Spirit's pneumatic means.

Hope and Love

In his letter in 1 Corinthians chapter three, Paul wrote in vv. 1 and 3 that he could not refer to them as spiritual people (πνευματικοῖς) but fleshly people (σαρκίνοις) as to infants (νηπίοις) in Christ . . . for they are still of the flesh (σαρκικοί). In v. 6, he explained that only God kept [it] growing (ηὔξανεν). He repeated it in v. 7 that only God gives growth (αὐξάνων). Like in Corinth, Christian believers nowadays still behave like Adamic humans. It is difficult for Christians to free themselves from the former behavior, but God can help them through the sanctification of their souls, which culminates during the second *huiothesía* at the parousia.

Humans sin and fall again and again. No matter what our situation is now, no matter where we are between a *népio* state and a *huio* state, our process of becoming sons (*huio*-fications) is progressing toward its goal: complete, consummated human beings. We face the same problem as the apostle Paul, where our mind serves the law of God, but our flesh serves the law of sin—the regulative principle of sin (Rom 7:24–25). Like him, too, we have to thank God, who, through Jesus Christ, our Lord, saves us. Human preachers can teach us how to become morally good people, but only Christ can save us. We, humans, cannot save ourselves. God is working on us and in us. Paul, in his "already/not yet" theology, has classified us who have been baptized as υἱοί like the Christ who was baptized and resurrected from

---

3. Refers to 2 Cor 6:18; Vincent explains, "Paul says *sons and daughters* for *son*." Vincent, *Word Studies*. Emphasis original.

death, even when we have not been resurrected. It means that Paul is telling us that our salvation is certain. Our hope—to have everlasting spiritual life and be free from sarkic desires—will not be in vain.

Modeled after *the* Christ (ὁ Υἱὸς τοῦ ἀνθρώπου and ὁ Υἱὸς τοῦ Θεοῦ), we should love those who are struggling because of sins and undergoing the sufferings of the present time. We must strengthen each other by reminding ourselves of the glory that will be revealed in us and towards us. Jesus said, "All that the Father gives me will come to me, and I will never cast anybody out" (John 6:37). We must rejoice in Christ because in Him there is hope. When the time had not come, the Messiah had not come, and there was not even a υἱός (a Son-heir) in the finite world. We discovered from this υἱοθεσία lesson that every creature will eventually vanish (not whole anymore) without the Messiah. Thanks be to God for transforming us to become like the Christ. As those who are becoming adults in the house, Christians must care for all the created beings.

Human Life in the Age of Technological Augmentation

Transhumanism is the study of various approaches to improving human capabilities by augmenting their *bodies*. Transhumans experience ontological transformation from natural beings to augmented beings. There are several kinds of augmentation. This endeavor can involve biotechnological enhancements, such as genetic alterations to enhance physical and mental characteristics and biological enhancements to increase illness resistance or lifespan. Transhumanism also encompasses cybernetic augmentation. The implantation of electronic devices can improve cognitive performance. Prosthetic limbs or organs may have enhanced capabilities. Nootropics, known as "smart drugs," can increase cognitive ability. Brain-computer interfaces enable direct communication between the brain, external devices or robots, and others logged into the network. Sensory enhancement is also conceivable. There is the augmentation of sensory organs to increase vision, hearing, and different sensory experiences, as well as the incorporation of new senses such as infrared vision or electromagnetic field detection.

Physical enhancements such as exoskeletons or powered suits can improve strength and endurance, while biochemical enhancements can raise physical performance. Emotional and psychological enhancements can influence mood, decision-making, perception, and environmental interaction. In the health sector, there are nano-scale enhancements. Nanotechnology can be employed for targeted medicine delivery and cellular healing.

Nanobots can be utilized for medical monitoring and maintenance within the body. There is also moral enhancement.[4]

There are ethical issues involved in these technologies. Still, these human enhancement technologies are very positive; they can solve many human conditions and help the weak and the sick. It is said that augmented human beings can live longer, surpassing the limit of natural humans. Still, this act of "playing God" must have its limit, or we must stop it to a certain degree. If the augmentations only change human physics, the person is technically still human.[5] Ultimately, the human body will transform, resulting in the emergence of a new form—pneumatic body. Conversely, these technologies cannot vivify the human spirit and cannot augment the human soul to achieve everlasting existence as a unified being.

Thus, how do we see the augmented humans on the subject of their salvation through the lens of υἱοθεσία? The Adamic race is confined to physical relationships in the temporal realm. Augmented humans, or human-machine hybrids, can establish connections with computers and other corporeal humans. Moreover, Christic beings can attain spiritual communion that transcends the limitations of their corporeal existence, extending beyond the confines of the temporal realm and the domain of created beings.

In light of the Pauline ontological transformation of υἱοθεσία, I propose that the νήπιος be classified as human *1.0* and the υἱός as human *2.0*. This classification could then be extended to include a transhuman. The augmented νήπιος may be classified as "human *1.x*," while the augmented υἱός may be classified as "human *2.x*." The factor "*x*" describes the levels of transhuman augmentation. A consummated υἱός—a fully Christic human—is determined by a vivified spirit, elevated soul, and new spiritual body and their ability to participate in communion with the triune God. The pneumatic new body will replace the transhuman's physical body made from the matters of this created world, also known as Kurzweil's human body 2.0.[6] Therefore, even if individuals endeavor to enhance their natural bodies, such improvements will ultimately prove inadequate for achieving

---

4. Savulescu at al., *Enhancing Human Capacities*.

5. Is there a distinction between "humanity" and "beyond humanity" or "posthuman?" Cf. Agar: "Radically enhanced beings are not only significantly better than us in various ways, they are different from us—so different, in fact, that they do not deserve to be called human. Moderate enhancement raises serious moral issues." Agar, *Humanity's End*, 17.

6. Kurzweil does not talk about Human 2.0 like other sources that quote him, but Human Body 2.0. He talks about *body* enhancements. See especially his subtitle "So What's Left?," in Kurzweil, "Human Body Version 2.0."

pneumatic everlastingness, given that pneumatic everlastingness necessitates a pneumatic body.

Salvation, or permanent wholeness in an everlasting, authentic existence before God, requires an elevated human nature rather than merely body enhancement. Those who pursue the transhumanist ideal of a protological sarkic-Adamic existence will ultimately face annihilation, whereas those who strive for the eschatological pneumatic-Christic ideal will achieve salvation (permanency). It should be noted that the term "trans" must be excluded from the description, such as "consummated eschatological pneumatic-Christic humans," as consummated humans possess new pneumatic bodies. Transhumans remain a transient entity. Faith in Jesus Christ that engenders an ontological transformation via υἱοθεσία is the key to attaining incorruptible and immortal everlasting life.

As we examine the potential implications of transhumanism, we must consider the defining characteristics that distinguish us as humans. While it is essential to establish boundaries to ensure our continued humanity, we can also capitalize on the potential advantages of technology. Acknowledging that only pneumatic humans can partake in a pneumatic relationship with God is imperative. Therefore, it is essential to maintain the attributes that define our humanity. In any case, transhumanism can assist humans in confronting their temporal existential condition while they remain in this *kairos*. A pneumatic body will replace the need for a technological augmentation.

THE HUMAN CONDITION: SIN, SUFFERINGS, AND MORTALITY

Salvation is not the conversion of lost people from slaves to adopted sons or from sinners to righteous ones through their transfer to God's divine family. It is not a change in human attributes (predicates), but rather a transformation of beings from a protological to an eschatological state. When God created Adamic humans, God intended them to be eschatological, Christlike creatures. Redemption is not a rescue from the fall of Adam but freedom from Adamic protological facticity (innate sin and decay). This freedom elevates human beings towards their planned perfection.[7]

---

7. Green writes, "Gunton sees in Irenaeus a theological model affirming the goodness of creation and an affirmation of God's continued relationship to, and working with, his creation in the working out of redemption. Redemption is not a 'rescue' of persons from createdness (an error Gunton associates with much of Western theology—especially Augustine), but is rather *the bringing of creation to its appointed end* (an emphasis Gunton also sees in Basil the Great)." Green, *Colin Gunton*, 8. Emphasis

Perhaps preexisting biases support the idea of adoption (along with the idea of restoring the lost prelapsarian state of being). Let us look at Matt 18:11 (AMP): "[For the Son of Man has come to save that which was lost.]" This verse is found in the King James family (the descendant of the Textus Receptus)[8] but is missing from several Bible translations such as the ESV, NET, ASV, and Weymouth. This verse can be found in the *Vulgata*, but is absent from the Modern Critical Text (UBS[5]), which is considered the most accurate text similar to the original Autograph. The idea of "lost (sonship)" comes from the Latin church. But Luke 19:10 (ESV) has a similar text: "For the Son of Man came to seek and to save the lost." The Greek "τὸ ἀπολωλός" has been translated into "that which was lost." It can also be rendered as "that which was perished," which is congruent with the wording in Matt 8:25, "Lord, save us, ἀπολλύμεθα (we are perishing)."[9] Humans are coming to an end.

Thus, the Mature Son of Human came to save what was lost and perishing. Adamic beings perish due to their protological state, which leads them to sin (be lost) and die (decay), so the remedy must focus on liberating humans from the protological state of being (the root human condition) rather than their sin and fall (symptoms). Again, the underlying issue is not their behavior but their primordial condition. This perspective will alter the way we perceive divine intervention for human salvation. It is erroneous to believe that one's good deeds can save one. Rather, salvation is the outcome of God's activity, which is known as υἱοθεσία, and which brings about the resurrection. Those who are virtuous but lack belief in the Son of God will ultimately perish, as they lack the spiritual union with God, through the Son, that is necessary for an everlasting existence (salvation). They are not connected to the source of all beings—the Being-Itself or the Ground of Being.

The gospel of υἱοθεσία (*huio*-fication) not only emphasizes the necessity of forgiveness of sins, but, more significantly, it centers on the elevation of protological beings to eschatological beings—transforming humans into a state of incapacity for sin. God can forgive human misdeeds without

added.

8. The Textus Receptus (TR) differs from both the Majority Text and the Modern Critical Text. It combines majority and minority readings, as well as back translations from the Latin Vulgate and textual emendations made by its authors.

9. Van Aarde renders, "'Lord, save [us] (Κύριε, σῶσον). We are perishing.' Harrington (1991, 123) notes: 'The background for the stilling of the storm [Matt 8:18–27] is the ancient Near Eastern idea that the sea (especially a storm at sea) symbolized the powers of chaos and evil. . . . By showing power over the sea Jesus does what God does according to Pss 74:13–14; 89:10–12." Van Aarde, "ΙΗΣΟΥΣ, the Davidic Messiah," 18.

requiring the Son's incarnation. Still, their Adamic temporal existence can only be resolved by the elevation of being through *huio-thesía* that requires the image of a *Huios*. The new beings, Χριστιανός (*Christianos*, the anointed ones), will be free from Adamic facticity, sarkic desire, and sin when they are consummated (Rom 8:23). God forgives humans' sins and recreates humans as new everlasting beings by transforming humans' nature (essence). Without forgiveness, there is no *re*-creation. Yet, forgiveness will not save humanity; *re*-creation (resurrection, elevation) saves the human and the subhuman creations from perishing.

Even in the absence of original sin, human beings require the incarnation of the person of Jesus Christ to develop and elevate their human nature. This new nature is capable of resurrection from death.[10] The gospel is for and about Adamic beings, which is to say, all humankind. This term describes the collective of humanity seeking liberation from their facticity: the actual, factual aspects of human existence. These aspects are the conditions, limitations, and restrictions of being alive. Such limitations include being confined to the physical realm, subject to the constraints of temporality, and unable to achieve a union with the divine. The Adamic potentiality, which initially takes the form of dormant human spirits bestowed upon them by the Spirit, allows them to be freed from the inherited Adamic facticity.

In a manner analogous to the Messiah, we shall be elevated. However, He endured suffering before attaining exaltation. Those who were His friends deserted Him on His way to His death. None of those He had assisted were present; they had withdrawn themselves. They sought to circumvent any potential issues with Him. The only individual who assumed the burden from His shoulders is with whom He is previously unacquainted, Simon of Cyrene. Similarly, the same sequence of events must occur for us to be elevated to the status of God's sons and heirs (υἱοὶ). In the event of a major catastrophe, it is possible that all of our hard-won achievements may be lost, and those who are our friends and family may be reluctant to provide us with assistance. Nevertheless, assistance from individuals we are not acquainted with will be available.

THE CORONATION OF PRIESTS AND KINGS

The making of a *huios* (*huiothesía*) is closely associated with the inauguration of a king in the biblical era. King David, in his psalm, wrote, "My son, you [are] today I have begotten you" (Ps 2:7). This prompts the question of how a father can speak to his son on that day and claim that he has begotten

---

10. Rom 6:3–9.

him on that day. According to Brown-Driver-Briggs, the word *yəliḏtīḵā* (יְלִדְתִּיךָ) in this verse is derived from *yālaḏ* (Strong's H 3205, יָלַד), which is used figuratively to mean "of [Yahweh] formally installing the king into theocratic rights."[11] Therefore, this verse can be interpreted as meaning, "My son, today I [Yahweh] have inaugurated (placed) you as king." Schreiner explains in *TDOT* that where God is the subject of this verb "*yālaḏ*," as in Ps 2:7, it means "during the enthronement of the king: *Today I have begotten you*."[12] This is a *benediction* bestowed at a coronation. The king of the theocratic nation Israel is regarded as the son of the divine King, Yahweh. It is considered a mandate from heaven.

Jesus of Nazareth, who was born as an Adamic human in the lineage of King David, is a child of God (νήπιος, a minor) who does not require adoption into God's family. Upon His resurrection, the human figure of the Lord Jesus Christ was *ontologically* elevated to the status of a consummated son (ὁ Ὑιός), thereby acquiring the rights and privileges associated with a primogenetic consummated son of God. The Lord Jesus Christ is a king, but not of this world (John 18:36). He is the King of the new pneumatic *aeon*. All human beings are the created children of God (νήπιοι). These include the elects (Christians), who are being constituted as God's adult sons (υἱοί). The culmination of God's sub-act of *huiothesía* will result in the coronation of Christians as co-priests and co-kings of the Lord of all beings.

The question of when the coronation of the Lord Jesus Christ as King will occur is the subject of considerable debate. The apostle John wrote, "They shall be priests of God and of Christ, and shall reign with him a thousand years" (Rev 20:4–6). It seems reasonable to posit that this inauguration of Christ as a priest and a king will take place at the parousia. If this is the case, the phrase "conform to the image of the Son" not only implies that Christians will become Christlike beings (new beings) in their resurrections; it also suggests that they will hold the offices of priests and kings. On the day of the parousia, a grand celebration will be held to inaugurate the Heir and coheirs. Paul describes this wonderful event in his Letter to the Romans: "That not comparable the undergoing sufferings of the present time towards the glory (splendor) that is about to be revealed to us-ward and in us" (v. 8:18). Therefore, it can be concluded that God's sub-act of *huiothesía* is a prerequisite for the coronation.

---

11. Brown et al., "3205. yalad."
12. *TDOT*, 80. Emphasis original.

EPHESIANS 1:4–5

The apostle Paul also discussed the idea of "υἱοθεσία" with the Ephesians. The verses from Eph 1:4–5 can be rendered in the following way.

> Just as He [God and Father of our Lord Jesus Christ] has chosen us [out of the collective mass of νήπιοι] in him (in Christ) before the foundation of the world [outside the *causa meritoria* on the part of human beings who had not yet been created] to be for us holy and blameless (to make us holy and *immaculatus*) before Him (God the Father). In love having predestined us to υἱοθεσία (to the making of a υἱός) through Jesus Christ, to God-self according to the good pleasure of the will of Him (God the Father). (AHT)

Salvation is a divine act, not a human effort. Before the creation of the universe, God planned to create everlasting pneumatic humankind. However, to make them into created beings, He initiated the process by creating mortal humans in space-time using the materials He had previously created, except for the human spirits. The Son's incarnation initiates the process of developing spiritual eschatological humans. The parousia, rather than the sixth day in Eden, represents the culminating phase of the creative process, wherein humans are regarded as holy and blameless before the Father of creation.

ADOPTION IS NOT PAULINE *HUIOTHESÍA*: CONCISE FINAL THOUGHTS

The doctrine of adoption elucidates the concept of lost sonship, an alien family, historical Adam and Eve, historical fall, and the restoration of [Adamic] human beings to a former original state or position as created sons of God through adoption into God's family to become adopted sons of God. The doctrine of adoption postulates that humanity, in its fallen state, has been alienated from the Creator God since the fall and before their adoption. Nevertheless, God desires to reinstate their status through a novel form of relationship, namely, adoption. It is unclear why adoption is necessary if we are discussing the concept of restoration or reinstatement. Adoption bestows upon Adamic individuals a novel status within the divine family, that of an adopted son, which differs from their original status as God's created sons.

Some proponents of adoption are opposed to the tenets of inclusivism or pluralism. The primary objective of the concept of two families is exclusivism.[13] In the writings of the apostle Paul, we find that the term "νήπιοι" is not used in the sense of being enslaved or belonging to Satan's family. Rather, it denotes all humans created by God but are in a minor state. They are always members of the family of God, and thus adoption is unnecessary. The doctrine of theological υἱοθεσία elucidates the process by which an infant of God becomes an adult while still within the familial structure of his Father. Symbolically, it illuminates the planned human being's constitution, or establishment, from an Adamic being to a Christic being, which will be completed at the parousia.

The initial account of creation in Gen 1:26 states that God created mankind in His image—a potentiality to make a fellowship like that in the triune God. This basic state of being is further developed. Paul, in Rom 8:29, affirms that those who believe in the Son will be transformed into the image of the Son through *huio*-fication, becoming a pneumatic human who is capable of participating in the pneumatic union with the triune God, which is mediated by God the Son incarnate. Humans are made according to these two images, which describe the two distinct stages in the overarching narrative of creation and elevation (redemption) within the framework of divine love.

We do not lose our [mature] sonship (*huio*-ship), which we have *not* had since the beginning of creation, but we are lost on our way to the elevation of beings. We are supposed to grow, but fall—we are heading into the state of subhuman creation instead of eschatological being. Humans also do not return to the prelapsarian state, where God just began to create self-conscious beings.[14] During that brief period, humans did not exercise their freedom as independent beings. Instead of returning, human beings pass through it and advance to perfection in the future. God progressively perfects humanity, transforming Adamic sarkic beings into Christic pneumatic beings. Despite the indivisible bond between humanity and God, an everlasting estrangement may occur if humanity does not evolve into eschatological beings.

---

13. For the discussion of exclusivism see the dialogue of John Hick and Alvin Plantinga put together in Kim, *Reformed Epistemology*, 100.

14. Cf. Tillich: "In Spinoza nature is presented geometrically whereas in Schelling it is presented partly biologically and partly psychologically. In this construction the process of nature proceeds from the lowest to the highest forms of nature, and finally to man in terms of a contrast of two principles. He called the one principle the unconscious and the other the conscious. He tried to show how slowly in all different forms of nature consciousness develops until it comes to man where it becomes self-consciousness. Then a new development starts, the development of culture and history." Tillich, *History of Christian Thought*, 442.

It would be a significant challenge to alter the meaning of υἱοθεσία to mean "adoption" without compromising the integrity and coherence of the gospel of the Christ. To propose that this specific interpretation (adoption) is the primary meaning of the gospel would be to cause considerable harm to the integrity of the true gospel. One must engage in more eisegesis and complex arguments to defend an engineered definition that alters the Pauline Greek υἱοθεσία into the Roman "gospel" of *adoptio*. Irrespective of the degree of care exercised in its construction, the resulting complexity highlights the argument's fundamental flaw. By reframing the concept of becoming Christlike beings who can transcend mortality and corruption, such as being adopted into the divine family of God, the interpretation in question effectively undermines the essence of this spiritual journey. The doctrine of adoption has had a significant impact on and replaced the Christian gospel of salvation.

TABLE 4: The Dichotomy in the Concept of Adoption

	Before Adoption	After Adoption
1	A slave, a son of wrath	A son of God
2	A member of Satan's family	A legal member of God's family
3	Not saved	Saved
4	Old status	New status
5	Old heart	New heart
6	Unloved	Loved
7	Under punishment	Being glorified
8	Raised outside of God's house	Accepted into God's house

TABLE 5: The Juxtaposition in the Concept of *Huiothesía*

	Before *Huiothesía*	After *Huiothesía*
1	An infant son (*népios*)	A mature son (*huios*)
2	A protological being	An eschatological being
3	Base nature	Elevated nature
4	An old being	A new being (an exalted being)
5	Humanity in potential	Humanity in fulfilment
6	Adamic sarkic	Christic pneumatic
7	Finite psychic existence	Transcendent pneumatic existence

8	Limited to temporal, physical fellowship	Capable of everlasting, pneumatic union with the Godhead through the Son
9	Cannot enter the pneumatic realm; ends in temporality	Able to live everlastingly in the pneumatic realm
10	Created and raised in God's creation	Exalted within God's creation to enter the everlastingness

The following table presents a comparative analysis of the doctrines of adoption and *huiothesía* (υἱοθεσία).

TABLE 6: A Tabular Comparison Between Adoption and *Huiothesía*

	Adoption in General	*Huiothesía* in This Work
1	As it relates to salvation, adoption conveys an unbiblical theme. The Roman idea of adoption, which has been chosen as a translation of *huiothesía* is not present in the Greek NT; an actual adoption is only mentioned in the OT concerning the adoption of Moses.	The teaching of *huiothesía*, as it is presented in the Greek NT, is a central tenet of Christian salvation. God's sub-act of *huiothesía* frees humans from their Adamic facticity, including protological nature, sinful desire, and temporality.
2	One-time legal adoption.	A process of ontological transformation.
3	The doctrine of adoption reflects Roman culture rather than biblical teaching; thus, it originates from an unknown gospel that diverges from scriptural truth. The Roman *adoptio* offers a perspective of salvation that the Bible does not address.	The doctrine of *huiothesía* is grounded in the universal analogy of human development, which the Apostle Paul employs to elucidate the ontological transformation experienced by believers.
4	Transformation of identity.	Transformation of being.
5	Adoption is a phrase that refers to the legal transfer of an adult son from one family to another. It metaphorically teaches that Christians are adopted sons of God.	*Huiothesía* is a phrase referring to the maturing of an infant into a son-heir position in their own family. It symbolically teaches about God's Adamic sarkic protological beings who become elevated Christic pneumatic eschatological beings.
6	Those who espouse the doctrine of adoption tend to eschew the notion of the human spirit.	The human spirit is an integral element of the true Pauline doctrine of *huiothesía*—the true gospel.

7	Those who advocate for adoption translate Pauline's "*huios*" into "son," which is equivalent to the Latin "filius." The term "son" is defined in several ways. It refers to a male child, whether considered a child of one parent or both. It includes any male descendant and an individual who assumes the role of a son through adoption, marriage, or other forms of familial affiliation.	The Pauline "*huios*" and English "son" have distinct meanings. The Pauline "*huios*" can be translated into "adult son," "son-heir," "eschatological son," "Christic son," "pneumatic son," "elevated/exalted son," or "consummated son." A *huios* is symbolically representative of a regenerated being in contrast to a *népios*, which represents the old Adamic being.
8	In the context of adoption, those previously not considered sons attain the state of sonship. The adopted son is a mature individual who originates from an unknown family or Satan's family.	In the context of Paul's *huiothesía*, *huio*-ship is a state of maturity that is bestowed upon those who were previously minors within God's family, thus not from another family.
9	Exclusivism. There are two families. God is the Father of adopted sons (Christians). Satan is the father of the sons of wrath.	Inclusivism. All conscious beings are in one God's created family. God is the Father of all human beings: *népioi* and *huioi*.
10	Adam was a son who sinned and lost his sonship.	Adam was symbolically a *népios*, with the potential to sin and decay or to become a *huios*. He does not have the status of a *huio*-ship yet. No lost sonship.
11	All descendants of Adam inherit original sin.	Adamic humans inherit a protological nature: sarkic desire, temporality, and potentiality. Jesus, born as an Adamic human, did not sin.
12	The attainment of salvation is contingent upon the acquisition of a new legal standing as an adopted son. Through adoption, salvation is attained by restoring the lost Adamic sonship—the prelapsarian state of being.	Salvation is achieved by transforming the mortal and corruptible Adamic being into an immortal and incorruptible pneumatic-Christic being. Salvation refers to the imminent new being, the everlasting eschatological being.
13	These statements (adoption and restoration) are incoherent. Why does restoration require adoption (and incarnation)? The status of being a created son of God is superior to that of being an adopted son.	Salvation is attained by being constituted into a new being. It requires the incarnation of the Divine Son to provide a pattern of a *huios* (the image of a *Huios*) for human elevation (not a restoration).

14	The illogical concept of human migration from God's family to Satan's family and back to God's family through adoption is a fundamental precept of the doctrine of adoption.	It is a fundamental teaching of *huiothesía* that all humans are members of God's created family, both before and after their salvation. They are perpetually subject to the divine economy.
15	God provides salvation for Satan's children by establishing a new legal status through the process of adoption into the divine family. Does Satan's family allow for adoption?	The concept of divine creation entails the formation, growth, and maturation of God's created children, from their initial state as minor beings (resembling Adam) to their eventual development into adults (resembling Christ). This process occurs within the context of God's created family. God initiates this process and culminates in the conferral of incorruptibility and immortality upon the individual through the divine sub-act of *huio-fication* (*huiothesía*, *huiopoiesis*).
16	Adoption bestows upon an adopted son a membership status that is distinct from that of Christ the Son, yet co-membership in the divine family (the triune God or the church). The relationship between God and adopted sons is now legally binding.	*Huiothesía* makes a *Christos* (*huios*), like the human figure *Iēsous ho Christos* (christification). Christians become extended participants in the Godhead's intrinsic, unseparated pneumatic oneness—the pneumatic union functions based on the compatible pneumatic essence of the creatures and their Creator.
17	It is posited that humans are created in the image of God. The image of God in humanity has been corrupted by sin and requires restoration.	There are two images: protological humans are created in the image of God and are constituted to conform to the image of the [mature] Son (1 Cor 15:49).
18	There is only one state of being with two legal statuses: adopted (transferred) into God's family or the sons of wrath.	There are two states of being: the protological sarkic-Adamic being and the eschatological pneumatic-Christic being.
19	Christians are Adamic beings with no ontological change.	Christians are pneumatic-Christic beings, ontologically distinct from the sarkic-Adamic beings.
20	Christians are God's adopted sons with new hearts.	In this *kairos*, Christians are elevated beings with both sarkic and pneumatic inclinations.

21	Christians have a direct sonship with God and are members of the divine family.	Christians are God's exalted, created, mature sons (*huioi*) with indirect, extended *huio*-ship through God the Son incarnate.
22	Adam is the historical ancestor of all humanity.	Agree to take the possibility of multiple human biological Adamic parents.
23	Sinners (all human beings) are separated from God before they are saved. All humans are separated from God since the historical Adam sinned.	God never separates His created children (*népioi* and *huioi*) from him. However, unbelievers (*népioi*) will be unable to participate in God's eternal pneumatic union. Thus, the separation is after parousia.
24	Believers are adopted sons of God (Rom 8:15). What happens with the adoption in Rom 8:23?	Believers (Rom 8:15) are *huioi* with sinful and spiritual natures who will later have a fully pneumatic nature when they receive the pneumatic body of resurrection (Rom 8:23).
25	Humans have fallen from a state of perfection in Eden; they are in a state of total depravity; they require restoration to perfection in Eden.	Protological, Adamic, corporeal, sarkic humans are in their early stage of development, and they are in a state of total incapability; they require vivification to the ultimate perfection as new beings in the new creation.
26	Adoption is a means of achieving salvation through membership in the family of God. As a result of this membership, Christians are granted eternal life. Salvation relates to legal membership.	*Huiothesía* solves both the problem of the Adamic human's facticity, including sin and temporality, through ontological transformation. By having a fully pneumatic state of being, consummated children of God (*huioi*) can proceed to live in the eternal pneumatic realm and are unable to sin. Salvation relates to changing human nature and establishing an everlasting pneumatic union with God.
27	Those who adhere to the Christian faith live and will die as adopted sons of God and will be resurrected as adopted sons of God.	Christians live and die as *nepioi-huioi* (half-sarkic, half-pneumatic) but will be resurrected as fully *huioi* (consummated pneumatic beings) of God.

28	The concept of salvation through adoption is also found in Gnosticism.	The concept of biblical *huiothesía* focuses on the humanity of the Lord Jesus Christ, while Gnosticism focuses on His divinity.
29	These points highlight a significant impact of the Augustinian tradition, particularly its emphasis on the historical or cosmic fall, on the development of the doctrine of adoption. It suggests that the Augustinian framework has shaped how adoption is understood within theological discourse.	This specific understanding of *huiothesía* has remained largely unaffected by the Augustinian tradition, particularly concerning the subject of original sin. This implies a non-Augustinian stream of thought regarding sin and salvation. It solves the problem of temporality (death) and the sting of death (sin).
30	The doctrine of adoption does not fit within the contemporary world-picture (*Weltbild*) where the possibility of a historical Adam is precluded, thereby undermining the foundational premise for the doctrine of original sin.	The doctrine of *huiothesía* does not require a historical Adam, but a literary Adam. It can be reconciled with the contemporary views of science.
31	Its Christology centers on the cross of Jesus Christ, which signifies the aspect of payment for human liberation from the bondage of sin.	Its Christology emphasizes the event of Jesus Christ—especially His birth, baptism, and resurrection. The resurrection marks liberation from human facticity.
32	It concerns the giving of the Holy Spirit to humanity.	It explores the work of the Holy Spirit (the unitive Being) in quickening the human spirit and establishing pneumatic union.
33	The doctrine of adoption conceals the true gospel of salvation.	The doctrine of *huiothesía* reveals the concealed knowledge of the true gospel of salvation.

SALVATION: HUMAN EXALTATION THROUGH THE MAKING OF CONSUMMATED SONS

In their protological state, humans are subject to mortality (temporality) and the potential for sin. However, they also possess the capacity for growth and improvement. The capabilities, possibilities, potentialities, and facticity of protological beings must be elevated. Miroslav Volf offers a rendering of the concept.

The basic problem of human beings resides not at the *moral*, but rather at the *ontological level*. Necessity and separation emerge because the individual is substance (however articulated) existing in time and space, and is set over against other objects; these qualities inhere in protological creaturely existence itself.[15]

God creates the planned humans in two sequences. Adam was created as a protological human (an old being, a νήπιος) capable of finite and sarkic existence only, but with a potential to grow (to be elevated).

The bodily existence of a human being (understood as *Dasein*, i.e., a human in the existential sense) cannot change on its own. An authentic existence of a protological finite being cannot bring salvation (free from decaying) to him because he is still under the bondage of his *temporal* primordial (developing yet limited) existence. Adamic humans are trapped in temporality (being-unto-death). Still, we are aware of our finitude. We must find external help, that is, from the Eternal Infinite.

Only through the intervention of the Creator can the human race be liberated from its current state of bondage as sarkic temporal beings. For this to be accomplished, a being must enter the temporal realm and possess the capacity to transcend the limitations of corporeal sarkic existence. Only the God-human person can fulfill this function, and this constitutes His most significant work—providing humanity with the archetypal image for ontological elevation. By conforming to this archetype, the image of Jesus the Messiah, God will elevate the elect to a higher ontological state. Such salvation—liberation from temporality—is found exclusively in Christ. This concerns becoming like Christ in His elevated human nature, not in His personhood.

BEYOND THIS WORK

Based on this disclosure of the meaning of *huiothesía* (υἱοθεσία), it becomes necessary to reconsider and potentially retranslate key Pauline texts—particularly the Epistles to the Galatians and Romans—to remove the anachronistic notion of adoption. Such translation efforts must carefully distinguish between related biblical Greek terms like *népios* (νήπιος), *huios* (υἱός), and *teknon* (τέκνον), to recover the original, nuanced meaning of *huiothesía* and restore the gospel of *Huio*-fication to its rightful theological prominence. This renewed textual approach aims to equip theology students and scholars with a more faithful understanding of Pauline soteriology and identity

---

15. Volf, *After Our Likeness*, 81. Emphasis added.

formation in Christ, enabling them to actively participate in recovering the authentic concept of *huiothesía*. Frequent revisitation of this issue is vital, as the pervasive presence of "adoption" in Bible translations, dictionaries, and theological literature continues to obscure the original concept and perpetuate misconceptions.

Moreover, scholars with access to diverse vernacular Bible Versions—including Old Latin (*Itala*), Syriac, Coptic, Armenian, Georgian, and Ethiopic translations—are uniquely positioned to critically examine how *huiothesía* or adoption has been rendered across textual traditions. While absolute certainty remains elusive, a multidisciplinary analysis of these vernacular ancient Bible Versions, Reformation-era translations, and patristic fragments offers a textured and historically grounded comprehension of *huiothesía*. The other thing we can do is to compare the teachings of the Greek patristic fathers and the Roman patristic fathers on the subject of *huiothesía*.

In addition, this gospel of *huiothesía*—emphasizing the full humanity of Jesus, the Son of God, and the consequent elevation of human beings—invites fruitful comparison with other transformative worldviews. These include the Baháʾí teaching of the new creation (*khalq-i-jadíd*), Friedrich Nietzsche's concept of the overman (*Übermensch*), Dietrich Bonhoeffer's vision of Christian maturity, and gnostic ideas of human becoming, which often diminish the significance of Jesus' humanity. Such comparative study enriches theological discourse and broadens the horizon of spiritual anthropology.

Furthermore, this perspective encourages a renewed christological inquiry, proposing that titles such as "the [consummated] Son of God" and "the Christ" primarily highlight Jesus' full humanity united with His divine mission. This approach opens new pathways for biblical scholarship and theological reflection, deepening our understanding of Jesus' identity and salvific role.

Ultimately, the teaching of *Huio*-fication (*huiothesía*) has the potential to transform our worldview, reshaping how we perceive our origins, purpose, morality, and destiny. By recovering this authentic Pauline concept, theology can offer a more coherent and life-giving vision of human existence in relation to God.

Bibliography

Academic. "Υἱοποίησις." https://greek_german.de-academic.com/74332/%CF%85%E1%BC%B1%CE%BF%CF%80%CE%BF%CE%AF%CE%B7%CF%83%CE%B9%CF%82.

Adiprasetya, Joas. *Berteologi Dalam Iman: Dasar-Dasar Teologi Sistimatika-Konstruktif.* Jakarta: BPK Gunung Mulia, 2023.

Agar, Nicholas. *Humanity's End: Why We Should Reject Radical Enhancement.* Life and Mind. Cambridge, MA: MIT Press, 2010.

Aho, Kevin. "Existentialism." *Stanford Encyclopedia of Philosophy*, January 6, 2023. Edited by Edward N. Zalta and Uri Nodelman. https://plato.stanford.edu/archives/sum2023/entries/existentialism/.

Aland, Barbara, et al., eds. *The Greek New Testament (UBS^5)* 5. Rev. ed. Stuttgart: Deutsche Bibelgesellschaft, 2014.

Amerson, Nathan D. "The Church as Tribe." *Journal of Biblical Theology* 4.3 (2021) 91–104.

Arnold, Brian. "Why Did God Become Man?—Dr. Stephen Wellum." Phoenix Seminary, November 17, 2020. https://ps.edu/why-did-god-become-man-dr-stephen-wellum/.

Augustine, Aurelius. *On The Trinity.* Vol. 7 of *The Works of Aurelius Augustine.* Edited by Marcus Dods. Translated by Arthur West Haddan. Edinburgh: T. & T. Clark, 1873.

Bacon, Benjamin Wisner. "Jesus as Lord." *Harvard Theological Review* 4.2 (1911) 204–28.

Barbour, Ian G. *When Science Meets Religion.* San Francisco: HarperSanFransisco, 2000.

Barden, Garrett. "On Intellectual Conversion." *Journal of Macrodynamic Analysis* 3 (2003) 117–41.

Barth, Karl. *Dogmatics in Outline.* Translated by G. T. Thomson. London: SCM, 1979.

———. *The Epistle to the Romans.* Translated by Edwyn C. Hoskyns. London: Oxford University Press, 1933.

Bavinck, Herman. *Reformed Dogmatics: Abridged in One Volume.* Edited by John Bolt. Grand Rapids: Baker Academic, 2011.

Becker, Dieter. *Pedoman Dogmatika: Suatu Kompendium Singkat.* Jakarta: BPK Gunung Mulia, 2015.

Beeke, Joel R. *Heirs with Christ: The Puritans on Adoption.* Grand Rapids: Reformation Heritage, 2008.

Behr, John. *Asceticism and Anthropology in Irenaeus and Clement*. Oxford Early Christian Studies. Oxford: Oxford University Press, 2000.

Benedict XVI (pope). *Jesus of Nazareth*. Translated by Adrian J. Walker. New York: Doubleday, 2007.

———. *Jesus of Nazareth: Part Two, Holy Week: From the Entrance into Jerusalem to the Resurrection*. Translated by Vatican Secretariat of State. San Fransisco: Ignatius, 2011.

Bennett, John G. *Making a Soul: Human Destiny and the Debt of Our Existence*. 1st ed. Santa Fe, NM: Bennett, 1995.

Betz, Hans Dieter. *Galatians: A Commentary on Paul's Letter to the Churches in Galatia*. Hermeneia: A Critical and Historical Commentary of the Bible. Philadelphia: Fortress, 1988.

Bible Hub. "Romans 8." https://biblehub.com/tyndale/romans/8.htm.

Blackwell, Ben C. *Christosis: Pauline Soteriology in Light of Deification in Irenaeus and Cyril of Alexandria*. Tübingen: Mohr Siebeck, 2011.

Blackwood, Andrew W. Jr. *The Epistles to the Galatians and Ephesians*. Proclaiming the New Testament 2. Grand Rapids: Baker, 1962.

Bloesch, Donald G. *A Theology of Word & Spirit: Authority & Method in Theology*. Downers Grove, IL: InterVarsity, 1992.

Blosser, Benjamin P. *Become Like the Angels: Origen's Doctrine of the Soul*. Washington, DC: Catholic University of America Press, 2012.

Boice, James Montgomery. *Romans, Volume 2: The Reign of Grace (Romans 5–8)*. The Boice Expositional Commentary Series. Grand Rapids: Baker, 2005.

Botterweck, Gerhard Johannes, and Helmer Ringgren. *Theological Dictionary of the Old Testament* 6. Grand Rapids: Eerdmans, 1990.

Bray, Gerald. *God Is Love: A Biblical and Systematic Theology*. Wheaton, IL: Crossway, 2012.

Brown, Collin, ed. *New International Dictionary of the New Testament Theology* 1. Grand Rapids: Zondervan, 1986.

Brown, Francis, et al. "3205. yalad." In *A Hebrew and English Lexicon of the Old Testament: With an Appendix Containing the Biblical Aramaic*. Oxford: Clarendon Press, 1906. https://biblehub.com/hebrew/3205.htm.

Brown, John. *An Exposition of the Epistle to the Galatians*. Marshallton, DE: Sovereign Grace, 1970.

———. *Analytical Exposition of the Epistle of Paul the Apostle to the Romans*. New York: Robert Carter and Brothers, 1857.

Bultmann, Rudolf. *Kerygma and Myth: A Theological Debate*. Edited by Hans Werner Bartsch. Rev. trans. New York: Harper Torchbook, 1961.

———. *Theology of the New Testament: Complete in One Volume*. Translated by Kendrick Grobel. New York: Charles Scribner's Sons, 1951.

Bundrick, David R. "Ta Stoicheia Tou Kosmou (Gal 4:3)." *The Journal of the Evangelical Theological Society* 34.3 (1991) 353–64.

Burke, Trevor J. "Adopted as Sons (ΥΙΟΘΕΣΙΑ): The Missing Piece in Pauline Soteriology." In *Paul: Jew, Greek, and Roman*, edited by Stanley E. Porter, 259–87. Vol. 5 of *Pauline Studies*. Leiden: Brill, 2008.

———. *Adopted into God's Family: Exploring a Pauline Metaphor*. New Studies in Biblical Theology 22. Downers Grove, IL: InterVarsity, 2006.

———. "Exegesis 14: Adoptive—Sonship." *Foundation* 29 (1992) 25–29.

———. "The Characteristics of Paul's Adoptive-Sonship (*Huiothesia*) Motif." *IBS* 17 (1995) 62–74.
———. *The Message of Sonship: At Home in God's Household*. Nottingham, UK: InterVarsity, 2011.
Calvin, John. *Commentaries on the Epistle of Paul to the Galatians and Ephesians*. Translated by William Pringle. Edinburgh: The Calvin Translation Society, 1854.
———. *Commentary on the Epistle of Paul the Apostle to the Romans*. Translated by John Owen. Edinburgh: The Calvin Translation Society, 1849.
The Cambridge Bible for Schools and Colleges. "Cambridge Bible for Schools and Colleges." Biblehub. https://biblehub.com/commentaries/cambridge/.
Campbell, Constantine R. *Paul and Union with Christ: An Exegetical and Theological Study*. Grand Rapids: Zondervan, 2012.
Candlish, Robert Smith. *The Fatherhood of God: Being the First Course of the Cunningham Lectures Delivered Before the New College, Edinburgh, in March 1864*. Edinburgh: Adam and Charles Black, 1865.
Cocceaianus, Lucius Cassius Dio. *Dio's Roman History, with an English Translation by Earnest Cary, Ph.D., on the Basis of the Version of Herbert Baldwin Foster, Ph.D.: In Nine Volumes*. 9 vols. London: William Heinemann, 1925.
Collodi, Carlo. *Pinocchio*. Hertfordshire, UK: Wordsworth, 1995.
Colunga, Alberto, and Laurentio Turrado. *Biblia Sacra Iuxta Vulgatam Clementinam Nova Editio*. Decima Editio. Matriti: Biblioteca de Autores Cristianos, 1999.
Cousar, James E. "The Reformed Doctrine of Adoption, by Robert Alexander Webb. Eerdmans, Grand Rapids, Michigan, 1947." *Interpretation* 4.2 (1950) 234–36.
Coverdale, Myles. "Coverdale Bible 1535." Bible Hub. https://biblehub.com/coverdale/romans/8.htm.
Cranfield, C. E. B. *A Critical and Exegetical Commentary on the Epistle to the Romans* 1. International Critical Commentary on the Holy Scriptures of the Old and New Testaments. London: T. & T. Clark, 2011.
———. *A Critical and Exegetical Commentary on the Epistle to the Romans* 2. The International Critical Commentary on the Holy Scriptures of the Old and New Testaments. London: T. & T. Clark, 2004.
Crawford, Thomas J. *The Fatherhood of God: Considered in Its General and Special Aspects and Particularly in Relation to the Atonement, with a Review of Recent Speculations on the Subject, and a Reply to the Strictures of Dr. Candlish*. 3rd ed. Edinburgh: William Blackwood and Sons, 1868.
Creswell, John W., and J. David Creswell. *Research Design: Qualitative, Quantitative, and Mixed Methods Approaches*. 3rd ed. Los Angeles: SAGE, 2009.
Dahl, Nils Alstrup. *Jesus the Christ: The Historical Origins of Christological Doctrine*. Edited by Donald H. Juel. Minneapolis: Fortress, 1991.
Daniell, David. *The Bible in English: Its History and Influence*. New Haven, CT: Yale University Press, 2003.
Danker, Frederick W., et al. *Greek-English Lexicon of the New Testament and Other Early Christian Literature*. 3rd ed. Chicago: University of Chicago Press, 2000.
Demarest, Bruce. *The Cross and Salvation: The Doctrine of Salvation*. Edited by John S. Feinberg. Foundation of Evangelical Theology. Wheaton, IL: Crossway, 1997.
Denney, James. *The Expositor's Greek Testament* 2. Edited by W. Robertson Nicoll. Grand Rapids: Eerdmans, 1956.

Dennison, James T., ed. *Reformed Confessions of the 16th and 17th Centuries in English Translation: Volume I, 1523–1552*. Grand Rapids: Reformation Heritage, 2008.
Deutsche Bibel Gesellschaft. "Deutsche Bibel Gesellschaft. Academic Bible." https://www.academic-bible.com/en/online-bibles/greek-new-testament-ubs5/read-the-bible-text/.
Dille, Sarah J. *Mixing Metaphors: God as Mother and Father in Deutero-Isaiah*. London: T. & T. Clark, 2004.
Diodorus. *Diodorus of Sicily* 11. Translated by Francis R. Walton. Loeb Classical Library 409. Cambridge, MA: Harvard Univ. Press, 1980.
Dodd, C. H. *The Interpretation of the Fourth Gospel*. Cambridge: Cambridge University Press, 1953.
Duncan, George S. *The Epistle of Paul to the Galatians*. The Moffat Commentary. New York: Harper and Brothers, 1934.
Dunn, James D. G. *Christology in the Making: A New Testament Inquiry into the Origins of the Doctrine of Incarnation*. 2nd ed. London: SCM, 1989.
———. *The Theology of Paul the Apostle*. Grand Rapids: Eerdmans, 2006.
———. *Romans 1–8*. Word Biblical Commentary 38A. Nashville, TN: Thomas Nelson, 1988.
Ebeling, Gerhard. *The Truth of the Gospel: An Exposition of Galatians*. Translated by David Green. Philadelphia: Fortress, 1985.
Ede, Andrew, and Lesley B. Cormack. *A History of Science in Society: From Philosophy to Utility*. 2nd ed. Toronto: University of Toronto Press, 2012.
Edwards, M. J., ed. *Galatians, Ephesians, Philippians*. Ancient Christian Commentary on Scripture 8. Downers Grove, IL: InterVarsity, 1999.
Ellicott, C. J., ed. *Ellicott's Commentary for English Readers by Various Writers* 2. London: Cassell and Company, 1897.
End, Th. van den. *Surat Roma 7*. Jakarta: BPK Gunung Mulia, 2010.
Erasmus, Desiderius. *Annotations on Romans*. Edited by Robert D. Sider and John B. Payne. Collected Works of Erasmus 56. Toronto: University of Toronto Press, 1994.
———. *Paraphrases on Romans and Galatians*. Edited by Robert D. Sider. Collected Works of Erasmus 42. Toronto: University of Toronto Press, 1984.
ESV Study Bible. Wheaton, IL: Crossway, 2008.
Etheridge, John Wesley, trans. "The Peschito Syriac New Testament 1849." STEP Bible. https://www.stepbible.org/version.jsp?version=Eth.
A Faithful Version. "A Faithful Version: Why Is This Bible Unique?" https://afaithfulversion.org/a-faithful-version/.
Fee, Gordon D. *God's Empowering Presence: The Holy Spirit in the Letters of Paul*. Peabody, MA: Hendrickson, 1994.
———. *Paul, the Spirit, and the People of God*. Peabody, MA: Hendrickson, 1996.
———. *Pauline Christology: An Exegetical-Theological Study*. Grand Rapids: Baker Academic, 2007.
Ferguson, Sinclair B. "The Reformed Doctrine of Sonship." In *Pulpit & People: Essays in Honour of William Still on His 75th Birthday*, edited by Nigel M. S. Cameron and Sinclair B. Ferguson, 81–88. Edinburgh: Rutherford House, 1986.
Feuerbach, Ludwig. *The Essence of Christianity*. Translated by George Elliot. Amherst, NY: Prometheus, 1989.

Fitzmyer, Joseph A., ed. *Romans: A New Translation with Introduction and Commentary*. 1st ed. Anchor Bible 33. New York: Doubleday, 1993.

Fokin, Alexey R. "The Relationship Between Soul and Spirit in Greek and Latin Patristic Thought." *Faith and Philosophy: Journal of the Society of Christian Philosophers* 26.5, Article 11 (2009) 599–614.

Fowler, James A. *A Commentary on The Epistle to The Galatians: The Gospel versus Religion, Christocentric Commentary Series*. Fallbrook, CA: C. I. Y., 2006.

Fowler, James W. *Stages of Faith: The Psychology of Human Development and the Quest for Meaning*. San Francisco: Harper&Row, 1981.

Frame, John M. *Systematic Theology: An Introduction to Christian Belief*. Phillipsburg, NJ: P. & R., 2013.

Friedrich, Gerhard, ed. *Theological Dictionary of the New Testament 8*. Translated by Geoffrey William Bromiley. Grand Rapids: Eerdmans, 1972.

Fung, Ronald Y. K. *Epistle to the Galatians*. Grand Rapids: Eerdmans, 1988.

Garner, David B. *Sons in the Son: The Riches and Reach of Adoption in Christ*. Phillipsburg, NJ: P. & R., 2016.

Genderen, J. van, and W. H. Velema. *Concise Reformed Dogmatics*. Edited by M. Van der Maas. Translated by Gerrit Bilkes. Phillipsburg, NJ: P. & R., 2008.

George, Archimandrite. *Theosis: The True Purpose of Human Life*. 4th ed. Greece: Mount Athos, 2006.

Girardeau, John L. *Discussions of Theological Discussions*. Edited by George Blackburn. Reprint, Harrisonburg, VA: Sprinkle, 1986.

Gorman, Michael J. *Reading Paul*. Eugene, OR: Cascade, 2008.

Grassmick, John D. *Principles and Practice of Greek Exegesis: A Classroom Manual*. Dallas: Dallas Theological Seminary, 1976.

Green, Bradley G. *Colin Gunton and the Failure of Augustine: The Theology of Colin Gunton in Light of Augustine*. Distinguished Dissertations in Christian Theology. Cambridge, UK: James Clarke & Co, 2012.

Green, Joel B., and Mark D. Baker. *Recovering the Scandal of the Cross: Atonement in New Testament and Contemporary Contexts*. Carlisle: Paternoster, 2003.

Greenlee, J. Harold. *Introduction to New Testament Textual Criticism*. Grand Rapids: Eerdmans, 1977.

Greenslade, Stanley Lawrence. *The Cambridge History of the Bible: The West from the Reformation to the Present Day*. Cambridge: Cambridge University Press, 1989.

Gribomont, Jean. "The Translations of Jerome and Rufinus." In *Patrology*, edited by Angelo Di Berardino, translated by Placid Solari, 4:195–254. Allen, TX: Christian Classics, 1983.

Grudem, Wayne. *Bible Doctrine: Essential Teachings of the Christian Faith*. Edited by Jeff Purswell. Grand Rapids: Zondervan, 1999.

Gunton, Colin E. *Father, Son, and the Holy Spirit: Essays Toward a Fully Trinitarian Theology*. London: T. & T. Clark, 2003.

Hahn, Scott. *First Comes Love: Finding Your Family in the Church and the Trinity*. New York: Doubleday, 2002.

Hall, Manly P. *The Wisdom of the Knowing Ones: Gnosticism, the Key to Esoteric Christianity*. Los Angeles: Philosophical Research Society, 2000.

Hamerton-Kelly, Robert. *God the Father: Theology and Patriarchy in the Teaching of Jesus*. Philadelphia: Fortress, 1979.

Harrill, J. Albert. "Coming of Age and Putting on Christ: The Toga Virilis Ceremony, Its Paraenesis, and Paul's Interpretation of Baptism in Galatians." *Novum Testamentum* 44.3 (2002) 252–77.

Harrison, Everett F., and Donald A. Hagner. *Romans*. Edited by Tremper Longman III and David E. Garland. Rev. ed. Expositor's Bible Commentary. Grand Rapids: Zondervan, 2008.

Hart, David B. *The New Testament: A Translation*. New Haven, CT: Yale University Press, 2017.

Hays, Christopher M., et al. *When the Son of Man Didn't Come: A Constructive Proposal on the Delay of the Parousia*. Minneapolis: Fortress, 2016.

Heard, J. B. *The Tripartite Nature of Man*. Edinburgh: T. & T. Clark, 1866.

Heim, Erin M. "Light Through a Prism: New Avenues of Inquiry for the Pauline Υἱοθεσία Metaphors." PhD diss., University of Otago, 2014.

Helm, Paul. "Classical Calvinist Doctrine of God." In *Perspectives on the Doctrine of God: Four Views*, edited by Bruce A. Ware, 5–52. Nashville: B. & H. Academic, 2008.

Hendriksen, William. *New Testament Commentary: Exposition of Galatians*. Grand Rapids: Baker, 1971.

Herberg, Will. *The Writings of Martin Buber*. Cleveland, OH: Meridian, 1963.

Hill, Brennan, et al. *Faith, Religion & Theology: A Contemporary Introduction*. Rev. and expan. ed. Mystic, CT: Twenty-Third, 1997.

Hogg, C. F., and W. E. Wine. *The Epistle to the Galatians and the Epistle to the Thessalonians: With Notes Exegetical and Expository*. Fincastle, VA: Scripture Truth Book, 1922.

Holcomb, Justin S., ed. *Christian Theologies of Salvation: A Comparative Introduction*. New York: New York University Press, 2017.

Horner, George William, ed. *The Coptic Version of the New Testament in the Southern Dialect Otherwise Called Sahidic and Thebaic with Critical Apparatus Literal English Translation, Appendix and Register of Fragments*. 7 vols. Oxford: Clarendon, 1920.

Houghton, H. A. G. "The Biblical Text of Jerome's Commentary on Galatians." *The Journal of Theological Studies* 65.1 (2014) 1–24.

Hus[set caron over s]ek, Vít. "Rebirth into a New Man: Deification in Jerome." In *Deification in the Latin Patristic Tradition*, edited by Jared Ortiz, 153–68. Washington, DC: The Catholic University of America Press, 2019.

Irenaeus. *Against Heresies*. Edited by James Donaldson. Translated by Alexander Roberts and William Rambaut. Vol. 1 of *Ante-Nicene Fathers*. Buffalo, NY: Christian Literature, 1885. https://www.ccel.org/ccel/schaff/anf01.ix.iv.xx.html.

Ironside, H. A. *Expository Messages on the Epistle to the Galatians*. Reprint, Blackwell, 2011.

Jenson, Robert W. "Once More the *Logos Asarkos*." *International Journal of Systematic Theology* 13.2 (2011) 130–33.

———. *Systematic Theology, Volume 1: The Triune God*. New York: Oxford University Press, 1997.

Johnstone, Nigel. "Does Ὑιοτηεσια [*sic*.] (*Huiothesia*) Really Mean 'Adoption' in Galatians 4:5?" Biblical Hermeneutics, January 11, 2022. https://hermeneutics.stackexchange.com/questions/35603/does-Ὑιοτηεσια-huiothesia-really-mean-adoption-in-galatians-45.

Jung, C. G. *Modern Man in Search of a Soul*. Translated by W. S. Dell and Cary F. Baynes. Reprint, New York: Harcourt, 1955.
Kärkkäinen, Veli-Matti. *Hope and Community*. Grand Rapids: Eerdmans, 2017.
Käsemann, Ernst. *Commentary on Romans*. Translated by Geoffrey W. Bromiley. Grand Rapids: Eerdmans, 1980.
Kaufman, Gordon D. *God the Problem*. Cambridge, MA: Harvard University Press, 1972.
Keizer, Heleen M. "'Eternity' Revisited: A Study of the Greek Word Αἰών." *Philosophia Reformata* 65.1 (2000) 53–71.
Kim, Joseph. *Reformed Epistemology and the Problem of Religious Diversity: Proper Function, Epistemic Disagreement, and Christian Exclusivism*. Cambridge, UK: James Clarke, 2012.
Kittel, Gerhard, and Gerhard Friedrich, eds. *Theological Dictionary of the New Testament*. Translated by Geoffrey W. Bromiley. 10 vols. Grand Rapids: Eerdmans, 1964–76.
Konstantinovsky, Julia S. "Negating the Fall and Re-Constituting Creation: An Apophatic Account of the Redemption of Time and History in Christ." In *When the Son of Man Didn't Come: A Constructive Proposal on the Delay of the Parousia*, by Christopher M. Hays et al., 109–45. Minneapolis: Fortress, 2016.
Kreyzig, Erwin. *Advanced Engineering Mathematics*. 8th ed. Singapore: John Wiley & Sons, 1999.
Kruse, Colin G. *Paul's Letter to The Romans*. The Pillar New Testament Commentary. Grand Rapids: Eerdmans, 2012.
Kubo, Sakae. *A Reader's Greek-English Lexicon of the New Testament and a Beginner's Guide for the Translation of the New Testament Greek*. Grand Rapids: Zondervan, 1980.
Kumar, Ranjit. *Research Methodology: A Step-by-Step Guide for Beginners*. 3rd ed. London: Sage, 2005.
Kurzweil, Ray. "Human Body Version 2.0." The Kurzweil Library + Collections. efaidnbmnnnibpcajpcglclefindmkaj/https://www.thekurzweillibrary.com/pdf/RayKurzweilReader.pdf.
LaCugna, Catherine Mowry. *God for Us: The Trinity and Christian Life*. HarperCollins paperback ed. New York: HarperSanFrancisco, 2006.
Larkin, Clarence. *Rightly Dividing the Word*. Glenside, PA: Rev. Clarence Larkin Est., 1920.
Leedy, Paul D., and Jeanne Ellis Ormrod. *Practical Research: Planning and Design*. 11th ed. Essex, UK: Pearson, 2015.
Leloup, Jean-Yves, ed. *The Gospel of Thomas: The Gnostic Wisdom of Jesus*. Translated by Joseph Rowe. Rochester, VT: Inner Traditions, 2005.
Lembaga Alkitab Indonesia. *Perjanjian Baru Indonesia-Yunani*. 3rd ed. Jakarta: Lembaga Alkitab Indonesia, 2010.
Lenski, R. C. H. *The Interpretation of St. Paul's Epistle to the Romans*. Minneapolis: Augsburg, 1963.
———. *The Interpretation of St. Paul's Epistles to the Galatians, to the Ephesians, and to the Philippians*. Minneapolis: Augsburg, 1961.
Liddell, Henry George, et al. *A Greek-English Lexicon*. Rev. and augm. ed. Oxford: Clarendon, 1996.

Liddon, H. P. *The Explanatory Analysis of St. Paul's Epistle to the Romans.* 2nd ed. London: Longmans, Green, and Co., 1893.

Litwa, M. David. *We Are Being Transformed: Deification in Paul's Soteriology.* Berlin: De Gruyter, 2012.

Logan, F. Donald. *A History of the Church in the Middle Ages.* London: Routledge, 2002.

Lonergan, Bernard J. F. *Method in Theology.* Toronto: University of Toronto Press, 2013.

Longenecker, Richard N. *The Christology of Early Jewish Christianity.* Studies in Biblical Theology, 2nd ser., 17. Naperville, IL: A. R. Allenson, 1970.

López, René A. "Is Faith a Gift from God or a Human Exercise?" *Bibliotheca Sacra* 164.655 (2007) 259–76.

Luther, Martin. *Galatians.* Edited by Alister E. McGrath and J. I. Packer. Crossway Classic Commentaries. Wheaton, IL: Crossway, 1998.

MacArthur, John. *Galatians: The Wondrous Grace of God.* MacArthur Bible Studies. Nashville, TN: Nelson, 2007.

Macleod, Donald. *Christ Crucified: Understanding the Atonement.* Downers Grove, IL: IVP Academic, 2014.

Macquarrie, John. *Existentialism: An Introduction, Guide, and Assessment.* London: Penguin, 1972.

———. *An Existentialist Theology: A Comparison of Heidegger and Bultmann.* London: Penguin, 1973.

———. *In Search of Humanity: A Theological & Philosophical Approach.* London: SCM, 1982.

———. *Principles of Christian Theology.* Rev. ed. London: SCM, 1986.

Marsden, Richard, and E. Ann Matter. *The New Cambridge History of the Bible, Volume 2: From 600 to 1450.* Cambridge: Cambridge University Press, 2012.

Mbua, Abigael Wangari. "Conceptualization and Translation: An Investigation of *Huiothesia* in the Pauline Epistles in View of the Kikuyu Folk Theories of Procreation and Adoption." PhD diss., Africa International University, 2018.

McGee, J. Vernon. *Galatians.* Pasadena: Thru the Bible, 1971.

McGrath, Alister E. *Historical Theology: An Introduction to the History of Christian Thought.* 2nd ed. West Sussex, UK: Wiley-Blackwell, 2013.

Meconi, David Vincent. *The One Christ: St. Augustine's Theology of Deification.* Washington, DC: The Catholic University of America Press, 2013.

Metzger, Bruce M. *A Textual Commentary on the Greek New Testament: A Companion Volume to the United Bible Societies' Greek New Testament (Fourth Revised Edition).* Second ed. D-Stuttgart: Deutsche Bibelgesellschaft, United Bible Societies, 2007.

Meyer, Heinrich August Wilhelm. *The Epistle to the Galatians.* Edited by William P. Dickson. Critical and Exegetical Commentary on the New Testament 7. Edinburgh: T. & T. Clark, 1873.

Mills, A. R. "Adam." In *New Dictionary of Theology: Historical and Systematic,* edited by Martin Davie et al., 3–5. 2nd ed. Downers Grove, IL: InterVarsity, 2016.

Moltmann, Jürgen. *The Way of Jesus Christ: Christology in Messianic Dimensions.* London: SCM, 1990.

Moo, Douglas J. *The Epistle to the Romans.* New International Commentary on the New Testament. Grand Rapids: Eerdmans, 1996.

Moore, Charles E. *Provocations: Spiritual Writings of Kierkegaard.* Farmington, PA: Bruderhof Foundation, 2002.

Morey, Robert A. *The Reformed Doctrine of Adoption.* Grand Rapids: Eerdmans, 1947.

Mounce, Robert H. *Romans*. New American Commentary 27. Nashville, TN: B. & H., 1995.
Mounce, William D. *Basics of Biblical Greek Grammar*. 3rd ed. Grand Rapids: Zondervan, 2009.
———. *Interlinear for the Rest of Us: The Reverse Interlinear for New Testament Word Studies*. Grand Rapids: Zondervan, 2006.
Murphy, Nancey. *Beyond Liberalism and Fundamentalism: How Modern and Postmodern Philosophy Set the Theological Agenda*. Valley Forge, PA: Trinity, 1996.
Murray, John. *Redemption: Accomplished and Applied*. Grand Rapids: Eerdmans, 1955.
———. *The Epistle to the Romans: The English Text with Introduction, Exposition and Notes*. Grand Rapids: Eerdmans, 1982.
Nancy, Jean-Luc. *Noli Me Tangere: On the Raising of the Body*. Translated by Sarah Clift et al. New York: Fordham University Press, 2008.
Nellas, Panayiotis. *Deification in Christ: Orthodox Perspectives on the Nature of the Human Person*. Translated by Norman Russell. Crestwood, NY: St. Vladimir's Seminary Press, 1987.
NET Bible, Full Notes Edition. Thomas Nelson, 2019.
Neville, Robert C. *Symbols of Jesus: A Christology of Symbolic Engagement*. Cambridge: Cambridge University Press, 2001.
Niebuhr, Reinhold. *Human Nature*. Vol. 1 of *The Nature and Destiny of Man: A Christian Interpretation*. Louisville, KY: Westminster John Knox, 1996.
Norton, David. "English Bibles from c. 1520 to c. 1750." In *The New Cambridge History of the Bible*, edited by Euan Cameron, 3:305–44. Cambridge: Cambridge University Press, 2016.
Nurhajarini, Dwi Ratna, et al. *Kajian Mitos dan Nilai Budaya Dalam Tantu Penggelaran*. Edited by Sri Guritno. Jakarta: Departemen Pendidikan dan Kebudayaan Republik Indonesia, 1999.
O'Collins, Gerald. *Jesus Our Redeemer: A Christian Approach to Salvation*. Oxford, UK: Oxford University Press, 2007.
———. *Rethinking Fundamental Theology: Toward a New Fundamental Theology*. Oxford, UK: Oxford University Press, 2011.
Omanson, Roger L. *A Textual Guide to the Greek New Testament: An Adaptation of Bruce M. Metzger's Textual Commentary for the Needs of Translators*. Stuttgart: Deutsche Bibelgesellschaft, 2006.
Origen. *Commentary on the Epistle to the Romans: Books 6–10*. Translated by Thomas P. Scheck. Fathers of the Church 104. Washington, DC: Catholic University of America Press, 2002.
Padgett, Alan G. "Eternity." In *The Routledge Companion to Philosophy of Religion*, edited by Chad V. Meister and Paul Copan, 335–43. 2nd ed. Routledge Philosophy Companions. New York: Routledge, 2013.
Pagels, Elaine H. *The Gnostic Paul: Gnostic Exegesis of the Pauline Letters*. Philadelphia: Fortress, 1975.
Panikkar, Raimundo. *The Rhythm of Being: The Unbroken Trinity*. The Gifford Lectures. Maryknoll, NY: Orbis, 2013.
Pannenberg, Wolfhart. *Systematic Theology* 2. Translated by Geoffrey W. Bromiley. London: T. & T. Clark International, 2004.
———. *Systematic Theology* 3. Translated by Geoffrey W. Bromiley. London: T. & T. Clark International, 2004.

Pate, C. Marvin. *Romans.* Edited by Mark L. Strauss and John H. Walton. Teach the Text Commentary Series. Grand Rapids: Baker, 2013.
Peppard, Michael. "Adopted and Begotten Sons of God: Paul and John on Divine Sonship." *The Catholic Biblical Quarterly* 73 (2011) 92–110.
———. "The Eagle and the Dove: Roman Imperial Sonship and the Baptism of Jesus (Mark 1.9–11)." *New Testament Study* 56 (2010) 431–51.
———. *The Son of God in the Roman World: Divine Sonship in Its Social and Political Context.* New York, NY: Oxford University Press, 2011.
Peters, Ted. *God as Trinity: Relationality and Temporality in Divine Life.* Louisville, KY: Westminster John Knox, 1993.
Presley, Stephen O. *The Intertextual Reception of Genesis 1–3 in Irenaeus of Lyons.* The Bible in Ancient Christianity 8. Leiden: Brill, 2015.
Rahner, Karl. *The Content of Faith: The Best of Karl Rahner's Theological Writings.* New York: Crossroad, 1993.
Rapa, Robert K. "Galatians." In *Romans, Galatians,* edited by Tremper Longman III and David E. Garland, 549–640. Rev. ed. The Expositor's Bible Commentary 11. Grand Rapids: Zondervan, 2008.
Reimherr, Otto, and F. Edward Cranz. "Irenaeus Lugdunensis." In *Catalogus Translationum et Commentariorum: Mediaeval and Renaissance Latin Translations and Commentaries,* edited by Virginia Brown et al., 7:13–54. Washington, DC: Catholic University of America Press, 1992.
Rendall, Frederic. *The Epistle to the Galatians: Expositor's Greek New Testament* 3. Edited by W. R. Nicoll. New York: George H. Doran, n.d.
Riches, John Kenneth. *Galatians Through the Centuries.* Wiley-Blackwell Bible Commentaries. Oxford, UK: Wiley-Blackwell, 2013.
Ridderbos, Herman. *Paul: An Outline of His Theology.* Grand Rapids: Eerdmans, 1975.
Roberts, Alexander, et al., eds. *Fathers of the Second Century—Hermas, Tatian, Athenagoras, Theophilus, and Clement of Alexandria (Entire).* Vol. 2 of *The Ante-Nicene Fathers.* Reprint, Grand Rapids: Eerdmans, 1978.
Roberts, Alexander, and James Donaldson, eds. *The Apostolic Fathers, Justin Martyr, Irenaeus.* Vol. 1 of *The Ante-Nicene Fathers.* Buffalo, NY: Christian Literature, 1885.
Roberts, Carol M. *The Dissertation Journey: A Practical and Comprehensive Guide to Planning, Writing, and Defending Your Dissertation.* 2nd ed. Thousand Oaks, CA: Corwin, 2010.
Rogers, John. *The Matthew Bible 1537.* Hamburg: Richard Grafton, 1537.
Rogers, Cleon L. Jr., and Cleon L. Rogers III. *The New Linguistic and Exegetical Key to the Greek New Testament.* Grand Rapids: Zondervan, 1998.
Roth, Andrew Gabriel, ed. אבתכ אשידק = *Aramaic English New Testament: MARI: Peshitta English Aramaic Critical Edition: A Compilation, Annotation and Translation of the Eastern Original Aramaic New Testament Peshitta Text.* 5th ed. Bellingham, WA: Netzari, 2012.
Russell, Norman. *The Doctrine of Deification in the Greek Patristic Tradition.* The Oxford Early Christian Studies. Oxford: Oxford University Press, 2004.
Ryrie Study Bible: New American Standard Bible. Chicago: Moody, 2012.
Sartre, Jean-Paul. *Existentialism.* Translated by Bernard Frechtman. New York: Philosophical Library, 1947.
Savulescu, Julian, et al., eds. *Enhancing Human Capacities.* Chichester, UK: Wiley-Blackwell, 2011.

Schaff, Philip, ed. *Fathers of the Second Century*. Reprint, Grand Rapids: Christian Classic Ethereal Library, 2004.

Schoeman, Roy H. *Salvation Is from the Jews (John 4:22): The Role of Judaism in Salvation History from Abraham to the Second Coming*. San Francisco: Ignatius, 2003.

Schott, Heinrich August. *Epistolae Pauli ad Thessalonicenses et Galatas*. Lipsiae: Sumtibus Joannis Ambrosii Barthii, 1834.

Schreiner, Thomas R. *Romans*. Grand Rapids: Baker Academic, 2008.

Scott, Bernard Brandon. *Hear Then the Parable: A Commentary on the Parables of Jesus*. Minneapolis: Fortress, 1990.

Searle, John R. "Metaphor." In *Metaphor and Thought*, edited by Andrew Ortony, 83–111. Cambridge: Cambridge University Press, 1993.

Shedd, William G. T. *A Critical and Doctrinal Commentary upon the Epistle of St. Paul to the Romans*. New York: Charles Scribner's Sons, 1879.

Silva, Moisés, ed. *New International Dictionary of New Testament Theology and Exegesis* 1. 2nd ed. Grand Rapids: Zondervan, 2014.

———. *New International Dictionary of New Testament Theology and Exegesis* 3. 2nd ed. Grand Rapids: Zondervan, 2014.

Sollier, Joseph. "Supernatural Adoption." In *The Catholic Encyclopedia* 1. New York: Robert Appleton Company, 1907. http://www.newadvent.org/cathen/01148a.htm.

Sproul, R. C. "The Order of Salvation." Ligonier Ministries, June 5, 1992. https://learn.ligonier.org/devotionals/order-salvation.

Steenberg, M. C. *Of God and Man: Theology as Anthropology from Irenaeus to Athanasius*. London: T. & T. Clark, 2009.

Stifler, James M. *The Epistle to the Romans*. Chicago: Moody, 1960.

Stott, John R. W. *Men Made New: An Exposition of Romans 5–8*. Downers Grove, IL: InterVarsity, 1966.

———. *The Message of Galatians: Only One Way*. The Bible Speaks Today. London: InterVarsity, 1988.

———. *The Message of Romans: God's Good News for the World*. The Bible Speaks Today. Downers Grove, IL: IVP Academic, 2001.

Strong, James, et al. *AMG's Strong's Annotated Dictionaries*. Chattanooga, TN: AMG, 2009.

Summers, Della. *Longman Dictionary of English Language and Culture*. Essex, UK: Longman, 1993.

Sutanto, Hasan. *Perjanjian Baru Interlinear Yunani-Indonesia dan Konkordansi Perjanjian Baru (PBIK)*. Jakarta: Lembaga Alkitab Indonesia, 2010.

Swinburne, Richard. *Simplicity as Evidence of Truth*. Aquinas Lecture. Milwaukee: Marquette University Press, 1997.

Tan, Ricky Andries. "The Call of 'Abba (to) the Father': A Study of Romans 8:15." *The Journal of Biblical Theology* 6.3 (2023) 221–46.

Taverner, Rychard. *The Most Sacred Bible*. London: Thomas Barthlet, 1539.

Thayer, Joseph Henry, ed. *A Greek-English Lexicon of the New Testament: Being Grimm's Wilke's Clavis Novi Testamenti*. Corrected ed. New York: American Book Company, 1889.

Tillich, Paul. *A History of Christian Thought, from Its Judaic and Hellenistic Origins to Existentialism*. Edited by Carl E. Braaten. A Touchstone Book. New York: Simon and Schuster, 1972.

———. *The New Being*. London: SCM, 1956.

———. *Systematic Theology: Three Volumes in One*. Chicago: The University of Chicago Press, 1967.

———. "What Is Wrong with the 'Dialectic' Theology?" In *The Ground of Being: Neglected Essays of Paul Tillich*, edited by Robert M. Price. San Bernardino, CA: Mindvendor, 2015.

Torrance, Thomas F. *Incarnation: The Person and Life of Christ*. Edited by Robert T. Walker. Downers Grove, IL: InterVarsity, 2008.

Trumper, Tim J. R. "A Fresh Exposition of Adoption: I. An Outline." *Scottish Bulletin of Evangelical Theology* 23.1 (2005) 60–80.

———. "From Slaves to Sons!" *Foundations* 55 (2006) 17–19.

———. "A Historical Study of the Doctrine of Adoption in the Calvinistic Tradition." PhD diss., University of Edinburgh, 2001.

———. "The Theological History of Adoption: I. An Account." *Scottish Bulletin of Evangelical Theology* 20 (2002) 4–28.

———. "The Theological History of Adoption: II. A Rationale." *Scottish Bulletin of Evangelical Theology* 20 (2002) 177–202.

Tsang, S. "'Abba' Revisited: Merging the Horizons of History and Rhetoric Through the New Rhetoric Structure for Metaphors." In *Exploring New Rhetorical Approaches to Galatians*, edited by D. F. Tolmie, 121–41. Acta Theologica 9. Bloemfontein: Publications Office of the Universiteit van die Vrystaat, 2007.

Van Aarde, Andries G. "ΙΗΣΟΥΣ, the Davidic Messiah, as Political Saviour in Matthew's History." In *Salvation in the New Testament: Perspectives on Soteriology*, edited by Jan G. van der Watt, 7–31. Supplements to Novum Testamentum 121. Leiden: Brill, 2005.

Verbrugge, Verlyn D. "1 Corinthians." In *The Expositor's Bible Commentary*, edited by Tremper Longman III and David E. Garland, Revised. Vol. 11. Romans, Galatians. Grand Rapids: Zondervan, 2008.

Vincent, Marvin R. *Word Studies in the New Testament*. Vol. 3 of *The Epistles of Paul*. Albany, OR: SAGE Software, 1996.

Volf, Miroslav. *After Our Likeness: The Church as the Image of the Trinity*. Sacra Doctrina. Grand Rapids: Eerdmans, 1998.

Vos, Geerhardus. *The Eschatology of the Old Testament*. Edited by James T. Dennison Jr. Phillipsburg, NJ: P. & R., 2001.

Waddell, James A. *The Messiah: A Comparative Study of the Enochic Son of Man and the Pauline Kyrios*. Jewish and Christian Texts in Contexts and Related Studies 10. London: T. & T. Clark, 2011.

Wallace, Daniel B. *Greek Grammar Beyond the Basics: An Exegetical Syntax of the New Testament*. Grand Rapids: Zondervan, 1996.

Ward, Keith. *God: A Guide for the Perplexed*. Oxford, UK: Oneworld, 2002.

Webb, Robert A. *The Reformed Doctrine of Adoption*. Grand Rapids: Eerdmans, 1947.

Weil, Simone. *Gravity and Grace*. Translated by Emma Crawford and Mario Von der Ruhr. London: Taylor & Francis e-Library, 2003.

Welz, Claudia. *Humanity in God's Image: An Interdisciplinary Exploration*. Oxford, UK: Oxford University Press, 2016.

Westhead, Nigel. "Adoption in the Thought of John Calvin." *Scottish Bulletin of Evangelical Theology* 13.2 (1995) 102–15.

Weymouth, Richard Francis. *The New Testament in Modern Speech: An Idiomatic Translation into Everyday English from the Text of the Resultant Greek Testament*. Edited by Ernest Hampden-Cook. London: James Clarke and Co., 1903.
Whitacre, Rodney A. *John*. IVP New Testament Commentary Series 4. Downers Grove, IL: InterVarsity, 1999.
White, Patrick. *Developing Research Questions: A Guide for Social Scientists*. London: Palgrave Macmillan, 2009.
Witherington, Ben, and Darlene Hyatt. *Paul's Letter to the Romans: A Socio-Rhetorical Commentary*. Grand Rapids: Eerdmans, 2004.
Wolter, Michael. *Paul: An Outline of His Theology*. Translated by Robert L. Brawley. Waco, TX: Baylor University Press, 2015.
Wright, N. T. *The Kingdom New Testament: A Contemporary Translation*. Grand Rapids: Zondervan, 2011.
Wuest, Kenneth S. *Wuest's Word Studies from the Greek New Testament for the English Reader. Volume 1: Mark, Romans, Galatians, Ephesians, and Colossians*. Grand Rapids: Eerdmans, 2012.
Wycliffite Bible. "Wycliffite Bible Digital Edition." https://wycliffite-bible.english.ox.ac.uk/#/.
Young, Robert, trans. *The Holy Bible, Consisting of the New and Old Covenants, Translated According to the Letter and Idioms of the Original Languages*. Rev. ed. Edinburgh: G. A. Young and Co., 1898.
Герасименко, Н. В. "АФАНАСИЙ I ВЕЛИКИЙ [Греч. Ἀθανάσιος ὁ Μέγας] (Ок. 295, Александрия?—2.05.373, Там Же), Свт. (Пам. 18 Янв., 2 Мая), Еп. Александрийский (с 8 Июня 328), Великий Отец и Учитель Церкви." In *Добро Пожаловать в Один Из Самых Полных Сводов Знаний По Православию и Истории Религии Энциклопедия Издается По Благословению Патриарха Московского и Всея Руси Алексия II и По Благословению Патриарха Московского и Всея Руси Кирилла*, n.d. https://www.pravenc.ru/text/76946.html.

Yeshua said,
Know what is in front of your face
and what is hidden from you will be disclosed;
There is nothing hidden that will not be revealed
[and nothing buried that will not be raised.]

~ *The Gospel of Thomas, saying 5.*

www.ingramcontent.com/pod-product-compliance
Lightning Source LLC
Chambersburg PA
CBHW050839230426
43667CB00012B/2066